D0929907

World Religions in War and Peace

World Religions in War and Peace

by

Henry O. Thompson

McFarland & Company, Inc., Publishers

Jefferson, North Carolina, and London

Library of Congress Cataloguing-in-Publication Data

Thompson, Henry O.
World religions in war and peace.

Bibliography: p. 219.
Includes index.
1. Religions.
2. Peace — Religious aspects.
3. War — Religious aspects.
I. Title.
BL80.2.T49   1988   291.1′7873   88-42516

ISBN 0-89950-341-1 (60# acid-free natural paper)

Manufactured in the United States of America.

McFarland & Company, Inc., Publishers
Box 611, Jefferson, North Carolina 28640

IN MEMORIAM

Orrin S. Thompson
1901–1973

Vera Bennett Manual Thompson
1909–1986

Table of Contents

Preface

A preface is a time of acknowledgment and disclaimer. The latter is easy enough. The author accepts blame and apologizes for any error of fact. The former is a joy. It is an opportunity to say thank you to all who have helped me to a deeper understanding of the religions described here, and the issue of war and peace that is the purpose of this book. The project started out as a joint effort with Dr. Jan Knappert, School of Oriental and African Studies, University of London. He has graciously read several of the essays and his suggestions, inter alia, are gratefully acknowledged.

Other friends have read chapters or portions of the material. It is a pleasure to acknowledge the help of Gordon Anderson, Anne Bancroft, Thomas Boslooper, Padmasiri de Silva, Y.N. Ozturk, Hae Soo Pyun, K.L. Seshagiri Rao, Wazir Singh, et al. Their insights, perspectives and sheer knowledge are deeply appreciated. That appreciation includes Joyce Elaine Beebe Thompson who drew the maps and provided encouragement for the task of putting all of this together. The headings on each chapter are drawn from a parchment on "Peace in the World's Religions" prepared by the Fellowship for Spiritual Understanding, directed by Dr. Marcus Bach. Permission to quote is gratefully acknowledged.

While insisting on honesty in treatment, one must also insist on accuracy and fair treatment. Hopefully that has been accomplished. Books, of course, are not always right and my interpretation of a given experience might not be correct. However, honest people can differ in interpretations of the same phenomena. The writer apologizes for any inaccuracy or unfairness but does not apologize for the bias toward peace.

This preface is also an opportunity to say something about the book. It would be a bit much to try to cover all the history of all the religions of the world in one volume. In some cases, we do not even know all of that history. What follows then is of necessity selective, in which religions to cover and how they are explored. The book is designed for readers. That may seem obvious since it is in print but such is not always the case. The concern has been to present the material in straightforward, readable prose. Whether students in the formal sense or students in the larger sense that one hopes all of us are, we can read through the text. The intent has been to give an overview of the history of a religion for those not familiar with it — to know only one's own religion is to know none. Relatively few people know about other religions, or know enough to be able to understand the issues of war and peace in that tradition. If the reader knows a tradition, the review might be helpful. But the knowledgeable person might simply skip over the introduction and move directly to the discussion of war and peace. Several friends, however, have shared their appreciation for the description of their *own* tradition as well as that of others.

Like virtually all aspects of life, religion is not simple and straight-forward. There are many nuances, shades of meaning, and differences of opinion. A rabbinical friend's favorite joke is, "What do you have when you have two Jews?" The answer is, "Three opinions." Over the years, I have found that to be true of all traditions — without exception. From a scholarly perspective, it has been tempting to put all the little varieties in the text, and even in the same sentence. The result would be a meaning-less snarl. Philosophical hairsplitting may help refine the truth but it does not help clarity of communication. The text is intended to communi-cate.

However, the scholarly quest cannot be denied — some call it the research imperative. There is no need to deny it. The notes have been used to carry the burden of the usual references. Here are sources, page numbers, etc. But here also are other views, nuances and comparative data. For a short course, a quick study, an overview or simple interest in the subject area, the reader can move through the text and get the gist of the tradition and its history of war and peace. The student — formal or informal — who wishes to consider the matter further, will perhaps consult some of the sources for further reading, to see for him or herself. The notes may be helpful in this regard. Thus the book can be used for longer term study, for additional study when the short course is over, and for further research in a given tradition. Gautama the Buddha is recorded as saying we should not mistake the finger pointing at the moon for the moon itself. In a sense, this book offers a pointer for directions in which to look at a vital subject.

Obviously one could write an entire book about each tradition, and entire volumes have in fact been written about each and about many im-portant and minor portions. Thus the other extreme would be an enormous amount of detail and a book many times the size of the present volume. I take comfort in the old adage that to be eternal, a book does not have to be everlasting. The effort here has been to present a reasonable overview in a reasonable amount of space and time.

In summary, the effort before you is really on three levels. For you who have less time, read the text. For you who have more time, read the text and the notes. For you who have even more, read the text and the notes and use the notes to go further into your research. If this book simply gives you an understanding of what world religions are and the role they have had in war and peace, I will feel my effort has been worthwhile. If you are stimulated to go further and expand your mind to include other nuances and views — the wider picture — I will be deeply grateful for your expanded interest. If you find yourself really taking off from the base provided here,

I will count myself among the blessed and sing out alhumdu'illah, Thanks be to God.

But no matter where this book takes you, or where you take it, I trust you will find peace. It can be found – in all the religions of the world. May they all find fulfillment in a world of peace.

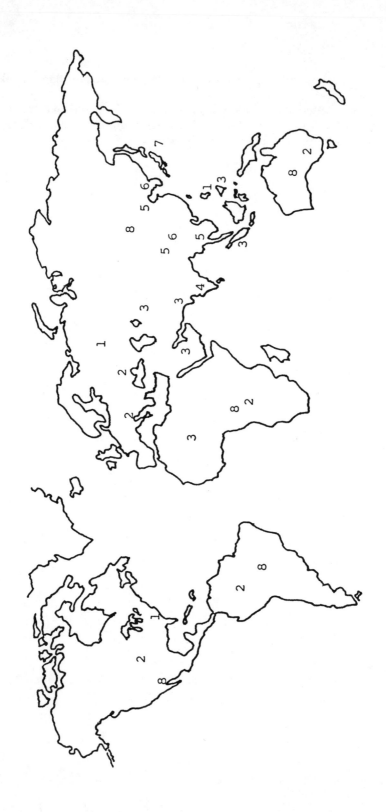

Introduction

*All that spiritual courage and
energy wasted in war could have
prevented it if properly used.*
—Roger Martin du Gard
(1916)

There is probably no greater issue facing the world today than world peace. It is tantalizingly within our grasp as human beings. The world has become, as Marshall McLuhan said, a Global Village. Thanks to satellite television and older forms of radio and telephone, human events wing their way around the Village in minutes. What happens in South Africa is soon known in London, Moscow, New York, New Delhi, Singapore, Tokyo, Beijing, Buenos Aires and all the other world capitals and the hinterlands as well. Racial prejudice in the United States is known all over the world through media showing Bull Connor sending his dogs against black Americans. Untouchability is part of the language of humanity. An earthquake in Peru and a flood in Wyoming call forth help from worldly neighbors. The struggles of East and West, North and South, are not just national problems but international ones. The nuclear threat is a mushroom-shaped cloud that hangs over much of the world. But local conflicts may mean more to those involved, such as the Israeli who is aware of the threat while being primarily concerned with the survival of his own country. From Afghanistan to Ireland, from Chile to Poland, the immediate task may well be survival, but the survival of the whole human race is at stake in the nuclear standoff between the world's superpowers.

Throughout the ages, religion has talked peace. Hinduism echoes with "shanti, shanti, shanti"—peace, peace, peace. Christianity began with angels singing, "Peace on earth, good will among all people." The ideal of the American Indian is harmony with the natural world. As we survey the religious traditions of humanity, however, we will also see that religion has

Opposite: Many of the religions of the world have spread across national boundaries but concentrations remain in some areas: (1) Judaism. (2) Christianity. (3) Islam. (4) Indian traditions—Hinduism, Jainism, Sikhism, Buddhism. (5) Buddhism is spread over Southeast and Far East Asia. (6) Confucianism and Taoism continue in China with some spread to Korea and Japan. (7) Shinto continues in Japan. (8) Traditional faiths continue in Siberia, Australia, Africa, the Americas and elsewhere such as India and Tibet. (Map by Joyce E. Thompson.)

been a source of conflict as well as a source of peace. This is both religion in a formal sense and in the broad spiritual sense of du Gard's statement cited above.[1]

Too often, religion has promoted an "us versus them" attitude as with the Greeks and the barbarians, the Jews and the goyim, the Muslims and the infidels, the Christians and the pagans, the true faith and the heretics, the good people (us) and the bad (them). However, the hope for peace has not been lost. For the sake of human existence as well as to fulfill the will of God or the gods or the spirit world, one might hope that the impetus for peace will be the stronger.

In the real world, those concerned with "realpolitik" would insist that one must face reality. When one's country or tribe or religion is attacked, self-defense is justified. Justification for war is largely ignored in this text. It is not that the author is a pacifist and sees no justification or distinction between military action when attacked and military action to conquer someone else's land. It is rather that humans have always managed to justify what they wanted to do. It is easy to slip into rationalization while reasoning. Christianity has especially promoted the "just war" theory. This may have been not only to take reality into account, but to limit war to the just variety. Historically one does not see much success here. Adolf Hitler was a Roman Catholic whom the Vatican has flatly refused to ex-communicate for World War II that brought death to over 54 million people, including six million Jews systematically exterminated by the Nazis. It is said that Christianity is against war in general and for war in particular. Thus the wars of one's own country are just and it is the others who are unjust, and we are back to an "us versus them" mentality once again.

One might enter here the caveat expressed by Bool Chand. An international community, a world order, is a recent concept. There are, of course, old dreams about world conquest in which devotees see their faith as supreme and prevailing over the world. He quotes Gilbert Murray at the turn of the century who thought the British government was the greatest supporter of peace in the world. But Chand suggests that was a matter of self-interest. Chand's call is for a world community based upon justice for all. Zakir Husain sees peace and justice as indivisible. "Peace without justice will be short-lived, and justice without peace will be a contradiction." If the religions of the world can rise above, outgrow, or find a way out of their own self-interest to a genuinely altruistic love for all humanity, it may be that the Global Village can live in peace. If the past has been lacking in vision, we can correct that past here and now for the future.[2]

There are signs that our Global Village may have moved into a new day. Husain witnesses to uplifting influences sweeping through Islam, Buddhism and Hinduism and drawing them closer together, and the winds of liberalization blowing within the Roman Catholic Church with a consequent rapprochement between it and the rest of Christianity. The universalism in some religions has always been open and acknowledged, while in others it has been more hidden. That too has varied with the times, but

Distribution of religions in South, Southeast, East Asia. (Map by Joyce E. Thompson.)

today there seems to be a greater willingness to consider that there is no longer "us versus them" but only "us," for we are all one human family. Theists might describe our common humanity as the one human family of God, but nontheists can and also have acknowledged the oneness of humanity. At this point justification for war becomes monstrous even among "siblings" while the nuclear destruction of the entire "family" becomes sheer folly.[3]

Oneness here is a reminder of a larger vision in the relationship between the individual and humanity. Numbers of religions have emphasized personal peace of heart or mind, individual salvation or enlightenment. At times the relationship of the parts and the whole of society has been forgotten. In Christianity, personal religion has been popularly opposed to the social gospel. The former by itself has been described as a ghostly religion — a spirit without a body — while the latter by itself has been called a corpse — a body without a soul. Both are needed for real religion. A similar conflict appears in some forms of Buddhism and Hinduism. Thus some have been led to ask whether peace is within the individual, or within the individuals' own group (family, nation, religion), or is it a total world community — interracial, international? Husain notes that these are all vitally interdependent. If the dynamic relationship of individual–group–the Global Village – is kept in mind, none of these will be isolated. That dynamic should be kept in mind even though this text focuses primarily on international peace.[4]

This volume presents both the ideal and the tragedy of religions and peace. There are those who would like to forget the tragedy and focus only on the ideal. However, the philosopher George Santayana noted that those who are ignorant of history are doomed to repeat it. That thought has been paraphrased to say that those who are ignorant of the mistakes of history are doomed to repeat them. These essays are presented in the hope and belief that we can learn from history. It will not do to cover up the mistakes and remain ignorant. It would of course be fraudulent to suggest that one's own tradition is perfect and others are wrong. Donald Swearer has pointed out that we must not become self-righteous with respect to other religious traditions. In fact, self-righteousness makes nonviolence virtually impossible. Zakir Husain has pointed out that for religion to play its historic role in bringing peace and goodwill among men, each religion must start with self-purification from within. We begin with honesty in our own tradition while honestly trying to see both the positive and negative in all traditions. By such an open view, one might hope to combine the power of the positive while learning to avoid or overcome the negative. By setting aside war as an instrument of faith, and proclaiming peace as the path for our own tradition and for all people, religion may yet learn to live by the ideal and lead all humanity to peace.[5]

A Comparative Calendar

[The following comparative dates may be useful to the reader. Complete calendars are available in Frank Parise, ed., *The Book of Calendars*, NY: Facts on File, 1982.]

Western	Judaism	Islam	Cycle	Chinese	Japanese
1	3762		44	58	661
4			45	1	664
40				37	700
63				60	723
64			46	1	724
100	3861				
123				60	783
124			47	1	784
140				17	800
184			48	1	844
200	3961				
239	4000				
240				57	900
244			49	1	
304			50	1	
340				37	1000
364			51	1	
424			52	1	
500	4261		53	17	1160
540				57	1200
622		1			
700		81			
718		100			
800		184			
840			58	57	1500
1000	4761	391	61	37	1660
1106		500			
1239	5000				
1500	5261	906	69	57	2160
1591		1000			
1900	5661	1318	76	37	2560
1979		1400			
1987	5748	1408	78	4	2647
2000	5761	1421		17	2660

I. Judaism

Origins

Modern scholars debate the origins of Judaism, represented today by about 14 million people. One suggestion is that it is the religion of the Pharisees, who survived the Roman destruction of the temple of Jerusalem in 70 C.E. and the destruction of Jerusalem in 135. At the time, the Pharisees, lay leaders of the synagogues, were one of several divisions of the religion of the people of Judah, the Jews.[1]

The name Jew comes from the Hebrew "Yehudi" and the Latin "Judaeus" and means "one who lives in Judah." Some suggest this name came at the end of the exile (539 B.C.E.) and the rebuilding of the temple of Jerusalem in 516.[2]

The exile itself followed the destruction of Jerusalem by the Babylonians in 587. The earlier tradition has been called the Hebrew religion, part of the larger tradition of ancient Semitic peoples of the Near or Middle East, today's Egypt, Israel, Jordan, Lebanon, Syria and Iraq. Some add Iran and Turkey to the list. In practice, the terms Hebrews, Jews, Hebrew religion, Jewish religion, and Judaism are often used interchangeably without the above chronological distinctions, developments or changes.

Earlier origins are suggested in the high ethical standards of the Hebrew or biblical prophets, especially those of the seventh-eighth centuries B.C.E. — Isaiah, Amos, Hosea, Jeremiah, etc. Even earlier, there may not have been a people until the first king, Saul (c. 1020 B.C.E.), and then King David (1000–960 B.C.) consolidated them into a kingdom. More commonly, Judaism is said to have begun with Moses, who may have lived in the thirteenth or fourteenth century. Moses led his people in an exodus from Egypt to Mt. Sinai. The location of Mt. Sinai is debated. One identification is today's Jebel Musa in the southern end of the Sinai peninsula, part of the modern state of Egypt.

The Hebrew Scriptures, the Bible, record the story of God's call to Moses (Exodus 3–4) to lead his people from slavery to freedom, and the

1

subsequent giving of the Torah, "instruction" or "law," at Mt. Sinai (Exodus 20ff). This gift was part of a covenant ceremony, perhaps modeled after ancient near eastern political treaties found among the Egyptians, the Hittites of Turkey and from a later date, the Assyrians and Babylonians. The covenant formed a disparate group into the Chosen People. There was an agreement that God would be their God and they would be his people (Leviticus 26:12).[3]

At the time of his call, Moses asked for God's name and God replied, "I AM WHO I AM. Say to the people that I AM has sent me to you." The "I AM" has been variously derived. One suggestion is the causative form of the Hebrew verb "to be," or YHWH without vowels in the consonantal Hebrew, giving a full name such as "Yahweh." In later times, pious Jews avoided saying the name lest they violate the commandment "You will not take the name of the Lord thy God in vain" (Exodus 20:7). They began substituting the term LORD for the name, and in writing later Hebrew texts used the vowels "adonai," or "lord," to indicate this sacred practice. In the fourteenth century C.E., an ignorant Christian transcribed the two and created the artificial name "Jehovah." This name continues in use in some Christian scriptures, songs, and worship.[4]

The people of the Exodus were a mixed multitude (Numbers 11:4). But a core or some number of them were descendants of an earlier family, according to the books of Exodus and Genesis. The family of Jacob, or Israel, had migrated to Egypt during a famine in Canaan (Genesis 45-47), later Palestine, today's Israel. Jacob's 12 children became the ancestors of the 12 tribes of Israel which later conquered Canaan under the direction of Moses and then his official successor, Joshua. This tribal grouping has been suggested for the Hebrews' origin.

Jacob himself was the grandson of Abram, or Abraham, whose ancestry is traced back to Adam and Eve, the traditional first man and woman. Abraham was called by God to leave Haran in Syria and go to Canaan (Genesis 12). There, in two covenants, or two versions of a covenant (Genesis 15, 17), God told Abram that he would be the ancestor of multitudes of people. This calling is traditionally the beginning of the Hebrew religion.

The Biblical Tradition

The opening words of the Bible are, "In the beginning God created the heavens and the earth." This creator God went on to create human beings in his own image (Genesis 1:27).[5] The opening chapter describes a wet creation while chapter two describes a dry one, but both agree that God is the creator. It is the second story, extending into chapter 3, which provides the names of Eve and Adam.[6]

Eve and Adam were placed in the Garden of Eden, a kind of paradise. When they disobeyed God they were expelled. Their descendants began to populate the earth. Human sin multiplied and the whole of humanity was destroyed in a great flood, except for Noah and his family. Their descendants repopulated the earth. One of Noah's sons was Shem, the traditional ancestor of the Semites. One descendant was named Eber (11:16), perhaps an early form of the term "Hebrew," which may mean "from across the river," as later, Abraham came from across the Euphrates River.

Later, Jacob's son, Joseph, became vizier, or prime minister, of Egypt (Genesis 41:41). His father and family were welcomed to Egypt and settled in the northeast in an area called Goshen. Later pharaohs enslaved Jacob's descendants and other Asiatics for public building projects (Exodus 1:8–11). The Exodus under Moses saved them from slavery and remains the central focus of Jewish tradition to this day, its Passover festival symbolizing the passing over of the angel of death who killed the Egyptian firstborn but spared the Hebrews.

After wandering in the wilderness for 40 years, Moses led a new generation from the Sinai peninsula, up the Arabah Valley from the Gulf of Eilat, or Aqaba, to the Transjordan plateau east of the Jordan River (Numbers 14ff). The Conquest began here and two and one-half tribes settled along the eastern side of the Jordan. The rest entered Canaan and conquered the land promised to Abraham and his descendants in the first covenant (Joshua 1–12). The area was divided among the remaining tribes who were united in a kingdom by Saul (I Samuel 10ff). David expanded his control and left an empire to his son Solomon (c. 960–920 B.C.E.), who built the temple destroyed in 587 (II Samuel–I Kings 9).[7]

After Solomon's death the empire split into the northern kingdom of Israel (traditionally 10 tribes), and the southern one of Judah traditionally comprising the tribes of Judah and Benjamin. Israel fell to the Assyrians (721 B.C.E.) and Judah to the Babylonians (I Kings 12–II Kings). The Assyrians exiled many people, leading to the tradition of the Ten Lost Tribes. The Babylonians also exiled people; this action is known in biblical tradition as the Exile. After the Persian conquest (539 B.C.E.) of the Babylonians, the exiled Jews were allowed to return to Jerusalem. A few did and Judah was gradually reconstituted. It was ruled by Alexander the Great (333–323), the Ptolemies of Egypt (323–198) and the Seleucids of Syria. In 165, the Hasmoneans, nicknamed Maccabees, rebelled against the Seleucids and reestablished an independent state which fell to the Romans in 63 B.C.E.. A group called Zealots led the First Jewish Revolt from 66–72 C.E. and the Second Jewish Revolt from 132–135 C.E.[8]

About 450–400 B.C.E., leaders Nehemiah and Ezra came from the Persian court to rebuild Jerusalem's city walls and to read the Torah. The reading by Ezra was followed by a new covenant. Ezra is sometimes called the Father of Judaism. It has been suggested that after this, Jewish identity was no longer political but a way of life — "halakah" — literally "walking," or living according to the Torah. The Jews were no longer a geographical nation but "The People of the Book."[9] The Torah read by Ezra may have been the Priestly document noted earlier, a portion of it called the Holiness

Code (Leviticus 17-26), or the entire Pentateuch—the Five Scrolls, or
Books of Genesis, Exodus, Leviticus, Numbers and Deuteronomy.

These five are generally seen as the first of three divisions of scripture,
though Deuteronomy, the last book, or a portion of it, was the basis of an
earlier covenant renewal under King Josiah (621 B.C.E.). By circa 200
B.C.E., the traditions from Joshua to 560 were gathered together to form
the Former Prophets (the Books of Joshua, Judges, Samuel and Kings), and
the oracles of the prophets were collected to form the Latter Prophets. The
Pentateuch is called the Torah and the second section is called the Nabiim,
or Prophets. The third section, the Kethubiim, or Writings (Psalms, Proverbs, etc.), was not finalized until after 70 C.E. when the Pharisees were
gathered in an academy at Jabneh or Jamniah on the Mediterranean
seacoast under the direction of Johannan ben Zakkai. A group of 15 additional writings (known today as the Apocrypha), including the traditions
of the Maccabees, were considered scripture by some Hellenistic Jews in the
Diaspora (outside of Palestine). These were incorporated into an early
Greek translation of the scriptures known as the Septuagint from the tradition that 70 scholars were involved in the translation in Alexandria. The
Apocrypha were rejected as scripture by the academy and the Kethubiim
was finalized into its present form. The three parts together are known as
the Tenak though sometimes the entire collection is called Torah.

Post-Biblical Developments

An accumulation of oral tradition, interpretations of the Torah by the
scribes (Soferim) and teachers (Tannaim), was put into writing circa 200
C.E. One of the main editors was Judah I, the Prince (or "nasi"—the head
of the Academy) who followed Rabbi Akiba's six orders (Sedarim). The
main sections are Seeds (agriculture), Feasts, Women (marriage, divorce,
etc.), Damages (civil and criminal law), Purities and Sacred Things. There
are 63 tractates (Massektoth) or subheadings. This collection is called the
Mishna (repetition).

Later interpretation of the Mishnah by the Amoraim (interpreters) and
other materials (astronomy, geography, gossip, folklore, traditions—the
Aggada) were incorporated in the Gemara (Supplementary Learning). One
collection, the Talmud Babli, was by the rav (masters) in Babylon (c. 500
C.E.) and a different collection, the Talmud Yerushalmi, was by the rabbis
(my teacher) in Palestine (c. 400 C.E.). Mishnah and Gemara together are
called the Talmud (learning), the usual reference being to the Babylonian
Gemara. Sometimes "Talmud" refers only to the Gemara. It has 36 tractates
with interpretations of 2000 teachers. Its huge bulk has made it very
difficult to assimilate. In the sixteenth century, Joseph Caro, or Karo,
(1488-1575) summarized it all in four sections to provide guidelines for
daily living in his *Shulhan Aruch* (A Table Prepared). While only the
Tenak is scripture in the technical sense, the Talmud has had an enormous

influence and some would say an even greater influence in the history of Judaism than the Tenak, but the reference point remains the Torah.[10]

Christianity is usually said to have begun with Jesus of Nazareth, born circa 6 B.C.E. His followers believed he was the messiah (Hebrew) or the Christ (Greek), the anointed, who fulfilled the promise of a leader who would save his people, the Jews. Many people in Jewish history claimed to be or were proclaimed the messiah. Simon ben Koseba, or Kochebah, leader of the Second Jewish Revolt (132–135 C.E.), was declared messiah by Rabbi Akiba, leader of the Academy. Shabbetai Zevi (1626–1676) declared himself the messiah as did Jacob Frank (1726–1791). The present political state of Israel has been called the fulfillment of the messianic promises.[11]

Christianity survived both revolts (70 and 135 C.E.) against the Romans and spread throughout the Roman Empire despite or because of sporadic persecution. In 313, Constantine and Licinius, contenders for the emperorship, produced an Edict of Toleration. By the time Constantine gained complete control of the empire and moved his capital from Rome to Constantinople (today's Istanbul), Christianity was well on its way to being the official state religion. The new religion turned on its mother or sibling with vicious persecution, dispersing Jews even more than they already were.[12]

In addition to the dispersion (Galut, exile, Diaspora) of Jews by wars and commerce from 721 B.C.E. onward, the two revolts of 70 and 135 C.E. created an even bigger Diaspora. While numbers moved east (especially to Babylon) and south, many moved into various parts of the Roman Empire and into Europe. Some settled in Spain where they eventually came to be known as Sephardim (Obadiah 20, Sepharad, identified later with Spain). They followed the Babylonian tradition which had a strong influence in Mediterranean areas. They enjoyed some peace and prosperity there, especially after the Muslim conquest of Spain (710–717 C.E.). Spain was reconquered by the Christian King Ferdinand in 1492 and Jews were forced to convert to Christianity or be expelled. Some converted, at least outwardly, and were called Marranos (pig) by the Christians. The expelled ones fled to other Muslim areas, especially Turkey and Palestine, and to the Netherlands when these became free (1579) of Spain.

The Jews of central, nothern and western Europe were gradually pushed eastward into Poland by persecution and expulsion (England, 1290; France, 1394), where they became known as the Ashkenazic Jews, after a descendant of Noah (Genesis 10:3, perhaps associated with Armenia). Many of these came under Russian control when parts of Poland were conquered by Russia. The Jewish portions were called the Pale, and they had limited protection. "Beyond the Pale" became a metaphor for beyond protection, but even within Pale there was savage persecution by the Christians. In spite of that, the Jews grew in numbers. The persecution culminated in the murder of over six million Jews during World War II led by Roman Catholic Adolf Hitler.

While studies of the Talmud and Torah were major concerns of

Judaism, many Jewish men were pushed into study also by Christian persecution which eliminated Jews from farming, the trades and other work. Women were more acceptable as domestics in Christian households. Independent professions were often the only thing left for males. One result was a larger number of Jewish philosophers, physicians and lawyers, as well as independent entrepreneurs in commerce.

Among the many great Jewish professionals, Moses Maimonides (1135–1204) is outstanding. Court physician to Saladin, Muslim victor against the Crusaders, Maimonides is famous for a 14-volume codification of the Talmud and Gaonic responsa (responses to questions of Jewish law), the Mishneh Torah (second Torah, English title, "The Strong Hand"), his *Guide for the Perplexed* and his 13 cardinal principles of faith. His 13 cardinal principles never became a creed in the Christian sense but were quite influential nonetheless. They included the doctrines of God as one, omniscient, eternal, Creator, spirit, whom people are obligated to serve, the unchanging Torah as revelation, Moses as the supreme prophet, the Messiah, and the resurrection.[13]

For centuries, the Christian Church forbade usury, lending money at interest. As the commercial interests of Europe grew, this became a problem which was solved by allowing Jews to become moneylenders and bankers. The persecutions of Jews by European Christians eliminated some Christians' debts to Jewish moneylenders. In time, the Church gave up its objection to usury which opened the banking field to Christians, whereupon Jews were attacked for their moneylending activities and accused of being avaricious. To this day, anti–Semites refer to Jews as international bankers, though there are very few Jews in international banking or in national banking either.[14]

Variety — The Spice of Life

It would be a misrepresentation to leave the impression that throughout this long history, Judaism was a single entity. Judaism has never been monolithic. The prophets condemned their people for worshipping other gods. Josianic or deuteronomic reform consolidated worship in the temple and destroyed other temples and worship areas known as high places. However, the later exiles in Egypt had a temple at Elephantine, an island in the Nile River. The returning exiles from 539–400 B.C.E. refused help or association from the Jews of Samaria who later came to be called Samaritans. The latter accepted the Pentaeuch (Torah) and the book of Joshua but did not accept later books as scripture. They built their own temple on Mt. Gerazim circa 300 B.C.E. The temple was destroyed by Hasmonean king John Hyrcanus in 130 B.C.E. There are several hundred Samaritans today, about half in Nablus near Mt. Gerazim, the rest on the seacoast south of Tel Aviv.

The priestly Sadducees traced their origins to Zadok, high priest under

Solomon (I Kings 1:7–8; Ezekiel 40:46). A movement of holy ones opposed to Hellenizing tendencies (Greek dress, food, games, language) in the Ptolemaic and Seleucid periods may have been the origin of the Pharisees and their contemporaries, militant Zealots and ascetic Essenes. Sadducees and Pharisees fought murderous internecine wars as the two groups struggled for power during the Maccabean period. While they were more ascetic, the Pharisees are sometimes called liberals because of their willingness to adapt religion to the changing culture. Hillel the Elder (30 B.C.E. to 10 C.E.) was one of many outstanding leaders. Among his many teachings was his summary of the 613 laws of the Torah: "Do not do unto others that which is hurtful to yourself" (the Golden Rule).

The Essenes have been associated with a monastic sect at Qumran on the northwest corner of the Dead Sea. A group of Dead Sea Scrolls were found in the vicinity between 1947–1952. Qumran was destroyed by the Romans in 68 C.E. The group had or was expecting at least two if not three messiahs – one a priest of the tribe of Levi, one a prince of the tribe of Judah. The founder of the group, probably called the Teacher of Righteousness, was a messianic figure.[15]

In later times, the Talmud was not accepted by everyone. Anan ben David in 767 defied the orthodox leaders (Gaonim, "excellencies") and began a kind of back-to-the-Bible movement called the Karaites (readers), the Bnai Mikra, or children of the texts. This has been compared to the Christian Reformation in Europe in which Protestants rejected the accumulation of canon law and went back to the Bible. The Karaites also emphasized reason and the use of Arabic, and resented the opulence of the exilarch, the secular leader of the community who was supported by Jewish taxes. There are still about 15,000 Karaites today. The movement was successfully opposed by Saadiah ben Joseph (882–942), the head (Gaon) of the Academy at Sura, in Babylon. The authority of the Talmud was confirmed. But in the process, Saadiah ben Joseph translated the Bible into Arabic and harmonized revelation and reason, making him the father of medieval Jewish philosophy.[16]

More significant, because it has been more lasting, was the rise of mysticism in Judaism. This included mystical interpretation of the texts, astrology, the mystical use of numbers, an extensive lore accumulated as Kabbalah (tradition). The influential *Zohar* was a commentary on the Pentateuch by Moses de Leon (1250–1305) who, however, attributed it to the second century author Simon ben Yohai. Another major figure was Isaac Luria (1534–1572 C.E.).

Interpretations vary, but one view is that the Hasidic movement stemmed from this wing of Judaism. It began with Israel ben Eliezer (1700–1760), known later as Baal Shem Tov, Master of the Good Name. He taught that God is everywhere and is the source of love and joy. This joy in God is expressed in singing and dancing. Israel ben Eliezer's followers were opposed and sometimes violently so by orthodox Judaism, by excommunication and by betrayal to the authorities. Petuchowski notes that the conflict led to open warfare, a conflict which has not altogether subsided even today. However, the Hasidim have persisted and represent a prominent part of orthodox Judaism today. Their leaders are in some ways similar to the guru or Zen master of eastern traditions.[17]

Orthodox Judaism continues to this day. In the United States, synagogues are organized in the Union of Orthodox Jewish Congregations (1898) and the Rabbinical Council of America (1935). Yeshiva University (1886) in New York City is a major school. A small minority of modern Jews, the orthodox are divided among several groups such as the Hasidim.

Three major movements in Judaism began in the nineteenth century. Reform Judaism had its roots in the Jewish enlightenment, the haskalah, and Moses Mendelssohn (1729–1786), a practicing Jew and philosopher who advocated separation of religion and state. He insisted Judaism is a religion and not a political state. Reform Judaism rejected the Talmud and dietary laws, called houses of worship temples instead of synagogues, and emphasized the ethics of the prophets. The Pittsburgh Platform of 1885 emphasized moral law as binding while rejecting ritual laws. Reform Jews adopted the local language of the geographical area and until recently rejected Jewish nationalism. Reform Jews see themselves as citizens of the country where they live, citizens whose religion is Judaism. The Conference of Reform Jews met in Chicago in 1918 and proclaimed the ideal of the Jew is not establishment of a Jewish state.

Among the great figures of Reform are Abraham Geiger (1810–1874), Isaac Mayer Wise (1819–1900), Stephen Samuel Wise (1874–1949), and Joshua Liebman (1907–1948). I.M. Wise established Hebrew Union College as the Reform seminary in America in 1875, organized (1873) the Union of American Hebrew Congregations, and (1889) the Central Conference of American Rabbis. S.S. Wise organized the Jewish Institute of Religion, now merged with HUC as HUC-JIR (1949).[18]

Conservative Judaism is intermediate between Reform and Orthodox Judaism. Judaism is a religion. The tradition is to be preserved where it does not interfere with modern living. Change takes place slowly within traditional Jewish law. Rabbi Samson Raphael Hirsch (1808–1888), Solomon Schechter (1847–1915), Louis Finkelstein (1895–) and Abraham Heschel (1907–1972) have been major leaders in this tradition. In America, conservatives are organized in the Rabbinical Assembly of America (1900) and the United Synagogue of America (1913), the latter founded by Schechter when he was president of Jewish Theological Seminary (1887) in New York City.[19]

Mordecai M. Kaplan (1909–1983) taught at JTS. Some see his Reconstructionist movement (1935) as simply a part of the Conservative tradition. Like Conservative Jews, he taught that traditions are to be preserved unless really useless or out of date. However, he also taught that God is not a personal being but is present within the person. Like the other groups, Jews are citizens with the religion of Judaism, but Judaism is more than a religion. It is a people – not a chosen people but simply a group that wants to survive. The world is a good place that could be better. We are here to make the world a better place. There is a strong emphasis on ethics, and on John Dewey and American pragmatism – if it works, there is something to it. The value of Judaism is measured by its practical results. The Jewish Reconstruction Foundation (1940), the Federation of Reconstructionist Congregations and Havurot (1954), the Reconstructionist Rabbinical Association, and the Women's Organization are developments of the movement. *The Reconstructionist* has been published since 1935. The Reconstructionist Rabbinical College (1968) started in Philadelphia and is now in Wyncote, PA.[20]

The third movement is Zionism, which originated with the work of Theodore Herzl (1860–1904). The name is an alternate for Jerusalem (II Samuel 5:7; I Kings 8:1). The term is sometimes extended to the whole land. The return from exile in 539 B.C. became a symbol for later Jews who were expelled by the Romans from Jerusalem, and perhaps from the land, though this is debated. The Passover festival includes the declaration, "Next year in Jerusalem." Over the centuries the desire for a return to empire gradually faded. It was periodically revived by such messianic contenders as Shabbetai Zevi but was practically squelched by Christian and Muslim rulers whenever a hint of such nationalism appeared. However, Jews normally assimilated to the culture where they lived. While Christians forced them to live in ghettoes (which also served to protect them from Christian attacks), the Jews were open to many of the cultural elements of the area.

Napoleon Bonaparte united his followers under the cry of Liberty, Equality and Brotherhood. The French National Assembly had already removed all restrictions against Jews with the slogan "To the Jews as Jews, nothing. To the Jews as men, everything." This and the impact of Reform brought many Jews out of the ghetto and into assimilation with the general culture. However, anti–Semitism raised its ugly head. Herzl was a journalist who covered the trial of Captain Alfred Dreyfus (1859–1935), a Jew falsely convicted of treason. Herzl began to develop a movement for a national homeland where Jews could live in peace. He himself was a nonpracticing Jew and his Zionism had neither God nor Torah nor rabbinical authority. He did note that Zionism was not just aspiration for land but for ethical and spiritual perfection. His book, *The Jewish State* (1896), brought the movement to international attention. He thought Uganda or Argentina or some other section of the Ottoman Empire was a suitable alternative to Palestine for this state. Herzl got the Second Zionist Congress to vote 295–177 for Uganda, which had been offered by the British. Baron de Hirsch, a Jewish philanthropist, gave liberally for Jewish resettlement in Argentina.[21]

The Zionist movement caught the imagination of many. Thousands of Jews eventually went to Palestine. Early Zionists bought land and developed kibbutzim, communal settlements. At first they were welcomed by the Palestinians, about 90 percent Muslims and most of the rest

Christians, with a few members of the Bahai tradition, and a few Jews whose ancestors had been there for centuries or had never left. In 1917, the British government got support from the Zionists for the war effort by the Balfour Declaration which said the government looked with favor upon the movement providing it did not deny the rights of the people already there. The British received Palestine as a mandate to administer for the League of Nations after World War I and the defeat of the Ottoman Empire which had controlled the area since 1517.

As the number of Jews entering Palestine grew, the Palestinians became alarmed. Opposition developed which led to riots in the 1930s. World War II brought some détente in the hostilities but afterwards, Jews and non-Jewish Palestinians fought guerrilla and pitched battles. The British tried to keep peace, failed, and took the matter to the United Nations, which divided the land between the Jews and Palestinians (1947). When the British moved out, the Zionists declared the modern state of Israel an independent nation. In subsequent fighting the Zionists held the territory designated by the U.N. and extended it, but the Jordanian army moved into the area known as the West Bank and the Egyptian army moved into the Gaza Strip around that coastal city. After several more wars, the Israelis extended control over both these territories in 1967 and continue in control today.[22]

While Reform, Conservative and Reconstructionist Judaism are illegal in Israel today, Conservative Judaism has generally supported Zionism. One can be both a religious Jew and support another nation-state than one's own country. Orthodox Judaism has a mixed record — some favor the state while others see it as idolatry. For some 60 years, however, with exceptions such as S.S. Wise, Reformed and other Jews were opposed, sometimes violently, to Zionism, partly on the basis that Judaism was a religion rather than a national group. But after the 1956 war with Egypt, many previously non-Zionist Jews changed, partly because they thought that the Jews of Israel were in mortal danger of another holocaust, and non-Jews did not care in spite of all the protestations of guilt over Hitler's murders. If Jews did not protect Jews, it appeared that no one else would either.

One interpretation of the events is that the German holocaust was the crucifixion of the Jews and the establishment of the state of Israel was the resurrection. One Jewish theologian estimated that 90 percent of the Jews of Israel and the United States are atheists and agnostics (other suggestions are 65–75 percent). Well over 90 percent of them are Zionists. One interpretation of the messianic tradition is that of a messianic age rather than a person and the state of Israel is the fulfillment of those messianic traditions, though a few Jews see the state as heresy, or a form of idolatry.[23]

Several other aspects of modern Judaism are important to note. One is the danger of assimilation. Between 1802–1812, one-third of the Jewish community in Berlin rejected their religion. The problem has continued under the "acids of modernity" and the existence of Jews in a larger non-Jewish culture. Many Jews marry outside their faith and many simply drift away from it. Rabbi Balfour Brickner has said that Judaism loses far more members to apathy than it has ever lost to conversions to other traditions. Allen S. Maller says the same. Rabbi Maller did an intensive study of efforts to convert Jews to Christianity and the higher-than-average percentage of Jews or people of Jewish background in the so-called New Religions such as Hare Krishna and the Unification Church. He found that from 7000–8000 U.S. Christians convert to Judaism every year. Approximately the same number of Jews convert to other traditions — witchcraft, new religions, Buddhism, Sufi (Islam), Shinto, etc.

An example of decline is a recent news article which says the Jewish population of Argentina had risen to 500,000 by 1950. Today, it is closer to 250,000. Several thousand have migrated to Israel. Some 50 percent of Argentine Jews marry outside their faith. There is a low birth rate. A majority of the community does not practice religion. Some speculate that Judaism will disappear, which others claim this is very unlikely.[24]

While support for Israel is nearly universal, there remain many wide differences among Jews such as Mexican Indian Jews, Black Falasha Ethiopian Jews, atheist Jews, etc. The Sephardim and the Ashkenazim maintain their own chief rabbis in Israel. Judaism is most certainly not a static, unitary or monolithic tradition. There are so many differences that this dynamic tradition today faces as a major question the issue "What is a Jew?"[25]

The founders declared the modern state of Israel would be as Jewish as England is English, a thought reminiscent of Jews as a people rather than a people whose religion is Jewish. The high percentage of atheists and agnostics among Israeli Jews is also supportive of this concept, as is the Law of Return. This law says that any Jew who comes to Israel is entitled to be a citizen. A Jew is one who is born of a Jewish mother. A convert to the religion of Judaism would not be included in this and a Jewish father does not count. However, a priest, born of a Jewish mother and a convert to Christianity, applied for citizenship and was refused. There has also been conflict over Ethiopian Jews, and the Jews of India, whose ancestry goes back for centuries but whose beliefs have been questioned as heresy. Thus there appears to be some ambiguity in how the state defines a Jew.

The religious tradition is patriarchal but society is changing. The role of women has been increasing in Judaism. The Reform tradition began ordaining women in the 1970s and more recently (1983), the Conservative tradition made the same move. Conservatives now count women in the minyan, the minimum of ten people to have a congregation. The Reform movement is now recognizing not only the children of a Jewish mother as Jewish but also the children of a Jewish father. While officially it is to retain the children of men who marry non–Jewish wives, it also removes the ancient stigma of "mother's baby, father's maybe." In Israel, the right to vote was extended to women, and Milwaukee-born Golda Meir was prime minister from 1969–1974. However, there is no civil law marriage. The only legal marriages are those performed by orthodox rabbis (other forms of

Judaism are illegal). The Orthodox do not recognize Jewish marriages in other countries, and they do not allow Jews to marry non–Jews though they allow atheists to marry. They also do not accept converts if the conversion was not performed by an Orthodox rabbi and hence refuse to marry a couple if one had a "doubtful" conversion.[26]

Peace and War

Genesis 14 has intrigued scholars for centuries. Four eastern kings raided the Transjordan area and captured Lot, Abraham's nephew. Abraham gathered his troops and chased the captors, defeated them, freed his nephew, and captured their goods. A tenth of this war booty was given to Melchizedek, king of Salem, who blessed Abraham in the name of God, "who has delivered your enemies into your hand!" Regardless of the historicity of the narrative, Hebrew traditions have war very early in the record and the war was believed to be blessed by God. The death-dealing power of God had already been demonstrated in the Flood story with its destruction of all humanity except for Noah and his family. The destruction is presented as the result of sin. A similar explanation was given for the destruction of Sodom and Gomorrah with the exception of Lot (Genesis 19). A different kind of war is recorded in Genesis 34. Jacob's daughter, Dinah, was raped. In revenge, her brothers killed the rapist and all the males of the city of Shechem, and the rest of the sons of Jacob plundered the city. Jacob feared revenge from the Canaanites but God protected him.

In the Exodus story, the people left Goshen for Sinai. The pharaoh had given permission for them to leave but the biblical tradition says he changed his mind and chased them. The Hebrews escaped across the Red Sea and the pursuing army was destroyed. Moses and the people sang a song to the Lord. Exodus 15:3 says, "The LORD is a man of war." Chapter 17 records a war with the Amalekites which resulted in a blood feud described in verse 16: "The LORD will have war with Amalek from generation to generation." A now lost book of the Wars of Yahweh is noted in Numbers 21:14. The conquest of the Transjordan and Canaan noted earlier was recorded as a military conquest, and wars continued throughout the period of the judges and kings until the last revolt in 581. Even the prophets could predict military victory in which the Hebrews would plunder their neighbors (Isaiah 11:13–15) and beat them to pieces (Micah 4:13).

During the next 400 years the decimated and weakened people fought little, though they were still feared (surrounding people resisted the rebuilding of the city walls circa 450) throughout the centuries that followed, until the Maccabees revolted in 168 and began the 105-year kingdom. The revolts against the Romans followed increasing unrest, resistance, murders. But the end of the Second Jewish Revolt ended Jewish military action for 1800 years.

Aho contends that warfare for the Hebrews was a holy obligation.

Rituals included summoning the 12 tribes, exempting those not there to glorify Yahweh, offering the enemy the choice of surrender, drawing lots to determine Yahweh's favorable will, and the battle cry, "Arise, Yahweh, and let thy enemies be scattered!" No holds were barred and the conquest was uncontrolled violence. Aho suggests that this is typical nomadic warfare and notes that chivalry in war was incorporated later by David, who learned it from the Philistines. One can compare Confucian concepts of warfare which were chivalrous when among equals but called for the total destruction of barbarians by any means possible.[27]

Holy war included the cherem, or ban, which called for total destruction of every living thing (Joshua 6:17; I Samuel 15:3). The Holocaust was a sacrifice to Yahweh since everything in the holy war was "dedicated" to him. There is some debate as to whether the ban was ever actually carried out or if this is a later writing of history. In either case, it represents a bloodthirsty element in Hebrew religion. Aho points out that other Semitic nations — Babylonians, Assyrians, Moabites, Egyptians, etc. — during the biblical period were just as bloody according to their own records discovered by archaeologists. Later, holy war was used with vengeance on both foreigners and heretic Jews by the Maccabees. Among the Dead Sea Scrolls is one called "The War of the Sons of Light and the Sons of Darkness." The Qumranites were the former and everyone else the latter. The latter — the rest of humanity — would be totally destroyed (complete genocide) in the apocalyptic war described in the scroll. In the 1947–48 fight for an independent state, Jews destroyed an Arab village, killing several hundred people. The concept has continued in Christianity and Islam throughout the centuries.[28]

While war was normal throughout the biblical period, peace was also a concern. In Genesis 13, Abram and Lot separate their flocks to avoid strife. Abraham and Abimelech make a peace treaty. Genesis 31 records a peace treaty between Jacob and his father-in-law. Several hundred references to peace show the prominence of the concern which ranged from dying and resting in peace to peace after or instead of war.

There is a trend toward peace and justice in the Bible itself. On his deathbed, Jacob denounced the violence of Simeon and Levi against the Shechemites. Jehu (842–815) massacred the royal families of Israel and Judah (II Kings 9–10) in the name of the Lord but the bloodshed was denounced (c. 740 B.C.) by Hosea (1:4). The bloodthirsty Assyrians are condemned but they repent at the preaching of Jonah to his disgust. However, God has compassion on them. The Psalms include warlike statements but also insist that the faithful should put their trust in the Lord rather than in military might. God is one who stamps out war (20:7–8; 33:16–18; 147:10–11; 46:9).[29]

In later times, Eisendrath notes that just as Gandhi reinterpreted the war sections of the Gita as the conflict between right and wrong, the rabbis spiritualized biblical violence. Abraham's trained men were not warriors but scholars of the Torah (Nedarim 32a). Jacob's victories over the

Amorites with sword and bow were reinterpreted as victories of prayer and supplication. Joshua is transformed into a man of peace. David the empire builder is remembered for his psalms. In the great Exodus from Egypt, rabbinic tradition says the angels wanted to exalt God in hymns of thanksgiving when the pursuing Egyptians were destroyed. God responded, "My creatures are perishing and you want to sing praises?" In the *Ethics of the Fathers* a hero is not the military warrior but the one who masters his passions, while Rabbi Nathan added that "the supreme hero is he who converts a foe into a friend." There was no need to transform Proverbs 25:21, "If your enemy hunger, give him bread to eat; and if he is thirsty, give him water to drink."[30]

The word "shalom" means wholeness or peace. It refers to political, military, or spiritual peace, to wholeness of health, prosperity, etc. All peace comes from Yahweh, whether secular or religious, personal or communal. The "Song of Peace" (Sam Shalom) in the Sabbath liturgy asks God to "grant us peace, Thy most precious gift, O Thou eternal source of peace." God's presence is peace but for peace, men must be right with God. The covenant is one sign of the right relationship between God and people, and the phrase covenant of peace, as in Numbers 25:12 and Ezekiel 37:26, makes it explicit. Peace is a major blessing and Yahweh's peace is salvation (Psalms 85:8-10). The messianic age and/or the eschatological end time will bring peace, though it may be preceded by war. Isaiah calls the messianic king the Prince of Peace (9:6). The greeting of peace, "Peace be unto you," remains a part of the Jewish tradition to the present.[31]

In the 1800 years following the Roman defeat, there was no center of military power for Judaism. Individual Jews served in the military forces of their respective countries. The Romans had exempted them from military service because of their refusal to fight on the Sabbath, the day of rest (Exodus 20:8-11). It was not, however, 18 centuries of peace. The persecution and murders were noted earlier. Sometimes these were accepted as punishment for sin, as in the defeats of ancient Israel and Judah. At other times the response was wonder, as when Habakkuk asked how long the more wicked would swallow up the more righteous. At still other times, the response was resentment. At times the messianic hope was for a peaceful world and at other times, the hope was for the restoration of Israel and military victory.[32]

But there are also the rabbinic reinterpretations for peace and specific injunctions that can be interpreted as promoting peace. For example, the Talmud records the rabbinic teaching on why God created Adam alone. This was to teach that "he who destroys the one life, it is as if he destroys the world. And he who saves one life, it is as if he saved the world." The related teaching is that since all humanity is descended from one, no one can claim superiority over another (Sanhedrin 38a). A number of rabbinic statements extol the virtues of peace (Deuteronomy Rabbah 5:12, 15; Baraita de Perek ha-Shalom; Numbers Rabbah 11:7: Leviticus Rabbah 9:9; Genesis Rabbah 38:6).[33]

A midrash (rabbinic commentary) dictates, "The Torah does not command you to run after or to pursue the other commandments, but only to fulfill them upon the appropriate occasion. But peace you must seek in your own place and pursue it even to another place as well." Psalms 34:14 states, "Seek peace and pursue it." Eisendrath notes that the rabbis did not invent an apology for a just war. They did divide wars into those commanded by divine decree ("milchemet chovah," obligatory war), and those permitted for human purposes ("milchemet reshut," optional war). The former are past history, applying only to the seven tribes of Canaan—the Hittites, Amorites, Canaanites, Perizites, Hivites and Jebusites (Deuteronomy 20: 16-18)—and the Amalekites (Deuteronomy 25:17-19). Maimonides added "war to deliver Israel from enemy aggression" (Misheh Torah: Hilchot Melachim 5:1). Optional war required approval of the Sanhedrin's 71 members, also past history, since the governing body called the Sanhedrin no longer exists. However, some today argue that the former justifies the use of military power in modern Israel. Dictators and oppressors have been identified as the "seed of Amalek" with whom the Lord has war from generation to generation (Exodus 17:16).[34]

The Zionist movement began with peaceful immigration to Palestine. The riots and conflicts of the 1930s were noted earlier. Guerrilla warfare broke out near the end of World War II and continued until the establishment of the Jewish state. War has been a nearly continuous part of modern Israeli history. Groups like Gush Emunim and Rabbi Meir Kahane's militant Jewish Defense League want to push all the Arabs out of Israel. Military action is approved, seen as necessary and promoted. War is appropriate for defense and expansion. Destruction of the enemy has been carried to other lands in what some call terrorist activity and others call freedom fighting.

There is also a Jewish peace movement in Israel as well as the West. The Jewish Peace Fellowship has joined with the Fellowship of Reconciliation along with the Buddhist Peace and Jain Peace fellowships. The JPF was founded in 1941 by Rabbi Cronbach and Jane Evans, and has 3500 members. Associates have included Albert Einstein, Rabbi Leo Baeck, Rabbi Abraham Joshua Heschel and others. Membership comes from all branches of Judaism. The JPF gives an annual Jewish Peace Seeker Award and publishes a Newsletter, *Shalom*, and numerous other materials. It has helped establish the right of Jews to be COs—conscientious objectors to war. It has worked against the draft, nuclear power and capital punishment. It has worked for prison reform, religious and social equality for women, freedom for Jews in Russia, Syria, Iraq and Argentina, for the rights of Falashas and COs in Israel and peaceful reconciliation in the Middle East. JPF's concern is for peace for Jewish people and for all people.

The Shalom Network supports the survival of the state of Israel while supporting Israeli peace groups and self-determination for Palestinians. They also object to the banalization of the Holocaust by using it as an ex-

cuse for politics and aggression. A broad-based coalition called Peace Now
(1970) has been described as humanist. The Oz veShalom (strength and
peace), described as "left-leaning, Orthodox academic," is concerned with
the fulfillment of Torah and Halakhah (Jewish law). It was formed in 1975
by Orthodox intellectuals at Bar Ilan University and moderates in the National Religious Party. The newer Netivot Shalom (paths of peace) is
also halachic but is more centrist. It was formed by rabbis upset by the
Lebanon war (1982) and its implications. Among the laws, these groups
stress the value of human life, one standard of justice for all, Hillel's Golden
Rule, etc.

There is a reminder here that Jews throughout the ages have often been
for moderation and tolerance as well as exclusiveness. While Ezra and
Nehemiah sought to preserve the people by excluding non–Jews, others,
such as the writers of Jonah and Ruth, reminded their people that God cares
for others as well. Hellenistic Jews in the time of Hillel and others through
the ages have stressed the universal elements of Judaism. In all ages, Jews
have intermarried with other peoples and traditions. In the modern period,
Jews have often worked with others to ease the lot of humanity in health,
social welfare, and peace. While supporting their respective nations in
time of war, many have also sought the establishment of a lasting
peace.[35]

Chaim Weizman (1874–1952), Israel's first president, said, "Jews who
aspire to rebuild our destroyed and dispersed people will respect and honor
similar aspirations among other peoples." But Bentwich notes that the Rabbinical Council of Israel is profoundly concerned with small points of the
law but says nothing on behalf of Palestinian refugees. An American
sociologist says the state does not cherish the moral and spiritual values of
Judaism. Israel is suffering from a retarded spiritual development. Bentwich claims that Israel must seek peace. He hopes it will practice "Love thy
neighbor." While the hawks of modern Israel continue to emphasize the
military, the doves seek reconciliation and peaceful solutions. Even the
hawks claim the military might is to ensure peace. General Yitzhak Rabin,
Israeli chief of staff, noted the triumph of the 1967 war but added the sor-
row and shock at dead comrades and "the terrible price paid by our
enemies." Israel's first prime minister, David Ben Gurion, commented on "a
foreign policy of peace, firm aspiration for peace with all our neighbors,
with all nations of the world; an active quest for friendly relations with all
the large and small nations of the East and West. This policy is in itself an
important element of our security."

Certainly peace would allow the state to devote itself to peaceful
development at home and abroad. The state, like Judaism in general, has
supported peaceful pursuits such as agriculture and commerce not only in
Israel but developing nations of the world.[36]

Summary

Judaism, like other world religions, has had its share of war and violence. But along with the military death and destruction there has been hope for peace and justice. While the focus has often been self-centered, including aggrandizement at the expense of neighbors, there is also a strong tradition of concern for peace in the world — in the Bible, in rabbinic tradition, in today's Israel. The "peaceable kingdom" pictured in Isaiah 11 begins with the wolf living with the lamb and moves on to the whole earth. "They shall not hurt or destroy in all my holy mountain; for the earth shall be full of the knowledge of the LORD" (verses 6–9).

The age-old dream of Jerusalem as a city of peace remains.[37] Psalm 122 is an ancient example with its words "Pray for the peace of Jerusalem.... Peace be within your walls.... For my brethren and companions' sake I say, 'Peace be within you'." The prophetic dream of a peaceful world remains very much alive. The prophets' words continue to ring across the centuries with their vision of peace, "They shall beat their swords into plowshares, and their spears into pruning hooks; nation shall not lift up sword against nation, neither shall they learn war any more" (Isaiah 2:4; Micah 4:3).

II. Christianity

Blessed are the peacemakers
for they shall be called
the children of God.
— Sermon on the Mount,
Matthew 5:9

Jesus of Nazareth

As noted in the chapter on Judaism, Christianity has been seen as a sect of Judaism which survived along with the sect of Pharisaic Judaism. Some see Christianity as the daughter of Judaism and some see it as the sibling of Judaism. Its beginnings, in any case, are in an itinerant Jewish preacher named Joshua, or Yehoshuah, Jesus in Greek.[1] He was born, according to the tradition, in Bethlehem in Judea, a few miles south of Jerusalem, but he grew up in Nazareth in Galilee.[2] The latter state, governed at the time by Herod Antipas, had a mixed population of Jews and Gentiles.[3]

Relatively little is known of his childhood. Luke notes that his parents went to Jerusalem every year for the feast of Passover (2:41). When Jesus was about 12, he went with them. Later they found him talking to the scribes in the temple. When he was about 30, his cousin, John the Baptist, began preaching beside the Jordan River. John called on the people to repent of their sins and to be baptized as a sign of repentance or as a ritual washing away of sins. The Essenes of Qumran practiced daily baptism, and some have compared John to them for this reason and because he lived in the wilderness as an ascetic. Jesus too has been identified with the Essenes, but he has more commonly been identified with the Pharisees.[4]

Jesus was baptized by John. Later tradition claimed Jesus was without sin. Matthew 3:14–15 quotes John as questioning the need but Jesus answered that the baptism would fulfill all righteousness. After the baptism, Jesus went into the wilderness to pray and meditate. He resisted the devil's temptations. Meanwhile, John was arrested (and later killed) by Herod Antipas.

Jesus began to preach John's message to "Repent, for the kingdom of heaven is at hand." He gathered 12 disciples and other followers and with them traveled around the land. He preached and taught, healed the sick, raised the dead to life, and performed other miracles over a period of about three years. He taught in aphorisms such as the Golden Rule (Matthew

18

7:12), and in parables – stories to illustrate a point. The parable of the good Samaritan is a well-known example. The common people called him a prophet (Matthew 21:11), though official dogma said prophecy had ended with Ezra over 400 years earlier. At least some thought he was the Messiah.[5]

His teachings included the Sermon on the Mount (Matthew 5–7), in which he proclaimed as blessed the poor, the mourning, the meek, the righteous, the merciful, the pure in heart, the peacemakers, those persecuted for righteousness' sake (cf. echoes of these concepts in Paul's Letter to the Romans, chapter 12). When asked what is the greatest of the Torah's 613 laws, he answered with two: "Love God with all your heart, with all your soul, with all your mind" (Deuteronomy 6:5), and "Love thy neighbor as thyself" (Leviticus 19:18). It has been said that he preached against intolerance and religious bigotry (Matthew 8:5ff, 9:10–13, 21:12–45, 23:1–39; Luke 7:31–50, 9:51–56, 10:25–37, 15:1–32; John 4) and that he rejected the idea that a nation or state is identified with God or his kingdom (Matthew 22:21; Mark 12:17; Luke 20:25). One can note, however, that Matthew 10:5–6 quotes him as instructing his disciples to "Go nowhere among the Gentiles, and enter no town of the Samaritans, but go rather to the lost sheep of the house of Israel." Matthew 15:24 quotes him as saying, "I was sent only to the lost sheep of the house of Israel." The Canaanite woman persisted and Jesus healed her daughter.[6]

Jesus gained a popular following. On what Christian tradition calls Palm Sunday, he entered Jerusalem riding on a donkey, perhaps again fulfilling a prophetic prediction of a king entering the city (Zechariah 9:9). He was greeted by crowds waving palm branches and shouting "Hosanna (Save us, we beseech thee) to the Son of David!" Both the branches and phrase reflect messianic expectations. In addition, he entered the temple courtyard and overturned the tables of the money changers and pigeon sellers, accusing them of changing God's house of prayer into a den of robbers.[7]

In the course of his teaching, Jesus had a series of encounters with religious leaders. In some verses they are the chief priests and elders (Matthew 21:23), while in others they are the chief priests and Pharisees (Matthew 21:45), Pharisees and Herodians (Matthew 22:16), and Sadducees (Matthew 22:23). Jesus called the scribes and Pharisees hypocrites (Matthew 23:13, 23, 25, 27, 29). He also predicted the temple would be destroyed. He was accused of this prediction when he was seized in the Garden of Gethsemane on the Mount of Olives and brought before the high priest, Caiaphas (Matthew 26:47, 57–62). This was presumably blasphemy but the real charge seems to have been whether he was the Messiah (Hebrew), the Christ (Greek). He was sentenced to death.

Apparently the religious leaders could not legally execute him so they accused him before Pontius Pilate, the Procurator of Judea. Pilate had Jesus crucified on what Christian tradition came to call Good Friday. The goodness of the day of death was based on the belief that Jesus died for the sins of humanity. On the following Sunday, Easter, he rose from the dead

or was raised from the dead by God (Matthew 27–28). Details differ
somewhat. According to Luke, he appeared to his disciples many times
over a 40-day period and then ascended into heaven.[8]

The Early Church

The New Testament Book of Acts describes the expansion of the nas-
cent movement and introduces the person of Saul of Tarsus (in Asia Minor,
today's Turkey), a diaspora Jew with a Gentile father. Saul had apparently
come to Jerusalem to study and became involved in persecuting the
followers of Jesus who were accused of heresy. A number were killed and
others fled to other areas. While on the road to Damascus to find more of
these heretic Jews, Saul was blinded by a bright light and heard the voice
of Jesus. Saul was later cured of his blindness by a disciple named Ananias,
and then became a follower of Jesus as well (Acts 8–9), changing his name
to Paul. After some years, he began to preach in the cities of Asia Minor
and Greece, where he started a series of churches initially composed of Jews
and "God-fearers," non–Jews who appreciated the high morality and
monotheism of Judaism. Some of Paul's letters to these churches are
preserved in the New Testament.[9]

One of the major debates about early Christian history is whether Paul
changed the Jewish religion of the historical Jesus into a mystery religion
of the Christ of faith. The traditional claim is that Jesus is the Christ, the
Messiah. Early Christian debates turned on the nature of Jesus. One group
(Ebionites) thought of him as human, a rabbi ("my teacher"), fulfilling the
functions of the Messiah. Another thought of him as divine. He only appeared to die or at the last minute, another person was substituted and the
substitute died on the cross, but Jesus himself is literally God (docetism).
What became the "orthodox" position with considerable political
maneuvering is that Jesus is truly God and truly man. He was God in the
flesh (incarnate). Some have compared this to the Hindu concept of avatar
with the distinction that there are many avatars and Christianity traditionally claims there is only one incarnation.[10]

As Christianity spread after the death of Jesus, it quickly began to include Hellenistic (diaspora) Jews as well as Palestinians. The first martyr,
Stephen, belonged to the first group. A more difficult problem was
non–Jews who were attracted to the faith. A great number of Greeks
"turned to the Lord" (Acts 11:21) in Antioch where "the disciples were for
the first time called Christians" (verse 26). In the beginning, it was assumed
they would first become Jews and then be followers of Jesus. Paul argued
against this. The ritual laws such as circumcision would be set aside in the
messianic age. Jeremiah the prophet had predicted the law would be written
in the heart in the days of the new covenant (Jeremiah 31:31–34). The
concept of a new covenant came in time to mean a new or true Israel just
as Qumranites, Pharisees and other groups before and since thought they

were the true Israel (a continuing issue in both Judaism and Christianity).

During the next several centuries, Christianity met with sporadic persecution. The Roman Empire had legalized certain religions such as Judaism. When Christianity became distinct from Pharisaic Judaism, the better authorities upheld the law and began persecuting this illegal religion. It was legalized by Constantine the Great in A.D. 313. In time, it became the official religion of the Roman (now the Late Roman, Eastern Roman, or Byzantine) Empire. The Christian bishop of Rome became the Pope, a title derived from Roman religions. Conflict arose over the supreme authority claimed by popes over Christianity including authority over the Patriarchs of Alexandria, Jerusalem, Antioch, and Constantinople (earlier Byzantium, today's Instanbul).[11]

Portions of Christianity had already split into groups such as the Monophysites (Jesus and God had one nature). The Nestorians were persecuted by orthodox Christians and fled further east, into the Parthian Empire, and then spread into China. The Arians converted the Germanic tribes which were emigrating from central Asia into central and northern Europe. Other Christians called these movements heresies and they were suppressed in Europe, but in the continuing conflict over authority, the western church and the eastern church excommunicated each other (A.D. 1054). The West continued as the Roman Catholic Church, while the East continued as the Eastern Orthodox. The latter divided into autonomous national groups, which recognized the Patriarch of Constantinople as first among equals — important but not a supreme authority. Further conflicts between the popes and northern Europe eventually led to the Protestant Reformation or schism, led by Martin Luther (Germany), John [Jean] Calvin (Switzerland), and King Henry VIII in England.[12]

Two movements in this history are worth noting for their resemblance to other religious traditions and their later involvement or transformation in war and peace. The monastic movement began with individual ascetics concerned with purifying themselves from the world. They usually withdrew from society to avoid its temptations to sin. Sometimes they attracted disciples, or disciples were attracted to them. The nucleus expanded to a monastic group. Over the centuries, a variety of such groups were formed such as the Benedictines, Franciscans, Cistercians, Dominicans, Jesuits, etc. There were both monks and nuns, which were sometimes related, e.g., Franciscans, nuns and monks who were followers of St. Francis of Assisi. Some groups restricted themselves to monasteries and convents. Others, especially the lay brothers and sisters, reached out to serve people in teaching, caring for the sick or poor, as missionaries, in service of the church, or the pope.

Some of the monastics were mystics. Some mystics founded orders while others were recluses. Christian mysticism has been defined in various ways. It might be seen as communion with the divine, which means for example that all prayer is a form of mysticism. It might be a concern for union, becoming spiritually one, with God. These forms of mysticism have much in common with other traditions such as the Hasidim of Judaism, the Sufis of Islam, the various Indian mysticisms. James A. Aho interprets Christian mysticism as the direct inward experience of being saved — what Christianity in general calls being justified by God. The concept of enthusiasm, "en-theos," in God or God within, filled with God, was sought by some Christians and condemned by others, as in Judaism and Islam.

Women as nuns and mystics raise a third element worthy of comment as an issue in other traditions and one which is prominent today. In Jesus' life and teachings, women play a relatively prominent role. Generally, they were excluded from the religious life of the times. Jesus included them among his followers. He healed women, blessed them, taught them. His parables included women. He allowed women to touch him. Presumably he included them in quoting the Jewish scripture to love one's neighbor. His first resurrection appearance according to John was to a woman.

In New Testament terms, his most prominent disciple was the Apostle Paul. Paul said that in Christ there is neither male nor female. He counted women among his friends and considered them ministers. A mosaic in a Christian catacomb outside Rome suggests women were priests and bishops until the eighth century A.D., although New Testament letters speak against them and Paul himself is quoted as saying he does not allow women to speak. Paul's attitude toward women is heavily debated, but there is some evidence now that he has been quoted out of context in order to demote women and keep them in a subservient position. One famous quotation is from the Letter to the Ephesians which some scholars do not think came from Paul. Ephesians 5 says that as Christ is the head of the Church, so man is the head of woman. The usual quotation of the passage neglects the following verse which says that husbands are to love their wives as Christ loved the Church and died for it. Not too many husbands die for their wives. A far greater indictment, however, turns on the nature of Christ as the "head" of the Church. Christians usually associate Christ with Jesus as the Christ or the Messiah. In the Gospels, Jesus tells followers not to "lord it over" others. The Son of Man (presumably himself) came to serve, not to be served. Christians are to serve one another. The Christian man is the servant of women.

With exceptions, as in monastic and mystic traditions, women in Christianity have not been well treated. Thomas Aquinas considered females as genetic defects for males, teaching the Church considers eternal. The Protestant reformer Martin Luther said that if having too many children kills a woman, that is all right because child bearing is her purpose in life. With exceptions like the Holiness Movement of the 1800s and the Pentecostal Movement which followed, and groups like Unity, it is only in the last several decades that mainline Christian groups have accepted women for ordination. The Eastern Orthodox and Roman Catholic churches still do not. Some women have left the religion while others have stayed in it, trying to work for reform. Still others accept the situation as it is.

Abraham Lincoln once said that a nation cannot exist half slave and half free. As Christianity has enslaved people and treated blacks, women and others as inferior, it has very clearly violated the teachings of its founder. Unfortunately, such infamy is not limited to this religion alone.[13]

A Continuing History

Through missionary activity and military conquest, Christianity had spread from Jerusalem throughout the Roman Empire and then to other areas. Nestorianism, banned in the Roman Empire, was more acceptable in the enemy empire of the Parthians in Persia, as noted earlier. From there it spread to China where it became identified with the ruling regime and died with the regime in the 10th century. The Jacobites spread to India and continue there today along with Roman Catholics and Protestants. The Coptic churches in Egypt and Ethiopia also continue although Christianity in North Africa largely disappeared with the conquests of Islam as the population gradually became Muslim. The same is true of the Near East where less than 10 percent remain Christian. The last major vestiges of Christianity in Turkey were wiped out by the Ottoman Turks with the conquest of Constantinople in 1453. Islam made major inroads into the Balkan region of southeastern Europe and major elements (70 percent in Albania; 30 percent in Yugoslavia) continue. Christian armies gradually reconquered these areas and Spain from Islamic control though the process was not complete until 1917 in the southeast and 1492 in Spain. By this time, Christianity had spread by missionaries and conquest to the rest of Europe. By 1492, however, Christianity was largely confined to Europe.

In 1492 Columbus sailed west and discovered the Americas. In time, by conquest, missionary activity, and European immigration, Christianity spread to the New World. In the Old World, explorers continued, and by 1498 Vasco da Gama of Portugal had sailed around Africa to India. Eventually, Christian missionaries spread western European forms of the faith to sub-Sahara Africa, India, Japan and China. In numbers, Christianity remains small in the last three, ranging from 1–10 percent. It is growing in Korea and remains the majority faith in the Philippines. Christianity is growing faster in sub-Sahara Africa today than in most places. It remains hindered there, vis à vis Islam, because of its identification with European colonialism and the slave trade which took millions of Africans to Europe and the Americas. Overall, Christianity is present in most of the world lending credibility to the designation of a universal (worldwide) religion incorporating all races, nationalities and ethnic groups. In the minds of many, however, it remains largely a Western phenomenon. By 1980, Christianity had a non–Western majority for the first time in 1200 years. By the year 2000, it is estimated that three-fifths of the world's Christians will be in the Southern Hemisphere (Latin America, Africa, India, Australia, etc.).

One might expect European cultural forms of Christianity to be somewhat limited in the future.[14]

War and Peace

In the first three centuries, some Christians may have been pacifists. Pacifism is one interpretation of Jesus' teachings. He put the Jewish teaching of "Love thy neighbor" in a central position. When asked to define neighbor, he offered as an example a Samaritan who helped someone in need (Luke 10:29–37). It would be equivalent to telling a Christian racist today that a black was the neighbor. Jesus went further in emphasizing a minor element in Judaism. He told his followers to love their enemies. If you love only those who love you, what do you do more than others? (Matthew 5:43–46). Instead of retaliating against insult or injury, turn the other cheek (Matthew 5:38–42). Do not do to others as others have done to you, but do to others as you would have them do to you (Matthew 7:12). Jesus never said (at least according to the preserved record) war is wrong. However, some people find it difficult to love enemies and kill them at the same time.[15]

Jesus himself went to his death rather than resist his captors. When he was taken prisoner in the Garden of Gethsemane, Peter (John 18:10; Matthew 26:51 says "one of those with Jesus") drew his sword and cut off the ear of the servant of the high priest. Jesus healed the man and told Peter to put up his sword. "All who take the sword will perish by the sword." He went on, according to Matthew 26:53, to add that he could appeal to his Father and have 12 legions (72,000) of angels, i.e., to protect himself. This has been interpreted that not even defensive warfare is allowed. He proclaimed the way of suffering as in the example of the Suffering Servant of Isaiah's "servant songs" (Isaiah 42, etc.), a nonviolent response to persecution.

As with later Judaism, Jesus' teachings have been interpreted as directing his followers to take the initiative for peace, not merely the way of nonviolence. That initiative includes reconciliation in case of differences (Matthew 5:23–26; 18:15), a ministry echoed by the apostle Paul (Romans 12; II Corinthians 5:20).[16]

Jesus also emphasized the Jewish concept of God as Father, the Father, or Creator of all humanity. Thus all human beings are sisters and brothers under the fatherhood of God. In time, Jesus was presented as the Savior of all humanity. John 3:16 notes that "God so loved the world, that he gave his only begotten son, that whosoever believeth in him should . . . have everlasting life." There is no distinction here between black and white, east and west, south and north, women or men. The apostle Paul later wrote that there is neither male nor female, slave nor free, Greek nor Jew, for all are one in Christ Jesus (Galatians 3:28). The prospect of war then brings with it the awareness that Christians would be killing those with whom Christians are one, their own family under God, those for whom Jesus died, those whom Jesus said to love — not to hate or kill.

At first, this was not a major problem. Christianity was identified with Judaism and as such, Christians escaped military duty. As an illegal religion, there were also some problems about conscripting them. Ferguson claims that for a century and a half, Christians would not touch military service and for another century, the predominant sense was that Christianity and war were incompatible. Christians were accused of undermining the empire by refusing military service as late as the fifth century. He traces the first Christians in the army circa 173 and adds that church rules prevented a believer from joining the army, and soldier-converts were required to renounce killing.

However, Acts 10 records the conversion and baptism of Cornelius the centurion, an army commander, and other gentiles. There is some question about gentiles but there is no suggestion of impropriety because of the military connection. Thus the picture is not quite that clean. Ferguson also notes that Cicero, a Roman pagan in the first century B.C., had explored the concept of a just war (just cause; war declared by constituted authority; conducted justly). The Christian apologists Tertullian (160-230) and Origen (185-254) appropriated this. They allowed that non-Christians might participate in such a just war but not Christians. However, the first recorded appearances of Christians in the army suggest they had been there for some time. The martyrs refer to others in the army. Problems arose not over killing but idolatry — to be an officer or even a common soldier meant swearing allegiance to army standards which were treated as gods as both Tertullian and Origen show. Thus it was not Christianity and war that were incompatible but Christianity and Roman army religion.[17]

With Constantine, faith and empire began to merge. Ferguson notes that Eusebius (d. A.D. 342) separated the clergy and laity. The former are to live according to the new covenant while the latter are excused to exercise the normal obligations of citizenship. This same distinction has been made in Buddhism. Ambrose (340-397), Bishop of Milan, and Augustine (354-430), Bishop of Hippo in North Africa, brought back the holy war. Defense of the empire equals defense of the church. The empire's enemies were equated with the enemies of God. New Testament teachings were spiritualized and internalized. Augustine even told General Boniface not to become a monk — his was a soldier's duty and "the object of war was peace."[18]

It was but a short step to conquest as a way of Christianizing a population or of converting them from heresy such as Arianism to the true faith. Military force converted the Saxons and even the clergy fought in these wars, though participation by the latter was usually prohibited. Some rulings ruled against the sword, so in 1182, the Archbishop of Mainz battled and killed with a mace.

The Frank Chief Clovis claimed that if he and his Franks had been there, no one would have crucified Jesus. He and 3000 followers were baptized on Christmas Day, A.D. 496. After that they fought for God as well as plunder. By the eleventh century, Frankish warriors were ordained knights with confession of sin, a bath of purification, a blessing of their weapons and armor to the defense of the church. With their help the church would rule the world. The oldest surviving German poem praises the apostle Peter for using his sword in Gethsemane.

Among the Vandals, Goths and Alemanni, war was the instrument of the gods. Aho traces Christian holy war to Teutonic warriors. In German sagas, soldiers who die on the battlefield go straight to heaven, a concept of early Islam as well. Pope John VII (705–707) and Leo IV (847–855) promised eternal life to all who defended the Church against Arabs and Vikings. The Holy Roman Emperor Charlemagne (742–814; Emperor 800–814) fought the pagans with papal blessings. Pope Leo IX (1049–1054) gave freedom from sin to soldiers fighting the Normans in southern Italy. Gregory VII (1073–1085) declared the properly ordained knight absolved of sin as St. Peter's servant.[19]

Christian subjects were expected to submit to government authorities. Paul had already claimed these authorities were installed or at least permitted by the will of God (Romans 13:1–2). Kings and emperors were designated defenders of the faith. They were the sword arm of the Church. Later kings claimed divine rights. Some manipulated these concepts to their own advantage, while others may have been quite sincere and quite unable to see the discrepancy between the faith professed and their own action, between loving their enemies and killing them. In the infamous Inquisition (formally established in 1233), non–Christians, suspected heretics and enemies of the regime were tortured, supposedly for their own good — to save their souls even if it meant destroying their bodies.[20]

As Christianity spread throughout Europe, Christians fought and killed each other. They had been doing this for some time, but now the tempo increased. At times, this was under the pretext of different forms of the faith and others were declared heretics. At other times it was simple conquest and raw aggression. The popes themselves carved out territory in central Italy and defended it with their own armies. On several occasions, stronger Christian forces conquered Rome and imprisoned or deposed the pope. Sometimes this was a contest as to who would appoint the pope and thereby control church appointments. The latter meant money from the faithful and rent from inherited lands. The former brought papal blessings for policies of state. In the East, the appointment of patriarchs by the ruler was a foregone conclusion.

It is of value to note here the tradition of Christian chivalry. In some ways it is like the warfare of the Confucian gentleman. While more than willing to slaughter infidels and their own common citizens by the thousands, Christian nobility played war games that have been glorified in such traditions as King Arthur and the Knights of the Round Table. When they were not fighting an official war, they held tournaments or jousting matches. While less destructive of the nobility than the commoners, it was all a far cry from Jesus' "put up your sword." Followers of Gregory VII even suggested Jesus was not telling people to get rid of the sword but to put it in its rightful place — in the hands of the Christian knight.[21]

Perhaps the most infamous of Christian wars were the Crusades. One could argue that when Christian nations conquered people and on occasion massacred large numbers of them, this was politics, an argument that appears again in Islam. It is said that Christianity is against war in general and for war in particular — when one's own nation is involved. The Crusades, however, were not only blessed by the Church; they were officially started by the Roman Catholic Church.

In 1071, the Seljuk Turks defeated the Byzantines in a battle at Manzikert and took over half the Byzantine Empire. The Byzantines appealed to the West for aid and finally the appeal of Emperor Alexius Comnenus to Pope Urban II in 1095 brought a response. Urban preached the First Crusade in Clermont in southern France. He called the Muslims an accursed race alienated from God. He listed their atrocities as desecration of churches, the rape of women, the torture and murder of men. He appealed to Europeans to stop quarreling among themselves, stop hating each other, stop their internecine wars. The crowd roared, "God wills it!" which became the battle cry of the Crusades. The popes sent representatives around Europe recruiting armies with promises of heaven or lesser time in purgatory, the forgiveness of debts and immunity from taxes.

The First Crusade conquered Jerusalem in 1099. Raymond du Aguilers described the conquest of Jerusalem: "Wonderful things were to be seen . . . numbers of Saracens were beheaded . . . others were shot with arrows, or forced to jump from the towers; others were tortured for several days then burned in flames. In the streets were seen piles of heads and hands and feet. . . ." The horses waded in blood up to their bridles. "It was a just and wonderful judgment of God. . . ." One could add that the atrocities of modern war are nothing new. Winnington-Ingram, Bishop of London in World War I, said, "Kill Germans . . . the good as well as the bad."

The crusaders set up the Latin Kingdom of Jerusalem, as well as the counties of Edessa and Tripoli and the Principality of Antioch. They did not recapture this land for the Byzantine Empire but for themselves. The Muslims recaptured Edessa in 1144, which led to the Second Crusade (1147–1149). It was preached by Bernard of Clairvaux at the request of the pope. Bernard rallied thousands with his cry, "To arms then! Let a holy indignation animate you to combat, and let the cry of Jeremiah reverberate through Christendom: Cursed be he that withholdeth his sword from blood!" (Jeremiah 48:10). He preached 86 sermons on chapters 1–2 of the Song of Songs, on love. But love did not stop him from his vicious hatred of the Muslims. The Crusade failed.[22]

Jerusalem was reconquered by Saladin in 1187. The Third Crusade failed to retake it. In 1204, the Fourth Crusade conquered the *Christian* Byzantines and established a Latin Empire which lasted until 1261. The Holy Roman Emperor Frederick II recovered Jerusalem by negotiation in 1228, but this was repudiated by the pope since Frederick was excommunicated as a heretic. Jerusalem was lost again in 1244. The crusaders' control ended completely when the Muslims captured the last stronghold of Acre (Akko) in 1291.

Intermixed among the four main crusades were a series of small ones, including a children's crusade that led thousands of small children to death or slavery. Subsequent crusades were used against Catholic rulers like Frederick, and against so-called heretics of Europe such as the Albigensians. Untold numbers of Jews were butchered, robbed, raped and kidnapped, and their communities destroyed in Europe, both as part of the war fever in local areas, and along the line of march of the crusaders.

Some have suggested that the crusaders were sincere, faithful Christians serving God. They saw their war as a holy mission. Either they were ignorant of Jesus' teachings or they reinterpreted them to suit the needs of the moment. Others have noted that the Crusades rid Europe of its excess sons and children. By primogeniture, the firstborn inherited the land or the title of kings, dukes, and feudal lords. Other sons were placed in church offices but these were somewhat limited in number. The excess spent their time fighting among themselves. This all took place before the rise of the great explorations of da Gama, Columbus, etc., and before the rise of commercial ventures that relieved pressure at a later time. Thus one could argue the Crusades were not Christian at all, but a way for Europeans to solve an excess population problem. The historic fact remains that these wars were started, encouraged and maintained by the Church, and they were fought in the name of Christ. At least in part, too, they were in response to Islamic activities so the religious dimension should not be dismissed entirely.[23]

One might note, in contrast to the Crusades, that the Church had made some attempts at peacekeeping within European lands. The wars were so frequent and devastating, several efforts were made to limit the destruction at the council of Charroux (989), the synods of Narbonne (990), Limoges (994), and Poitiers (1011). The Peace of God (c. 990 through the eleventh century) protected classes of persons and property, e.g., clergy and churches. The synod of Elne in 1027 and of Narbonne in 1054 declared the Truce of God to limit times of combat. Fighting was forbidden from Thursday to Sunday, in Advent, Lent and Eastertide, and on other holy days. If the warring factions took all this seriously, fighting would have been forbidden three-fourths of the year. It was most influential in the twelfth century, but like the earlier Muslims who proclaimed defending Allah was more meritorious than observing holy days, Christians managed to keep on fighting.[24]

The Crusades themselves may be seen as part of the church's efforts at peace in Europe. Early Muslim leaders united the warring tribes of Arabia and focused their fighting energy against the infidels. Ferguson suggests this was the policy of Gregory VII (1073–1085). In 1093, Urban II promulgated the Truce of God and initiated the First Crusade. The monastic tradition was brought into play in the formation of military orders of soldier monks — the Knights of the Temple, or Templars (1119), Hospitallers, or the Knights of St. John, Knights of the Sword (1202).[25]

The fighting continued throughout subsequent centuries. The wars against Islam largely unsuccessful, the Christians fought each other. There were several exceptions or distinctions, however. As noted earlier, the Christians gradually succeeded in Spain and by 1492 had conquered Grenada, the last Muslim district. The Ottomans reached the gates of Vienna in 1529 and again in 1683 but were repulsed. The Protestant Reformation provided fresh opportunities and Catholic and Protestant armies soon met in battle. Huldreich Zwingli (1484–1531), the first reformer in Zurich, Switzerland, died in battle[26]

The killing was not merely on religious grounds. Social conditions at the time were horrible. In 1525, the peasants of Germany revolted. The Lutheran princes asked Martin Luther (1483–1546) what to do and he told them to slaughter the thieving peasants. And they did — an estimated 100,000. Luther thought Jesus' pacifism was no more required than Jesus' celibacy or carpentry. Thomas Muntzer (1489–1525) did not think Luther's reforms went far enough. He claimed a revelation from God. God wills the overthrow of the social structures. He tried to set up communal societies as in the book of Acts and aided the peasants, but along with crushing the revolt, Muntzer was beheaded.

While the Catholic and Lutheran armies charged back and forth in battle, the left wing of the Reformation, a loose grouping of radical movements generally called Anabaptists was gaining momentum. The name was from their insistence on adult baptism by complete immersion, and that normally meant rebaptism. More important to them, however, was an insistence upon separation of church and state and restoration of the church to its New Testament purity. Catholics retaliated by burning them at the stake, while Protestants favored drowning them in parody of their baptismal belief of complete immersion.

In contrast to the separation doctrine, Anabaptists came to power in the city of Munster in 1534, where they also tried to set up a communal society. Catholic and Lutheran armies were fighting each other when the news arrived. They called a truce, put their forces together and marched to Munster. They butchered the inhabitants. Anyone not killed in the fighting was tortured to death. Then the victorious Catholics and Lutherans returned to their own battlefield, resumed their places, ended their truce and went back to killing each other. All this, of course, was done in the name of Jesus, the Prince of Peace.[27]

One can note here that the Protestant reformers in general accepted the doctrine of just war (see later). However, they differed somewhat. Luther separated politics and religion. The government could fight against the Turks though the church should not use violence. Since the state is supposed to serve God, the distinction did not mean much. Soldiers served Christ by being good soldiers. Luther did more than this, for he liberated the state from all moral obligations. The state does not need to love its neighbor. An alternate interpretation here is that he saw the state as self-policing and from there the state moved to self-serving. But Luther went even further. God himself has ordained princes to quell violence. War and killing have been instituted by God. It is God who wields the sword, who hangs, tortures, beheads, kills and fights. He interpreted Paul in Romans 13 as saying anyone who resists the government resists God. Luther claimed that no one since Paul had so exalted the craven power of the state as he, Luther, had.

Zwingli and Calvin (1509–1564) not only accepted the just war doctrine. They and others believed in holy war. Technically this means right theology justifies war. In practice it meant might makes right and the end justifies the means. Chanon said, "Only Christians are permitted to rage against each other with every variety of inhumanity provided it be for the advancement of one party and the detriment of another. Those who are moderate are held suspect." In the later phases of the English Reformation, Oliver Cromwell (1599–1658) and the Puritans carried on a holy war. Cromwell's commoners, like the Templars and other monastic orders, were forbidden to swear, get drunk, commit adultery, etc. It is claimed that like Islam, they were welcomed by the local populations who joined with them. Since the traditional just war doctrine did not allow rebellion against duly constituted government, they did not oppose the king, but his advisers, and concluded that any government that behaved unrighteously was not legitimate. Cromwell found help in the Old Testament. He went to church to sing Psalm 68, "Let God arise and let his enemies be scattered."[28]

Aho suggests that Protestantism contributed to a revolution in war reflected in the absolute inhumanity of total war noted above. He sees Luther, Andreas Karlstadt, Muntzer, and other reformers as having their origin in mysticism to which one could add monasticism since these leaders were monks. They were justified by God and totally righteous or made so by God. On the other hand, people are evil. John Calvin and later Calvinists such as Jonathan Edwards described even newborn babies as totally evil, odious and abominable to God. All human beings are "sinners in the hands of an angry God." Aho describes their god as one who compels the criminal to act and then condemns him to Hell for doing what this god forced them to do. This sadistic theology brought a common result in war from both the separation of church and state in Lutheranism and the union of church and state in Calvinism. Since the world and man himself are inexorably evil, the state is free, and indeed encouraged to destroy evil, that is, destroy human beings, at the hands of this angry god.

Aho suggests that Catholicism tried to harness military force to serve spiritual ends—hence the monastic military orders, the Crusades, the banning of lethal weapons like the crossbow, the banning of enslavement of Christian captives. Protestantism freed the state of any moral restrictions whatsoever in achieving its ends of destroying evil. What is more, says Aho, is that "the Protestant whose spirit is seized by God will strike out at evil with . . . impassioned frenzy. . . ." Inwardly, one must conquer the evil within the self while outwardly exterminating the sin of others, which often means exterminating those others. He sees self-doubt as leading to many atrocities. The ascetic flagellates starved and tortured the self. The crusader tortured and killed others in an effort to scapegoat — put the evil from the self onto others. It was a martial frenzy and Cromwell knew what he was doing when he picked men who "had the fear of God before them" for his troops instead of men of estate. His Ironsides won repeated victories over the royal Cavaliers because they were driven by their ideology, their righteous cause, as the Old Testament heroes and the heroes of Islam before them.

The enemies of the state become the enemies of God and their destruction is God's doing. This was already a part of the holy war concept, and was picked up by Islam in its jihad. While Luther denied that humans are holy and thus there is no holy war, the result was the same as seen by the efficient and deadly destruction carried out by Lutheran states, such as Sweden under Gustavus Adolphus (1591–1632) and Frederick William I (1688–1740) of Germany. They were matched in the Calvinist camp by Maurice (1567–1625) of Orange in the Netherlands and the neo–Calvinist Independent Oliver Cromwell in England.[29]

Lutherans and Catholics in Germany finally came to a compromise in the Peace of Augsburg in 1555 in which the faith of an area would be determined by the faith of the ruler. When this changed, the entire population would simply shift to the other tradition, suggesting something of the lack of commitment people had to different interpretations of the faith. In France the Calvinists (Huguenots) and Catholics battled it out from 1562 until the Edict of Toleration (Nantes) in 1598. When it was revoked in 1685, the Catholics were firmly in power and the Calvinists suffered accordingly. The Dutch wars of independence from Spain pitted the latter Catholic nation against the Calvinists of Holland from 1560 to 1618. The religious dimensions of the English civil war (1642–1648) were noted earlier with Cromwell's use of the Old Testament and holy war.

Continental Europe's wars climaxed in the Thirty Years War (1618–1648), largely a Calvinist-Catholic conflict centered on Bohemia. But wars within countries and between countries were so common that war was virtually normal and peace abnormal. War was carried outside Europe in conquests of the American Indians, African tribes, the maharajahs of India and Indonesia. Christian arms moved into the Near East and the Far East whenever and wherever opportunity offered. In addition to fighting local peoples, European Christians fought each other. Sometimes the local people were caught in the middle between opposing Christian groups. The history of Sri Lanka (Ceylon) is a case in point which went from Portuguese Roman Catholic, to Dutch Calvinist, to English Anglican. Similar conflicts took place in Africa, the Far East, the South Sea Islands and the Americas. Russian Orthodoxy moved with the tsar's forces from Europe to the Pacific and into North America, partly by conquest and partly by incentives such as tax cuts and excuse from military service from those who became Christian.[30]

War continued back in Europe and the West throughout these centuries. The English fought the Dutch, Spanish and the French and gained new territory such as Jamaica and Canada. The colonists fought for independence from England and formed the United States. The French civil war was followed by the Napoleonic wars and later the Franco-Prussian war. The United States fought another war with England, with Mexico, a civil war and with Spain. The devastation of World War I (1914–1917) involved the Christian West and its colonial outposts and the Near East. The war's horrors gave impetus to pacifism for a few decades, but the movement was buried with the dead and debris of World War II. The Nazis, under Roman Catholic Adolf Hitler, and with the tacit support of many German Protestants, systematically murdered six million Jews (the Holocaust) and millions of gypsies, the handicapped, Slavs and enemies of the regime. The war included Asia and much of Africa. When the dust settled, over 54 million people were dead. Hitler has never been excommunicated for his butchery. A Lutheran bishop said the Jews died because God was punishing them for their sins.

Again, one might ask to what extent these were Christian wars and to what extent religion was merely being used to cover political aims. Some suggest the Nazi movement was a repaganization of Europe while others see it as a natural extension of the Christian record. Protestant theologians Reinhold Niebuhr and Paul Ramsey rejected pacifism as unrealistic. Methodist Ramsey suggested violence may be the only way for Christian love to protect a neighbor from oppression. What is clear is that Christianity was unable to stop either war in general or wars in particlar. It has even been suggested that Christianity has started or fomented more war than any group in history. Ferguson notes that while Christianity is one of the most pacifist of the religions in origin, it has a record of military activity second to none. It has an appalling record of bloodshed as the religion of the militant nationalisms of Europe.[31]

More Peaceful Pursuits

There are several alternative lines in this picture. The monk Gratian published his *Decretum* circa 1140, in which he developed the thought of Augustine on just war. A just war includes immunity for clergy, women, pilgrims, monks and the unarmed poor. It requires a just cause, proper authority and obedience. It can be fought for defense and to recover stolen property, to avenge injury, to assert a right. Subsequent thinkers tried to sharpen the definitions of these ideas. Hostensis distinguished several kinds of just war: the faithful against heretics, declared by just authority, and defense. Unjust war was against legal authority or for private gain.

Officially, unjust wars should not be fought. A defensive war was just unless the attackers were blessed by the Church. This standard had been promoted by the earlier Muslims and like them, Christians found ways to defend the faith even when it meant reaching across continents and oceans to attack people who had never heard of Christ. The just war theory became part of the spiritualizing of Jesus' teachings. Thomas Aquinas decided that "resist not evil" was only internal and public authorities were free to use the sword against the guilty. He added the just intention — the end justifies the means. This was further advanced by sixteenth century thinkers. It continues today in many circles. Modern Communism is atheistic and is seen as a threat to world peace by many. Thus a defensive war would be a just war in both its defensiveness and as opposed to the enemies of God. Ferguson suggests that just war is the church's conformity to an unredeemed world — the concept has literally nothing to do with Christianity. Perhaps, from this concern for a just war, one gets the caricature of Christianity as being against war in theory but for war whenever a real one appears and self-interest takes over.

It is worth noting that interest in a just war seems to have been far greater than interest in a just peace. It may simply be because wars have been so common that a theology of war has taken precedence over a theology of peace. But the founder of the movement did not order his followers to fight just wars. He called them to be peacemakers.[32]

Occasionally a different light shines. While the later Franciscans tried to refine the concept of just war, their founder, Francis of Assisi (1181–1226), presents a different picture. He went to the Near East to seek a peaceful end to the Crusades. He is the antithesis of "Kill the infidel. God wills it." The famous prayer attributed to him holds peace in a central place:

> Lord, make me an instrument of Your peace.
> Where there is hatred let me sow love;
> Where there is injury, pardon;
> Where there is doubt, faith;
> Where there is despair, hope;
> Where there is darkness, light; and
> Where there is sadness, joy.
>
> O divine Master, grant that I may not so much
> Seek to be consoled as to console;
> To be understood as to understand;
> To be loved as to love;
> For it is in giving that we receive;
> It is in pardoning that we are pardoned; and
> It is in dying that we are born to eternal life.

The Waldensians, a sectarian group in Italy, were a pacifist group which left the Church and then were persuaded to return with exemption from military service. The Lollards in 1395 presented Twelve Conclusions to the English Parliament. The tenth condemned war. The Hussites in Bohemia developed a pacifist wing under the direction of Peter Czelcicky (c. 1390–1460). The Roman Catholic scholar Desiderius Erasmus wrote a famous tract, "The Complaint of Peace," in which he condemned the horrors of war and pleaded for commitment to the Prince of Peace. Ferguson notes that as a loyal Catholic, he accepted the doctrine of just war but did not acknowledge as just the wars of his day.[33]

A different perspective in part came out of the destruction of Munster. Like the Jews after A.D. 135 and the final destruction of Jerusalem, the Anabaptists turned to peace. Menno Simons (c. 1496–1561), a former Roman Catholic priest, joined the group in 1636. He traveled throughout Europe, rallying the scattered Anabaptists and inspiring them to new life. A dedicated pacifist, his preaching led to the complete repudiation of violence and the beginning of the peace churches movement. Many of the descendants are called Mennonites in memory of this itinerant preacher.[34]

Several groups of Anabaptists found refuge from Catholic persecution by seeking protection from tolerant rulers in Moravia. They formed economic communities called "Bruderhof." Under the leadership of Jakob Hutter (d. 1536), they became known as Hutterites. Others in southern Germany and Switzerland were known simply as brethren. Conrad Grebel (1498–1526) of the Swiss Brethren had earlier written to the militant Thomas Munzer that the Gospel teaches peace. In time these groups lost their zeal but in recent decades have experienced a revival. Between 1950 and 1975, estimated growth doubled their numbers to about 600,000.[35]

George Fox also believed in separation of church and state, and more. He thought one should not only claim Jesus as savior. One should follow Jesus and practice his teachings. He claimed that Christ had taken away his sins and for this blasphemy, in 1650, he was sentenced to jail. He told Judge Bennett to tremble in fear of God, but the judge laughed and said it was Fox and his followers who were the quakers. The name stuck and is still used today, though officially they are the Friends or Society of Friends following Jesus' teaching, "You are my friends, if you do what I command you." Heavily persecuted, imprisoned, murdered, the movement grew. Finally William Penn, Jr., was given what today is the state of Pennsylvania (Penn's woods) as payment for a debt King James owed Penn, Sr. Penn established the colony as a refuge for Quakers and others. In contrast to many groups, when they themselves achieved control, the Quakers did not turn on their enemies but extended freedom of worship to all. They worked against slavery and for relief of all kinds for the poor. The movement extended to the American Indians and today there are more Native American Quakers than English Quakers. Our concern with the movement is its dedication to nonviolence. It is no accident that Pennsylvania became a refuge for Mennonites, Moravians and Brethren.[36]

The historic peace churches sometimes participate in today's peace movement. This generic term applies to a wider concern and includes more than Christians or Christianity. The Fellowship of Reconciliation, for example, was noted earlier. Among its affiliates are the Ethical Culture/ Humanist, Buddhist, Jain and Jewish peace fellowships as well as peace fellowships of the Roman Catholic Church and several Protestant groups, and individuals without any formal religious identification. The FOR began in 1914, initiated by a Quaker and a German Lutheran. It recognizes the essential unity of all humanity as it explores the power of love and truth for resolving human conflict. It seeks a just and peaceful world community with full dignity and freedom for every human being. It is committed to nonviolence and seeks not only the abolition of war but a just and compassionate social order. The FOR's concern is not merely the absence of armed conflict but loving concern without bitterness or contention, a concern that extends to education and respect for all persons without regard to racial, sexual, creedal or national backgrounds.[37]

The modern move for peace has spawned much research for peace, numerous organizations both religious and secular, and many books. Since the explosion of the first atomic bomb in 1945 there has been a growing concern with nuclear weapons. Various efforts have been made to stop producing them, to freeze current levels of production, to somehow avoid a nuclear war. The "anti-nuke" concern has generated a movement of its own. While Christians and churches are prominent, the concerns are worldwide and both interfaith and secular.[38]

Peace is not the concern of all Christians and Christian groups, however. Simmons notes that "Certain eschatological visions of the future almost hope for a nuclear conflagration so that Jesus will come again. Dispensationalist thought, for instance, is little interested in peacemaking but is eagerly awaiting Armageddon – the last great military confrontation (Revelation 16:16). Some have united with New Right politics in opposing SALT II and START talks and the Panama Canal Treaty. They advocate an escalation of the arms buildup and a hawkish foreign policy. Behind their view is a perverse optimism based upon a theology of a thorough-going sinfulness of the age and an apocalyptic eschatology." He calls this the "Judas syndrome" – they believe they can force God's hand to destroy the enemy while they themselves will be saved. Some claim they will be caught up in the sky to meet the returning Jesus in the "Rapture," while all other human beings are killed. Simmons thinks a nuclear holocaust is made more probable by misguided religious fanaticism. But he paraphrases Jesus' words, "Those who live by the (bomb) will die by the (bomb)" (Matthew 26:52).

Glen Stassen adds as an example the work of Hal Lindsey, who claims the biblical prophets are making predictions about Iran, Russia, etc., but not the United States. Lindsey then proceeds on explicitly nonbiblical grounds to call for a huge nuclear buildup, thus placing his trust in "horses and chariots" rather than God – "precisely what the prophets identified as idolatry." Stassen goes on to note what he calls "idolatrous silversmithism" (Acts 19:23ff) – the concern with profits to the hurt and endangerment of the lives of others. He adds that the problem appears in the Soviet Union as well as the United States.[39]

Stassen suggests that our root problem is relational or, rather, a broken relationship. The essence of biblical peacemaking is the reconciliation of God and humanity. It is vertical relationship with God and horizontal relationship with people. Instead of self-righteously blaming each other, we are called to embrace one another — yes, even, and especially, our enemies. "If we are on God's side, if we are a follower of Christ who died on that cross, then the future we hope for and pray for is redemption for our enemies and fellowship with them. When we pray regularly that way, it transforms our attitude toward our enemy. We can't wish nuclear incineration and radiation would melt the flesh of brothers and sisters for whose redemption we are sincerely praying."[40]

III. Islam

God will guide men to peace.
If they will heed him,
He will lead them from the
darkness of war to the light
of peace.

Background

Non-Muslims often see the origin of Islam in the person of Muhammad the Prophet. Chronologically, there is some truth in that, though spiritually Muslims see the origin in God, whom they call 'Allah, who revealed himself in the Holy Quran. One could note historically that there are precedents for the faith. Judaism and Christianity were monotheistic and both were known to the Prophet through representatives in the area and traditionally from his caravan travels to Syria. The religion of the Arabian peninsula more generally was polytheistic with the worship of many spirits, goddesses and gods. One of these was Allah, the creator God worshipped by the Quraysh tribe.[1]

While other deities were worshipped in the form of idols and spirits were known at springs, unusually shaped rocks, etc., Allah (Arabic al-ilah, the God) was imageless. Inside the Ka'ba, or Kaabah ("cube"), in the shrine at Mecca, Allah was worshipped along with other deities such as Hubal, a chief male deity, and three goddesses, Lat, Manat, and 'Uzza — mother goddess, goddess of fate, and the morning star — three daughters of Allah.[2]

Mecca itself was one of the major shrines of the peninsula. It is located on the western side of Arabia, 45 miles from its seaport of Jidda and about halfway between the Mediterranean and Arabian seas. It was a caravan center for both the north-south spice trade from Yemen and India, and several trade routes converging from the east coast and Iraq, to the Mediterranean world. If trade declined, as when the Egyptian sea route to India was opened through the Red Sea, the town suffered. It had no agricultural area for economic reserve. The pilgrimage (hajj) site, however, was important to all Arabia, and pilgrimage was combined with trade fairs and other commercial activities.[3]

Built into the Ka'ba is a black stone usually thought to be a meteorite

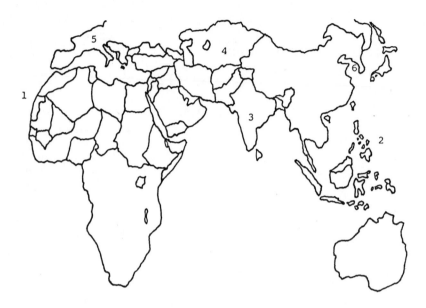

The traditional "World of Islam" stretches from (1) North Africa to (2) the Philippines, from (3) India (90 million Muslims) to (4) the Soviet Union (40 million Muslims), from (5) Europe to (6) Korea, and now to the Americas. (Map by Joyce E. Thompson.)

worshipped as a heavenly stone, in hope for heavenly blessings. Worship consisted of running around the stone seven times and kissing the sacred rock. The Black Stone was ascribed to Adam of the Hebrew creation story. When it was built into the cube building, the building was ascribed to Abraham by some, while others credited Adam with the building and Abraham and his son Ishmael with a rebuilding. Arabic tradition shared with the Hebrew tradition the belief that Abraham was the father of Ishmael, ancestor of the Arabs.[4]

Muhammad the Prophet

Muhammad (Arabic, "praised") was born about A.D. 571 and died in 632. He was the son of Abdallah ibn ("son") Abd-al-Muttalib and Amina bint Wahb. His father died before he was born and his mother died when he was six years old. He was raised first by his grandfather, Abd-al-Muttalib, who died when Muhammad was eight, and then by uncle Abu ("father") Talib. They belonged to the Hashim clan of the Quraysh tribe which ruled Mecca. Later Muslim rulers — the Umayyads, Abbasids, and Fatimids — were of this tribe. The kings of Morocco and the Hashemite kings of Jordan (and of Iraq after World War I) are descendants.[5]

Muhammad grew up in poverty according to Sura ("chapter") 93:6f of the Quran, which may help account for his later opposition to irresponsible use of economic power, hoarding wealth, extravagance and waste, and failure to give to the poor. When he was 12, he traveled to Syria with his uncle's caravan, and went again when he was 25 and guiding caravans for a wealthy widow named Khadijah (d. 619). He married her that year (596). She was 15 years older than he. They had seven children—four girls and three boys. The girls grew up enough to get married but only Fatimah (606–632) survived to produce descendants. She was married to Muhammad's cousin, Ali, whom Muhammad also adopted as a son. He also adopted a Christian slave boy, Zaid ibn Haritha, as his son.[6]

At the age of 40 (A.D. 611), he began having visions of the angel Gabriel. In the first, Gabriel said "Recite: In the Name of thy Lord who created Man of a blood-clot. . . ." According to one interpretation, Muhammad could neither read nor write. He memorized the messages and eventually began preaching them in the sacred precincts of the Ka'ba. First, he shared them with his wife, his first convert, and family members and friends. Some believed and some did not. His adopted son Zaid, adopted son and cousin Ali and friend Abu Bakr were among the first, but in four years he gained only about 40 converts.[7]

There was considerable opposition, including violence. Many of his followers took refuge for a time in Ethiopia. While some people thought he was crazy, the revelations themselves may not have been so much a problem as the claim to be a prophet. This might have been interpreted as a bid to take control of the city and the holy shrines with their revenue. His preaching included social justice and helping the poor, as well as his monotheism. The former would have threatened the wealthy vested interests in the power structure. The worship of 'Allah which Muhammad preached was not in and of itself new, but the monotheism was. This would have threatened those who made money from the polytheistic shrines. Muhammad himself feared for his sanity, according to an early tradition noted by the historian al–Tabiri, as coming from Muhammad's later wife, 'A'isha, but Khadijah reassured him as did her cousin Waraqa, an old blind man who may have been a Christian.

Opposition finally forced him to flee, in A.D. 622, which became the year 1 in the Muslim calendar—1 A.H.—the year of the Hijra (flight or migration).[8] He went to Yathrib some 250 miles to the north. The year before, he had met men from there at the commercial fair in 'Ukaz. The city was divided by the blood feud of the Aws and Khazraj. The six men were looking for a leader who could unite the warring factions. He did and the city was renamed Medina, or Madinat an Nabiy (City of the Prophet), in his honor.

He developed the mosque (place of prostration) as a meeting place, worship services on Friday, the call to prayer by the muezzin, prostration in prayer in the direction of Jerusalem. Later, when the Jews of Medina opposed him, he changed the direction toward Mecca where it remains.

Above all, he developed the umma, the community, the brotherhood. The new community included Muslims and those who would fight along with them. Men are enemies of one another but under leadership they become as one hand. The umma, united against all others, gave the new community its identity. To get funds, he led his men in an attack on a Meccan caravan, which brought war with Mecca. After several indecisive battles, Muhammad's forces won. In 630, he conquered the city. Within months, nearly all Arabia was under his control. Nearby opponents were conquered and more distant tribes were invited to pay tribute. He died June 3, 632 (10 A.H.), at the age of 61, and was buried in Medina.⁹

After Khadijah's death, Muhammad had remarried. Some say 12 times, others nine. His favorite wife was Aisha or Ayesha (614–678), the daughter of Abu Bakr, whom he married when she was seven. He died in her arms when she was 18. She was a powerful political figure in the later intrigues of empire, working against her stepson Ali. In Muslim tradition she is called the Mother of Believers. Another wife was Hatsa, the daughter of Umar or Omar. Muhammad's death was a crisis in the movement. While the Hadith ("traditions," nonrevelational sayings attributed to Muhammad) legends considered him sinless, he had never declared himself to be anything other than a human being.¹⁰

Abu Bakr, whom Muhammad had often designated to lead prayer, stepped into the breach with the announcement that Muhammad was dead but Allah lives. Muslims, those who submit, do not worship Muhammad. They submit to Allah, and Islam ("to submit") is the religion (din) of Allah. Muhammad is his prophet (rasul), the last, and the greatest, but only a man. Muhammad is honored but only Allah is worshipped. Abu Bakr became the first of four Companions of Muhammad who ruled as Caliphs (successors). They had spiritual and temporal powers but not prophetic. Muhammad was the last prophet. Abu Bakr ruled from 632–634. Revolts erupted all over Arabia but he just as quickly quelled them, formed the conquered into armies and sent them into Palestine and Syria.¹¹

Umar ibn al–Khattab, another father-in-law of Muhammad, ruled from 634–644. In 635, Syria, Palestine and Iraq fell to the conquerors though Jerusalem held out for a while. The armies entered Iran in 637, but it was 651 before the entire area was subdued. It took from 640–652 to conquer most of Asia Minor. In 640 Egypt fell and in 643, Tripoli. Umar established the calendar as beginning on July 16, 622 (1 A.H.). He was murdered by a Persian slave. His successor Uthman or Othman, a member of the Umayyad clan of the Quraysh tribe, ruled from A.D. 644–656. He had the official recension made of the Quran in 651 (30 A.H.). Other collections were destroyed. In that same year, Muslim diplomats were in China. Uthman appointed his family to high positions and the resulting scandals led to his murder by Egyptian Muslims who gathered to force his abdication.¹²

Cousin Ali triumphed initially over three rivals and ruled from 656–661. He lost the support of the puritan Khariji movement founded by al Rasibi and was assassinated by the Khariji, Ibn Muljam. He and Fatimah had two sons, Hasan (d. 669) and Husayn (d. 680). The prophet's lineage continued through the latter. Ali's murder by disgusted followers brought the first major rift in Islamic ranks, dividing the orthodox Sunni from the followers of Ali, the Shiites (Arabic, "party") or Shi'a, who number between 10-20 percent of Muslims today. Before further expansion, we need to stop and consider the all-important Quran as well as other teachings and practices.[13]

Word and Traditions

Uthman's recension of the Quran (Arabic, reading, recitation) was noted above. Tradition says the Arabic editors used a collection made by Muhammad's secretary, Zaid ibn Thabit, from writings on palm leaves, carvings on stone, and memories. The verses were arranged in chapters called suras, from the longest to the shortest. Thus generally earlier ones come after later ones. Some historians divide Muhammad's life into the Mecca and Medina phases. In Medina, tradition describes revelations in public. He would break out in a sweat on a cold day. He became entranced or fell into a trance. Once, it is said, he was on his camel and the weight of the revelation brought the stunned animal to her knees.[14]

From non–Muslim perspectives, the suras are sayings of Muhammad, but to Muslims these are the pure word of God. The sayings of Muhammad are preserved in six separate canonical (accepted as authoritative) collections of Hadith plus several other noncanonical collections. These were not made for several centuries. Al-Bukhari (d. 870) reduced 600,000 reputed sayings to 7,275 supposedly genuine ones, based on the trustworthiness of the contributors, somewhat like the sayings of Buddha passed down by oral tradition.[15]

The deeds of Muhammad are preserved as sunna (custom), hence the name Sunni for orthodox Islam. These, and the biographies of the first century A.H., are important sources of information though not all scholars accept everything in them as correct. That, of course is true for hadith and sunna as well.

The Quran tells of the last judgment, and of paradise for the faithful. The last is a place of cleanliness, rich food and drink, and wide-eyed houris (dancing girls) waiting on them (56:15–23, 34f, and 2:255). This suggests a male paradise. Some verses see the houris as faithful wives, returned to the beauty of youth. Sura 73:5–15 quotes Allah as saying, "We have sent you a Messenger as a witness even as We sent to Pharaoh a Messenger." The parallel suggests Muhammad is a new Moses. The latter, along with Abraham, Jesus and many others are genuine prophets and the Hebrew and Greek Bibles are the word of god. They and the Quran were revealed from an original book in heaven but the first two became distorted through human misunderstanding. The Quran is accurate and final but people of the book – Jews, Christians, Sabaeans and others – were respected even as they were also allowed to accept the final message of Muhammad. Non-Muslim sources often claim Muslims forced the conquered to accept Islam but Muslims deny this. "There shall be no coercion in religion" (Sura 2:257; see also 10:100 and 18:30). Aho notes the suggestion that this protection was continuous with the ancient bedouin concept of hospitality, which also appears in the Hebrew Bible.[16]

On a larger scale, Muslim authorities identified faith and practice – Islam is for all of life – literature, economics, politics, etc. – not just the holy day or the worship hour. However, there are three categories here – articles of faith (iman), right conduct (ihsan) and religious duty ('ibadat). The first begins with the creed, "There is no god but God (la ilaha illa Allah) and Muhammad is his messenger (rasul)." God has 100 names but he is one.[17]

There is continuing debate over God offering guidance to man who has freedom of will and predestination (Sura 8:17, 9:51), Turkish kismet, in which the all-knowing God has determined in advance what will happen. Sunni Muslims tend to the latter view. Some have equated this with fate. Individuals often speak of the future, whether good or bad, as Inshallah, "God willing." In the former view, Allah does not guide the wicked (Sura 9:110). He reveals his will to the faithful through Muhammad, the Quran and angels. The three are part of one process since angels revealed the Quran to Muhammad.

Right conduct includes prohibitions against killing newborn children (common practice among the poor bedouin, especialy of females), alcohol, gambling, idolatry, cheating the poor, hoarding wealth, usury (it exploits those in need), extravagance and waste. Religious duty includes witness (shahada) by repeating the creed, prayer (salat) five times a day, alms (zakat), fasting (saum) during the month of Ramadan, and the pilgrimage (hajj) to Mecca. The fast is in the Quran (Sura 2:181) while the others come from the tradition, including Muhammad's practice. The five are called the Five Pillars (al–Arkan). Jihad, or holy war, has been added as a sixth by the Kharijis and others. They follow the example of Muhammad who spent several years in war. He is supposed to have said, "My fate is under the shadow of my spear." But the Five are for individuals while most Muslims see jihad as a function of the state.

Sometimes the Quran, hadith and sunna were not clear in a given situation. The use of reason (ijtihad) was favored by many, sometimes by the use of analogy (qiyas). A hadith has Muhammad himself approving of the exercise of judgment. The consensus (ijma') of the people could also be relied on for Muhammad said, "My people will never agree to an error."

This way of change has been used by Muslim modernists who see Islam as a dynamic faith relevant to the times rather than a static faith limited to the interpretations of old. This is relevant in many areas of life but we note here particularly the issue of women's rights. Muhammad was a radical reformer who upgraded the status of females. He forbade the exposure or burial alive of infants, for example. Female infants were most often the ones killed since they were an economic burden on the bedouin. He also made provisions for multiple marriage and respectful treatment of women to care for the excess women when so many men were killed in war. In a short time, women were relegated to their previous status. The imposition of the veil, a Syrian and Persian custom, is but one example. Today, some women are going back to Muhammad, and in the light of modern conditions they are seeking rights such as better divorce laws. More Muslim women are taking part in government, education, commerce and industry, and even politics. But in many areas, conservative backlash continues to restrict them or is trying to reinstate old restrictions.[18]

Continued Expansion

Umar had appointed the Umayyad Mu'awiya, or Moawiyah, as governor of Syria in 639. He was Ali's third opponent at Uthman's death. He began extending his control in Syria and Africa. Ali objected but he got Ali to promise to negotiate a truce. While Ali waited, Mu'awiya cemented his control of the empire. On Ali's death, he declared himself caliph with his capital at Damascus. Under the 14 caliphs (A.D. 661–750) of the Umayyad, or Omayyad, dynasty, Islam extended its sway over North Africa (Carthage fell in 689) and Spain (710), moved into France (718) where it was stopped in 732 by Charles Martel (Battle of Tours), and Switzerland, into Turkestan and Mongolia, and into India, Sind (today's southeast Pakistan), the lower reaches of the Indus River (A.D. 712). Abd al–Malik (685–705) built the famous Dome of the Rock in Jerusalem in 691. The family was killed by the Abbasids, except for one member, Abd er–Rahman, who established his rule in Cordova, Spain, where the Umayyad caliphate continued until 1031. Subsequent dynasties, the Almoravids (1056–1147), Almohades (1130–1269) and Masrids (1232–1491) maintained a Muslim presence until the Christian, Ferdinand of Castile, conquered the last.[19]

Abu Muslim, later Caliph Abu al–Abbas al–Safah, conquered Mecca and united the rest of the empire. His son, Mansur, moved the capital to Baghdad. The fifth caliph, Harun ar–Rashid (736–809; ruled from 786) is famous in the West for his role in the "Arabian Nights" stories. The Abbasids' 37 caliphs ruled from 750–1258 but lost North Africa west of Egypt in 787. In later centuries, the empire broke down into many independent sections.

Ahmad ibn Tulun was governor of Egypt in 878, became independent and conquered Syria. The Tulids ruled until 904. Said ibn Husayn claimed descent from Fatimah and established the Shiite dynasty of Fatimids (910–1171) over Egypt, North Africa, Sicily, Mecca and Syria (961). The sixth caliph, al–Hakim bi–Amo Allah (996–1021), burned the Church of the Holy Sepulchre in Jerusalem in 1010, an event which was background for the Crusades (1095–1291). The Seljuk Turks came out of central Asia. Togrul entered Baghdad in 1055. The Abbasid caliph declared him sultan (Arabic for victorious or ruler). The Seljuks took Syria from the Fatimids and then declined in power. In the more successful army of Nur ad–Din (1118–1174) was a Kurd named Salah ad–Din, or Saladin (1137–1193), who established the Ayyubid dynasty (1171–1250) over Egypt and Syria. He defeated the crusaders in the Battle of Hattim in 1187.

The Mongols ravaged the Near East in 1216. Jenghis Khan had pulled the tribes together to form an empire. His sons and grandsons established khanates in China (Yuan dynasty), Turkestan, Russia (Empire of the Golden Horde) and Persia. The Mongols were stopped by Mameluke (Arabic, "owned") general Baybars near Nazareth in Palestine. The Mongols were converted to Islam in 1295 but that did not stop Tamerlane (1336–1405) from conquering the Muslim empires of central Asia and India.

The Mamelukes were slaves used as soldiers by the Fatimids and Ayyubids. In 1250, Aybak took over and their sultans — Turks, Mongols and Circassians — ruled until they were defeated by the Ottoman Turks in 1517. The Ottomans had conquered Constantinople in 1453. They took most of Hungary (1526–1543) but were beaten back from the gates of Vienna in 1529 and 1532 or they might have taken Europe. They remained in power until 1917.

Babur, a Turk who claimed descent from Tamerlane, established the Mughal Empire (1526–1857) in India. The Safavids ruled Persia (1502–1736) and made Shiism the official state religion. They were followed by three other dynasties until the Pahlevi (1925–1977). The Arabs fought the Turks in World War I and helped bring down the Ottoman Empire. The Near East broke up into states under French (Syria, Lebanon) and British (Iraq, Jordan, Palestine, Egypt) influence. The puritanical Wahhabi under Abd al–Aziz ibn Saud (1888–1953) conquered (1900–1925) much of Arabia and established Saudi Arabia. They trace their name to Muhammad ibn 'Abd al–Wahhab (1703–1787). After World War II, Israel was established in Palestine. India divided into India and Muslim East and West Pakistan (1947), with 90 million Muslims still in India today. In 1971, East Pakistan revolted and became Bangladesh.

In addition to conquest, Islam spread through trade, commerce, travel and peaceful migration. Indonesia and the Philippine island of Mindanao are Muslim. The former, with 150 million Muslims, is the largest Muslim country in the world (about 800 milion worldwide). Today, there are Muslims in western Europe and the Americas. It is the second largest religion in Europe and the third largest religion in the United States. Since a Muslim brother could not be kept as a slave, early Muslims enslaved non–Muslims. Slaves were a primary source for the harem system and for the Mameluke armies. Arab slavers were prominent in the slave trade of black Africa. They avoided the issue of brotherhood by avoiding conversions. This is largely forgotten today. The West abolished slavery over a century ago but it remained legal in some Muslim countries until recent decades. However black Africa was colonized by European countries. Islam is not identified with these colonial powers. Slavery is forgotten except for the Muslim prayer that the righteous are they who set slaves free. Islam is growing in black Africa today through contact and active missionary programs.[20]

Divisions

Before his death, Muhammad proclaimed all Muslims to be brothers. A Muslim prayer says, "The believers are brothers. So make peace between your brothers and observe your duty to God. . . ." The almost constant internecine warfare outlined above suggests that at times the brotherhood was very nominal. Some dissension was doctrinal. The Kharijis, or Kharijites, were separatists who deserted Ali and later murdered him when he delayed. They were puritans who objected to the Johnny-come-lately Umayyads and others who became Muslims for financial or political reasons. Their own lives were austere. They thought the Islamic state should be permanently organized for war to ensure that heretics were converted or killed. They were ruthless in fighting, killing noncombatants and prisoners without mercy. The Umayyads slaughtered them without mercy as heretics though their belief still persists in moderate form among the Ibadis in areas such as Algeria, Tunisia, Oman and Zanzibar. The Murjites (irja', to postpone) favored delayed judgment — only God can decide who is a true believer. This position was more widely accepted and generally helped the Umayyads and the development of the traditions and the later Sunni.[21]

The Shi'a ("party"), estimated today at between 10-20 percent of Islam, and located in Iran, Iraq (30 percent of the population), India, East Africa, Yemen, etc., goes back to Ali. The Shi'as' claim was that the caliphate belonged to the descendants of Muhammad, the people of the house (Ahl al–Bayt). Muhammad chose Ali as successor. The creed here is "There is no god but God; Muhammad is the Prophet of God, and Ali is the Saint of God." The murders of Ali and his sons, Hasan and Husayn, are as focal to Shiism as the death of Jesus on the cross is to Christianity. The first three caliphs are still cursed in the Friday prayers.

Over time, they developed several theological concepts such as dissimulation (taqiyah) which allowed them to conform outwardly to the demands of their Sunni persecutors, and thus survive. It also facilitated the rise of secret societies. Shiites saw Allah as just and man as having free will. This helped explain Sunni persecution and assured the faithful that Allah would act to vindicate the righteous (themselves). The imam ("example," from Arabic "amma," to walk), is simply the leader in worship in Sunni tradition. For the Shiites, every legitimate leader is an imam mahdi, a divinely appointed and guided leader with special knowledge and insight, sinless and infallible in interpreting the law. Sunnis call this heresy. Ali (d. 661) was the first imam, Hasan (d. 669) the second, Husayn the third. The third fell in battle at Karbala fighting against Yazid, the second Umayyad caliph. In time, Shiites supported the Abbasids, blood relatives of Muhammad but did not get much better treatment.[22]

In time, too, the Shiites split into various sects. The Zaidites, or Zaydis, followed Zaid as fifth imam instead of Muhammad al-Baqir (d. 731). They have had a dynasty in Yemen since the ninth century and for varying periods in Tabaristan, Morocco, etc. The Twelvers (the majority of the Shiites) say the twelfth imam, Muhammad al-Muntazar (d. 878 at the age of five) did not die but withdrew. He will return as the Mahdi. In the meanwhile, he guides his followers through selected representatives. In the Safavid period, the Shah claimed to be this representative.

The third largest group of Shiites are the Seveners, or Isma'ilites, or Isma'ilis. They follow Isma'il (d. 760) as the seventh imam instead of Musa al-Kazim (d. 797). When his father, Ja'far al-Sadiq (d. 765), was told Isma'il was drunk, he transferred the imamship to Musa. Isma'ilis think the drunkenness charge a lie. Isma'il is not dead but hidden and will come again as the Mahdi.[23]

The Isma'ilis interpret the Quran allegorically and spread their esoteric doctrines by secret missionary activity, concealing their work with taqiya. One secret group developed as the Qarmatians, named for Hamdan Qarmat in the ninth century. For a time they held all of eastern Arabia, controlled the caravan and pilgrimage routes from Iraq to Mecca, looted Mecca during a pilgrimage and stole the Black Stone. They returned the latter 20 years later when the Fatimid caliph al-Mansur requested it. The Fatimids were also Isma'ilis. The Druze, known to modern newspaper readers from the crisis in Lebanon, get their name from an Isma'ili missionary from Bukhara, Muhammad ibn Isma'il al-Darazi, who convinced the mountain dwellers that the sixth Fatimid caliph, al-Hakim (d. 1021), who mysteriously disappeared, would return some day as the Mahdi. The Assassins were founded by Hasan Sabbah (d. 1124). The name is from the Arabic hashishi, since they took hashish. They murdered rulers and officials they considered unrighteous. The Assassins were often killed in the process but they believed they went straight to paradise. At times, they held considerable territory in northern Persia and Syria, where they became known to the crusaders and hence to the West.

The majority of Isma'ilis today, about two million, moderate offshoots of the Assassins, are found in India, Pakistan and East Africa. They are divided into Musta'lis and Nizaris, named after two sons of Caliph Mustansir (d. 1094). The latter are known in the West as followers of the Aga Khan (Chief Commander). The title was given to the 46th Isma'ili imam by the Kajar Shah of Persia in 1834.

Other divisions are worthy of note. There are four schools of interpretation of Islamic law (shari'a). The Hanifite was founded by Abu Hanifa (d. 767), a Persian in Iraq. He made little use of Hadith but applied the

Quran to the situation in Iraq. If there was no direct application, he used analogy (qiyas) and reasoned judgment (istihsan, careful judgment for the public good). The Quran prescribes cutting off the hand for theft (Sura 5:37), but that was for a situation not analogous to Iraq, so he derived imprisonment as punishment. Hanifite was followed by the Abbasids and the Ottomans and is used today in Iraq, Iran, Central Asia, Pakistan and India.

The Malikite school in Medina is from Malik ibn Anas (715–795), who used the Quran and Hadith together. In difficulty, he leaned on the consensus (ijma') in Medina, then analogy and finally, the public good. This school prevails in North Africa and eastern Arabia. The Shafi'ite was founded by al-Shafi'i, a Persian born Quraysh. He studied the other two, used the Quran, Hadith and Sunna, consensus and analogy. The first two have equal weight but on occasion, he favored the Hadith. This school prevails in the East Indies and influences southern India, East Africa, southern Arabia and Cairo. The most conservative is the Hanbalite school of Ibn-Hanbal, a student of al-Shafi'i, who was shocked by the loose living of Baghdad in the days of Harun al Rashid. He follows the letter of the Quran and secondarily the Hadith. This school is followed in Saudi Arabia.[24]

Doctrinally, one can note Islamic liberals and conservatives. The Mu'atazilites used reason to defend the faith. There is no dichotomy between the two. They assumed the unity and justice of Allah and man's free response to his moral demands. They began during the Umayyad period and before their final overthrow as heretics in the tenth century, they used their rationalistic methods on the Quran. Literal descriptions of Allah sitting on a throne are figurative. Their ideas continued among the Shiites, and many modernists have revived them. Their rationalistic methods resembled philosophy which was also condemned. Among Islam's greatest philosophers were Persian ibn-Sina, or Avicenna (980–1037), and the Spanish ibn-Rushed, or Averroes (1126–1198). They created a synthesis of Islam and Greek philosophy.

The Mu'tazilites were refuted by one of their own, Abu'l al-Hasan al-Ash'ari (872–935), who converted to conservatism at the age of 40. Believers in paradise will see Allah on his throne though their seeing is not comparable to the seeing of this world. The Quran is eternal though it is eternal in the mind of Allah while its expression on material things like paper is human. Allah is the creator of evil as well as good. All human actions are predestined though man is guilty for acting as if he were free.

On a nonrationalistic level, Islamic mysticism had a different kind of influence. Ascetics such as al-Hasan of Basra (d. 728) were revered as saints. Abu Hashim al Kufi (776) was the first Muslim ascetic to wear the coarse woolen (suf) robe and be called a Sufi. Sufi asceticism includes a vow of poverty and they are sometimes called dervishes (Persian for pauper). In time, these mystics produced a series of orders called brotherhoods. Like Christian monks, they meditated, but on the Quran, mixing in Greek philosophy and Gnosticism. They sought a personal experience of Allah and union with him. The movement produced great poets like Jalal al–Din Rumi who said, "He is a true lover of God to whom God says, 'I am thine, and thou art mine'!" The Sufis accepted truth from whatever direction. The Spanish poet Ibn al–'Arabi said, "Love alone is my religion." The immanence and omnipresence of God were quite opposite to the transcendence and omnipotence of the Sunni view. The Sufis were condemned and frequently killed as heretics but managed to survive. Al-Ghazali synthesized Sunni and Sufi thought and saved the Sufis from being driven out of Islam.

Abu Hamid al–Ghazali (1058–1111) was Persian, trained as a Shafi'ite and Ash'arite, and went to Baghdad to lecture in a new university. His curiosity led him to reach out in all directions but in the end he became a Sufi. However, he retained his hold on Sunni doctrine and law. The Five Pillars must be practiced but are of no value unless done from the heart. Sufi meditation too, if done with common sense, provides self-discipline of great value. Revered as a saint, he is the Thomas Aquinas of Islam and is still followed today.

All of these divisions are a reminder that Islam is not monolithic. It is diverse and dynamic. The West needs a reminder of that in a day when the media portrays Islam as a single entity — the terrorist backed by petro-dollars. But while the divergences are great, Ninian Smart observes that of all the great religions, Islam remains the most cohesive — one founder, one Book, one God, one brotherhood.[25]

Islamic Culture

Islam sees all of life as under God. Like Judaism, it is a way of life. Thus politics, economics, medicine, science, philosophy, the arts, etc., are Islamic politics, etc. The Quran has provided the Arabic that united many different tongues in praise of Allah, like the Latin of the Roman Catholic Church. It provided a common language for scholarship as Latin did in the Middle Ages of Europe. Its influence on literature has been like that of the King James Version of the Bible on the English language. Crusaders came in contact with Arabic wisdom and the ancient wisdom of the Greeks preserved by Islam. But much of it was translated to the West through Spain by Jewish scholars. Islamic medicine synthesized the best of the empires' cultures and was scientifically far ahead of Europe in its day. Islamic architecture is known through its mosques, schools and tombs such as the one at Samarakand, the shrine of the Dome of the Rock in Jerusalem, and the incomparably beautiful Taj Mahal of Agra, India, a tomb built (1630–1648) by the Mughal shah Jahan in memory of his wife, Mumtaz Mahal, who died in 1629. The Golden Age of Islamic arts, science and culture shows it capable of producing or allowing great cultural development. Modern Islamic art and architecture, science and culture, medicine, etc., show the continuing dynamism of this great faith.[26]

Islam Today

The puritanical Wahhabi of Arabia were mentioned earlier. They opposed anything not in accordance with the Quran and were especially against saint worship and the Sufis. Today, under the impact of oil billions, the modern Saudi government has built huge, magnificent, extravagant airports, capitals, universities. A similar scenario is played out in other oil rich Muslim countries, but elsewhere, Muslims starve to death. Secularism hit Turkey after World War I. The Young Turks, led by Mustapha Kemal, or Ataturk (1881–1938), overthrew the Ottoman caliphate in 1924 and openly westernized and secularized the country. The separation of church and state brought a new legal system, education, women's rights, etc. They cut themselves off from the rest of Islam in the process. Today, Turkey is one of the few Islamic governments that have recognized the state of Israel. The secularism is not total, however. Only Muslims are recognized as Turks. Others are Greeks or Jews. Since World War II, Islam has assumed a more open role with state-sponsored religious instruction, etc.[27]

Secularism has had less influence in other Muslim states. A pan-Islamic movement was founded by Jamal al-Din al-Afghani (1839–1897) in Egypt. On the one hand, it is concerned with a return to Islam and opposition to the West, even as it is also concerned with modernizing Islam in Western terms. Muslim unity is matched with regional reform to carry out the will of the people. The conservative countermovement is in the fundamentalist Muslim Brotherhood, founded in Egypt by Hassan al Banna, in 1928. It worked for independence from British influence. The movement was banned by Nasser, allowed to reappear under Sadat, while President Mubarak has encouraged dialogue.

The conservative influence has been acknowledged in the Shiite stronghold of Iran with the ouster of the Pahlevi dynasty and the establishment of rule by the ayatollahs — aya, feminine ayat, meaning "sign," and ollah = Allah, so an ayatollah is a "sign of God." The Ayatollah Khomeini allowed the formation of a constitution but it is modeled on his interpretations of the Quran. Meanwhile, Shiite Iranians fight Shiite and Sunni Iraqi in a protracted war.

Conservative elements helped bring forth Pakistan as an Islamic state separate from India. But leaders have been moderate and even modernist. It is not even clear who is a Muslim. There is some agreement on who is not a Muslim. The Ahmadiya have been called heretics. This group began with Hazrat Mirza Ghulam Ahmad (1835–1908) of Qadiyan. At 40, he felt called to be the Mahdi and reading the New Testament convinced him he was the Messiah fulfilling the second coming of Jesus. In 1904, he declared himself an avatar of Krishna. Since he was only a reappearance of Muhammad the Prophet, the movement claims to be Muslim while others have officially excommunicated them. The original Qadiyani branch is openly syncretistic but the Lahore branch is devotedly Muslim. Both branches have missionaries in Africa, the East Indies, Europe and the Americas. The

Qadiyan branch has had a Second and Third Successor. The Fourth (Khalifatul Masih IV) was chosen June 10, 1982, in the person of Hazrat Mirza Tahir Ahmad. The movement claims ten million members.

Another syncretistic movement that has been labeled heretical is the Baha'i. A Shiite sect of Twelvers thought the imam was a gate (bab) through which the faithful had access to the true faith. The hidden imam seeks other gates to conduct people to himself. In 1844, the Persian Mirza Ali Muhammad accepted the call and named himself Bab-ud-Din (Gate of the Faith). He said his mission was to prepare the way for a greater one (like John the Baptist in Christian tradition). He was executed in 1850 as a heretic. His followers continue as the Babis. A follower, Mirza Husain Ali (1817–1892), took the name Baha'u'llah (Glory of God) and in 1862 said he was the one to come. He went to Palestine, where the Turks put him in prison and where he died (1892). But his writings reached the outside world. He sought the unity of all religions since all prophets are witnesses to the truth and humanity is one under God. The message is one of unity, brother and sisterhood, racial and sexual equality, world peace and social justice. His followers call themselves Baha'is.

The Baha'is are outlawed in Iran and hundreds have been executed. Headquarters are in Haifa, Israel. The movement is active in many countries from Sri Lanka to the United States. There are a number of splinter groups. These are primarily from conflict over the successor to the Bab, to Baha'u'llah and to his son Abbas Effendi ('Abdu'l-Baha') who died in 1921, to Effendi's grandson Shoghi Effendi (d. 1957), and to the subsequent Hands of the Cause, the International Baha'i Council and the Universal House of Justice. There is some debate over the identity of Baha'ism. Some see it as an independent world religion while others see it as a sect of Islam. The latter is the view of the present Shiite leadership of Iran which has been imprisoning, torturing and murdering Baha'is since coming to power.

The Black Muslims began in Detroit in 1930 with W.D. Fard (Master Wali Farrad Muhammad) and his successor, Elijah Poole (Elijah Muhammad), who called the movement The Lost-Found Nation of Islam. In 1934, Fard disappeared. The movement's theology centered on blacks as descendants of the Original Man, Muslims from the ancient tribe of Shabazz. A mad scientist rebelled against Allah and created a weak and hybrid white race of devils who will be overthrown in the last judgment. Elijah built self-esteem through a strong work ethic, a sober life-style, no aggression but quick defense when attacked. He was succeeded by his son Wallace (Warith) in 1975. He has moved in the direction of Sunni orthodoxy, allowed followers to enter the armed forces and changed the name to the American Muslim Mission (1980). Followers are now called Bilalians after Bilal, the first meuzzin of Islam, and an Ethiopian. Racial inclusiveness has been accepted as part of the brotherhood of Islam.

It is of interest that there is no central authority in Islam but individuals and groups are labeled heretics and treated accordingly. Historically this has been done by leaders, ulema (jurists, learned ones), and consensus. Most Muslims have been called heretics by someone, e.g., the Shiites see the Sunni Muslims as such. It has even been suggested that to some authorities, everyone else is a kafir (infidel), like the Christian fundamentalist who sees himself as the only true Christian. This may be a caricature though it has figured in official rulings for both traditions. It raises additional problems in Islam since one can declare a jihad against any kafir, who can be killed any time, any place, anywhere.[28]

War and Peace

War is such a major part of Islamic history that some see it as the whole picture, not unlike some views of Judaism as it appears in the Tenak, the Christian Old Testament. God seems to bless war and holy war appears intrinsic to the tradition. In Islam, it is called the jihad (Arabic, striving). It is a prominent part of Islam. Some say it is the permanent state of Islam — the intent of the Quran is one world, one faith, one God, one ruler. Until that intent is fulfilled, there will be the House of Islam (Dar es-Islam) versus the House of War (Dar al-Harb). Until then, peace is temporary and should not last more than ten years. Others view the suspension of jihad as normal. Ibn Khaldun (1332-1406) saw it as the passage to civilization.[29]

The jihad was invoked by Usuman dan Fodio in Nigeria against the Hausa in 1804. He called himself Commander of the Faithful and established an Islamic state. Hausa Muslims objected to his jihad against them. However, father and son, Sultan Bello, called them heathen and conquered them and pagan tribes to create the Muslim society of today's Nigeria. These rulers called it a true jihad because it was a defense against aggression, a conversion of the heathen and a strengthening of Islam.

Mustafa Kemal Ataturk led the war against Greeks and Allies in 1921 as a jihad, formally receiving the rank of Ghazi (warrior for the faith), given only to participants in a jihad. It has been revived in the modern period, against the Zionists of Palestine and the modern state of Israel. The cry of "jihad" was raised in the partition of India into India and Pakistan. Jihad is used today in Lebanon and elsewhere by several groups called terrorists in the West and freedom fighters by their supporters. As in Judaic and Christian tradition, a distinction is made between just war (defense when attacked or to right an injustice), and aggressive or unjust war. As with other traditions, of course, one must ask who decides, and on what grounds, which war is just and which is unjust.

Shaykh Abu Zahra claims that all of Islam's wars have been defensive. Muslims did not attack Byzantines, Persians, etc., until Muslims had been attacked. Historically, one notes Muslims had to travel vast distances across desert and rough terrain, in order to be attacked after arriving at a city and demanding conversion, surrender or death. Khadduri says that when Islamic armies arrived in a new area, they offered conversion, submit and pay tribute (if the inhabitants were people of the Book) or fight.

Obviously the invitation to fight would have been unnecessary if Muslims had already been attacked. It is a bit difficult to see why in a defensive war there would be cause to make others submit to Islam or pay a tax. Conquest is assumed here. At one point, the Islamic empire stretched from the Atlantic Ocean to China and from Russia to India. To call this a defensive action is simple sophistry. One is reminded of the Christians who came unbidden from Europe to the Americas, declared the Indians "Canaanites" and slaughtered them. The defense was obviously on the other side. When the Indians resisted, they were accused of being aggressive and subject to the motto "The only good Indian is a dead one."

Muslim legal scholars have noted four different types of jihad — with heart, tongue, hands and sword. The first is the individual's fight against evil while the second and third support the right and correct the wrong. The fourth is war against unbelievers and enemies of the faith. The faithful are obligated to offer their wealth and their lives in this war (Sura 61:11).

Others distinguished four other kinds of jihad. One was against polytheists. The Quran says fight them (9:5, 124) and "strike off the heads of misbelievers in a total massacre" (47:4). Aho notes the real jihadist is "the instrument of . . . Allah. A servant of God who purifies the earth from the filth of polytheism . . ." There was a jihad against believers in apostasy (Abu Bakr fought the tribes that fell away at Muhammad's death), dissension (Ali versus the Kharijis) and banditry (Sura 5:37 orders punishment by execution, crucifixion, banishment, or cutting off their hands and feet). The jihad against the people of the Book differed in their option to convert or keep their beliefs but accept the authority of Islam and pay the taxes. If they refused either option, they got the jihad. Strengthening the frontiers, the ribat, was jihad for some (Sura 8:62). Generally it was interpreted as defense but others said it was fighting unbelievers. Ibn Khaldun described four kinds of war — tribal wars, feuds and raids, the jihad, and wars against rebels and dissenters. The first two are unjustified while the second two are justified.

Ferguson notes a great deal of intertribal raiding among the Arabs of Muhammad's day. He had no mandate for abolishing it. If he let it continue, it would disrupt the umma, the community. So he controlled it by banning it within the umma but leaving it legitimate outside and channeling aggression against others. The neighboring tribes could join Islam and become part of the umma, or suffer the consequences. And that is what happened when the united Arab armies moved out of Arabia and created an empire. War became a means of spreading the faith, "an effective part in the striving of the faithful for their faith." However, S.A. Haque claims that the accusation that jihad was used for the expansion of Islam is fiction promoted by anti-Muslim propaganda.

Many individuals and whole populations *did* join the new faith. This could have been out of honest conviction that Allah is supreme — his armies were victorious. It may have been to find forgiveness for their sins, to get into Paradise, because of the inadequacy of their old faith and the attractiveness of the new, to gain political or economic advantages such as avoiding the religious tax, or to share in the loot by joining the armies as they marched on to new conquests. It should be noted, though, that those who fought only for loot were rebuked as hypocrites (munafiq). The point here in terms of jihad is that noted earlier, that there is no coercion in religion (Sura 2:227). It is widely believed outside Islam that in practice there was, and surrender or die might have a bit of coercion to it, along with the economic burdens imposed on the conquered who did not convert. Different motives and differences between theory and practice, of course, have been true in other religious traditions as well.

Jihad is usually thought of in military terms but one can note variants. Mirza Ghulam claimed it is not the use of force of arms but forceful preachers. Thus the Ahmadiya are at once pacifists and strong missionaries. Jihad is sacrificing one's all for the protection of the weak and oppressed and is never directed at the political expansion of Islam. Proponents see the necessity for armed self-defense but not aggression. Jihad has been interpreted as "investing oneself in order to make it possible for others to enjoy life. That is, to invest one's effort in making the poor or the people who suffered, or the people who are different from yourself, better off."

Sufis and other modern writers claim the true holy war is against sin in the self. Ferguson quotes al-Qushayri (d. 1074) as saying the jihad of the elect is purifying the inner state. Al-Jilani (d. 1166) quoted the Prophet, "We have returned from the lesser jihad to the greater jihad." The conquest of the self is a greater conquest than external enemies. Saiyadain observes that only love can conquer evil. The real fight is against man's own nature — its cruelty, its desire to exploit, its denial of justice, its narrowness and stupidity. This contrasts with the view cited by Aho that Muslims are innocent (forgiven of all sin by faith in Allah) while all others are guilty harbies (foreigners).

Ferguson notes that the Maziyariyya have dropped jihad altogether. He also notes the remarkable work of 'Abdul Ghaffir Khan, the Gandhi of the Indian frontier. The Pathans of North India had a strong tradition of violence but 'Abdul Ghaffir Khan, a puritan reformer, persuaded them in 1930 to practice nonviolence. They faced executions, jail and persecution for years, "striving" (jihad) for peace. The Ahmadiyya found the test of jihad in the willingness to suffer rather than in fighting.[30]

One should note too that as in Judaism, so in Islam, just warfare was carefully defined — it must be led by an imam or caliph, enemies must be invited to accept Islam, monotheists may refuse but submit to being ruled on payment of a tax. It is a function of the umma, the community (fard al-kifaya), so individuals are not to conduct jihad which is why jihad is not usually accepted as a sixth pillar after the Five individual Pillars of Islam.

Unfortunately, Aho points out the rules of law also allow captured combatants to be killed, enslaved or exchanged for ransom. In addition, prisoners could be killed (unless they accepted Islam) if they would be a burden during the battle. There were no limits on either weapons or tactics. Allah wanted the dar al-harb cleansed and was indifferent to how it was done as long as it was done effectively. Before the first Syrian campaign, Abu Bakr read ten rules that limited violence, but the jurists greatly limited the applicability of these prohibitions. Abu Hanafi, whose legal system was cited earlier, said that all is permitted against the enemy. Since the enemy is by definition deceitful, it should be treated in the same way (Sura 8:58), even though "Allah loveth not the treacherous." This legitimized the military horrors of Babur (1483–1530) in setting up the Mughal Empire, and those of the earlier "liberator" Tamerlane (1336–1405) who built "towers of heads and walls of live bodies bound with brick and mortar." The Khariji-Shiite sects (Assassins and Almoravids) and the Wahhabis said that all resisting nonbelievers are enemies of Allah to be liquidated. The Quran reminds warriors to be compassionate as Allah is compassionate (8:69–70) and "Be not prone to kill (merely) because permitted" (17:33).

Women can be made concubines (battlefield marriage) without ritual delay as in Hebrew warfare. Land was left to the "owners" (it really belongs to Allah) who paid taxes or rent but the rents could be assigned as a grant to individuals or a tribe and in the end, the owner had little to say about the disposition of his property. In practice, Aho notes, neither lives nor property was exempt from military destruction.

War in general is destructive. "Whenever they kindle the fire of war, Allah extinguishes it" (Sura 5:65). "Surely Allah loves not the transgressors" (2:191–194). Saiyadain offers some contrast to the above. He claims no Muslim was allowed to initiate war. He can only fight in self-defense or to defend his freedom of belief and worship. Even in the heat of battle one must never deny the enemy food or water or commit any excess against women or children, the wounded, noncombatant civilians. Even in a defensive war, if the enemy shows the slightest inclination to peace, respond in full measure (8:62–63). Even if it is false, Allah will care for his own. Thus even the fear of treachery should not stand in the way of peace. He adds that modern war removes the frontier between combatants and noncombatants. It tortures, it annihilates the human race. It obviously cannot "be carried on within the kind of conditions envisioned by Islam." There is no justification for such total war.[31]

The concern for peace is part of the pre–Islamic heritage of Arabia. Throughout the peninsula, the tribes agreed to a four-month truce each year for trade and pilgrimage with no violence allowed. The concern for peace was continued in Islam. Muhammad extended the peace by having the four months at the beginning and the four months at the end of the year set aside from war for trade and pilgrimage (9:2). Muslims soon got around this by quoting Sura 2:217 that war in the sacred month is bad but to turn aside from the cause of Allah is worse.

Saiyadain points out that the central purpose of Islam is the promotion of peace and good fellowship in the world. Its concern is to bring about peaceful understanding between the religions and other divisions of humanity. This is the message, he says, that is woven like a refrain through the Quran and the Hadith. "In love, service, unwillingness to offend, settling of disputes by amicable discussion, and the promotion of peace lies the reality of life. They are the objectives of Islam — not conflict, exploitation, hatred, injustice, and war." He adds the Prophet's message that "'he is no believer, whose neighbor does not live in peace because of his mischief making.' And today everyone — however different, however far away — is our neighbor. . . ." As in other traditions, so in Islam, Zafrulla Khan reminds us that no one can be at peace with his brother unless he is at peace within himself — peace begins in the heart. He adds too that no one can be at peace with himself unless he is also at peace with his Maker. "Those who have faith and do not let it be debased by the least injustice are the ones who shall have peace" (Sura 6:83).[32]

The concern continues in the common form of greeting equivalent to the Hebrew "Shalom," among Muslims today: Salam 'alaikum, "Peace be upon you" (Sura 6:54). The reply is Alaikum es-salam. Saiyadain notes it is a greeting to all whether one is Muslim, Hindu, Christian, etc. — even an atheist. This is in contrast to an older view that the greeting is only for Muslims and not for infidels. Perhaps we could see it as the distinction between the normative and the historical. Salam is used to describe the litany given from the minarets on Friday. In India, seven salams from the Quran are written or recited for protection. The blessing of peace is invoked in prayer and praise of Allah. As in Judaism, peace is a gift of God (Sura 49:10–13). An alternate name for Dar al Islam (The House of Islam) is Dar al Salam, or Dar us–Salam (The House of Peace). As noted earlier, the very name Islam is derived by some from "silm," the word for peace.[33]

Saiyadain sees Islam as probing beyond immediate conflict to the causes of war — racism, religious bias, nationalism. Kahn adds justice and care for the poor. Muslims should ensure that a neighbor, irrespective of who he is, does not go to bed hungry at night. "'Amr ibn Murrah told Mu'awiyah that he had heard from the Prophet that if a ruler closed his door on the weak and needy, then God would close the doors of heaven on him at the hour of his greatest need and destitution." (Tirmidhi)

This echo of the Golden Rule is also found in Abu Hurairah, who reported the Prophet as saying, "When your Muslim brother comes to you to excuse himself, accept his excuse, for otherwise you will not receive from me the water that I shall hand out at the Pond of Plenitude." These problems must be faced with both the proclamation and practice of brotherhood, compassion and forgiveness. A story is told about the Imam Zain'ul-'Abidin, son of Husain son of Ali, the only member of Ali's family to escape the slaughter of Karbala. He was told of a person who spoke ill of him. Zain asked to be taken to this person and when they met, Zain said, "Peace be upon you. If what you say is true, then I pray that God should forgive me. And if it is false, I pray that he should forgive you."

These thoughts are shared by Brohi, who notes that while justice is required and evil is to be fought and vanquished, it is a higher virtue to forgive (42:41, 44). Sura 41:34 commends exchanging enmity for friendship, while verse 37 admonishes believers to forgive when they are angry. Verse 40 announces that evil is recompensed with punishment like it but whoever forgives, his reward is with Allah. The Prophet said, "God fills with peace and faith the heart of one who swallows his anger, even though he is in a position to give vent to it." The Prophet himself forgave those who had persecuted him in Mecca before the Hijra. When he conquered Mecca, he declared a general amnesty except for ten people, who were later pardoned. Imitation of the Prophet implies generosity regarding others.[34]

Isma'il Al Faruqi claimed that Allah has revealed himself to all people (Quran 4:164, 14:4, 16:36) The message is the same in its essence though it varied according to their particular conditions. The message is that God alone is God and people are to serve him, doing good and avoiding evil. The moral code is for charity, with the rich ministering to the material needs of the poor in a just society ruled by law. All human beings have the power to freely fulfill the moral law (see earlier on the debate over predestination). Through this fulfillment, man fulfills the purpose of his creation, to represent God on earth (2:30, 6:165, 23:116, 51:57). All human beings are part of this. Each person has innately a natural religion comparable to Rudolph Otto's "sense of the numinous" (3:19, 30:30). Because of this, all religions can live in peace. The Pax Islamica recognizes the legitimacy of every religious community. Al Faruqi went on to say the Islamic state has had its tyrants, like all other systems. Muslims as well as non-Muslims suffered under these evil rulers. The Pax is a world order rather than the political empires of history. Faruqi's thought is echoed and repeated by others. Mohammed Rafi-ud-Din claims the only hope for peace is through world domination by a single ideology—Islam. Non-Muslims might call this totalitarianism.[35]

These views have engendered some discussion. In part that has been caused by the problem of distinguishing between the essence of a religion and what has been done in the name of that religion. Reliable statistics are not available and would probably not help much, but the murder or execution of heretics or nonbelievers, both within a religion and those outside, is found and perhaps matched or outnumbered in other religions. The torture and murder of Baha'is in Iran can be compared to the Spanish Inquisition and to the enslavement and murder of and continuing bigotry against blacks in the United States. The Turkish massacre of the Armenians was only paled by the German slaughter of the Jews and millions of others in the Holocaust. Some Christians deny responsibility for the Holocaust as some Muslims deny responsibility for the massacre of the Armenians, and some in each group deny that the Holocaust/massacre ever happened!

The distinction in this and many other instances of war and mass murder is complicated by the relationship between a religion and a state. If a Muslim nation squanders its oil revenues on gigantic and opulent buildings while Muslims and non-Muslims in another country are starving to death, is that Islam failing to care for the poor while living in extravagance? If a Muslim state kills people, is that Islam killing people? If a Christian nation kills people, is that Christianity killing people? What is a Muslim state? What is a Christian state? No agreement has been reached in the modern Muslim state of Pakistan. No agreement is known among Christian countries. Predominance of a religion in the population is one view but it leaves many questions.

If Germany kills millions of people, do we distinguish between nation and religion? If the Turks massacre non-Muslims, as in the extermination of Smyrna in 1923 (120,000 people), and many other mass liquidations, do we distinguish between nation and religion? When the Wahhabis were asked about the terrible atrocities in the Najd Desert in 1925, they replied they had been promised paradise with many glorious houris if they were killed fighting against the infidels — non-Wahhabi Muslims — especially Shiites — and the rest of humanity. Do we ascribe the atrocities to Islam, or to the imam (Bin Sa'ud) who told them this?

Saiyadain quotes the Prophet as refusing to accept or support wrongdoing by one's country as proof of patriotism or an act of virtue — "bear witness for justice and let not hatred of a people seduce you so that you deal with them unjustly." "He who supports a tyrant or oppressor knowing he is a tyrant casts himself outside the pale of Islam." Abu Bakr, the first caliph, is reported to have told people, "I am no better than you. . . . I am just like any one of you. If you see that I am pursuing a proper course, then follow me; and if you see me err, then set me straight." This, of course, is in contrast to Al-Ash'ari and Din ibn Jama'a (d. 1333), who forbade uprisings against tyrants. The duty of Muslims is obedience no matter how unjust the usurper.[36]

The problem today is even more complicated when private or not so private groups blow up planes, capture ships on the high seas, kidnap people off the street and hold them for ransom or murder them. They proclaim a jihad, or call themselves a Muslim or Islamic jihad, or identify themselves as Muslim. Sometimes they are sponsored or supported by a nation that calls itself Muslim. They act in the name of religion. They claim they seek justice and are trying to right wrongs while others call them terrorist groups. Obviously most Muslims are not doing this. Do we distinguish between small groups and the total group? Such distinctions are made within Christianity and other traditions.

Zakir Husain claims that all religions teach the reality of God and obedience to his will which translates as goodwill and peace among men. He notes hatred, violence and evil but asks what the situation might have been without religious influence. While others note that many of the conflicts seem to have started or been encouraged by religions, he points out the increasing cooperation among the world's religions. He suggests religions have a role to play in world peace. But to play that role, they must look beyond dogmas, rituals and practices which obstruct the flow of life to a new sense of harmony. "This will mean nothing less than the self-purification of every religious community from within. Who can deny that all religious communities need today to undergo such self-purification?" He adds that the Sermon on the Mount, Buddha's compassion, Hindu ahimsa and the passion of Islam for obedience to the will of God can combine as the most potent influence for world peace. Since peace and justice are indivisible, he calls on people to build a just and peaceful human society. His words echo an hadith of the Prophet, "When God wishes well unto his servant He causes him to see the faults of his own soul."[37]

Echoing these words, K.G. Saiyadain declines any defense of misguided rulers or others who defied Islam's insistence on peace as the only right way of life. The crimes of individuals should not be blamed "on their respective religions. In judging a religion, we should do so as it is at its best and in the context of its genuine teachings. . . ." Of course, we are then faced with the issue of who decides which teachings are genuine. On the international scene, Brohi recalls a story from Tolstoy. God sent the angel of peace to 100 kings to ask why they were at war. Each one said he was for peace but there were 99 others who were for war.[38]

In summary, one can note the concern for peace among Muslims. This is true even as they fight each other, fight Russia in Afghanistan, fight Israel, fight India, etc. It is true even as Muslims claiming to be freedom fighters use terrorist tactics against civilians of other countries like the Assassins of old. Such may not differ much except in location, however, from Christian action against other Christians (as in Ireland, the Holy Land, Central America), or against non–Christians as in Vietnam, etc. Islam as a whole and Muslims in general seek to fulfill the name they bear — submission to Allah whose will is peace.

IV. Hinduism

Without meditation,
where is peace?
Without peace,
where is happiness?

The origins of Hinduism are lost in the mists of time. Many teachers throughout the history of Hinduism have contributed and continue to contribute to its history and development. But there is no single founder of the faith, in contrast to such traditions as Judaism or Confucianism.[1]

There is even some debate as to whether Hinduism is a single religion. Some have called Hinduism a federation of religions. Animistic cults flourish alongside monotheism and monism. Vaishnavites hold the god Vishnu as supreme. Shaivites hold Shiva supreme. Charvaka philosophy is atheistic. The Advaita Vedantins hold to no personal god but to an abstract one. The Purva Mimansakas put their trust in rituals. The very name, Hindu, was applied by outsiders to refer to the religion or culture "beyond the Indus River." The term has been adopted by people in the tradition, though their earlier self-designation was "sanatana dharma," "eternal law."[2]

Historically, Hinduism is a blend of the Indo-Aryans who invaded circa 1700 or 1500 B.C. and the native Dravidian religion. The latter itself may not be a single faith but a panorama of tribal religions that mingled with one another, or at least spread across the geography with the passage of centuries.

Some see the Aryans as fire (the god Agni) worshippers as in the later Zoroastrianism, with the great gods of Brahma (the creator), Vishnu (the preserver), Shiva (the destroyer), Indra (king of the gods), et al., as a further development. However, the gods Mitra (friendship), Varuna (guardian of the cosmic order), Indra and the Nasatyas ("unfailing") are named in Indo-Aryan (Hurrian) texts in Mitanni (northern Iraq today) circa 1380 B.C., suggesting these deities were part of the pantheon before the movement into India. The Aryan gods were personifications of nature (fire, sun, sky, thunder, etc.). But Aryan religion was the polytheistic religion of nomad warriors, while the Dravidian tradition was an animistic fertility cult, focusing on nature spirits, yakshas (male) and yakshis, related to trees, springs, rivers, etc.[3]

The ancient Indus Valley civilization is dated from circa 2500–circa 1500 B.C. (It may cover fewer centuries.) Archaeological excavations have produced art which shows a deity seated in the lotus position like Shiva. Sometimes the figure is surrounded by animals like Shiva as "pashupati," the "lord of the animals." Figurines represent the ancient Mother Goddess. Humpshouldered bulls were a favorite motif. This may be the cow worship of Hinduism. Some interpreters consider the Indus Valley culture to be Dravidian. These artifacts suggest some similarity which the new Indo-Aryan faith may have interfaced, to allow or encourage a merger of the traditions.[4]

Some have suggested that deities such as Krishna may have been a more southern religion. As this pastoral deity emerged into prominence, he, along with other Dravidian and earlier resident deities, were merged with such Aryan deities as Vishnu, as avatars, incarnations, of the Aryan deities. There are many gods and goddesses.[5]

On the surface, this is obviously a polytheistic tradition. However, Hindu philosophers such as Shankara (A.D. 788–820) claim that the surface multiplicity is but an expression of an inner or higher unity. Brahman is seen as an expression of an abstract oneness, a philosophical monism. This impersonal absolute stands in contrast to all external or empirical things which are an illusion, or maya. It is human ignorance that prevents us from seeing this and realizing our oneness with Brahman. This realization brings moksha, liberation, from the wheel of karma or the law of reincarnation. Sometimes the oneness is seen as permeating all things in a form of monistic pantheism. Sometimes it is a more personal monotheism.

The Sources

The script of the Indus Valley culture has been deciphered several times. So far, no decipherment has been universally accepted. Thus while the artifacts give some clues on the early religion, the oldest written sources for Hinduism are the Aryan traditions found in the Vedas. The oldest of the four is the Rig-Veda. The others are the Sama, Yajur and Atharva. The origins of the hymns and incantations may be in the pre–Indian Aryan tradition. The written form may be as late as 1000 B.C., while the oldest manuscript dates to the fourteenth century A.D. Tradition says the Vedas were compiled or arranged by Vyasa.[6]

The 250 metaphysical texts called the Upanishads date from 800–300 B.C. Only about 13 or so of these are of real significance. Here the philosophers have spelled out the tradition of Vedanta ("end of the Veda"). Animal sacrifices are replaced by meditation, self-control and good action.[7]

At the end of this period, though with an older oral history, we find the great Hindu epics, such as the Mahabharata (the Great Bharata) and the Ramayana. The first is a poem of 100,000 stanzas traditionally held to be composed by the wise man Vyasa. It is a story of royal dynastic wars. The sixth book is the famous Gita, "song," or Bhagavad-Gita, "the Song of the Lord," which some consider a revelation from Krishna. The poem is sometimes called the Veda of Krishna or the fifth Veda. Some date the poem as late as the third century A.D. Others put it before 300 B.C.[8]

The Ramayana has 24,000 couplets, traditionally composed by Valmiki, circa A.D. 1. Rama is the seventh incarnation of Vishnu. Rama's wife, Sita, is kidnapped by the demon king of Sri Lanka. Rama rescues her with the help of the monkeys and returns to his own kingdom, only to put her away under the suspicion of adultery. Some see the story as a reflection of Hindu conquest of Sri Lanka.

The tales called the Puranas ("ancient") present a more popular religion than the philosophical Upanishads. Traditionally, these too were compiled by Vyasa but probably date from the Golden Age of Hinduism (the second Gupta empire, c. A.D. 300–650). Out of 18 of the most important ones, six exalt the god Brahma, six Vishnu and six Shiva. The Bhagavata Purana lists 22 avatars of Vishnu. Krishna is the tenth.

The 64 books of Tantra share conversations between Shiva and his wife, Shakti (divine energy), Devi or Durga. Magical formulas and charms help people gain superhuman powers and unite with the Supreme Spirit, as well as cure disease, curse one's enemies, etc. Tantrism was later carried over into Buddhism as well. Like the Puranas, the Tantra texts probably date from the Golden Age.

Other important writings include the Laws of Manu ("manu" means "man"), credited to the first human, but usually dated between the Vedas and Upanishads. The works of philosophers such as Shankara, sometimes called the Aquinas of Hinduism, and Ramanuja (eleventh century A.D.), who justified popular devotion — bhakti — to the gods, are significant as are more recent figures such as Ramakrishna Paramahamsa (1834–1886), Rabindranath Tagore (1861–1941), Vivekananda (1863–1902), Sarvepalli Radhakrishnan (born 1888), Aurobindo Ghose (1872–1950) and Mohandas K. Gandhi (1869–1948).[9]

The Caste System

The social structure of Hinduism is the well-known caste (varna) system. There are basically four castes — kshatriyas (warriors), brahmins (priests), vaishyas (farmers, businessmen and professionals), and shudras (laborers). Below the system are the untouchables, sometimes called the outcastes. Within this structure, there are hundreds of subcastes, called jatis.[10]

Mary Carroll Smith has noted that both the Rig-Veda and the Mahabharata show that originally the priests were subject to the warriors. At some point, a reversal took place. The priests wrote down and compiled the traditions. She suggests they adopted warrior codes of morality which helped them in their shift to power. But in the Upanishads, the original warrior code of violence was spiritualized.[11]

The origin of the caste system has been attributed to the Dravidians, but there is also evidence for at least the four basic groups in pre-Indian or non-Indian Aryan traditions. Historically, it has been suggested that the light-skinned, conquering Aryans enslaved the dark-skinned Dravidians, who then formed either the worker castes or the untouchables. Yet others have suggested that the untouchables represent the pre-Dravidian Veddians, the original aborigines from the Stone Age. Some have suggested the brahmin priests developed the system to increase and maintain their own power. The Mahabharata urges the "King of Dharma," the eldest Pandava brother, Yudhisthira, to worship the brahmins who are the source of great benefit in this world and the next. Worship the brahmins and thus obtain kingdom, fame, and children.[12]

Some have interpreted the caste system as basic to human personality types, i.e., some men (males, not women) are meant to rule while others are meant to be followers. People have security in their defined roles in society. According to karma, the law of cause and effect, each person is in the system where he deserves to be, because of his previous life. Others note the basic evil of the system which reinforces the status quo rather than improving the quality of human existence. They claim that neither reincarnation (samsara) nor the caste system is part of the oldest vedic traditions. Numerous spiritual and philosophical leaders through the ages have proclaimed equality and refused to practice caste.[13]

Mahatma Gandhi believed in the Vedas, the Upanishads, and the Puranas. The Gita was his favorite scripture. He did not disallow image worship and honored the cow as the central fact of Hinduism. He accepted what he claimed was the original concept of caste but rejected untouchability. Gandhi was excommunicated by his own caste because he traveled to a foreign land, though he was reinstated in part with the help of his brother. A fanatic of the Hindu Mahasabha murdered him because he thought Gandhi was a heretic, helping Muslims instead of being loyal to Hinduism.

Gandhi was not a fundamentalist insisting on a literalistic interpretation of scripture. In fact, he was rather free in spiritualizing it. He noted that millions of Hindus consider the whole Mahabharata, including the Gita, to be historical. Gandhi considered it fiction, leading on to truth, containing significance but not historical fact. He also took note of progressive revelation. The animal sacrifices of the Aryans were spiritualized or replaced in the Upanishads with meditation. In the Gita, concentration on God is the king of sacrifices. Gandhi also denied the exclusive divinity of the Vedas. The Bible, Quran, and Zend Avesta are as inspired as the Vedas. In addition, he refused to be tied to anyone else's interpretation if it denied reason or morality.[14]

Some claim that one need only believe in the Vedas, while others reject even these as scripture. The founder of the reform movement, Brahmo Samaj (1828), Ram Mohun Roy (1772–1833), denounced image worship, caste, and widow burning. The modern state of India has rejected caste though the social structure remains. Nehru considered himself a Hindu but he was a secularist who rejected caste, images, etc. There is considerable variety as to what is essential to Hinduism.[15]

The Goal of Hinduism

The Aryan warriors were interested in religion as a source of magical power to ensure victory in war, which meant capturing much booty and many women. In the course of time, the moral code changed from world affirming to world denying. The Pandava king, Yudhisthira, in the Mahabharata, ruled out of duty, dharma, but in the end turned to a higher duty and became an ascetic hermit.[16]

It has been suggested that the masses of Hindus perform puja (worship) simply as part of their daily lives. Sen suggests this Dravidian tradition replaced the Aryans' animal sacrifice. Others see the goal of Hinduism to be mystical union with the One or the Divine, as noted earlier. Another view is that the atman, the soul or self, and Brahman are one. In the realization of oneness (moksha, liberation), there is no room for hate for anyone. There is an equality with all humanity, and indeed to all life, without delusion, discrimination, or attachment to the things of the world. To the enlightened one, the whole of humanity is one family. There are no foreigners or outsiders. Vivekananda (1862–1902) suggested that if all people realized their oneness, instead of bombs of hatred, people could live in peace. Unfortunately, enlightenment comes only to the very few.[17]

Liberation or enlightenment may come through Shankara's jnana yoga — through knowledge, or through karma yoga — by works of duty or service (Gandhi) or rituals. It may come through Ramanuja's or tantra's bhakti — devotion — worship based on love. For some, liberation comes from asceticism while for others it is a joyous affirmation of life. But whatever the method, one could say the result is a person at peace, with the self, with society and with the world.[18]

War in Hindu History

The record of Hindu history is close to unmitigated war. The Aryans were conquerors. They conquered the hill forts of the inhabitants, which suggests in turn the latter were also warriors. The Puranas offer some information on the dynasties of Hindu history. The nomadic Aryans established settled kingdoms by the seventh century B.C. if not earlier. These fought one another for supremacy. The Mahabharata records dynastic struggles. The epic tells the story of the five Pandava brothers who were dispossessed by their cousins, the Kauravas, but the Pandavas, urged on by their common wife, were successful in slaughtering the Kauravas and regaining the kingdom. Some commentators believe the poem reflects intra–Aryan tribal warfare.

The other great epic, the Ramayana, records the conquest of the demon king of Sri Lanka. The view was noted earlier that this may reflect the conquest of the island by the Sinhalese, Aryans from northwest India, with a second (or more) wave from northeast India. The conquest is recorded in the Mahavamsa and Dipavamsa records of the sixth century A.D. or later where the conquest is glorified. It is assumed that the island was inhabited by spirits, yakshas and nagas (snakes). The Balangodas, ancestors of the Veddian aborigines still numbering several thousand in the island, were thus dehumanized, a common technique of conquerors. The point here is simply that Hindu conquests were carried abroad and not limited to the subcontinent. Portions of Southeast Asia were also conquered, though Hinduism arrived in some places through traders.[19]

While he spiritualized the teaching of the Gita, even Mahatma Gandhi admitted there is no sign of nonviolence in the Mahabharata or the Ramayana. The avatars are bloodthirsty. The battles are described with great zest. The warriors were equipped with weapons as destructive as the mind could imagine. Tulsidas (1543–1623), a brahmin poet, rewrote the Ramayana in Hindi. Gandhi notes that Tulsidas' fine hymn in praise of Rama emphasizes Rama's ability to destroy the enemy. Even the philosopher Shankara (788–820), who sought to purify Hinduism, did not hesitate to use unspeakable cruelty in banishing Buddhism from India.[20]

The kingdom of Magadha succeeded in conquering several of its neighbors. It formed the base of the Mauryan empire (325–183 B.C.) founded by Chandragupta Maurya. His grandson, Ashoka, conquered most of the subcontinent as well as present-day Afghanistan. After a particularly bloody conquest of the Kalingas, tradition says he was sickened by the carnage and became a Buddhist — not a nonviolent Hindu. The invading Kushans lived in almost constant warfare for several centuries. A second Gupta empire (A.D. 300–650) conquered most of northern India and inaugurated the "Golden Age" or the "Classical Age" of Hinduism. A multitude of small kingdoms such as the Pandyas, Pallavas and the Chola rose and fell. The Rajputs called themselves the "sword arm of Hindustan," the protectors of Hinduism and the brahmins. They fought one another, other Hindu groups and invaders. In 1769, Hindu rajputs conquered the Gurkha district of the Himalayas and created the nation of Nepal. The Gurkhas are famous as fierce warriors.

War has followed upon war. Throughout known history, Hindus have fought fiercely against invaders — Aryans, Greeks, Huns, Muslims, the British. The kshatriya caste were the warriors, originally the highest caste. It was still second highest after the brahmin priests gained power. Modern Indian history has continued the bloodshed and violence. In the division of post–British India into Pakistan and India, almost a million Hindus and Muslims butchered each other in cold blood. Nakhre goes on to claim that India today is riven with conflict and violence on an unprecedented scale.

The public violence between Hindus and Sikhs, Hindus and Muslims, and in Sri Lanka, Hindus and Buddhists, is well known. There is violence between Hindus and Christians, and Hindus and other Hindus such as untouchables and different groups such as Ananda Marga. Nakhre's concern is far broader than physical violence and extends to social, economic and other violence. He suggests that nonviolence is not typical of Indian culture. Several Hindu groups have won world renown for their fighting ability. Hindus serve in the formidable Indian Army, which in addition to war with Pakistan and China has made notable contributions to the United Nations peacekeeping actions. At first glance, the history of Hinduism suggests war has been glorified and peace in the sense of world order is hard to find.[21]

Hinduism and Peace

Peace appears, however, in the individual search for moksha or liberation noted earlier. If an individual is at peace, it is hard to be at war with another. If a society is at peace with itself, it will not be aggressive with other societies. The universalism of the Upanishads has a worldwide appeal that has helped spread interest in Hinduism in the West. Roy founded his Brahmo Samaj (God Society) on the unitarian doctrine of the Upanishads. Sen quotes from a Upanishad a great potential for peace: "He who is one, and who dispenses the inherent needs of all peoples and all times, who is in the beginning and the end of all things, may He unite us with the bond of Goodwill" (Svetasvatara Upanishad, IV.1).[22]

But perhaps the greatest impetus to peace in Hinduism is the concept of ahimsa, literally "no injury," nonviolence. Another non–Vedic concept, according to Sen. Ahimsa, appears as early as the Chandogya Upanishad, III.18.4, where it is listed as one of the five ethical virtues along with austerity, almsgiving, uprightness, and truthfulness. The Padma Purana (1.31.27) says, "Ahimsa is the highest duty."

Walli claims that the concept of no harm was already present with the ancient Aryans (Rig-Veda VII. 104.7–10) though the record of conquest seems to contradict this. However, as noted, one can simply define war and animal sacrifice as "no harm" though the victims might disagree. Kotteran notes that ahimsa is not in the Vedas though it may be seen indirectly. The first historical appearance of ahimsa is in Jain morality with Mahavira (599–527 B.C.). One could speculate that he got the idea from his parents who were disciples of Parshva (872–772 B.C.). The Chandogya Upanishad is usually dated earlier than Mahavira. Still, it was not originally a central Hindu doctrine like dharma, karma, samsara, maya, moksha or nirvana. However, it has become a mainstay in the concern for both individual and international peace. It is based on the oneness or unity of all life (monism). Albert Schweitzer called it reverence for life.[23]

The reverence is for all of life, leading some practitioners to avoid harming insects or life in any form. This contrasts, of course, to the Aryan Vedic tradition of hunting and animal sacrifice still carried on in some quarters, such as the sacrifice of goats to Kali, and the traditional approval, given to some, of eating meat. These have been interpreted as not harmful. Killing an animal for sacrifice to the gods meant the animal soul would be reincarnated as a higher being so one was doing it a favor. One cynical observer has even suggested that ahimsa means it is wrong to kill cockroaches but it is alright to kill human beings. Another example is letting a swarm of locusts destroy a crop out of compassion for the insects, though such compassion leaves humans starving to death. That is a caricature, of course. In contrast, Gandhi claimed that a religion that worships the cow cannot possibly allow cruel and inhuman treatment of human beings. What Hindus do to other Hindus in maintaining untouchability is wrong. Neither cow worship nor protecting rats and mosquitos will make up for that.[24]

There is a more subtle problem, however, noted by Gandhi. He believed there are times when it is appropriate to kill for human existence. Gandhi favored mercy killing of suffering cows, incurably ill humans, poisonous snakes and rabid dogs, or destructive monkeys. Unnecessary killing was avoided even here. Snakes were not killed at Phoenix or Tolstoy farm in South Africa. But the point is that killing is not necessarily injury ("himsa"). In this, he was one with those who approved the Vedic sacrifices, but Gandhi strongly disagreed with animal sacrifices. He went on to note that people who let cows starve are being cruel, and in doing so, they are disowning God. He also suggested that ahimsa is not simply the negative of no harm. It demands the positive protection of the weak and helpless, including the untouchables, whom he renamed Harijans, the children of God.[25]

Both the necessity to kill and the concept of ahimsa have ancient roots. In the Mahabharata Vanaparva, the hunter Dharmavyadha believed his profession was the result of bad karma, misdeeds in an earlier reincarnation. But, he tells Brahmana that people kill in many ways, quite unconsciously in their ignorance, as well as deliberately. Brahmana responds that since the hunter's evil actions belong to the duty of his profession, the evil karma will not be held against him.[26]

In the Gita, the third brother, Arjuna, the leader of the Pandavas, is ready for battle. He is guaranteed by the gods to win. But then he realizes it is wrong to kill his own people. He would rather be killed himself. His chariot driver, Krishna, tells him he must do his duty. There is no greater good for a kshatriya than to do his duty to carry out the war. To fail to do this is to sin. Nonviolence is alright for a brahmin but not a kshatriya. Krishna points out that sooner or later everyone is going to die anyway. The cycle of life and death is fixed. Arjuna cannot save anyone. Besides, death does not affect the real self. A similar concept appears in later Buddhism, in which killing is alright as long as one remains internally calm, and in the idea of the predestination of each person's life and death.

In the Ramayana, the demon king Ravana is killed. Hanuman, the monkey god, wants to destroy the demonic followers. Sita says no. They were just obeying orders. You should not retaliate when someone else is the source of your injury. Good conduct is the adornment of those who are good. Even if those who do wrong deserve to be killed, the noble ones should be compassionate, since there is no one who does not transgress. The Laws of Manu note that killing is not conducive to heaven. Ahimsa is listed along with purity, truthfulness and honesty in the summary of the law.[27]

The Vishnu Purana and the philosopher of yoga, Patanjali (second century A.D.), say ahimsa is one of the restraints for someone practicing yoga. Other restraints are no stealing, no greed, truthfulness, continence. Patanjali considered these universal absolutes. Others considered ahimsa more relative. A soldier, for example, might vow not to do harm except in battle.[28]

Gandhi

Mohandas K. Gandhi, better known as Mahatma, Great Soul, came from a Vaishnava (Vishnu worshipping) family but they also visited the temples of Shiva and Rama. His nurse taught him to take refuge in Ramanama (repetition of the name of Rama). The family was vaishya rather than brahmin. Yet, he probably did more to popularize the concept of ahimsa than anyone.

Gandhi was not an absolutist. As noted earlier, he approved of mercy killing and killing to protect crops and humans. He participated in several wars as a noncombatant and recruiter. He did not approve of using nonviolence as a cover for cowardice. Violence ("himsa") to right a wrong was preferable to tame submission to injustice or aggression. He approved of Polish and Czech resistance to the Nazi armies and of India's use of military power in the struggle in Kashmir. He told the Pathans that sincere violence was better than insincere ahimsa. Women may defend their honor in any way they can, including violence. He expected leaders to practice nonviolence. He did not expect this of the masses, though Gangal notes there is nothing impossible about it. After all, if ordinary people can submit to the discipline of the army, there is no reason why they cannot follow the discipline of ahimsa. In turn, while most writers have said the masses had no faith in nonviolence, Nakhre's empirical research found the opposite. The rank and file were deeply committed to nonviolence.[29]

Gandhi's religion was not a world denying faith but one of affirmation. Instead of withdrawing to the forest (vanaprastha) or becoming a sannyasin (renouncing ties with society), he became a vanaprastha in a different sense. As early as 1900 informally, and openly in 1906, he became celibate and gave up the desire for possessions. However, as a karma yogin, he stayed in society, to serve humanity, and developed a political program based on nonviolence. In doing so, he borrowed from the New Testament teachings of Jesus and Western figures such as Leo Tolstoy, John Ruskin and Henry David Thoreau. He read the New Testament in London (1888-1889) and the others in South Africa (1893-1914), where he worked out his philosophy and techniques of ahimsa. He read selections from Ruskin's *Unto This Last* in 1904. He was so moved by it that he closed his prosperous law offices and moved to the country to start an ashram. Later in India, he translated this work in Gujarati as *Sarvodaya*, "the welfare of all." In India, he led the movement for political independence from England.[30]

His concern was far more extensive than political independence, however. He worked for social justice, including acceptance for the untouchables. In other words, he used ahimsa against the Hindus as much as against the British. His campaigns included extensive religious preparation in terms of purification, prayer, fasting, and giving up self-interest. If a nonviolent protest became violent, Gandhi withdrew. Ethically, it is of interest that he rejected the common philosophical concept that the end justifies the means. That is blasphemy. In fact, he understood that we have control over the means but not the ends.

For Gandhi, ahimsa is a positive moral force linked with truth (satya) and asceticism (tapasya). He talked about soul force or truth force (satyagraha). This is the natural law of humanity as opposed to the violence of wild animals. It is practical idealism for everyone and not just for saints. It means a conscious choice of suffering and not passive submission to evil. He changed the name of his movement from passive resistance to satyagraha for several reasons. One was that he saw the violence ("himsa") in much passive resistance. There is no coercion of any kind in true satyagraha. He saw soul force as so powerful, it would even work in an atomic war. If an enemy begins killing nonviolent resisters, he will get tired of the slaughter. Gandhi apparently did not know of Hitler's systematic untired murder of millions, a policy repeated by other regimes. One could argue that Communists and Mongols and others who have slaughtered millions of people were not met with satyagraha, though that seems like "blaming the victims."[31]

Rothermund notes that in the Upanishads, "sat" means "essence" or "ultimate reality." It is an ontological concept. But it is more, for in Tantra and the Atharvaveda, satya is a magical concept. Gandhi brought ontology together with ethics as one concept. She finds the background for this in the Vedas. Satya is found there but the more common word is "rta," perhaps best translated "binding truth." The "binding" has a divine element. The gods Mitra and Varuna are the guardians of rta. Mitra is the god of contract whose function is protective. Varuna is the god of the oath whose function is punitive (parenthetically, she notes Varuna's magical invincible power—nothing even confronts, let alone stands against him). From this Gandhi could say that "God is the essence of the vow" (vrata).

He moved on to say that "Truth (satya) is God." He described his own religion as a religion of truth. In turn, rta=satya which in turn equals dharma as the universal law which governs the cosmos (Varuna is the guardian of cosmic order). Satya functions according to cosmic law. Gandhi saw it as his duty (dharma) to seek truth. The way to attain truth is ahimsa. Ahimsa is truth. He saw no distinction between them. Satyagraha is not just a bit of human psychology but what in other traditions would be called a divine decree. Thus when he led a satyagraha campaign, the gods fought with him against the evil (ignorance, untruth) at hand. Gandhi did not seek a human utopia. He sought a divine society on earth. At the same time, he was willing to leave God entirely out of satyagraha so there was no theological requirement for a satyagrahi.[32]

In this regard, it is of interest that Gandhi interpreted the Gita as a spiritual battle in human hearts rather than an historical war. The bloody battles of the Gita are examples of ahimsa, nonviolence. The basic teaching of the Gita is selflessness (anasakti). Gandhi recognized the right of others to interpret the Gita in their own understanding. This led to what some consider inconsistencies. He thought it better to be a sincere soldier than an insincere pacifist, as noted earlier. While Emerson thought consistency to be the hobgoblin of little minds, Gandhi said he would rather be right than consistent. Others, however, have insisted he was consistent. For example, he thought the way of peace is the way of truth, but truthfulness is even more important than peacefulness. He was consistent in his search for truth. In conclusion, one can note that the nations have not followed Gandhi's example — not even India — though some individuals have, such as Vinoba Bhave, to which we would add Martin Luther King, Jr. William R. Miller has noted that nonviolence has been interred and enshrined with Gandhi's ashes. He goes on, however, to note that it has been buried many times in recent years, i.e., it may rise yet again.[33]

Some question has been raised about Gandhi's Hinduism. He claimed to be orthodox but he was murdered with the accusation he was unorthodox, and his own caste repudiated him. He himself noted how he had drawn on Jesus and such Western figures as Tolstoy, Ruskin and Thoreau. In his earlier years, he was heavily influenced by the Jain and Buddhist traditions, and some have suggested his whole concept of ahimsa is from them. However, Gandhi did not consider these two traditions separate from Hinduism. He claims his love of truth comes from the story of Harischandra in the Mahabharata, in the form of a play he saw as a schoolboy. A Gujrati poet, Shamal Bhat, was the source of his concern to return good for evil. He insisted to the end that he was a Hindu. The last words on his lips were a call to to Rama. However, Arvind Sharma suggests he distinguished between a lower and a higher Hinduism. He wrote in 1946 about two aspects of Hinduism. He tried to reform "historical Hinduism with its untouchability, superstitious worship of stocks and stones, animal sacrifices and so on." He tried to cultivate "the Hinduism of the Gita, the Upanishads, and Patanjali Yoga Sutras which is the acme of Ahimsa and oneness of all creation, pure worship of one immanent, formless, imperishable God."

He was open to truth from anywhere, and he expressed that by saying the windows should be open to let in fresh air, but he would not be swept off his feet. At the same time, he considered it a travesty of true religion to consider one's own superior and others' inferior.[34]

Others too have insisted Gandhi was a loyal Hindu. These include Christians such as missionary C.F. Andrews. The list even includes Jawaharlal Nehru (1889-1964), who openly repudiated Gandhi's methods and is even quoted as saying that Gandhi was an awful old hypocrite. While no one person speaks for Hinduism, there is at least this much testimony that Gandhi's perspectives were Hindu. But the historical fact remains that while Gandhi is highly honored, as a saint or even an avatar, and Gandhi idols are enshrined in village temples, very few Hindus follow him.[35]

Beyond the debate about his Hinduness, one can note other perspectives. E. Stanley Jones said that "Gandhi brought to focus in himself universal principles . . . as inescapable as the law of gravitation." Much of Gandhi's work was more local than universal, much of it within Hinduism itself. However, the above notations indicate a breadth of interest. He was in touch with many other religious traditions and worked tirelessly on behalf of peace between Hindus and others, especially Muslims. He saw life in India as a microcosm of the world. To put it in terms of sarvodaya, the awakening of all, Kantowsky has outlined the movement from the individual moksha, to the village (gramodaya), to the nation (deshodaya), to the world (vishodaya). Gandhi drew from other sources; he incorporated these into his Hindu perspective; he reached out to the whole world with a vision of peace. As Rao puts it, besides working at village reconstruction and the independence of India, Gandhi called upon the religious leaders of the world to share the deepest and best within their heritage to achieve a just and peaceful world order — perhaps the only condition for human survival.[36]

A Continuing Concern

While the Gandhi tradition may be the most illustrious proponent of peace in the Hindu tradition, this is, of course, not the only one. Rabindranath Tagore (1861-1941) is renowned as a poet, politician and prophet. Will Durant called him the most impressive of all the men now on earth. His *The Religion of Man* (London: Allen & Unwin, 1931) uses the universal language of humanity. It is a theistic view of ultimate reality, but he dispensed with mythological symbols and sectarian names and forms. Aurobindo (1872-1950) fused political and religious nationalism. Yet he sought the liberation of India as a step in the liberation of the world. Sharma goes on to say that Tagore and Aurobindo Ghosh began as nationalists but became internationalists. Shri Jagadguru has suggested that all the great religions are pervaded with truth, nonviolence, compassion and unity. But these need to be translated into action. When that happens, the world will have peace. He suggests, "There is no religion without peace, no peace without religion." The peace must be just if it is to endure. That includes helping others such as undeveloped nations though the help must be given in a spirit of cooperation and love without exploitation.[37]

V. Jainism

All men should live in
Peace with their fellows.
This is the Lord's desire.

As noted in the comments on Gandhi, he was heavily influenced by the Jain and Buddhist traditions. Some claim his concept of ahimsa is from them. Gandhi himself did not consider these two groups separate from Hinduism.[1]

Jainism, the faith of over two million people, is the religion of the Jaina, the conquerors or victors over their lower natures, those who escape the cycle of rebirths or the transmigration of souls. Jains understand their religion to go back to the beginning of time. They have a total of 24 Tirthankara, "ford makers" or "bridge makers" in this aeon. The last of these, Mahavira, is usually seen as the historic founder of Jainism. With the teachings of the Tirthankara, people can cross over or through this life of suffering to the perfect state. Another interpretation is that they have crossed beyond the heavens to the top of the universe called Isatpragbhara. They have cleaved the way to where the siddhas, enlightened souls, dwell in eternal bliss, beyond the cycle of rebirth. The Tirthankara are not founders of the religion but teachers of truth and a path. They are not gods and are not worshipped. They are beyond reach of intercession but they are contemplated.[2]

The first of these was Rishabha, sometimes called Adi Natha, the primal helper or primal refuge ("adi"=first or original). He is said to have lived 80 million years. The Kalpa Sutra credits him with teaching men the 72 sciences with writing first and mathematics most important. In the Hindu devotional, Bhagavata Purana, he was a righteous king with 100 sons. He handed his kingdom over to Bharata, the eldest, and became an ascetic.[3]

Some historians credit the rise of Jainism to the twenty-third Tirthankara, Parshva or Parsvanatha who was born in Benares circa 872 B.C. He was the son of King Ashvasena and Queen Vama, and thus a kshatriya, a member of the warrior caste. According to the traditions, he lived 100 years and then starved himself to death (sallakhana). He founded an order of monks, the Nirgranthas (the unattached), who some suggest are the original "white clads," the Shvetambaras of today.[4]

Among Parshva's followers were Siddhartha, a warrior chief of the Jnatrika clan, and Trishala, the sister of Chetaka, king of the Vaisali (in modern Bihar). Thus they belonged to the kshatriya caste. They were the parents of Nataputta Vardhamana, later called Mahavira (great man or hero), the twenty-fourth Tirthankara. Mahavira was born at Kundagrama near modern Patna. He married Yeshoda and had a daughter named Priya-darshana. When he was about 30 years of age, his parents also starved themselves to death and he became a monk. After 12 years, he found kevala (infinite and perfect knowledge or enlightenment) and spent the last 30 years teaching and gathering an order of monks and nuns. The 2500th anniversary of his nirvana was celebrated in 1975. According to the Shvetambara, he lived from 599–527 B.C. Modern scholars tend to date him 60 years later, 540–468 B.C.[5]

Historically, this was the period of the Kingdom of Magadha, circa 600–325 B.C., and its King Bimbisara, 550–490 B.C. This period also marks the rise of Buddhism and Ajivika Hinduism and other sramana movements — protests against Brahmanic ritualism. Part of this protest was the rejection of any supreme or creator god like Brahman. Thus Jains are sometimes called atheists. In later times, however, Jainism incorporated the worship of Hindu gods such as Rama and Krishna, and 16 Hindu samskaras (rites) and brahmin priests officiated at marriages, deaths and in temple worship. This process was largely completed through the work of Jinasena in his massive work, Adipurana, circa A.D. 820.[6]

Historically, one might note also the Jain tradition that Chandragupta (321–298 B.C.), founder of the Maurya Empire (321–183 B.C.), became a Jain monk and fasted to death. This was not, however, until after he had conquered Magadha and established a considerable empire which extended into Afghanistan. He obtained the latter when he defeated the Hellenistic ruler of Syria, Seleucus I Nicator, in 305. Chandragupta's grandson, Ashoka, reportedly became a Buddhist.[7]

Nevaskar and P.S. Jaini have suggested that royal patronage was a major portion of early Jain success. The kings were perhaps sincere but also found Jain and other heterodox groups helpful against the power of the priestly brahmins. When royal patronage declined, as when a ruling house was conquered, Jainism moved northwest and then south to Gujarat, as well as down the east coast to Mysore.[8]

The Shvetambara wear white robes and hence the name, "white clad." They admit women who take the same vows and have a chance at moksha, "release" from the transmigration of souls or samsara, the cycle of rebirth. They are the strongest in the West — Gujarat, Rajasthan and Punjab.

Among the Digambara, or sky clad Jains, nuns are of a lower order. They do not take the vow of nudity. A woman's only hope for moksha is to be reborn as a male and then become a monk. The laity cannot achieve release or enlightenment or nirvana either. Their hope is in becoming a monk so they can practice the required austerities (tapas) such as fasting, celibacy, standing in the hot sun or the cold for long periods of time. Merit also comes from acts of charity and good works. The term sky clad comes from the progressive nonattachment to the things of the world including clothing. Eventually, the saints become wanderers in the nude. The group is strongest in the south – Maharashtra and Karnataka. The origin of the split between white and sky clad is told differently by the two groups. Jaini suggests the southward migration separated the originally unified tradition which then developed separately. Nevaskar says this was circa 300 B.C. Basham dates the division to circa A.D. 79.[9]

A third sect, the Sthanakvasis (dwellers in halls), do not believe in idols (of the Tirthankaras) or in temples. Some have suggested this group originated in response to Islam with its ban on idols. Nuns take the same vows as monks and as with the Shvetambara, women are spiritual equals. The origins of the group were in the reforming zeal of a Jaina layman, Lonka Saha, in 1451. Officially he was concerned with harming life in the process of digging and quarrying for statues. He also saw the growing wealth and power of the temples as a source of worldly attachment.[10]

One can note the Jain belief in an eternal universe, somewhat similar to modern science. Where the latter says matter is neither created nor destroyed but only changed in form, Jainism says souls and matter are neither created nor destroyed. The Jain tradition here is a dualistic one, contrasting matter and spirit. The siddhas, or liberated souls, go to the ceiling of the universe where they exist in a state of indescribable bliss in union with the divine. Jain beliefs reject the Vedas as authoritative but include karma along with samsara, moksha, nirvana and other Hindu traditions. For a time, Mahavira associated with the Ajivika Makkhali Gosala, who was a deterministic ascetic. The latter taught that people are tied to the wheel of Karma and there is nothing that can be done (fatalism). Mahavira broke with this concept. Man can liberate himself by becoming a monk and practicing the teachings and gaining moksha, freedom from karma and the cycle of rebirths. This is human action without help from any gods. In contrast to the Hindu traditions, the Jains rejected caste. However, in later centuries, caste was largely reinstated.[11]

The belief that is important for our concerns with world peace is the one noted for Gandhi, the concept of ahimsa, no injury. George Kotturan claims the concept makes its first historical appearance in Jainism in the teachings of Mahavira. While that may be beyond clear documentation, there is no question that ahimsa plays a leading role in Jainism. It is the first of the Five Great Vows (anuvratas). The monastic vow says: "I renounce all killing of living things, whether movable or immovable. Nor shall I myself kill living beings nor cause others to do it. As long as I live I confess, and blame and exempt myself of these sins, in mind, speech, and body."[12]

The laity refrain from causing injury to beings with more than one sense faculty (plants). This means they do not work with the soil, lest they kill insects. Monks and nuns wear mouth masks lest they breathe in an insect and kill it. Water must be strained through a cloth or boiled by someone else, lest life in it be killed in the process of drinking. In addition, "The man who lights a fire kills living things, while he who puts it out kills the fire." (Sutrakritanga 1,6). Jains are not merely vegetarians. Monastics do not eat fresh fruit became there is still life in it.[13]

Females in Jainism have benefited considerably over other traditions. Among the Shvetambaras, the nineteenth Tirthankara was a princess named Mallinatha. There is no female infanticide, for this would be himsa — violence. Unmarried women are provided for and Jain women have been allowed to become nuns. They receive some education and many women have become teachers. Suttee as a form of suicide is considered killing. Thus in contrast to the historic Hindu tradition of a widow burning herself alive on her husband's funeral pyre, Jain women have not been expected to do this. In addition, Jain women inherit their husbands' estates, giving them financial security and control over their children. This may be reflected in the low incidence of juvenile delinquency among Jains, though it may also come through the concept of ahimsa — no harm.[14]

Some of the most outstanding Jains have starved themselves to death as an act of piety to gain moksha. This type of suicide is not considered self-killing or wrong. However, this is only for the saints at the end of life. Death is inevitable and sallakhana is a discipline preparing a person for a peaceful and ennobling parting. It is quite inappropriate for those in good health who are not faced with any contingency such as severe famine or incurable disease.[15]

Parenthetically, it should be noted again that merit is not limited to acts of negation. It is also gained through positive good works by caring for the sick and aged, both humans and animals, and by support of the monastics and temple system. Jains provide food, clothing and shelter for those in need, not only other Jains. They give generously to education and have been major contributors to the development of literature wherever they have wandered over the centuries. They also have youth organizations and cooperatives for helping each other in housing, etc.[16]

Ahimsa itself is not merely nonviolence. Bool Chand notes that ahimsa is more than refraining from violence. A Jain is to order his life so as to make the need for violence superfluous. He goes on to quote the resolution of the Third General Conference of the World Fellowship of Religions (Delhi, 1965), "Love, truth, and nonattachment to worldly possessions are the essential constituents of Ahimsa . . . the keynote of religion." Chand goes on to claim that all humanist thinkers of the world have preached ahimsa, without actually using the word. Kothari notes that ahimsa is based on the positive quality of universal love which in turn is based on the recognition of kinship among all living things. Inspired by this ideal, one cannot be indifferent to the sufferings and pain of others. The follower of ahimsa is compassionate towards all living beings and is merciful to the afflicted. This universal love is the foundation of liberation and self-realization. It is the kernel of religion. We add here, too, Kothari's insistence that moksha, liberation, is not limited to ahimsa. It is a threefold path. The three jewels of Jainism are right faith, right knowledge and right conduct.

In contrast to the love and compassion noted by Chand and Kothari, Basham notes that while there are passages in the Jaina scripture which show warmth and human sympathy, ahimsa has little love and merely involves vegetarianism and precautions against accidental killing of small animals. Ellen Evert Hopman has a different view. To practice ahimsa means not hurting your own body, mind, health, peace and joy. We are to nourish the positive and beautiful within, daily filtering away the negative and adding love and beauty, enhancing life in every way. Jain teacher Gurudev Shree Chitrabhanuji says, "Truth is one but it has been explained in different ways. . . . Where there is unity, there is health, wealth, peace, happiness, prosperity." He claims that "in forgiveness we are one with the light of our soul. As we wash away subtle grains of anger, resentment and hatred with feelings of forgiveness, the radiant soul within shines forth its ray of joy and peace." "To experience positive energy, think of God as love. . . . To grow, have the feeling of God as love. . . ." While Basham may be right in his interpretation, others seem to find a great deal of love in Jain tradition.[17]

The limitations on occupation extend beyond agriculture to railroads which sometimes kill life, leather working since life was killed for the leather, blacksmithing, forestry and similar strictures. However, the strictures turned out to have economic value. Commerce and finance are open to them and Jains are among the most prominent bankers and industrialists of modern India. In addition to ahimsa, Jains are to refrain from gambling, alcohol, theft, adultery and debauchery. Their life-style has brought considerable social respect. Some have acquired considerable political stature as well. Jains have been called the Quakers of India for their accumulation of capital. This is in contrast to the view of some that Jainism is a world-denying religion. However, while the acquisition of wealth is not forbidden, nonattachment is required even here. There is also a distinction which Nevaskar calls a twofold training. The laity who cannot attain nirvana anyway renounce the world in principle only. Monastics renounce everything. They practice a stricter form of ahimsa. "Lay people can never be strong enough to be entirely nonviolent in thought, word and deed." Nonviolence is a goal or ideal.[18]

This may account for the political activity and military heroes of Jainism which seem so totally discordant with the main tradition. Jaini notes the establishment of the Ganga dynasty in Karnataka (formerly Mysore State) in southern India. A Digambara monk, Simhanandi, set up Madhava Kongunivarma as ruler in the city of Gangavadi in A.D. 265. The dynasty provided almost 700 years of pro–Jaina rule. Some of the kings took the vows and ended life in starvation. Many built temples and tried to follow the rules Simhanandi laid down. The rules included vegetarianism and the statement: "If you flee from the battlefield/ Then your race will go to ruin." In other words, warfare was not ruled out.[19]

Camundaraya stormed the fortress of Ucchangi in the tenth century A.D. He routed the enemy "like an elephant putting a herd of deer to flight." His titles included vairikulakaladanda, "the club which brings death to the host of enemies." He was given the Jaina epithet, samyaktvaratnakara, "ocean of true insight," for erecting the 57-foot Bahubali (son of Rishaba) image (locally called Gommatesvara) at Shravanabelgola in 948.[20]

The Hoysala dynasty was also established in Karnataka by a Jain monk named Sudatta. Tradition says he and a chief named Sala met a raging tiger. Sudatta handed over his staff and told Sala to "poy [smite him] Sala." The dynasty lasted until the fourteenth century when it was replaced by the brahmanical Vijayanagara empire.[21]

Ferguson notes a significant series of commanders in the twelfth century, serving King Vishnuvardhana. Their activity included conquest as well as defense. One of these was Ganga Raja. His family — parents, wife and children — were devout Jains. Ferguson notes Ganga was, too, up to a point. He was called "the terrifier of his enemies, the purifier of his family, the raiser up of the Kingdom of Vishnuvardhana." The king was compared to the storm god and Ganga was his thunderbolt. Ganga's son, Boppa, was raised as a Jain but also became a soldier.[22]

In Gujarat, the Shvetambara were also involved with royal houses. King Gardabhila of Ujjain in the first century B.C. raped a Jaina nun, the sister of Kalaka, a Shvetambara acarya (teacher). Kalaka went to the neighboring Scythian kings, called Sahi or Sakas, and incited them to invade Ujjain. They ruled Ujjain until they were conquered by Vikramaditya, said to be a Jain, in A.D. 57. Centuries later, the monk Silagunasuri rescued the orphan of a displaced Shaivite royal lineage. When the orphan grew up, he took the name of Vanaraja, regained his throne and established a Jaina kingdom from 746–806. Jains gained positions of power as ministers and financiers which lasted even though Vanaraja's successors reverted to Shaivism. A Jaina teacher, Hemacandra (1088–1172), saved Kumarapala from execution by hiding him in the monastery. When the latter became king (1143–1172), he forbade animal sacrifice and built many temples before he died. One can note in this context that this ideal Jain king never gave up warfare.[23]

Jaini notes that great efforts are made to avoid personally harming living things. The record on condoning violence is less clear. The establishment and maintenance of kingdoms very likely included violence and in some of the cases just cited, the injury is explicit. The violence of the military generals was not condemned, and it was clearly beneficial to the religious tradition. The responsibility of the laity in time of war has never been presented directly.

Jaina literature, however, is not pacifist as the Quakers are. Only aggressive war is proscribed. Defensive war is passed over almost without comment. Scholars imply the defensive war is acceptable. Somadevasuri (tenth century A.D.) saw it as a last resort, although stories of the tradition are clear that one who kills even for a good cause goes to hell. A modern scholar, Bool Chand, claims that ahimsa is not unthinking pacifism. Neither men nor nations are to submit to being the booty of others. Ahimsa does not approve of the cowardice of running away from danger. When war does take place, ahimsa thinkers take all rational steps to sustain the morale of the army and the civilian population. On the other hand, Chand notes that religion cannot support an existing order unless it is based on justice. The way to obtain justice, however, is through nonviolent means, as Gandhi did, whenever possible. However, the military heroes cited above fought aggressive wars, as well as defensive ones, and thus should have been condemned. The failure to condemn war in any form appears to be a serious indictment to Jaini.

However, Jaini notes the problems presented by the reforming monk Bhikhanji, who founded the Terapantha. His theory was that helping someone or some thing formed karmic attachment and if the helped one harmed another, the helper was responsible for that himsa. Some pacifists are willing to do first aid or health care in war, but others claim that if you help a wounded soldier get well and go back to duty, he then kills and the helper is responsible for that killing. The influence on Gandhi of Jaina layman Raychandbhai Mehta (1868–1901) was noted earlier. He told Gandhi in 1894 that since the body is perishable, it would not be right to kill in order to protect it from death. Thus self-defense was not legitimate for Mehta. As was noted in the discussion of Hinduism, Gandhi did not kill snakes on his South African farm but he did approve of killing mad dogs and terminally ill cows.[24]

C.R. Jain claims that ahimsa does not forbid a king (and presumably his people) from defending one's country. Korean monks Won-Kuang (d. A.D. 630) and Sosan (1520–1604) similarly interpreted Buddhist ahimsa. Sosan formed a monk army which defeated Japanese invaders. V.P. Kothari urges ahimsa as a solution to the problems of modern warfare and as an alternative to the atomic bomb. Ahimsa is not a sterile passivity but a powerful moral force for social transformation. However, he too notes that ahimsa does not mean cowardly submission to aggression or surrender to evil. While one must be ever ready to negotiate an honorable settlement, when one's security is endangered, when justice is violated, he is obligated to use force for defense.[25]

C.R. Jain considers ahimsa the highest dharma. Those who practice ahimsa become contented, thoughtful, self-centered and brave. Jyotiprasad Jain equates ahimsa and dharma. He also notes that himsa, harm, is not just physical harm. It may be spiritual or emotional, a matter of thought or word as well as deed. Anger, greed, deceit, envy, jealousy, and other negative emotions and their expressions in gestures, facial expressions, speech, etc., are himsa. We see a parallel here with other traditions such as the Hebrew prophets, Jesus and Paul in Christianity, Gautama the Buddha, etc. Jain also makes a distinction between intentional, careless or merely fun-type violence and accidental injury. For the latter, the person is not responsible, morally or spiritually. He also notes that the ascetic is expected to practice complete ahimsa while the laity have many exceptions. But he offers several caveats or cautions. While some say war is necessary, he doubts it. The aim of religion is to bring peace on earth and goodwill among all people. Religion must emphasize the ultimate good and declare evil as evil even if it appears unavoidable under some circumstances. Good cannot come from evil.[26]

Mahavira's teaching remains. "Don't talk about loving others. Talk first to yourself, whether you love yourself or not." "He whom you wish to kill, is no other than yourself." The modern Jain movement for world peace includes the recognition that "treaties and laws only create an artificial peace." Real peace must begin in human hearts. It does not end there, of course. Jyotiprasad Jain says the Jaina philosophy of life is peace that is both internal and external, personal and universal. His prayer for peace includes both his own unending peace, peace for others, and for all the citizens of the world. The Jain Peace Fellowship is working for global peace. Its methods include a weekly time of prayer or meditation in which people everywhere are asked to join. By building a powerful "Thought-Image of Peace," the collective human mind can generate an overwhelming influence for peace. Some believe in maintaining military strength and building ever mightier war machines. The Jain method works within the human heart.[27]

VI. Sikhism

*Only in the Name of the Lord
do we find our peace.*

Introduction

The origins of Sikhism have sometimes been traced back to a series of poets (bhaktas) such as Jaidev, a Bengali Brahmin and Hindu reformer in the twelfth century A.D. He considered all ceremonies worthless without the pious repetition of God's name. Noss suggested Sikhism is an Islamic teaching adapted to Hinduism. To reverse the metaphor, it is a resurgence of the thousand-year-old bhakti marg (path of devotion) movement in Hinduism, partly as a response to Muslim Sufism. A major figure in the latter tradition is Sheikh Farid (1173–1265), whose 134 hymns are included in the Adi Granth, the holy book, the Guru of Sikhism. Sikh scholars do not generally subscribe to the syncretistic origins of Sikhism. They understand it to be a new revelation.[1]

Bhakti origins are part of the nirguna sampradaya, the Sant tradition of northern India which merged bhakti and the Nath tradition. The latter, an expression of ancient Tantra and hatha yoga, emphasized interiority, the rejection of idols, ritual, temples and mosques, pilgrimage, and caste. These traditions also were distinguished by the use of vernacular languages. Bhakti and Sufi thought emphasized a personal and emotional relationship with God and saw doctrine as unimportant.[2]

Another figure is Namdev (1270–1350), a tailor of Maharashtra in western India, a follower of Vishnu who also represents devotional Hinduism. He did not think God is in stone images. There is no satisfaction in ceremonies without inner sincerity. The love of God frees one from reincarnation. Another fourteenth century reformer was a Hindu saint named Ramananda (b. 1299), who is credited with popularizing southern bhakti in northern India and establishing a new Vishnu sect. He opposed the caste system and vegetarianism.

A more immediate predecessor of Sikhism was the poet Kabir, 1440–1518, who was born to a Muslim family. His name means "great" in Arabic and may reflect his Islamic heritage. He worked as a weaver in the holy Hindu city of Benaras, or Varanasi. As a young man, he became a disciple of Ramananda. His songs, in the vernacular Hindi language, show a synthesis of Islam and Hinduism. He taught that people are one family under God. He opposed all sectarianism, the worship of images, ritual, and caste. His basic thought was that the same God is worshipped under different names such as Allah in Islam and Ram in Hinduism. He anticipates here the unified religion, Din-i-ilahi, of the Mughal Emperor Akbar (1556–1605). He called himself a "pir" of Islam and Hinduism. Pir is Persian for elder and is used for a Murshid, Arabic for a Sufi leader or spiritual director. In India, pir refers to a Muslim saint and is equivalent to the Hindi "guru" (teacher; Sanskrit, honored). He was persecuted for being anti-institutional and left Benaras in 1495. He traveled around north India for the rest of his life. His verse is preserved in the *Kabir-Granthavali*, a later work called *Bijak*, the scriptures of the Dadupanthi and the *Adi Granth* of Sikhism. He still has over a million followers, known as the Kabir Panthis (path, followers or community of Kabir).[3]

Guru Nanak

While these earlier origins are important, the actual founder of Sikhism is Guru Nanak, 1469–1539. He was born in Talwandi, 30 miles from Lahore, now in Pakistan, and died in Kartarpur. His parents, Mehta Kalian Das Bedi or Kalu and Tripata, were Hindus of the mercantile khatri caste. His father was a farmer, accountant and the revenue superintendent for Rai Bular, the zamindar of Talwandi. Rai Bular was a Hindu who converted to Islam but remained tolerant of Hinduism. As a child, Nanak went to school and learned Hindi and Urdu. Through a friend of his father's he learned about Shiite Islam as well as the Sunni tradition and Sufism. In addition to his native Hinduism, he may have had contact with Parsis, Jews and Christians.[4]

When he was 16, he went to live with his sister, Nanaki, and her husband, Jai Ram, in Sultanpur. Jai Ram was a steward for the nawab, Daulat Khan Lodi, Afghan governor of the province, and Nanak was given a job as storekeeper. At age 19, Nanak married Sulakhni. They had two sons, Sri Chand (1494) and Lakmi Das (1497). During the day, he worked hard and capably, but his evenings were spent singing hymns along with his friend, the Muslim minstrel Mardana, who followed him from Talwandi. A small group of disciples ("sikhs") formed around them.[5]

Nanak's spiritual experience is recorded in the Old Chronicle, Puratan Janamsakhi (birth testimony) of 1635, and in his own hymns. He was about 30 years old when he was bathing in the river one morning. He had a vision of going to heaven. God offered him a drink of nectar and told Nanak that he was to go into the world to teach people how to pray. His life was to be one of praise of the Word (nam — pronounced naam), charity (dan = daan), ablution (isnan = isnaan), service (seva) and prayer (simran). He rejected the ascetic life and lived as a householder in service of the people.

Service is to be free and voluntary for all persons without regard to race, color or creed. The same Being permeates everyone so all are equal. However, Nanak objected to exploitation and sided with the deprived. The service concept is illustrated in a tradition that he told a wealthy farmer he could not take his wealth with him into the next world, but "Give some of thy wealth in God's name, feed the poor, and thy wealth shall accompany thee." Service might be seen somewhat in the tradition of karma marg, the path of work, made famous in more recent decades by Mahatma Gandhi. Sangat, the fellowship of believers, is part of this, for "In good company one becomes good." Instead of karma marg, Sikhs prefer to think of their tradition as one of Nam (Name) Marg, repeating God's name and contemplating him. Repeating the True Name equals bathing in 68 Hindu places of pilgrimage. Believers are reborn into a life where they can hear and read and obey the lessons of the Guru, and are thus within reach of liberation, freed from the cycle of rebirth and united with God.[6]

Simran is defined as the remembrance of God's name by constant repetition but it must be done from the heart, not as mere mechanical repetition. At its very best, simran is true contemplation and is at the base of Sikh mysticism. During the cycle of rebirths, the soul evolves from primitive to human. The soul is part of the Eternal Soul, so its union with God in the final liberation is a return, a reabsorption.

As G.S. Sidhu says, salvation can be obtained through good deeds as well as by the grace of God. He goes on to say that "In order to deserve God's grace, the Guru outlines the course of eradicating lust, anger, greed, infatuation and ego, and act in His will remembering Him every moment of life." He adds that transmigration can be halted by acting on the advice of the guru, repeating the true name, and doing good deeds. He notes that salvation is impossible without love, the pivot of Sikhism and one of the cardinal virtues of the gurus and their followers. McLeod suggests that for Nanak in the Adi Granth, grace and service are parallel. Both are vital for salvation. Service came first and God's grace is a response to it. He goes on to say that the Adi Granth has the single message that salvation is through meditation on the divine name. Originally, asceticism was rejected but later became respected in the form of nonattachment. Whatever the exact relationship of deeds, prayer and asceticism, the service motif and social responsibility are major parts of the social code of Sikhism.[7]

Nanak taught monotheism like Kabir — there is one God behind all the different names. The monotheism can be seen as reflecting Muslim tradition while he retained the concept of samsara, the cycle of rebirth, or reincarnation, from Hinduism. God is at the same time transcendent (unseen, shrouded in mystery) and an immanent, loving God who cares for his people. Like his poet-reformer predecessors, he opposed caste, a priesthood, idolatry, and ritual. All people are equal before God.

While others had said this in regard to caste, race and other distinctions, he extended it to include women. Such acceptance and tolerance is extremely rare in religious traditions. This translates into monogamy and a higher education rate for Sikh women. Men are not to look lustfully at women. They are to be seen as mothers, daughters and sisters. The equality also came to be symbolized by the langar, or free community kitchen, in which people eat together, and thus break caste. The Sikh worship service in later years ended with the sharing of parshad, a warm sweet made of wheat flour, sugar and ghee (rarefied butter). One can add here that Nanak preached the doctrine that the lower creation serves man, the highest creature. This removes taboos against eating meat and values human life over cockroaches.[8]

After his call, Nanak became a wanderer. He and Mardana traveled around preaching and singing, Nanak dressed like a Hindu sannyasi and a Muslim Qalander, or dervish. In the bhakti tradition, Nanak repeated the Sat Nam, the True Name. The concept is familiar now in the West through the chanting of Hare Krishna by members of the International Society of Krishna Consciousness. In their wanderings, tradition says they met Kabir in the vicinity of Benaras. Nanak apparently did not impress too many people until he returned to the Punjab where he began to gather disciples ("sikhs" in Punjabi).[9]

He settled in Kartarpur with his family and preached regularly until his death in 1539. His disciples formed the Nanak Panth, or Sikh Panth, or simply the Panth. They were expected to follow a strict life-style. In time, Nanak appointed a successor. He bypassed his sons and chose his chief disciple, Lehna, or Lahina (1504–1552), renamed Angad ("of my own limb"). This started a nonhereditary tradition of leadership by guru.[10]

The Teachers

There were ten Gurus altogether. Angad, the son of a trader and originally a worshipper of Durga, created the Gurmukhi (from the mouth of the guru) script and wrote down Nanak's life and teaching. He and his successors emphasized education in the vernacular. They also emphasized the langar, the free kitchen. Amar Das, born in 1479 and Guru from 1552–1574, organized the movement into congregations (sangats) meeting into gurdwara (temples or meeting houses). They in turn were organized into 22 manjis, or dioceses, or circles, each under a leader. He dug a step-well (bawali) as a place of pilgrimage at Goindwal, appointed three feast days in the year, provided simplified marriage and funeral ceremonies, and discouraged the use of wine and sati (widow burning). He was also a poet and over 900 of his verses have been preserved. His son-in-law, Ram Das, born 1534, Guru 1574–1581, dug a tank or reservoir (1577) on land donated to his wife by Akbar and began building Ramdaspur, later the sacred city, Amritsar (pool of nectar).[11]

Nanak had compiled the Japuji (Punjabi for meditation, from the Sanskrit japa, repeated prayers), the Sikh morning prayer, consisting of 38 stanzas which he said were revealed to him by God. Arjan, the younger son

of Ram Das and fifth Guru, born 1563, Guru 1581–1606, compiled the Adi
Granth which opens with the Japuji. The Holy Word (sabda) became a
symbol for Nam, the True Name of God.[12]

Arjan wrote a preface, the Mul (basic) Mantra ("mind" + "feeling"), for
the Japuji. This preface is a basic creedal statement for Sikhism. It says

> There is One God
> His Name is Truth,
> The All-pervading Creator,
> Without fear, without hatred
> Immortal, unborn, self-existent,
> By grace, the Enlightener,
> Truth in the beginning, truth throughout the ages,
> Truth even now, Nanak, and forever shall be true.

God is to be called "Sat" for he is truth eternal. He is the creator but he is
present or immanent as well as transcendent. Unlimited by time, he is not
subject to birth and decay. God is known through meditation, religious
devotion and the grace of the Guru. Arjan wrote that bathing in the Amritsar tank washed away all sins.[13]

Arjan built the Golden Temple (Har Mandir) in the center of Amritsar
tank. The foundation stone was laid by Saint Mian Mir, a Muslim sufi. Its
four doors symbolize its openness to all four castes. Arjan brought
thousands of Jats, Punjabi peasants, into the Sikh fold. He encouraged
trade in Turkish horses. This broke the Hindu caste sanctions against cross-
ing the Indus River and leaving Mother India, which in turn broke caste.
The horse trade increased prosperity and developed horse riding and eventually cavalry among the Sikhs. It also brought contact with a newly militant Islam. Arjan was tortured to death by the Mughal Emperor Jahangir
(1605–1627) who considered Arjan a Hindu who was attracting ignorant
Muslims away from the true faith. Arjan was the first Sikh martyr. Before
his death, he told his son to arm himself. Here is the transition from
pacifism to militarism.[14]

The son became Guru Hargobind, born in 1595 and Guru, 1606–1644.
Next to the Golden Temple, he built the shrine, Akal Takht, "the throne
of the Timeless." Military clashes with the rajas of the Himalayan foothills
and the Mughals (1628, 1631 and 1634) increased the militarism of the
Sikhs. Har Rai, born 1630, was Guru, 1644–1661. His son, Harkrishan was
only five at his father's death but he nonetheless became the Guru, 1661–64.
He was followed by Tegh Bahadur, "Hero of the Sword," born 1621, Guru
1664–1675. Bahadur was killed by the Mughal Emperor Aurangzeb
(1658–1707) and thus became the second martyred Guru. His son, Gobind
Rai, born 1666, was Guru, 1675–1708. He took the name Gobind Singh
(lion).[15]

Guru Gobind Singh enlarged the Adi Granth by adding the collection
called Dasam Granth. In October 1708, he declared the Granth to be *the*
Guru. There would be no more human Gurus. Earlier, on the Hindu New

Year's Day in 1699, he formed the Khalsa, the fellowship of the pure. These would rise before dawn to bathe in cold water and live by the five K's (panj kakke): the Kesh (uncut hair and beard), the Kangha (a wooden comb), the Kach (shorts), the Kara (a steel bracelet on the wrist), and the Kirpan (a steel sword or dagger). Khalsa members are to eat no kosher meat killed by Muslims, have no sexual relations with Muslims, avoid smoking and beverage alcohol. They are called the chosen of God. They take the name Singh, while the women of the family take the name Kuar, princess. The turban often associated with Sikh males is not strictly prescribed but is convenient to cover the long hair. Long-haired Sikhs are called keshadhari.

The five K's have been variously interpreted. The sword says Sikhs are slave to no man. It is an emblem of power and freedom of the spirit. It is an instrument of defense. The bracelet means Sikhs are slaves to God and the hand is never to be used for evil. It indicates restraint and the wearer's indebtedness to the Guru. The short trouser is a symbol of modesty and chastity. It is a mark of perpetual readiness and ensures briskness and agility. The comb is a symbol of physical cleanliness, and the uncut hair represents "sacred men of complete body." These are marks of dedication and group consciousness.[16]

Not all Sikhs are in the Khalsa. Clean-shaven Sikhs are called sahajadharis (sahaj, slow adopters, or, spiritual ecstasy from simran). They do not think identity is a matter of external signs. They may go back to Nanak or one of the other eight for inspiration. The Nanakpanthis are more pacifist than the Khalsa.[17]

Further Developments

While the Granth Sahib was henceforth the Guru, the Sikhs were led by military commanders. Guru Gobind Singh had appointed Banda Singh as army commander. He sacked Sirhind and held power from Lahore to Panipat. However, he was captured by the Mughals and tortured to death in 1715. Sikhism was prohibited and persecuted. People were paid to murder Sikhs. Then the central government was weakened by all the revolts and by the 1738 invasion of Nadir Shah, who conquered Delhi. Sikh fortunes waxed and waned. The armies of Ahmad Shah massacred 30,000 Sikhs and polluted the Golden Temple in 1762. But they recovered and later restored the temple and captured Lahore. Ahmad's attacks actually strengthened the Sikhs by giving them cohesion against a common enemy.[18]

In the early nineteenth century, Ranjit Singh (d. 1839) extended the Sikhs' territory and established a state. He practiced religious toleration, had a Muslim as his leading minister, and brought in American and British officers to train his army. However, while the Mughals were weakening in power, the British were growing. In the Sikh Wars, the British were eventually successful. The last Sikh ruler, Maharajah Dulip Singh, surrendered in 1849. As a pledge of Sikh loyalty, he gave Queen Victoria the Koh-i-noor diamond. In time, the British recruited Sikhs for the Indian army and Sikhs became some of the best soldiers in the British Empire.[19]

With the collapse of the Khalsa, the Sikhs began to disintegrate. Mughal persecution had pushed them toward Hinduism. Population pressures exacerbated the economic situation, which was also affected by the disbanding of the military. British employment of Sikhs for the army, and the development of irrigation agriculture helped restore the economics. The recruitment of only Khalsa Sikhs strengthened the Khalsa compared to the non-Khalsa. The restoration was aided by a series of reform movements. Dyal Das (1783-1855) formed the Nirankaris (the formless), opposed to idol worship, Hindu ceremonies and pilgrimages. His son, Bhai (brother) Dara (1855-1870), carried on his work which also had a pacifist element. In the 1840s, Balak Singh, or Sain Sahib (d. 1862), started the Namdhari movement which opposed caste, sati (reintroduced at the death of Ranjit), and idols. It has been called a back-to-pure-Sikhism movement. Under his successor, Ram Singh, the movement also became an anti-British political movement. He proclaimed himself to be a successor to Guru Gobind Singh and promised to drive the English out of the country. The British jailed him. He was a protector of the cow and in 1871, some of his followers murdered some Muslim butchers. In chanting and working themselves into a frenzy, participants uttered loud shrieks, "kuks," and the group is sometimes called the Kuka Movement. They follow the simple life of Nanak and Gobind and were first in the freedom movement to use noncooperation methods, developed by Ram Singh in the 1860s, and used later by Gandhi. The Singh Sabha (association) was a major reform group for 50 years after its founding in 1873. It was a group of Sikh organizations dedicated to religious, social and educational reform. They sent out missionaries and formed the Khalsa Tract Society to distribute religious literature. They worked against both Christian missionaries and the Hindu proselytism of the Arya Samaj whose efforts in converting Sikhs left a deep distrust towards Hinduism.[20]

Some conflict with British authority continued. In 1922, the British refused the Sikhs permission to use one of their temples. In the campaign of the gurdwara Guru-ka-Bagh, the Sikhs used Gandhi's methods of non-violence. Hundreds were injured in the protest. Violence returned during World War II when General Mohan Singh organized the Indian National Army to throw out the British. He failed and casualties were heavy.[21]

Another movement in the 1920s concerned control of the gurdwaras, worship centers. Many of these had fallen into the hands of hereditary mahants (priests) who were more Hindu than Sikh. The Sikh Gurdwaras Bill of 1925 restored control to the Sikh community and centralized that control in the Shiromani Gurdwara Parbandhak Committee (SGPC). The move was led by the Akalis, which in turn became the center of political control, now represented in the Akali Party or the Akali Dal.[22]

In 1947, the Punjab was divided between Pakistan and India in spite of Sikh protests. Supported by the Hindu Jats, they fought the Muslims in a holy war that resulted in over a million casualties. Over 2.5 million Sikhs moved from West Punjab in Pakistan to East Punjab in India. In recent years, some of the 12 million Sikhs have asked India for freedom and the establishment of a Sikh nation. In 1982, a Sikh, Zail Singh, was elected president of India. However, India has refused to grant independence to the Punjab and some Sikhs have responded with rebellion and guerilla-type warfare. In 1984, the Indian army attacked the Golden Temple complex, claiming it was a stronghold for armed militants. The Temple's interior was nearly unscathed. The facade of the Akal Takht was torn away by heavy fire. Thousands of Sikhs were reported killed. Priceless, one of a kind manuscripts were destroyed.

The leader of the militants, reported to be a small minority of Sikhs, Jarnail Singh Bhindranwale, was killed and thousands of his followers were arrested. A Sikh journalist, historian and member of Parliament said Jarnail was not so good a man but the brutal attack on the temple alienated all Sikhs. Nearly 5000 Sikhs created the first mutiny in the modern Indian army. While Sikhs are only two percent of the total population of India, they number ten percent of the army. Two Sikhs were charged with the later killing of the prime minister, Indira Gandhi, October 31, 1984. In the four days of rioting that followed, almost 3000 Sikhs were killed in 100 cities. Unrest continues.[23]

It should be noted further that the Punjab (land of five waters) is one of the richest agricultural areas of India. Much of it is doab, plain between two rivers. The Indus River forms the northwestern border. The five waters (rivers) are the Sutlej on the south and its tributary the Beas, and the Ravi and Chenab, both tributary to the Jhelum. The Jhelum and the Sutlej join below Multan and enter the Indus as it enters Baluchistan.

The Sikhs in turn have followed Guru Nanak's threefold dictum to work, worship and be charitable. The three have also been translated as service, simran and the sacrifice of one's self for and sharing one's possessions with others. To this one could add Nanak's view that "Adversity is a medicine and comfort a disease for in comfort there is no yearning for God," and Gobind Singh's lines "But with Thee shall I in adversity dwell./ Without Thee life of ease is life in hell" (Sabad Hazare). Instead of accepting adversity and living in poverty and apathy, they work to overcome the difficulties, which include helping the needy.

Thus we have the happy combination of good land and good workers which has made the Punjab materially better off than some other areas of the world. In recent years, this has resulted in educational and other advances, including several new universities such as Punjabi University in Patiala and Guru Nanak Dev University in Amritsar.[24]

Sikhs have now spread to all parts of the world. The Sikh Missionary Society was founded in 1969 in England while the Sikh Research Centre was formed in Canada. Similar groups, such as the Sikh Foundation which emerged as a voice of Sikhism in the 1970s, are found in the United States.

Harbhajan Singh Puri or Yogi Bhajan, a priest of the Sikh Dharma in
Amritsar, came to the United States to teach yoga. In 1969, he started the
Healthy-Happy-Holy Organization, or 3 H O, with headquarters in Los
Angeles. Today it has over 150 centers in the United States and other coun-
tries. The movement uses Sikh symbols, rituals and beliefs, and some of its
members have formally become Sikhs.[25]

War and Peace

There are several ways of viewing this history with its changes from
a peaceful tradition to a military one and the concern for peace continuing
both in separate groups and in the main tradition. One view is that Nanak
promoted goodness, preaching love for one's neighbor. Early Sikhs lived
by the words, "If anyone ill-treat you, bear it three times, and God Himself
will fight for you the fourth time." Gobind Singh called for uprooting evil
and protecting the weak and oppressed from tyranny, though it is said
some of his advisors protested military involvement and his mother left in
tears when he refused her plea for peace with the Mughals. The call to arms
had already begun with the sixth Guru, Hargobind, though it was Gobind
Singh who established the army on a regular basis. Nanak himself was a
man of peace but was not a pacifist. He is quoted as having said, "To fight
and accept death for a righteous cause is the privilege of the brave and truly
religious." Sikhs, like Christians, sing of God as their shield and defender.
The Guru declared that those who died fighting went to paradise, an old
Muslim tradition.[26]
      One expression of the concern for peace is the tolerance of other tradi-
tions. All religions come from God. God is worshipped through a thousand
names, according to the Guru Granth Sahib. Nanak claimed there is neither
Hindu nor Muslim but only people. Gobind Singh called God the God of
no-religion, for if God is identified only with a particular religion, his grace
and mercy are denied to others. Sikhism does not claim exclusive possession of truth. Sikhs do not attempt to destroy other religions, though the
division of the Punjab resulted in a de facto war with Muslim Pakistan. It
has been said that "Sikhism was born as a gospel of reconciliation." The
ideal is freely given service to others without regard to race, religion,
politics, or gender. The ideal is love but love means little until it is put into
action. At the battle of Anandpur, Gobind Singh blessed Kanihya for giving water to the wounded of both sides. Sheikh Farid said that we are to
"do good to the evil-doer and nurse not anger in the heart."[27]
      The way of peace is found in numerous portions of the tradition. In
a Sikh worship service, both inner peace and peaceful relationships are
stressed. In the Sukhmani, Guru Arjan said, "In the company of saints, man
learns how to turn enemies into friends, as he becomes completely free of
evil, and bears malice to none." The ideal of all humanity as one family
under God is found in tolerance, acceptance of others, humility, obedience

(not servility), forgiveness-compassion, gratitude, learning, wisdom, truthfulness, temperance and nonattachment. The latter resembles Greek Stoicism and the commitment to duty which Krishna calls for from Arjuna in the Bhagavad Gita. One accepts with equanimity all that happens as from God, even as one works to change what needs to be changed when God gives the power to change.

The two fundamental imperatives of this ideal life are control of one's own ego and the recognition of divine law. This divine dimension to life requires purity. While combating the evil influences of the world, Sikhs are expected to keep themselves pure. Sikhs are to keep good company, contemplate the spiritual, treat others as equal, do honest work, give up conceit, serve humbly. In addition to the five K's noted earlier, Arjan's Sukhmani says, "I come to take refuge with the Lord: May the Divine Guru out of His mercy grant that the passions of lust, anger, greed, pride and undue attachment in me may vanish and leave me in peace." If human beings overcome these five sins, the world would certainly be much closer to peace.[28]

Harbans Singh suggests the human person is divine in essence. Humans are sacred and inviolable, entitled to honor and attention. We come from God and have a divine spark within us. The Granth includes the words, "God resides in every heart. Try not to injure the feelings of anyone." Each person is to respect the rights of others and guard them as one's own. Human dignity means freedom, equality and justice. This has several dimensions such as resistance to government oppression and a positive attitude toward the world. Guru Arjan said, "O God, I seek neither dominions, nor emancipation. I crave only the love of Thy feet." Guru Nanak's word is that "He who rules over another is a fool, an indiscriminate wretch." The material world is not rejected but related to a higher spiritual and moral goal.[29]

Gopal Singh notes that international efforts to integrate mankind through hatred and class war decimate everything spiritual in people which distinguishes the human from the animal. He points out that Sikhism does not divide the world into for and against, the individual versus society, nor even into good and bad. God is concerned for all people. Emancipation, or mukti, is to be realized not only for the self but for the whole of society. Singh sees this unity as essential. He suggests that strictly speaking, Sikhism is not a system of philosophy but a way of life. Nanak said, "Truth is above everything, but higher by far is the living of truth." Singh believes every world religion has advocated world peace. The problem is one of practice — living the truth. But if we look upon the world as illusory, or on people as being divided into the chosen and condemned, how can we claim the world is worthy of being saved at all?

G. Singh goes on to ask, "What kind of a world order does Sikhism seek to bring about?" He quotes the Scriptures. Arjan said, "My compassionate Lord has given the command that no one will give pain to another. And whosoever is, will live in peace: And the poor in spirit will reign supreme." Ravidas described, "The city of my love is without grief. There, no one paineth another, nor feareth. There is no tax on goods, and no anxiety afflicteth man. And erreth here no one, nor is afraid of another, and compassion is never in want."

Historically, Singh is well aware of the military side of Sikhism. But he points out that the sixth and tenth gurus drew the sword only as a last resort to protect the rights of Sikhs and others. The sword is employed with no rancor in the heart, even against the enemy. In the "Letter of Victory," Gobind Singh wrote to the Emperor Aurangzeb, "Do not wield the sword to murder the innocent, for the God on high would for sure punish thee . . . annoy not the weak. . . ." Thus, while he sees coexistence as the only alternative to nonexistence, he also notes that no sure peace is possible or desirable if it denies even to a single man his liberty of conscience, or if one group dominates another—politically, socially, economically, or through religious imperialism. In part, this is a matter of doing unto others as one wants done to the self, but it is more than this. Each person must sacrifice ego in service to the family, the interests of the family in service to the nation, and the interests of the nation in service to humanity.[30]

In his "Religious Pluralism & Co-existence," Wazir Singh acknowledges the former and calls for the latter. To illustrate the former, he quotes the ancient Indian dictum, "Truth is one, the sages call it by many names." To promote the latter, he recasts the aphorism as "One Truth, many paths." One of the paths is prayer. There are moments in life when people pray for themselves alone. But prayer often extends to others—to family and friends. Wazir Singh points beyond the closed circle to an open one that extends to all humanity. In light of today's pluralism, Singh quotes the third Sikh guru, Amar Das, whose prayer accepts the several pathways leading to the supreme goal.

> Save this burning world, O Lord,
> Through Thy Act of Grace!
> Save the people through the path
> They may choose to take. (Guru Granth, p. 853)[31]

VII. Buddhism

*There is no happiness
greater than peace.*

The stereotype of Buddhism is a statue of the Buddha in meditation in the lotus position, or on his side. He is at peace. The peace is an inner peace. He achieved nirvana (Sanskrit) or nibbana (Pali) in his lifetime and parinirvana (final) at the time of his death.[1]

Siddhartha, of the clan Gautama of the Sakya tribe, was born about 563 B.C. in the Himalayan foothills in what today is Nepal. He lived to be 80 years old. He was a royal prince, the son of Suddhodana, king of the Sakya, a member of the kshatriya caste of Hinduism, the warrior or ruler caste. His mother, Queen Maya, died within a few days and he was raised by her sister, Prajapati Gautami, who was also his stepmother and who later became his first female convert and nun. Tradition tells us that a prediction at the time of his birth was that he would be a world conqueror or a world renouncer. To avoid the latter and keep his son in line for the throne, Gautama's father surrounded him with luxury and did not allow him to see suffering of any kind. At the age of 16, he married his cousin, Yasodhara. They had a son who was named Rahula, "chains."[2]

In time, he did see suffering, the traditional four sights: a sick man, an old man, a dead man and a monk. The monk was at peace. These four sights led him to contemplate the mystery of life. At the age of 29, he left his wife and child, gave up the royal life and sought a teacher. When he had learned what he could, he left to become an ascetic, meditating with five others. Asceticism did not lead him to the peace which he sought, so he left the ascetic way. While meditating under a pipal (fig) tree at Gaya (now called Budh-Gaya), he attained the enlightenment he sought. He has since been called the Buddha, the enlightened one, while the pipal became the Bo- or Bodhi-tree of enlightenment.

He sought for his five ascetic companions and found them in a deer park near Varanasi. He shared his insight or teaching in a sermon, "Discourse on the Turning of the Wheel of Dharma [Sanskrit] or Dhamma [Pali]." There are Four Noble Truths: All is suffering. Its cause is desire. Suffering can be stopped. The way to do so is by giving up desire and following the Middle Way or the Eightfold Noble Path. The eight points are right views, resolve, speech, action, livelihood, effort, mindfulness and

South Asia, showing important places in the life of Gautama, the Buddha. (Map by Joyce E. Thompson.)

concentration. The five were converted. He continued to preach and soon had many followers. They were organized into the Sangha, the Order of Monks, the bhikkhus, the thera or male elders.[3]

He allowed women to join the Sangha, forming an order of nuns, the bhikkshuni, the theri. One tradition says he did this reluctantly but another quotes Gautama as saying that women might obtain enlightenment. This respect for women stands in contrast to the later tradition of some branches of Buddhism but it is certainly consistent with Gautama's concepts of equality, which refused to recognize castes and such other human distinctions as those between rich and poor. The Buddha both taught and practiced tolerance for all people, including other religious faiths (The Dhammapada, Digha and Majjhima-nikaya).[4]

For the rest of his life, about 40 years, Gautama continued to meditate and taught his followers to do so. He also continued to preach and teach the Four Noble Truths and the Eightfold Path. Early teaching said that right action included the five precepts: do not lie, kill, steal, commit adultery or drink intoxicants. The negative precepts are balanced by positive ones such as the Four Sublime Moods in the Brahma-vihara: loving kindness (metta), compassion (karuna), equanimity (upekkha) and joy in the joy of others (mudita). Gautama also sent his followers out into the world. The Mahavagga records his words: "Go ye, O bhikkhus, and wander forth for the good of many, for the happiness of many, in compassion for the world, for the welfare, for the good, for the happiness of gods and men" (Vinaya, Mahavagga).

Buddhism can be considered a world-renouncing religion. It has been called a self-centered tradition in which the individual seeks only his [sic] own salvation, as in the Christian concept that each one must work out his own salvation (Philippians 2:12). However, Buddhism is also a religion of service to humanity, as in the Christian call to social service (Matthew 25:35–45). The Noble Path and precepts have a number of social implications. "Do not steal" has a positive corollary of charity and generosity. The laity practice this by providing food for the monks. The monks practice it with their teaching.

Padmasiri de Silva has emphasized that even those who renounce the world are driven by compassion for all beings. In a different vein, Nolan Jacobson claims "Buddhism is the first orientation in history to suggest that ultimate reality — what is 'really real' — is social in the deepest sense. Nothing is independent of its contemporaries...."[5]

When Gautama died, perhaps of food poisoning, he entered parinirvana. His remains were cremated and the ashes buried under stupas in eight cities. The Sangha carried on his work.

There are variations on the above traditions. Parts of the tradition claim there have been many Buddhas, some earlier, some later, some, such as Maitreya, yet to come. Others consider Gautama the only Buddha, though he may have been active through many lives as in the Jataka Tales. Some think Buddhism's missionary impulse came later, perhaps with the Emperor Ashoka, circa 273–232 B.C. Some claim that the Eightfold Path is a later addition to the tradition. Some claim that one does not need to give up all desire, for that would mean death from thirst or starvation. The problematic desire is specifically "tanha," selfish desire. We are to give up greed (lobha), conceit (mana), hatred (dosa) and aggression or revenge. Some note an empirical dimension of Gautama's teaching. People were and are invited to see for themselves (Kalama-sutta, Anguttara-nikaya; Sutta-nipata; Samyutta-nikaya). Thus no original teaching of the Buddha is authoritative for all time. One result was a splintering of the movement into divisions.[6]

Traditionally there were 18 sects of Buddhism by the first century B.C. Today, Buddhism is usually divided into two great branches, Theravada and Mahayana. The first is the tradition of the elders. It is called southern

Buddhism and is usually considered older. It is predominant today in Sri
Lanka, Burma, Thailand, Cambodia and Laos. Among its teachings is the
idea that there may be other Buddhas but Gautama is the only one for this
eon. There are gods but no creator god. Theravada has sometimes been
called a-theistic.[7]

Mahayana, or northern Buddhism, is found in Tibet, China, Korea,
Japan and Vietnam. One of its scriptures, the Lotus Sutra, refers to two
million Buddhas. There are also many bodhisattvas, persons who have or
could have achieved nirvana but stay in the world to help others. The Buddha himself has become a god, at least to some interpreters of Mahayana,
though Nagarjuna in the second century A.D. said that the gods are false
and the wise do not believe in them.

Both Theravada and Mahayana have now spread to other parts of the
world as well. Tibetan Buddhism is sometimes considered a separate division called Vajrayana, the Diamond Way. In the West, it is sometimes
called lamaism, now commonly applied to all monks though originally a
term only for the abbot. Chan or Zen Buddhism in China and Japan is
sometimes considered yet another form of the faith.

One interpretation of Theravada is that only males, and some say only
monks, can reach nirvana. Women must be reincarnated as males. They
then have the option to become monks. For some, this means two tiers or
levels of Buddhism. There is the Buddhism of the lay persons and there is
that of the monks. About the best the laity can expect is that if they make
a reasonable effort at the Eightfold Path, they may get a better reincarnation the next time around. The monks have a higher ethic and numerous
rules, though even these do not guarantee escape from the wheel of life,
samsara, into nirvana. One might presume, however, that monks have
some greater opportunity to achieve peace in this life, in the sense of an inner calm. Distinctions between women and men and between monastics
and laity seem to contradict the Buddha's teaching of benevolence for all
without discrimination (Theragatha). K.N. Jayatilleke has pointed out that
the Buddha was one of the earliest religious teachers to preach equality. De
Silva phrases it, "The moral excellence of a person is the only basis for
grouping people, and not birth, caste, colour or sex." Presumably if one is
benevolent towards insects, one might also be benevolent towards women
and the laity.[8]

In Mahayana, the "great vehicle," everyone can supposedly achieve
peace, including nirvana. For some portions of Mahayana, this means
following the Path. For some portions of the tradition, nirvana comes as
a means of grace or compassion (karuna) from the Buddha, or from a
bodhisattva, who gives nirvana directly or offers passage to the Western
Paradise. One may be content to stay there or move to parinirvana (final
nirvana after physical death).

The concern here is not a complete introduction to Buddhism but a
highlighting of the many paths to peace available in a very broad tradition.
Buddhism's ability to adapt to various cultures has made it the most

adaptable world religion. This has also brought differing perspectives on war and peace. We pause here, however, to note again the renunciation stereotype.

To be a Buddhist, or at least a good one, it has been assumed that one must renounce the world. That means celibacy, no property or occupation, no participation in politics, economics, education or anything else that is usually related to life. On the other hand, we have already noted the two different tiers for monks and laity. Again, when one studies the history of both Gautama and the Sangha, a quite different picture emerges. We might note here, inter alia, that the modern significance of this debate is far reaching. De Silva notes that without peace, there can be no development. The view of Buddhism as world renouncing means there is no interest in development, or in peace, for it is all an illusion. Thus the different picture is crucial to our concern of Buddhism and world peace.⁹

Gautama was a preacher and teacher. All monks are called to preach and teach. Some of the greatest centers of learning in history have been Buddhist. The isolated forest dweller represents a small percentage of the total number of monks. By including women in the Sangha, the Buddha created an alternative life for them which had a major effect on society, including its economic life. The withdrawal of large numbers of men to the monastic life had an effect on the economics and population of Buddhist societies. The same must be said when devoted lay people gave property to the monasteries which in time became quite rich. We might add that the temples (viharas) and centers were also places of shelter for the poor and the sick who should be fed and cared for (Bodhicaryavatara; Bodhisattvabhumi).

The Samyutta-nikaya does not negate political activity. It rather insists that politics should be advanced according to the dhamma, without killing, hurting or conquering. A closer reading of history also makes clear that the Sangha has been heavily involved in politics and the military throughout the centuries.¹⁰

Rulers often used monks for direct rule, for advice, for determining the propitiousness of the stars, etc. Both ancient and modern rulers have sponsored Buddhist councils such as Rajagriha after Gautama's death. Ashoka and Kanishka of the Kushans circa A.D. 120 are alleged to have convened councils. The Burmese fifth council in 1868–1871 was sponsored by Mindon Min. U Nu sponsored the sixth in 1954. Royal houses have supported Buddhism while being supported by Buddhism, "serving as spiritual tranquilizer for the oppressed by promising happiness in the world to come." One must add that kings have been made, and unmade, by the power of the Sangha and have even been assassinated by monks.

In one invasion, Sri Lankan monks led the charge and one became a general. They assured King Duttha-Gamani that he would not be held back from nirvana for killing the enemy who were criminals and no better than animals. This contrasts with the Buddha's claim of benevolence for all creatures and Sariputa the Elder's claim that Buddhists are to have compassion even for their enemies (Milindapanha).¹¹

However, Arthur L. Basham points out that many Buddhist kings of India and Sri Lanka were great conquerors and as ruthless as their Hindu neighbors. Two of India's greatest conquerors were the Buddhist kings Harsha of Kanauj (A.D. 606–647) and Dharmapala of Bihar and Bengal (770–810). In southeast Asia, Buddhist groups conquered and slaughtered each other and destroyed the Buddhist temples and shrines of their enemies. Trevor Ling's history of Buddhism in Burma and Thailand is one of war, often very brutal. He suggests that one reason for the savagery was the psychological release of hostilities suppressed by Buddhist strictures against anger. The negative stricture was honored in letter but not in spirit, and the positive not at all. These brutal wars were often conducted with the explicit approval of the Sangha, which then reaped part of the spoils of the victor even while the Sangha in the other area was destroyed. Nor is this just ancient history as Ling and others note. The Sangha supported the overthrow of the government of Thailand in both 1932 and 1957. The Sangha was then reorganized by government decree.[12]

In contrast to the situation in Burma and Thailand, the Sangha-state relationship in Vietnam has been characterized by protest — against Vietnamese emperors, the French, the Americans, and now the communists.

Tibet has been thought of as a completely Buddhist country. However, there are still elements of the original Bon religion there. Snellgrove reports that Buddhist hostility and repression of Bon or bonpos (followers of Bon) were severe but have receded. Now, others take as little account of their existence as possible. The hostility may be a return, tit for tat, phenomenon. When Buddhism first arrived, it met strong resistance. It originally established itself with superior magic, a phenomenon known in other traditions as well, such as Christianity.

In China, Buddhism was not received with great enthusiasm at first. The shaved heads of monks and lack of family ties were seen as weird. The new religion was considered barbarian by the civilized Chinese. But then rulers discovered that Buddhist monks made loyal subjects because they had no family ties. Buddhism was coopted by the rulers. Emperor Wen, or Yang Chien (541–604), established the Sui dynasty (581–618). He claimed to be spreading the ideals of the Buddha with armed might. His military victories promoted the Ten Virtues. Weapons of war were the offerings of incense and flowers presented to Buddha and his land was identical with the Buddha-land.[13]

While ostensibly pacifist, the monks who supported the T'ang dynasty (A.D. 618–907) were given military honors. An uprising of monks in 619 included not only killing but a monk, Kao T'an-cheng, who declared himself the emperor. Monks fought the Mongols at the end of the Sung dynasty (960–1279) with the slogan "Crush the demons." General Fan Tche-hiu formed an entire army of monks. A monk, Tchen-pao, led the defense of Song because he had promised to die for the emperor of Song. In the Ming period (1368–1644), monks fought well enough to repel some Japanese pirates. The Ming dynasty was founded by a former monk. These were all orthodox groups. Sectarian fringe groups also included military action. Nor was the killing limited to monks and generals. "Buddhism was frequently at the center of peasant rebellions from the thirteenth century on."[14]

In Korea, monks enlisted in the armies against the Jurchen (twelfth century C.E.), Mongols (fourteenth century), Japanese (sixteenth century) and Manchus (seventeenth century). The Venerable Sosan (1520–1604) successfully led his monk army against the invasion of Toyotomi Hideyoshi from Japan. Sosan's rationale was protecting the nation. He based it on the teaching of Won-Kuang (d. A.D. 630), who called for deliberation in killing rather than no killing at all. Park translates "deliberation" where the original can also be translated "Kill only if necessary." Followers of this line of thinking claim that necessity includes protecting the nation. They quote the Nirvana Sutra and the "Three Sutras of protecting the nation" — the Lotus Sutra, the Golden Splendor Sutra and the Jen-Wang Sutra.

In Japan, most of the monasteries from the tenth to the sixteenth centuries had their own armies, both to defend themselves and to conquer their neighbors. Fielding thousands of troops, single campaigns are recorded as destroying hundreds of religious buildings, thousands of homes and religious objects. They were especially harsh on new movements such as Zen, which itself helped form the bushido code of honor of the Samurai knights. Zen insisted on stoic resignation in the face of suffering and death, and in absolute loyalty to one's superior. Both brought Zen extensive support from the Shoguns. Zen priests had influential roles in government. The most religiously zealous Zen generals were the most murderous.

Wars were fought with the government as well as other monasteries. Buddhism permeated the masses and formed a dimension of the peasant revolts. Within the monasteries, disorder rather than peace was the order of the day. Finally, in 1571 Nobunaja Oda (1534–1582) destroyed the monasteries and annihilated the monastic armies in his unification of Japan. The Samurai continued, though in the Tokugawa period (1600–1867) bushido became a moral discipline designed to bring satori, insight. History continued, however, in the twentieth century for "organized Buddhism in Japan ... supported aggressive war in the 1930's and the 1940's...."[15]

Thus while both right action and right livelihood, and the precept against killing can be related to ahimsa, nonviolence, exceptions could always be made. In modern China, supporters of the communist regime interpret ahimsa as harmlessness to good people, i.e., Party supporters. The Mahaparinibbana Sutta tells how the Buddha himself killed some heretics in his former lives. Thus killing is justified to protect the doctrine. Another tradition is that he killed a bandit to save 500 other people. We will elaborate shortly on the doctrine of no soul and no self. If there is no self, one argument is that there is nothing to kill. It is all an illusion. Nichiren (A.D. 1222–1282) believed in predestination so it was no sin to kill, though the person doing the killing must not disturb his own inner calm. Self-defense is yet another justification for killing. That is extended to the defense of others. It is better to kill than to allow another to kill.[16]

Today's Buddhism *is* seen as a peace-loving religion. John M. Koller claims that in its 2500-year spread to 400 million people, "no wars have been fought and no blood shed in the propagation of the teachings. Violence is absolutely contrary to . . . Buddhism. It is a common conviction of Buddhists everywhere that anger and violence only provoke more of the same, and that anger and violence are only appeased and removed by kindness and compassion." Burma's attorney general in 1950, U Chan Htoon, said "Buddhism is the only ideology which can give peace to the world and save it from war and destruction." U Thant of Burma served as secretary-general of the United Nations (1962–1972). In this position, he promoted world order and peace. Though not always successful, he was certainly a loyal Buddhist in his efforts. Burmese Prime Minister U Nu claimed that while theistic creeds sanction war, Buddhism does not sanction violence of any kind, even self-defense.[17]

However, not everyone agrees today any more than historically. Peacemaker U Nu was overthrown by the Buddhist military General Win in 1962. Trevor Ling noted that when Sinhalese students in England read his first edition in 1970, they said that it was "no longer possible for young Buddhists to be content with non-violent, non-revolutionary forms of Buddhism." U Ba Swe of Burma thought violent Marxism to be compatible with Buddhism. A revolutionary program based on both would be quite appropriate for Burma. The revolutionary monk, U Pandia of Burma, cited the self-defense motif as justification for his explosive career. The same understanding was used for the military buildup of Thailand under Sandhurst-trained King Vajiravudh (Rama VI) from 1910 to 1925. He had the explicit backing of the Buddhist Patriarch who claimed wars must be prepared for even in time of peace. The preface of the printed sermon included the reminder that the Buddha was not against war but only militarism, unreasoning hatred, savagery, blood lust. Nothing was said about the historic savagery in the area. In building up the army, Rama laid the groundwork for the coup of 1932.[18]

During the Vietnam War, several Vietnamese monks burned themselves to death. While this certainly violates the sanctions against killing, Thich Nhat Hanh justified the deeds by citing the Jataka Tale of Buddha in a previous incarnation in which he gave himself to a hungry lioness or tigress to keep her from eating her own cubs. Thus the suicides were acts of compassion. He himself did not believe in killing one's own enemies, even in self-defense. In contrast, Theravadin Padmasiri de Silva has spoken clearly. What the Vietnamese monks did, was wrong.[19]

However, the Asian Buddhist Conference for Peace, meeting in Moscow in 1975, hailed the end of the Vietnam War as a great victory for the people of Vietnam, Laos and Cambodia. The Ven. Kyotaku Nakano of Japan condemned the World Conference on Religion and Peace, in which Thich Nhat Hanh participated, along with its central figure, Rev. Homer A. Jack, for its dangerous role as an instrument of Western imperialism.[20] The Ven. Pham The Long of the Democratic Republic of Vietnam hailed military action by the Vietnamese people as a victory of the charity, intellect and strength of Buddhism against the crimes and war of the devil, U.S. imperialism. "Friendship with all and enmity with none is the basic principle we follow in establishing peace at home and peace outside, but the forces of evil, when they stand in the way, are to be destroyed with all the strength." The Ven. Vishudhananda Mahathero of Bangladesh went on to say, "Here we do not deal with politics, our aim is peace through the Buddhist cult of Metta, Karuna, Mudita, and Upekkha." Phramachakhamtan Thevabonaly of Laos quoted the Buddha as saying, "Those who do good receive good, those who do evil receive evil." One might note there is no mention of Tibet in the ABPC report, nor of the destruction of Tibetan Buddhism by Chinese Communists. Nor is anything said about their decimation of Chinese Buddhism, including the destruction of 130,000 temples and murder of untold thousands of monks and nuns.

Maoist Buddhists in China approved of killing those opposed to the great revolution on the ground that it is alright to kill in order to save others. Modern Chinese monks fought in the Korean War to wipe out the American imperialist demons who were breaking world peace. Hsin-tao (1951) not only said such killing was blameless, it had merit towards nirvana.

David L. Snellgrove claims that modern Tibetophiles portray Tibetan Buddhism as a kind of self-resigning meekness in suffering. However, he claims Tibetan monks and laity have always been tough fighters. They fought external aggression, readily destroyed the monasteries of their rivals and killed laymen and priests alike. A united Tibet (1642 onward) was feared by Buddhist Ladakh, Sikkim and Bhutan. However, the fifth Dalai Lama (d. 1682) influenced his followers to interfere as little as possible with other religious orders.

In Japan, as noted earlier, the Zen tradition has given strong support to the military. Enemies are evil and to be eliminated.[21]

We can see here the continued variety in Buddhism. One could repeat the earlier comment on the empirical nature of Buddhism in which people are invited to seek their own answers, but the speakers on both sides of the killing issue seem quite convinced of their own opinion without inviting further consideration by others.

Another example of this is vegetarianism. Ahimsa, nonkilling or nonviolence, might suggest that Buddhists should be vegetarian, and some are. Some are not. Gautama was not. Some Buddhists eat meat, providing the animal was killed by someone else. The concept may be extended to various occupations. Gautama said a Buddhist could not be a butcher, for example. In Bangkok, Christians are the butchers. They live in squalor and degradation as a fringe group of the city. Apparently this is not seen as harmful by Buddhists though others see degradation as harm. The occupation is seen as low caste or outcaste, though Gautama himself presumably did away with caste and class distinctions. Fishing is done in Sri Lanka by the Hindu Tamils and in Cambodia by the Vietnamese and Chinese.

Gautama said a Buddhist should not participate in the arms trade, liquor trade or any activity that is harmful to another, such as deceit or usury. But presumably one can get someone else to do these things. At various times in history, pacifists have hired others to do their fighting for them. The historical examples above suggest that Buddhists have not done this but have done their own killing of humans.[22]

One of the teachings of Gautama has particular relevance here in an indirect way. Both ahimsa and nirvana are part of his Hindu tradition, as is samsara, the wheel of life, to which humans are bound by the law of karma. Escape from the wheel is nirvana. Gautama both agreed with and differed from the Hindu tradition. One difference is in the concept of no soul, anatta, which he may have favored (Samyutta Nikaya). There are differences of interpretation in the teachings. Some say that Gautama rejected metaphysical speculation. He taught neither soul, nor no soul. Others see the doctrine of anatta, no soul, as a crucial part of his teachings or at least the tradition.

In Hinduism, the individual personality, the soul, is reincarnated according to the law of karma. The soul is tied to the wheel of life until good karma or merit has been achieved. The concept is carried over into Buddhism but with the differences that there is no soul that is reincarnated. This in turn contributes to the concept of emptiness in Buddhism, emphasized in the madhyamika tradition traced at least to the teachings of Nagarjuna. He is sometimes called the father of Mahayana or the second patriarch, for his teaching of the Middle Doctrine and its distinctive concept of the Void, Shunyata, or Emptiness. The doctrine is midway between idealism and realism. It avoids agnosticism with a qualified realism. However, the visible world has no self-substance and the ideal world has no limitations of individuality. It is a monistic theory which proclaims the essential oneness of everything.[23]

Our concern with it here is in the lowering of barriers between individual selves. De Silva notes that according to the Buddha, egoism is the basic factor that separates people. Once that barrier is broken, healthy human relations are possible. He quotes Erich Fromm's idea that the goal of all religions is to overcome narcissism.[24]

In Buddhism, there are no such phenomena as individual selves. We are all one with each other. Without the self, there is no selfish desire (tanha) and hence no greed for fame or pelf or power. There is no need to "get the better of the other" for we are the other and the other is us. Ferguson describes it, "There is a unity among living beings. Love of oneself entails love of all; love of all is the true love of oneself." He quotes The Udana in which the Buddha says, "I have never yet met with any thing that was dearer to anyone than his own self. Since to others, to each one for himself, the self is dear, let him who desires his own advantage not harm another." The Dhammapada quotes Gautama as saying, "If one compares oneself with others one would never take life or be involved in the taking of life."[25]

This, of course, means no violence, no killing or bloodshed, no murder, no war. This interpretation is in sharp contrast to the use of the no-soul doctrine as justification for killing, noted earlier — there is no self there to kill so the killing is an illusion.

The doctrine of dependent origination is also part of this interrelatedness of life. The contrast between the stereotype of Buddhism as narcissism, and Jacobson's claim that Buddhism's ultimate reality is social, was noted earlier. He sees the denial of the self as related to dependent origination, the "central conception of Buddhism," the source of its "self-surpassing oneness." We are all part of a network of relationships.[26]

Reincarnation is part of this tradition which in turn is part of the compassion (karuna) for all living creatures. Animal sacrifice is cruel and causes needless suffering. The best sacrifice is obedience to the Precepts or better yet, sacrifice all selfish desire (Dighanikaya). Force should not be used against either the weak or the strong (Suttanipata). This did not apply to accidental killing but it rules out intentional killing of any form of life.[27]

The social implications are, of course, enormous. Societies would live at peace within for there would be no "rat race" or scramble for the world's goods. People would have no need to prove their superiority to others or to insist on the inferiority of others. No-self relates to the Noble Path's Right Effort expressed in Ten Perfections which include generosity, equanimity, honesty, patience and loving-kindness. In meditation, one seeks to be free of hatred and ill will. But more than this, one seeks freedom for all humanity from these and from affliction and anxiety. Positively, one seeks not only one's own happiness, but the happiness of all (Patisambhida). This extends to enemies as well as friends.

If people were to practice this, nations would have no need for war. World peace would be the natural order of things. "Lebensraum" would be unnecessary, for all people would live in one world. There would be no population explosion as people realized there is no need to reproduce themselves, for there is no self to reproduce. Potential parents practicing ahimsa (do no harm) would refuse to produce children whom the parents could not or would not care for. Material goods would be readily shared for they are not "real" anyway.

The middle way precludes hoarding so there would be no discrepancy between rich and poor individuals, nor rich and poor nations. At present, the average American consumes 30 times the world's resources as the average Indian. Obesity is a major health problem in the United States. This would end if all things, including eating, were done in moderation, following the Eightfold Path. If no-self and madhyamika were socially accepted, humanity might be truly one and war would be no more.

There are drawbacks of course. We know today that insects such as cockroaches and mosquitos carry disease. Some Buddhist areas refuse to spray for mosquitos, to the detriment of human life. In a malaria-infested city in Burma, a Western-educated monk explained to an American, "It's not merely a question of killing mosquitos; it's a question of what happens to us when we kill." Others point out that killing an insect is not a violation of the precepts. It is murder, i.e., killing human beings that Gautama opposed. Gautama did not prohibit farming, which naturally kills many insects. He did not carry the commandment against killing to the extent of the Jains who wear breathing masks and dust their path lest they accidentally kill an insect. Some Buddhists do this however. And some say Gautama forbade monks to farm though in China they did.[28]

One source of war has been meeting fire with fire, evil with evil. The Dhammapada, the summary of the teaching, says instead that evil must be overcome with good, greed by generosity, lies by truth. One harbors resentment by repeating thoughts about being treated unfairly. Resentment can be removed through meditation, practicing benevolence (maitri) which includes the Four Sublime Moods, by ignoring the offender, by realizing his actions are his own, and by concentrating on his positive aspects (Anguttaranikaya). Resentment does not harm the other but harms the self — spitting into the wind dirties your own face. O.H. de A. Wijesekera sees benevolence as "the antidote to all forms of conflict (patigha) and hatred (dosa) which in the ultimate analysis are found to lie at the bottom of every type of tension." De Silva notes the removal of tension and healing of wounds as the building of peace.[29]

Reincarnation reminds us that the enemy may be a member of your own family, so neither hate nor kill for you are hating and killing your own loved ones. Instead, love your enemies. If nations or societies were to apply these teachings to one another, there would be peace in the world rather than war. Nakamura's *The Ideal of World Community* is such a place.[30]

Officially, Buddhism is a pacifist religion. The Brahmajala-sutra has the most unequivocal expression of this. Buddhists are not supposed to go to war. They are not to take part in rebellions, revolts or uprisings. They are not supposed to look at an army or watch a battle, let alone join an army. They are not to give assent to or approve of killing in any way. This has not stopped Buddhists from doing this any more than following the Prince of Peace has stopped Christians from war and killing. But the sutra is clear that when Buddhists participate in war of any kind, they are violating their tradition. The power and the glory of the faith are clear. But the tragedy is also clear.[31]

The Buddha taught with both words and example. Later Buddhists who served in government had Gautama's practice before them. King Ajatasattu asked Gautama's advice in his plan to attack the tribe of the Vajji. Gautama told the king not to attack. The Vajji met in assemblies, practiced consensus, honored older people, kept their traditions and prospered. The same should be true for the Sangha, a universal brotherhood. This is interpreted by some that Gautama advocated a democratic form of government in which people chose their own rulers.[32]

The king went to war anyway and conquered the Vajji. The teaching has been preserved in spite of the fact it was ignored. It remains as part of the teaching for later rulers.

One of these was Ashoka, the grandson of Chandragupta, founder of the Maurya dynasty. Ashoka expanded the empire to include Afghanistan and almost all of the Indian subcontinent. He has been called the ideal universal monarch (Pali, Chakkavatti; Sanskrit, Cakravartin). After his especially bloody conquest of the Kalingas, tradition says he repented of the suffering he caused and became a Buddhist. He has been compared to the Roman emperor Constantine (A.D. 306–337) in the Christian tradition, who first tolerated and then promoted Christianity.

Paul Clasper has suggested that Ashoka spread Buddhism because it insured a more contented and docile people, making it easier to rule the vast land mass under his control. Ferguson notes that later, Kublai Khan used Buddhism to keep Tibet militarily neutral. John S. Strong has noted that in promoting Buddhism, Ashoka clearly also promoted his own kingship. Others suggest his conversion was genuine and sincere. He was the upaya, the master of good means. His love of the Doctrine led him to zealous protection of the law. It is this concern with universal law, rather than the size of his territory, that makes a ruler a Cakravartin.[33]

One can note that it is true that Ashoka did not convert until after he had finished his conquests. The promotion of tolerance may very well have contributed to the pacification of his realm though this facet of Buddhism has been integral to the faith since Gautama. One can also note that much of our knowledge of his conversion comes from his edicts carved on pillars and boulders throughout the land. In these edicts, we do not find the Four Noble Truths or the Eightfold Path. We do not find central doctrines like nirvana. We do find an emphasis on the sacredness of life, on honesty, compassion, tolerance and generosity. The latter included an early version of the welfare state. He built rest houses and shelters, developed hospitals and medical centers for both humans and animals, largely banned animal sacrifice, stopped hunting, built water reservoirs and planted trees. He established religious tolerance and called for respect for elders, teachers and ascetics. While Gautama rejected asceticism, it had long been practiced in the Sangha and in Ashoka's Hindu background.[34]

In contrast to Gautama, Ashoka promoted family affection. That included describing himself as a father to his people. The Dhammapada quotes Gautama as saying that love is the source of grief and fear so it should be given up as part of desire. One example of the problem is his favorite disciple, Ananda, who did not receive enlightenment until he gave up his love for the Buddha. We should note, however, that de Silva finds in the Sigalovada Sutta a warm network of human relations centered on the family. Dependence and domination are replaced by mature relationships. Pride, vanity, conceit (mana) and jealousy are unhealthy states that block genuine concern, respect, love and understanding.[35]

Another contrast is that Ashoka promoted hard work which would obviously benefit people's lives as well as the finances of the Empire. The Visuddhi-magga describes work as an obstruction to spiritual progress, while Nakamura claims Gautama disdained manual labor, as one might expect of a kshatriya raised in luxury. De Silva, however, claims a Buddhist work ethic is positively concerned with enhancing meaning. Group activity overcomes ego centeredness. Instead of raping nature for short-term gains, the nonviolent Buddhist protects nature, plants trees, etc. People are called to live in harmony with nature and other people. Minoru Kiyota notes that when Buddhism moved to China and the Far East, begging was no longer an acceptable way to live. Ch'an Buddhism developed an independent monastic order. The "Commentary on the Sayings of Huai-hai" (720–814) includes the statement, "a day without work is a day without food." Saicho (766–822) in Japan had an educational program that included road building, ship building, farming, digging wells, irrigation, etc. In Japan, one should note another ruler of significance for Buddhism and peace. Prince Shotoku (572–621) was concerned with the poor and justice. Among his many activities, he founded a hospital.[36]

Regardless of Ashoka's real motives, he remains the ideal Buddhist king. Perhaps this is as much because he supported the Sangha, built many monasteries and stupas, and sent Buddhist missionaries abroad, as it is for the care he gave his people. It is the latter that inspires such modern Buddhist movements as Sarvodaya Shramana in Sri Lanka. In either case, the military conqueror, Ashoka, became a symbol for peace and is a part of modern Buddhism's continuing thrust for peace in the world.

While part of China's eventual acceptance of Buddhism turned on its contribution to the military, Maurice Percheron claims that the faith did modify the war-loving character of the Mongols and Tibetans. He notes the peacefulness of the Soyots and the Khalkhas, who are so different from their ancestors, the fierce warriors of Jenghis Khan. Fou Yi (c. A.D. 625) and Yuan Tchen (c. 779–831) accused the Buddhists of using their religion to avoid military duty. The pacifist side of Buddhism is historically present as well as a part of modern Buddhism. The drive for peace is to be sure only part of modern Buddhism, but it is a part that can work together with all the peace-loving people of the world. While the tragedy of war is part of the tradition, the ideal of peace is the greater part.[37]

There are many examples of modern Buddhism working for peace. The Japanese Nichiren tradition was noted earlier. Rissho Kosei-kai has been actively involved in the peace movement, reaching out to other Buddhist groups and other traditions. They find support for this stance in the Lotus Sutra and the idea that Buddha is not just a man but the Eternal Buddha, not just one religious leader but ultimate Reality. He is the Reality behind all religions. The founder and president, Nikkyo Niwano, has met with leaders of other world religions and has been actively involved in such groups as the International Association for Religious Freedom and the WCRP noted earlier.[38]

Under the guidance of President Daisaku Ikeda, Soka Gakkai has tempered its shakubaku (shake and break) techniques and is working for world peace. Like Niwano, Ikeda has traveled the world to meet with both religious and secular leaders in the cause of peace.[39]

A new example of this concern for peace is The Buddhist Peace Fellowship. Its international headquarters is in Berkeley, CA, while local chapters are located in other parts of the United States and England. It began in 1978 as a small group of Caucasian Buddhists but has grown into an international, intercultural and interracial group. The group slogan is the Metta Sutta, "Just as a mother would protect her only child even at the risk of her own life, even so let one cultivate a boundless heart toward all beings." Nakamura cites this verse (from the Suttanipata) as illustrating benevolence, which he sees as the basis of the peace concept in Buddhism.[40]

BPF has "been involved in disarmament, ecological, and human rights activities, including campaigns opposing political oppression of Buddhists in such places as Bangladesh and Tibet," Vietnam and Thailand. BPF members are trying to get food to the starving children of Vietnam. Part of the BPF purpose is to resist the forces of exploitation and war. The *BPF Newsletter* presents this resistance in the form of protests, marches, workshops, and educational activities rather than suicide or shooting the enemy. The concern is "engaged Buddhism," a term which originated in Vietnam, but which includes the social action noted earlier for the Sri Lankan movement of Sarvodaya Shramadana.

One writer noted the important contributions of political leaders such as U Nu in Burma and S.W.R.D. Bandaranayake in Sri Lanka and the Komeito Party (Soka Gakkai) of Japan. But he went on to claim it is inappropriate for Buddhism to identify with a political party. "Buddhism's priority is not the creation of a particular kind of state, but a culture based on non-violence, sharing and participatory democracy, putting the full development of human potential in community before the pursuit of gross national product."[41] Related to this, one might note de Silva's point that a Buddhist does not make a blind commitment to *any* form of social change or to mere change. The commitment is to change based on Buddhist values. Religion provides a continuous criticism for ongoing change.[42]

A still different perspective comes from Nolan Pliny Jacobson, who focuses on the Buddhist doctrine of anicca, change, or impermanence. Jacobson, a United Methodist in the Protestant side of Christianity, sees this as the most turbulent time in history, with volatile change as the major adversary of nations and social classes. There are few predictables left in life, though two of them are revolutions which exchange one tyranny for another, and, the threat of nuclear proliferation. He sees the United States and the Soviet Union leading humanity to self-destruction in a nuclear war. But there is a drive to global interdependence which no nation or social class can prevent or control. Even the most advanced technology cannot control it. Jacobson sees Buddhism in all probability offering the only viable alternative to the overtaxed economic, political, diplomatic and military measures employed to cope with the underlying disorder. Bureaucracies and power structures are irrational, self-serving, and amoral. Buddhism offers fresh alternatives and new options to the compulsive greed that is destroying the earth.[43]

VIII. Taoism

*Weapons at best
are tools of bad omen.
Loathed and avoided
by those of the Way.*
— Tao Te Ching 31

Taoism has been described as a philosophy, as magic, as religion. It has been seen as some combination of these. Herrlee G. Creel claimed Taoism is not "a school, but a whole congeries of doctrines." Taoism may be simply what Taoists do or are. It has been defined as and is closely related to the teachings of Lao-tzu, circa 604–531 B.C., in the Tao Te Ching. He may have written this or edited it, though some suggest it dates centuries later. Taoism may be worship of the Tao, though Lao-tzu does not seem to have worshipped it. Lao-tzu himself was worshipped in later centuries both directly and as the Tao incarnated, and as the Buddha or as reincarnated in other figures.[1]

The Tao itself has a variety of definitions. The word literally means way or path. In the Confucian tradition, it has meant a norm for ethics. Lao-tzu suggested it was the way the universe functions, the path or course of natural events. That includes spontaneous creativity and regular alternations like day and night, the ebb and flow of the tide, etc. The law of return is the continuous return of everything to its original starting point. Chapter 25 of the Tao Te Ching says:

> Man conforms to the Earth;
> The Earth conforms to Heaven;
> Heaven conforms to the Way;
> The Way conforms to its own Nature.

These are but human ways to describe the undescribable. In this same chapter, he called it "the mother of the world," and went on to say

> I do not know its name;
> A name for it is "Way."

The thought is repeated in chapter 32. It is the ultimate unity that lies behind all appearances, the origin of the universe, experienced in a trance through meditation.[2]

106

The ultimate unity is often expressed in duality. One famous example of this is the concept of Yin and Yang which first appears in literature in the fourth century B.C. in an appendix to *I Ching*, usually regarded as Confucian. Later, in Japan, Taoism is first known as onmyodo, the way (do) of yin and yang. Literally, Yin is the dark side of the hill and Yang is the sunny side. They are complementary and interdependent principles which represent all pairs of opposites in the universe. The female Yin is associated with Earth while the male Yang is related to Heaven. While common to all Chinese philosophy, the Yin-Yang symbol, the T'ai-chi T'u diagram, has come to represent Taoism in particular. Yang is identified with aggression and Yin with submissiveness. The mysterious female is considered the ideal which men ought to follow.[3]

This is reflected in part in another major concept, "wu wei," "effortless action." Water is an example of this. Water unresistingly takes the lowest level as it runs along. While it simply flows, it wears away hard substances like rock. One expression of this is that action which leaves no trace of the worker. A jade carving leaves no mark of the tools that created it. This of course contrasts with the idea of the purely natural without any human intervention. Another way to put it is that human beings are to give up striving and live with the simplicity of an infant and thereby find the undiminished vitality of the neonate. This is to return to the "uncarved block" of the original state of nature. One is to flow with, live in harmony with nature.[4]

This concept has led to Taoism being called a philosophy of indifference, passivity, anarchy. Paradoxically it has also been described as hedonism and political activism. Material possessions are a matter of indifference. One passively goes where led or pushed by life, people, events. Law and order, duty to society or country, and social responsibility in general are to be ignored as irrelevant. In contrast, this might lead to a hedonism that takes pleasure in the moment without regard to others or to the future. Politically, that government is best which governs least. Chapter 58 says "When the government is lazy and dull, / The people are unspoiled." Chapter 59 says "In managing human affairs, / there is no better rule than to be sparing." Chapter 60 says "Rule a big country as you would fry small fish." The last has been interpreted as "leave it alone or it will become paste by constant turning about." A government that does not rule by the Tao should be overthrown. This also becomes a part of the concern for world peace.

Lao-tzu and his later disciple, Chuang-tzu (369–286 B.C.), saw knowledge itself as either worthless or having only negative value to demonstrate the relativity of all knowledge except that gained through meditation. The ideal society has no books. The Tao can be caught but not caught. By emptying the mind, the seeker can be filled with Tao, the power of the universe.

The magic dimension of Taoism may have developed from a natural phenomenon. When people, in this case Taoists, are relaxed, flowing with life, free of anxiety and fear, they may be free of other kinds of problems. A relaxed person who falls is less apt to be hurt than one who stiffens in fear. It has been said that fear engenders attack from wild beasts and wild men. People walking in cities are advised to walk purposefully to their destination without showing fear to avoid being mugged.[5]

Regardless of the origins, people came to believe that the Tao would protect them from harm. The Tao could even protect them from the final harm of death itself. Folk tradition sought ways to find the Tao for the protection of the devotee and even to provide immortality. These included talismans, magic charms, rituals, esoteric sexual practices, gymnastics (to circulate the blood) and hygiene to ensure long life.

The early Taoists were like or even part of the shamanist tradition with its healing power and out-of-body experiences. Philosophers added to the belief in an achievable immortality by turning to alchemy in search of the elixir of life. Secret societies grew up as Taoist leaders received revelations on, or thought they had found, or offered to people, techniques or ways to find the Tao and immortality. These in turn became sources of military and political power as loyal followers provided leaders with the strength to govern territory and to rebel against rulers who did not govern according to the Tao.

The line between valuing, honoring, revering and worshipping is not always distinct. There is some agreement that Taoism was or became a religion though it is not clear just when this happened. The distinction between philosophy and religion has been called a Western perspective, suggesting that for Taoists themselves, their tradition is and has always been a religion. Their faith is in the Tao no matter how others might divide the disciplines of study. Western analyses also include the perspective that magic and religion are either identical or closely interwoven. However, some historians also point to the time when Taoism borrowed heavily from Mahayana Buddhism and other traditions to establish a pantheon which incorporated numerous popular gods and goddesses, fairies and demons, and various concepts of heaven and hell. Monastic orders were developed and a tradition of master teachers was established.[6]

Lao-tzu

The earliest reference to Lao-tzu ("Old Master") is in the writing of Chuang-tzu, who presents his master as an older contemporary of Confucius, an archivist for the Chou dynasty (1122–221 B.C.). A fuller biography appears in the second-century B.C. history of Ssu-ma Ch'ien, which is the standard for those who accept Lao-tzu as an historical figure. He was born in Honan province. His name was Erh and his family name was Li. He was disturbed with the decline of the Chou government, so he gave up his job and headed west. Yin Hsi, the guardian of the frontier, would not let him leave the country unless Lao-tzu wrote down his teachings.

The result, according to this tradition, was the Tao Te Ching ("Way Power Classic"). It is only 5,000 words long. It consists of 81 sections of short, concise sayings, over half in rhyme. It serves as scripture for all branches of Taoism even though modern scholars in both East and West doubt that Lao-tzu wrote it. At best, they figure, he wrote only the core which expanded over several centuries. Strickman says that all ancient Chinese philosophies were theories of government. Thus the Tao Te Ching gives directions on proper government when properly interpreted, even though this could be seen as contradicting the earlier statement on being indifferent to the world.[7]

One tradition says that after he left China, Lao-tzu became the Buddha. Buddhism was first seen as a degraded form of Taoism. It was even suggested that Lao-tzu had established celibacy as a way of eliminating the barbarians, although the Taoist monk Sung Wen-ming began advocating celibacy in the sixth century A.D. Taoist monks had 300 commandments. The first was not to kill any living thing or damage its life. The second was against eating the flesh and blood of any living thing. The resemblance to Buddhist ahimsa, no injury, is clear whether or not these laws were borrowed directly from Buddhism.[8]

A first century A.D. text, the Book of the Transformations of Lao Tzu, presents him with cosmic powers of omnipotence and as omnipresent, the origin of all life, i.e., the Tao. Lao-tzu became Tao in the flesh. A number of his incarnations are described between A.D. 132–155. A temple was dedicated to him in west China in 155. Later, Lao-tzu was part of a triad of gods which included Yuan Shih T'ien Tsun and Yu Huang.

In A.D. 166, the Han emperor held a sacrifice for Lao-tzu and the Buddha. Even earlier, in 142, the deified Lao, Lord Most High, gave a revelation to Chang Tao-ling, who developed the Way of the Celestial Masters. He and his descendants developed a Taocracy with spiritual and territorial powers in their hands. In 215, Chang's grandson submitted to the Wei dynasty which gave approval to the dynasty's rule. The result was that Lao-tzu was not presented as incarnate in the Celestial Masters but rather chose them as his representatives on earth. While the dynasty governed by Tao, it was acceptable. When that was lacking, the Celestial Masters would claim temporal control as well.[9]

Later Developments

Chuang-tzu, perhaps originally Chung-chou, was a native of Meng between today's Honan and Shantung provinces. He saw the Tao in everything. The Book of Chuang-tzu contains fables and stories of kings and gods and commoners. Some suggest less than half of the present text comes from Chuang-tzu.

Chuang-tzu saw the ordinary workman as in tune with Tao when the work is done to perfection. He debunked the concern with immortality even as he described the perfected ones, spiritual beings free of the limits of bodily existence, who later became the model which devotees strove to emulate, though this violated the no striving, flow with nature concept. Chuang-tzu himself saw the oneness of all life so there was no distinction of any kind, even between life and death. Death is natural and should be accepted as such. When his wife died, instead of mourning, he sang. When asked why, he noted that nonbeing became being and then returned to nonbeing. There was no point in mourning the natural order of things. But he did not explain why he sang. Similarly, when offered a job in the imperial court, he declined. He noted the sacred turtle that had died and was now kept in a chest in the temple. Would the turtle rather be dead and venerated or alive and wagging its tail in the mud? The officials with the invitation to the imperial court immediately said, "Alive and wagging its tail in the mud." Chuang-tzu dismissed them. He too would wag his tail in the mud. But he did not explain why. If he followed his own teaching of going where pushed or led, he would of course have taken the job.

Over the centuries, both philosophical and religious Taoism developed numerous sects or movements. In the third century A.D., neo-Taoism began absorbing elements from Buddhism and Confucianism, while neo-Confucianism absorbed elements of Taoism, thus breaking down some of the rivalry among them. One view of Ch'an or Zen Buddhism is that it is a synthesis of Taoism and Buddhism. During the T'ang (618–906) dynasty, The Three Religions (San Chiao) combined all three in a single, syncretistic sect which was popular through the Sung (960–1279) and Ming (1368–1644) dynasties. The founder of the T'ang dynasty, Li Yuan, claimed descent from Lao-tzu and made Taoism the state religion.[10]

Taoism contributed to the development of Chinese science with its search for herbs or metals that would give longevity or immortality. Politics, art, literature, and many other aspects of life were influenced. Paintings often show people as tiny figures against a background of huge mountains, showing man's place in nature.

Taoism continues today in Taiwan and among the Chinese dispersion in Singapore, Thailand and other areas. In Mainland China, a Chinese Taoist Association was formed in 1957 under strict government control. The Tao Te Ching has been reinterpreted in Marxist terms as opposing private property (chapter 17) and as containing a plea to dissolve class distinctions (chapter 56). At one point the Communist government approved the teaching of Taoist hygiene, perhaps part of an effort to revitalize traditional medicine. In the West, it has had some vogue, especially through the Tao Te Ching, among antiestablishment subcultures, which have picked up on the hedonistic tradition and the relativity of responsibility to society. The concepts of spontaneity and creativity have also had an appeal in some circles. In an imaginary dialogue, Welch has Lao-tzu urge America to get rid of advertising in general as well as the brand of advertising called public relations. The former builds people's desires instead of lessening them; the latter violates the principle of anonymity.[11]

Peace and War

Strickman sees religious Taoism as a distinct phenomenon with a hierarchy of priests and believers, quite distinct from Buddhism and a constant opponent and competitor for official patronage. During the Ch'in and Han periods (221 B.C.–A.D. 220), representatives of different traditions met as competitors for official favor in the Imperial court itself. The Taoist master considered himself with his spiritual lineage, institutional relationships and complex rituals to be far apart from the exorcist of folk religion. The distinction is maintained in Taiwan where the Taoists are blackheads (from their headgear) and the others are redheads. Taoists, Buddhists and Confucianists worked together to rechannel or suppress unauthorized worship in "abusive cults." Unregulated religion was considered dangerous to society and to the individual who might become addicted to enthusiasm.[12]

A second source of conflict for Taoism was in the secret societies mentioned earlier and the idea that a government which did not practice Tao could legitimately be overthrown. Strickman describes "revolutionary messianism" which appeared at least as early as the first century B.C. The "Classic of the Great Peace" of Kan Chung-k'o was one source of this concept. In A.D. 184, the Yellow Turban Rebellion broke out in the East. Chang Chueh's followers wore yellow turbans as a symbol that the blue heaven was to be replaced by a yellow heaven. The revolt was put down with an estimated loss of life of over 500,000, but sporadic revolutions continued for centuries. Sometimes they resulted in territorial control as noted earlier. The Boxer Rebellion of A.D. 1900 was led by the Harmonious Fist Society and was partly Taoist in origin.[13]

It could be seen from this that there is no particular objection to war and/or violence in Taoism, but this is not the case. Chapter 31 of the Tao Te Ching says

> Weapons are tools of ill omen,
> . . .
> those who admire them truly
> Are men who in murder delight.
> As for those who delight to do murder,
> It is certain they never can get
> From the world . . . power and rule.
> . . .
> The victory after a conflict
> Is a theme for a funeral rite.

People of the Way will have nothing to do with weapons unless driven to use force in self-defense. Chapter 30 urges those of the Way who want to help a ruler

Let him not with his militant might
Try to conquer the world;
This tactic is like to recoil.
. . .
The good man's purpose once attained,
He stops at that;
. . .
He won the day because he must.

Welch suggests the meaning is that in human relations force defeats itself.
Every action produces a reaction. If our attitude is bloodthirsty, the conflict
will escalate. Aggression produces more aggression to mutual ruin.

In war only for defense, we hear echoes of other traditions such as
Buddhism and Jainism. The Christian concept of the "Just War" may also
be similar. But Welch also suggests that Taoism is less opposed to the use
of force. The difference is in the regret at having to use it, for it is a last
resort. The concept of wu wei, actionless action, is that war means someone has failed to follow the Tao. Chapter 63 says

Take hard jobs in hand
While they are easy;
And great affairs too
While they are small.
The troubles of the world
Cannot be solved except
Before they grow too hard.[14]

Chuang-tzu was also aware of a peaceful way. He described the
pacifists of his day. They believed in love and universal brotherhood.
"They forbade aggression, and preached disarmament in order to redeem
mankind from war. This teaching they carried throughout the world. . . .
The world was not ready to accept their teaching. . . ."[15]

The larger context for this is crucial. The concept of harmony with
nature calls for harmony among human beings as well. If this were consistently carried out, Taoism could be the basis for world peace. Closely
related to this is the concept of nature itself as harmonious, where aggression is out of place. This is an idealized nature, since the nature of the real
world contains considerable aggression whether one considers the natural
violence of storms and earthquakes, or carnivores killing for food. Lao-tzu
and Chuang-tzu, however, saw man and society as corrupting an essen-
tially good nature. Human beings are good by nature, a concept shared
with Mencius in the Confucian tradition and such Western figures as Immanuel Kant and Jean Jacques Rousseau.

If men will become like women, integrating their Yang qualities with
the female Yin, they will stop trying to dominate nature or subjugate
others. The ruler who lives by Tao does not oppress people. Rather he seeks
their happiness and thus ensures his own well-being. Men who try to
dominate defy the natural order of things and upset the harmony decreed

by the Tao. The natural tendency of the Tao is peace, prosperity and health. If it were not for perverse men and demonic beings that refuse to adjust to the Tao, peace would be here. If the Tao is followed, heaven and earth and the human race will exist in a single harmonious unit.[16]

The world is faced today with two major sources of total destruction. One is the destruction of the environment. In "The Hollow Men" (1925), T.S. Eliot (1888-1965) said, "This is the way the world ends/ not with a bang but with a whimper." As the air and water resources of the earth become more and more polluted from industrial and other human wastes, the environment becomes less and less livable. Unless people learn to live in harmony with nature rather than exploit it, nature will become inimical to human life and perhaps to all life. The Taoist call to live in harmony with nature could be the salvation of life on earth.

The second great threat to human existence and perhaps to all existence is the threat of nuclear war. If nuclear weapons could be seen as hateful as any other kind of weapon, one could present the Tao Te Ching as having the insight necessary for survival. War itself violates the harmony of heaven and earth and the human race. A nuclear war would do more than violate that harmony. A nuclear war could destroy it for all time. Thus Taoism could be the hope of humanity.[17]

One particular dimension of the tradition is of interest for both the individual and humanity in general. In the ideal kingdom on earth, there will be no law or duty. Lao-tzu saw these as the useless trappings of a fallen society. His critics have accused him of being an anarchist and perhaps he was.[18]

But Welch notes that morality is frequently used to justify violence. He goes on to compare Lao-tzu's thought to the American Indian idea that in the old days, there were no fights about hunting and fishing rights. There were no laws then, so everyone did what was right.[19]

The "no laws" idea is also reminiscent of the Hebrew prophets and the New Testament Apostle Paul. In Jeremiah's prediction of the new covenant, there would be no law or Torah, for God's law would be written on the human heart. With internal goodness, people would not only stop aggressively competing for the material goods of the world or for fame or status or power in accord with Tao. They would regulate the size of their families and cooperate with each other for food and territory to obviate the necessity for "lebensraum" and other causes of war. The starvation so rampant in today's world would become a thing of the past as would the graft and corruption that continue to build military empires backed by huge stockpiles of "hateful" weapons.

With peace in the heart of the Taoist sage, there would be no more fear or anxiety and every person would even be safe from wild beasts and wild men. If this did not actually achieve immortality in the physical sense, it would at least add to human longevity and make that longevity worthwhile in what bioethicists call an adequate quality of life compared to mere existence.

IX. Confucianism

*Seek to be in harmony
with all your neighbors...
live in peace with your brethren.*

The Man

The Jesuits called him Confucius (551–479 B.C.), and this Latinized form has continued in the West. He was K'ung Fu-tze (Great Master K'ung) or simply Master K'ung (K'ung tze). Earlier he was Ch'iu ("hill") to his mother and publicly Chung-ni which has been translated as "The Younger Brother of Mud." His mother, Cheng-tsai, had climbed Ch'iu Ni, Mud Hill, to pray to the mountain spirit to grant her a son.[1]

Cheng-tsai is said by some to have belonged to the rich and powerful Yen clan, but others say she was the daughter of a peasant named Yen. She took Ch'iu to live close to Ch'u-fu, the capital of Lu, a city that still exists in southwestern Shantung, on the northeast coast of China, south of Pe-king/Beijing. She died while he was still young, perhaps still a teenager. Ch'iu gave her a temporary burial and then went back to his birthplace to find his father's grave. He did and reburied his mother next to his father.[2]

We know very little about his younger life because he did not talk about it much. But he did say, "When I was young, we were very poor. Perhaps that's why I can turn my hand to so many odd jobs" (Analects 9.6). About his teen years, he simply said, "When I was fifteen, I set my mind on learning" (Analects 2.4). He married young but not even tradition has a name for his wife, though it does say he had a son and a daughter. He was working for the government as a tax collector (grain and livestock, taxes in kind). Duke Chao of Lu sent him a carp as a gift honoring the birth of a son. The carp was the traditional symbol of domestic felicity and fer-tility and the son was named Po Yu, "First Carp." Po Yu was not much of a scholar though his son, Tze Sse, followed in Grandfather Confucius' footsteps. Po Yu died in 482 and the Master gave him a simple burial, fitting for a scholar's son. Confucius himself died three years later and was buried by his disciples near his native town. His tomb temple is still there, pre-served by the Communists as a museum.[3]

It was the teenage love of learning that eventually made his name

114

synonymous with wisdom. He became a teacher of liberal arts and political science. Tradition, however, says that at the age of 50 he joined the cabinet of the Duke of Lu, first as minister of public works, then justice, and finally prime minister. Court intrigue caused him to "lose face" and he resigned. Scholars doubt the ministerial status but acknowledge that at age 55 he began a period of wandering that lasted 13 years. In some places the feudal powers received him with respect and in others with suspicion. He was chased out of Sung by armed guards and held under house arrest to keep him out of Ch'u. One of his disciples had attained a position back in Lu and arranged for Duke Ai to invite Confucius back home. He spent his last years in retirement sometimes serving as a consultant to the Duke.

The Rise to Faith

Kao Tsu, first emperor of the Han dynasty (206 B.C.–A.D. 220), sacrificed an ox, a sheep and a pig at Confucius' grave in 195 B.C. Later emperors also venerated Confucius. Emperor Wu Ti (141–87 B.C.) made Confucian teaching the policy of the state. In 124, he established the first national university to train potential government officials in the Confucian tradition. In A.D. 630, the T'ang Emperor T'ai Tsung ordered a temple built in every one of the 2000 counties or prefectures. In later centuries he was deified and given many titles. The rituals and temples became increasingly elaborate until finally, in A.D. 1530, the state cult was reformed. The temples were returned to their original simplicity. All titles were dropped and he was simply called Master K'ung.[4]

Religion or Philosophy

Some have argued that Confucianism is not a religion but a philosophy. In some ways, this is a Western argument because in recent centuries the two concerns have been split into two disciplines. In the East, including South and Southeast Asia, the two remain one. Even in the West, the two are not as divided as some think. Christianity is a syncretism of Eastern (Semitic) religion and Western (Greek) philosophy though some have forgotten this. Religion in the broad sense is education, which begins in the womb and carries through to the grave. Confucianism was Ju (or Yu) Chiao (Jiao), the School or Religion of the Scholar. In Japan, it was Ju Do, the Way of the Gentleman or the Superior Man. Confucius was far more concerned with molding character than with training in technology. It is true that he rejected the old animistic cult handed down from the Yin dynasty. It had degenerated into witchcraft and sorcery. Confucius did not say much about God or gods, but he kept the practice of ancestor worship, and he was concerned with the Way (tao) of Heaven. Later, disciple Mencius said the superior man did his best and left the result to the will of heaven (Bk. VII, Prt. II, Ch. 33, Sec. 3). One could see a parallel here with the Hindu Bhagavad Gita. Tien-Hsi Cheng notes will of heaven (ming) is to be understood theologically and not as fate or predestination. Thus it differs from Indian karma and Christian Calvinism. Cheng adds that Confucius had a divine mission to carry out the will of heaven (Analects 3.24, 7.22, 9.5). One might add that for many, ritual is mere mechanical repetition while for Confucius, it was a serious concern to be practiced from the heart.

However one decides the issue of Confucius' own views, as indicated above, Confucius himself clearly became a religion—deified, he was a god worshipped in temples with rituals.[5]

In Other Lands

In time, Confucianism spread to Korea, Japan and Indochina. Confucian temples can still be found in Japan. Seoul, Korea, has the most imposing Confucian temple outside China. Confucian temples are well cared for and Confucian universities well attended. Confucianism was introduced to Korea some 2000 years ago and today "outranks Buddhism and compares with shamanism as a controlling force in Korean life." Confucianism entered Japan in the sixth century, probably already fused with Taoism. The Constitution of Prince Shotoku Taishi, A.D. 604, is already Confucian in ethics and theory of government. One should note that in Japan Confucianism coexists with Shinto and Buddhism. It has provided practical ethics for both traditions. Loyalty to the emperor has been the most important virtue.[6]

Jesuit missionaries to China, such as Matteo Ricci (1552–1610; entered China in 1582), shared Confucius with the West. They studied Confucius as well as the neo–Confucianism of that day, opting in favor of the older works. Creel claims that through their reports to their order in Europe, Confucian ideas influenced the European Enlightenment and the French Revolution. Through Benjamin Franklin's friendship with French philosophers, and through Thomas Jefferson, Confucianism in turn influenced democracy in the Americas. Jefferson promoted the idea of education for all and political rule by those with the ability and integrity for it in contrast with hereditary rule.

Confucianism has continued to play a part through more recent thought, such as that of Ezra Pound, poet and translator of Confucian classics (see further later). These, especially the I Ching, Book of Changes, have had some popularity in the counterculture in recent decades. Confucianism remains of significance among persons of Chinese ancestry as well as some occidentals in various parts of the West and the rest of the world.[7]

The Teacher

The tradition of teacher remains foremost, not unlike the rabbi of Judaism and the guru of Indian traditions. Confucius is said to be the first full-time teacher in Chinese history. Some claim he created the role of the private teacher. More significantly he accepted students from all social classes. In education, there should be no class distinctions (Analects 15.38). In time, this broke the feudal system in which only the wealthy were educated. The Confucian educational system lasted until 1911.[8]

Confucius taught that human beings are social creatures. We are bound to each other by jen — sympathy and human-heartedness, which calls us to seek the good of others. It has been equated with "love thy neighbor." There are five relationships with others which can be symbolized by five fingers on one hand. They are the parent-child relationship (thumb), the husband-wife relationship (first finger), the elder-younger brother (second finger), friend-friend (third) and ruler-subject (fourth). Of these, filial piety (hsiao) is stressed. The word jen is represented by the Chinese character for man and for two, which has been interpreted as meaning love for others.[9]

Another basic concept is li, the ideal social order. It means etiquette and ritual, hospitality, religion, reason and morality. The basic concept is righteous harmony. If there is righteousness in the heart, there is harmony in the home. If there is harmony in the home, there is order in the nation. If there is order in the nation, there is peace in the world. On the cosmic scene there is harmony among men, earth and heaven (Ta Hsueh, The Great Learning). The family is the basis of Chinese culture. There is reciprocity ("shu" or mutual consideration) here, represented in the Golden Rule (Analects 6.28) as well as in a reverse way with the Silver Rule, "What you do not want done to yourself, do not do to others" (Analects 15.23). Confucian ethics have an interesting twist. Lao-tzu and Jesus called for returning good for evil. Confucius was asked about this and replied, "Then what are you going to repay kindness with? . . . Repay kindness with kindness, but repay evil with justice" (Analects 14.36). Note, however, that he did not preach vengeance. In the Book of Li (Rites), we find, "To recompense injury with kindness is a virtue of magnanimity." The Analects call for forgiveness and forgetting past wrongs (5.2, 7.28, 14.2).[10]

One should note that harmony does not come through compulsion. It comes from a sense of virtue (te) inculcated by observing models of deportment. There are five cardinal virtues: jen (the most important), li, yi (the moral imperative; justice, a sense of duty — not just a mechanical ritual but from the heart), chih (wisdom) and hsi (faithfulness).

Political Science

In government, Confucius taught that the ruler himself must be above reproach. One scholar interprets this by comparison. Western thought is system oriented. The Orient is person oriented. Change the man and you change the system. The West is concerned with rule by law while the East rules by person. Thus it is crucial that the ruler be virtuous. Without virtue, one has tyranny. Creel suggests the alternative of loyalty to principle, rather than persons, as an essential of democracy. Confucius denounced blind loyalty. The ideal retainer served his ruler completely as long as he could do so in accord with the Way. If he had to choose between them, he followed the Way and left the ruler's service. There is no reward for such virtue. It is an end in itself.[11]

If a ruler is virtuous, in tune with the Way of Heaven or the Mandate of Heaven (T'ien ming), the country will be at peace. If the ruler is not, he may be replaced, i.e., Confucius taught obedience to the ruler but not blind obedience. The ruler is to care for his people as a father for his children. People are not to be exploited. There must be honesty in government. Some would say we need Confucius today.

The ruler as father has been called benevolent paternalism but one should note that it is never for the aggrandizement of the ruler. By purifying the heart, regulating his own family and governing well, the ruler brings peace to the world. The ruler is to be a superior man – one who respects all, including himself. "The superior man understands what is right; the inferior man [siao yun] understands what is profitable" (Analects 4.16). Not only does the superior man understand, he wants to and feels like practicing the right. It is not just a formalistic routine but a living dynamic.[12]

From a Western perspective, of course, paternalism remains paternalism, rather than a true, participating democracy. Throughout history, one can cite examples where Confucianism was used as the direct opposite of democracy, as in Japan's conquest of Korea and Manchuria. One can see the negative aspect of paternalism especially in the treatment of women who remained second class or even subhuman. Cheng claims equality for husband and wife in the Chinese system. However, the word he translates "equality" is "superior and inferior" in the Book of Li (Rites Bk. 26). Yeh simply notes Confucius did not think highly of women, did not educate them, etc. Later, Mencius thought their role was to obey their husbands. While in one sense this reflected the culture of the times, Confucianism did not improve their lot.

In a way, this is surprising, given the apparent respect Confucius had for his mother. The Doctrine of the Mean does quote the Book of Poetry: "When wives and children and their sires are one, / 'Tis like the harp and lute in unison." Being one with their sires should mean mutual respect, but there is no evidence that for women it was anything other than subordination. Thus, while Sun Yat-sen and some modern scholars see Confucius and Mencius as exponents of democracy, Confucianism has often been used to support tyranny. Where Confucius, like the Judeo-Christian Bible, called for *mutual* respect and care, the persons in power have emphasized only the inferior's absolute obedience to the power – father, ruler, the state, but not the responsibility of the power to provide honest government and genuine care for the people.[13]

One could also add by way of critique that in later times, Confucius' love for the high moral standards of the past sometimes became mere antiquarianism and Confucianism became a barrier to progress. One example to the contrary, however, is in modern Japan where Confucianism provides the ethics for the economy. In essence, this ethic is to produce more and consume less. We hear echoes here of Ernst F. Schumacher's *Small Is Beautiful*. Kaibara Ekiken (1630–1714) said that "If a ruler wants to govern his people with benevolence, he should practice economy. There are limits to the productive capacity of the land. . . . All wise rulers have been thrifty. Economy is, indeed, a virtue essential to the ruler." Confucius said, "Extravagance leads to insubordination, and parsimony to meanness. It is better to be mean than to be insubordinate." Mencius acknowledged the Confucian teaching that one must maintain a fixed heart no matter the economic circumstances (we can be happy on vegetables and water [Analects 7.15]), and yet people need a livelihood. "To nourish the heart there is nothing better than to make the desires few." This was before Buddhism reached China, but it would echo the Buddhist doctrine that suffering comes from desire. It also resonated with Japanese Bushido, with its loyalty to the ruler and attainment of his goals.[14]

The Written Word

Confucius himself claimed he was only a preserver and transmitter of ancient wisdom (Analects 7.1). Tradition ascribes to him five or six books, the Confucian Classics: Book of History (Shu Ching), Book of Poetry (Shih Ching), Book of Rites (Li Chi), Book of Changes (I Ching) and the Annals of Spring and Autumn (Ch'un Ch'iu) or the Annals of Lu. The Book of Music (Yueh) survives only as chapter X of the Book of Rites. The present form of the material is judged to come from a later time but some portion may come from Confucius. How much, if any, is a matter of scholarly debate. Some suggest he only edited the classics rather than authored them. This fits his own claim.

Later, during the Sung dynasty (A.D. 960–1279), Chu Hsi (1130–1200) made a collection called the Four Books. The Analects (Lun Yu), or Selected Sayings, record the sayings of Confucius though modern scholarship considers less than half of the 20 sections to be from Confucius himself. The Great Learning (Ta Hsueh) is chapter 39 of the Book of Rites. Some credit this to a disciple, Hsun-tzu (298–238 B.C.). It was the first book studied in classical Chinese education. The Doctrine of the Mean (Chung Yung) is chapter 28 of the Rites. This philosophy of the relationship between human nature and the moral order of the universe has been attributed to Confucius' grandson, Tzu Ssu. The older first part could go back to him but the second part dates from the second century B.C. In some ways, it resembles the Buddhist doctrine of the Middle Way, and the Golden Mean of the Greek philosopher, Aristotle. The fourth book is the Meng Tzu, the sayings of Mencius, one of if not the most important of the later Confucians.[15]

Disciples

Mencius (371–288 B.C.) is the Westernized name of Meng K'o, Mandarin Meng-tse or Master Meng. He was born in Ts'ou, near Confucius' old home. He was also reared by his mother after his father's death. She noticed that he was growing like his environment, so she moved near a school and he became a scholar. Like Confucius, Mencius was also faced with and appalled by the anarchy of his day. He preached Confucius and developed the idea that human beings are good by nature, a view held by Immanuel Kant and others in the West. Neither Kant nor Mencius ignored the evil in the world. For Mencius, human nature cannot be left to itself. It must be trained with jen and yi. "If jade is not cut and polished carefully, it is useless." In his view of government, the ruler is to ensure the prosperity of his subjects. If the ruler fails, he can be deposed. One who has betrayed the trust of the people is no longer a king but a scoundrel. For Mencius, there should be no war except for defense. War makers are robbers of the people. By the eleventh century A.D., Mencius was venerated. His image was put alongside that of Confucius in Confucian temples. However, Mencius was not accepted as fully orthodox until Chu Hsi.[16]

Chu Hsi (1130–1200) finalized the interpretation of Confucianism which became orthodoxy for 700 years. He was a realist who has been compared with Thomas Aquinas. He not only declared Mencius orthodox, he declared Hsun Tzu (c. 298–238 B.C.) a heretic. The latter retained such basic Confucian concepts as li and the idea that anyone "can become like the sage-king Yu." Like Mencius, he thought the way to cope with desires was not to eliminate them, but guide them. The heretic label was for saying human nature is evil and Heaven does not watch over human affairs. Chu was part of a New or neo–Confucianism, sometimes seen as a syncretism of Confucianism, Taoism and Buddhism. Confucius had no metaphysics but the new Confucianists did. For Chu, the rational principle of li represents the true human nature. His metaphysics was based on li as the principle of form in many things. During the Ming dynasty (1368–1644), the idealist Wang Yang-ming (1472–1529) stressed meditation and intuition. Jen equals universal love. Virtue grows out of our realization of the oneness of all things in an ultimate Mind. Like Socrates, Yang-ming thought that to know good is to do it. "There has been no one who really has knowledge and yet fails to practice it." On universalism, one might also cite the Analects 12.5 where the disciple Master Hsia claims that within the four seas all men are brothers.[17]

Historical Context

Historically, one can note that Confucianism has had its ups and downs. Ancient China remembered some legendary emperors from circa 2500 B.C. The Hsia dynasty (2205–1765) was overthrown by the Shang (1765–1122). Founder Tang claimed his violence had divine approval. So did Confucius' beloved Chou dynasty (1122–221), which overthrew the Shang and built its capital at Loyang in today's province of Honan. Ti was a god and founding ancestor of the Shang dynasty. The Chou dynasty united Ti with a heavenly deity, T'ien, and insisted on the righteous life demanded by Shang Ti, the Supreme Ti. The Emperor, as the Son of Heaven (T'ien Tzu), was given the Mandate (ming) of Heaven. Ti could withdraw that mandate if the ruler was unjust. The Duke of Chou used this Mandate to take over from his nephew, organize the empire and then hand it back to the nephew. In contrast to the force of conquest, Huang Ti, the legendary Yellow Emperor and ancestor of the Chou, brought harmony from chaos by his superior virtue, adapting and yielding to natural conditions and to the will of Heaven.[18]

Confucius echoed the Mandate in his saying, "If it is the will of Heaven that the way shall prevail, then the way will prevail" (Analects 14.38). He lived in the later centuries of the Chou empire when central control was a fiction and each duke, such as Duke Chao of Lu, ran his own province as he wished, which included making alliances and fighting other dukes for conquest and defense. Within a province, as in Lu, the real power might be in the hands of powerful nobles such as the three families—the Meng, the Chi, and Shu—descendants of the three sons of Duke Huan (711–697 B.C.) of Lu. Confucius wanted to return to the "good old days" of the Mandate of Heaven and righteous rule rather than rule by court intrigue. He believed those days were times of justice rather than corruption. Confucius has been called a reactionary for his desire for the "old ways." In fact, he was a revolutionary as in his educational policies.[19]

The Ch'in dynasty (221–207 B.C.) gave its name to China and nearly destroyed Confucianism. Duke Cheng, the founder, united all the provinces under his rule, as the Emperor Ch'in Shih Huang Ti. He modernized the state and saw Confucianism as reactionary. Cheng ordered the Great Book Burning (213 B.C.). Fortunately, tradition says, he did not burn the books in the state archives. Within five years of Cheng's death, the Confucian Classics were restored, though not accurately, giving rise to the Old Text and the New Text schools.[20]

It was the Han dynasty (206 B.C.–A.D. 221) that recognized Confucianism and venerated Confucius. The T'ang dynasty (618–906) made Confucianism the state religion. The Sung and Ming saw the rise of neo-Confucianism. In between, the Yuan (Mongol) dynasty (1280–1368) was Buddhist but even it used the Confucian examination system for recruiting officials. The 1530 reform with its return to simplicity was led by Ming emperor Chia Ching. Part of the reform was to replace images of

Confucius with a simple wooden tablet with his words on it. Confucianism was closely allied with the Ch'ing (Manchu) dynasty (1644–1911). When the Manchu fell, official Confucianism fell also. Many of its principles, however, continued under the Republic. Sun Yat-sen believed he had a "Heaven appointed task" to save humanity from injustice. In 1937, under Sun Yat-sen's disciple, Chiang Kai-shek, the national shrine built in Nanking had the tablet of Confucius in the highest place. The birthday of Confucius is still celebrated by the Nationalist government on Taiwan, as Teachers' Day. In recent years, the Taiwan government has promoted Confucian teachings through a Council for the Promotion of the Chinese Cultural Renaissance and a New Life Movement. In the same time period as the Chinese Republic, the Japanese had integrated Confucianism into their philosophy of government and used it as their authority for their "benevolent" rule of Korea, and after 1933, Manchuria.[21]

Confucianism Today

Chinese Communism began by trying to destroy all religions. The current policy is one of restoration and what is promoted as religious freedom. Some have wondered if Confucianism has any future. Kenneth L. Woodward touches on this in his concern with mental health in China. He asked a Communist Party member, a retired newspaper editor, what values his parents had taught him. He answered, "Confucius." Woodward went on to ask what values he was teaching his grandchildren, and the answer was the same.[22]

Woodward goes on to note that Confucianism has been incorporated into Communism, e.g., Confucius called for self-reflection as the key to self-governance. That is the chief characteristic of good mental health in the People's Republic of China. Noss also claims Communism has incorporated Confucianism by calling for filial piety toward Mao and the state. This was noted earlier for Tokugawa Japan and Japanese militarists in Korea and Manchuria.[23]

Peace and War

Noss notes that Confucius thought the reform of society begins at the top with the rulers. Baron Chi asked him how to rule and Confucius said, "If you lead the people straight, which of your subjects will venture to fall out of line?" The Baron asked about cutting off the lawless to preserve law and order. Confucius asked, "What need is there of the death-penalty . . . ? If you showed a sincere desire to be good, your people would likewise be good. The virtue of the prince is like unto the wind; that of the people like unto grass. For it is the nature of grass to bend when the wind blows upon it." People are good but they need guidance. The influence of the environment is clear. It also appears in the story of Mencius and his mother and Mencius' own teaching. Thus the way to peace is to have a peaceful ruler.[24]

The focus on government also appeared when Confucius said that a state needs three things: sufficient food, sufficient military equipment, and the confidence of the people in their government. When asked what he would give up first if he had to, it was military equipment. The second thing he would give up would be food, for everyone must die, but life is not worth much if people have lost confidence in their government (Analects 12.7). We are back to the concept of the virtuous ruler.

Confucius himself claimed to know nothing of armies and troops. The only military skill he had was archery which was also a sport and used for hunting. In the latter, he practiced sportsmanship, e.g., he did not shoot at a sitting bird. Perhaps this could be seen as equivalent to the chivalry he expected in all walks of life. While he clearly was not a practitioner of ahimsa, no injury to any living thing as in Indian traditions, he did hold that a moral person's first concern was peace.[25]

In noting the tradition of the Yellow Emperor who brought harmony through virtue rather than bloodshed, James Aho claims that Confucianism repudiates military solutions to human problems, for such solutions are unworkable. He goes on to note the Confucian criticism of violence. "The people may be made well affected by virtue, [but] . . . not . . . so by violence. To use violence with that view is like trying to put silk in order and only unraveling it." "Military weapons are like fire; if you do not lay fire aside, it will burn you."[26]

However, Confucius was not a pacifist. While urging Duke Ting of Lu to be wary of Duke Ching of Ch'i, Confucius commented, "If you want peace, prepare for war." The idea has been expressed by Horace and George Washington and Anthony Eden. The Annals include records of military actions without disapproval. His "gentleman" (chun tzu) has been called "a knight trained for war." He accepted vengeance and blood feuds. Society must be defended by war when necessary. But war is to be a last resort and for a just cause. There should be no war of aggression against other nations. Instead of challenging war, as such, he refined it by insisting on understanding the cause. The restriction on war became a check on war. This continued with Mencius, who condemned war in general. In the whole Spring and Autumn period (722–481 B.C.), there was not a single righteous war (Mencius, Bk. VII, Pt. II, Ch. 2, Sec. 1). He called successful generals criminals. They and those who direct aggression should be punished. Mencius appealed to loving-kindness (jen) and righteousness (li). There was a spiritual dimension to this for "Heaven sees as the people see, and Heaven hears as the people hear."[27]

Aho has compared the restrictions on war to the Roman concepts of a just war and the tactics and weapons allowable in just war. A just war is for a just cause. The tactics and weapons relate to the Confucian concept of the superior man. The superior man should never attack another without warning. The superior man should not loose an arrow toward one with greater virtue, or if he does, he allows the other to shoot first. The element is a minimum of violence. The vanquished should not be made to suffer needlessly. Here, however, Aho notes the distinction among enemies. Expeditions are superiors (the Chou dynasty) versus inferiors. Wars are among the feudal lords, descendants of the Chou, "brothers" in nobility and thus equals. Drives are military actions against barbarians who may be exterminated, which is easier to do through surprise attack. Aho suggests a strong parallel here to the Catholic Middle Ages, with the unity of Christian knights fighting each other, compared to their savage treatment of heretics and Muslims. Chivalry among the Chinese nobility was lost in the period known as the Warring States, 403–221 B.C., in the final breakdown of the Chou empire.[28]

The loss appears in the writings of Sun Tzu (400–320 B.C.) in the first century of the Warring States. His *Art of War* became a classic required of military students until 1912. It was full of Machiavellian treachery that completely contradicted the chivalry of the superior man. And yet, it retained the third point of no excess injury. That included quick victories. There is a practical side to this, for a quick victory saves weapons and morale, and money. But it also means minimal oppression of people and minimal destruction. These ideas were still being included in Manchu laws in 1731, 1748 and 1784. They reappear in Mao Tse-tung's "Three Main Rules of Discipline and Eight Points for Attention." Even a portion of the superior man doctrine is retained, for it is the business of the general to be serene, upright and fearless. But such a balance is not possible unless he clings to the Way of Heaven. The Way or the Tao is of course the way of humanity and justice. Those who excel in war are those who cultivate their own humanity. In the end, Sun Tzu presented victory without bloodshed as the highest skill.[29]

A different concept appears in the Book of Rites (Li Chi, Bk. XXI). A quotation from the essay on the Evolution of Rites (Li Yun, Ch. 9 of Bk. XXI) is at the United Nations in New York City.

> When the great principle (tao) prevails, the world is a commonwealth in which the rulers are selected according to their wisdom and ability. Mutual confidence is promoted and good neighborliness cultivated. Hence, men do not regard as parents only their own parents, nor do they treat as children only their own children. Provision is secured for the aged until death, employment for the able-bodied, and the means of growing up for the young. Helpless widows and widowers, orphans and the lonely, as well as the sick and the disabled, are well cared for. Men have their respective occupations and women their homes. They do not like to see wealth lying idle, yet they do not keep it for their own gratification. They despise indolence, yet they do not use their energies for their own benefit. In this way, selfish schemings are repressed, and robbers, thieves and other lawless men no longer exist, and there is no need for people to shut their outer doors. This is called the Great Harmony [Great Commonwealth].[30]

The Great Commonwealth, or Grand Unity (Ta T'ung), is a kind of utopia. Scholars doubt that it comes from Confucius himself, but it reflects Confucian thinking from a later time, perhaps that of the Han dynasty (205 B.C.–A.D. 220). The Li Yun is divided into two epochs – the Small Tranquility (Hsiao K'ang) and the Great Commonwealth. The latter was set in the golden ages of the past during the reigns of the sage kings Yao, Shun, Yu, Tang, etc.

The concept was picked up by K'ang Yu-wei (1858–1927) and Sun Yat-sen (1866–1925). For the first of these, this utopia consists of the principles of universal love and equality. "The Tao of Ta-t'ung is the epitomy of fairness, justice, love, and good government." There will be justice for all on a foundation of love. Jen will abound. K'ang Yu'wei borrowed the idea of three ages: The Age of Disorder, the Age of Approaching Peace, and the Age of Great Peace. In the first, Confucius established good government in his own state of Lu. In the second, he established good government in China. In the third age, the world is the center of Confucius' reforms to unite humanity in one harmonious whole.

K'ang wrote in 1884 that he saw Confucius' prophecy happening. The reforms going on in the West and the growing communications between East and West showed the world is evolving from Disorder to the Age of Approaching Peace. Next comes the Great Peace. Confucius was the prophet of One World. In the first Age, priority is given one's family but in the end, all will be treated in the same way. The nine boundaries will fall away – boundaries of nations or tribes, nobility and commoner (or pure and impure), races, gender, family, occupation (private ownership) and disorder (inequality, unjust laws), kind (people, birds and beasts), and suffering (will end). K'ang went on to outline a complete system for a universal parliament and government.

Both Sun Yat-sen and Chiang Kai-shek wrote about Ta T'ung and promoted Confucian virtues. While Communism wiped out virtually all the externals of religion, Mao Tse-tung wrote in his autobiography that his cousin gave him a book on the Reform Movement of K'ang Yu-wei, edited by Liang Ch'i-ch'ao. "I worshipped K'ang Yu-wei and Liang Ch'i-ch'ao..." Mao's writings reflect Confucian concepts, including the Ta T'ung, which, however, he identifies with Communism.[31]

Concluding Thoughts

With Confucianism, as with other traditions, there is a temptation to ask, "Will the real Confucianist stand up?" The founder's words, as with the Buddha's, seem clear enough. Confucius saw war as evil. He worked for peace, without being a pacifist. War was a last resort for defense. Confucianists have led armies and fought wars. Confucianism has been used to promote and justify wars of aggression. Cheng claims China never had a religious war, a claim found in Buddhism and Shinto also. However, all of the religious traditions of China persecuted one another many times. The government tried to destroy first one religion, then another, often with the encouragement, support or initiation of another tradition. Cheng sees these attempts as simply individual conflicts. And yet, the basic teaching of Confucianism would seem to be for peace and justice. This includes special care for the common people who often bear the brunt of war, paying with their lives as well as their taxes, with their suffering as well as their homes and land.

The Confucian code of conduct was the ideal norm for individuals at all levels of life—from poor to rich, from peasant to emperor. Confucian values were the ideal for human relationships at all levels of life—individual, family, community, nation, international. The Confucian creed has been worked into the fabric of Chinese life and society. Yi Pao Mei points out this has happened apart from the religious dimension of Confucianism, for one may be a Taoist, a Buddhist or Christian and remain a Confucianist. Anyone who wishes to be a superior person can be one by learning and devotion to moral ideals. That includes jen—loving people joyously from the innermost part of one's heart. It means being virtuous (te) and righteous (yi). It means to set things right by setting one's self right. Perhaps Confucious would agree with a song by Sy Miller and Jill Jackson, "Let there be peace on earth, and let it begin with me."[32]

X. Shinto

Let the earth be free
from trouble and men
live at peace under the
protection of the Divine.

Introduction

The word "shinto" comes from the Chinese, shen tao, the way of the gods, to distinguish traditional Japanese religion from the Way of the Buddha. In Japanese, it is the Kami-no-michi, the way of the kami, the gods. Michael Pye suggests, "Shinto is the name given to a wide conglomeration of religious practices with roots in prehistoric Japan." Originally, it was an animistic or shamanistic faith that peopled all the rocks and rills and templed hills of Japan with spirits. Objects like swords, spears, and bows and arrows might be symbols of the kami, or kami themselves. Ancestral spirits were also kami, who required offerings, as well as proper burial of the dead, to keep them benevolent. Human beings such as the emperor and later the shoguns and founders of new religions were kami. Kami of ideas such as growth, creation and judgment are also known but are of uncertain date. This reflects Ferguson's judgment that the essence of Shinto is activity — life is a striving, a growing, a seeking for kami. Fujisawa describes the High Production Kami, called the High Tree Kami, who is the sanctification of cosmic vital energy. He says kami means the productive power of Taiichi (Confucianism), identified with the Tao, the Great Ultimate.

Kami is more inclusive than the English word "gods." Earhart suggests the closest English term may be the idea of the sacred. Bellah equates it with "sincere," having a pure heart. Melton calls it the life force. Noss compares it to the Polynesian concept of mana. This perspective may have developed in Japan, but it may also be that the people who came from the South Seas, Malaya and Mongolia brought their faith with them. They either united with or drove north the aboriginal tribes whom some see in the Ainu of Hokkaido today (still numbering about 14,000) but earlier in Honshu as well. Others suggest the Ainu were also immigrants, from Siberia.[1]

Early History

Relatively little is known of the prehistoric period. Human remains date to about 30,000 B.C. The Jomon period (8000–300 B.C.) religion had ritual burials (flexed bodies sprinkled with red ochre) and fertility cult objects. The Yayoi culture (300 B.C.–A.D. 250) originated in northern Kyushu. The cultivation and irrigation of rice were developed. This may be when the rice rituals—from planting to harvest—were developed. The Kofun (Tomb) period (250–645) is named for the large burial places prepared for the rulers. These may have been Asiatic warriors who brought the horse and metal smelting.

By the first century B.C., there were three centers of culture. On the island of Kyushu, the gods of the sea were the focus of worship. On the western side of the main island of Honshu, the Izumo clans worshipped the storm god, Susa-no-wo. The Yamato at the northern end of the Inland Sea worshipped the sun goddess. By the fourth century A.D., the last group gained a shaky hold over the rest with their chief on an imperial throne. The first Chinese literary references date to the Tomb period. These refer to women ruling in south Japan as influential shamans.[2]

Korean and Chinese influence arrived in the fifth century. Buddhism, Taoism and Confucianism came with that influence, along with writing, silkworm culture and advanced types of farming and metal working. The Way (Tao) of the Kami in its prehistoric form was a mix of nature worship, ancestor worship and fertility cult. Taoism reinforced the last and magical elements of folk religion. Confucianism reinforced ancestor worship and provided an ethic for the ancient tradition, making the people obedient to their "benevolent" rulers. It also gave support to the idea of the emperor as the Son of Heaven, though in China the Mandate of Heaven could be withdrawn, while the Japanese imperial line could supposedly never be broken.

Buddhism took over the shrines for a thousand years but kept them and the rituals largely intact. In turn, Shinto priests claimed Buddha taught the Way of Kami and his fourfold truth was revealed by the sun goddess. Buddhist temples were built into Shinto shrines, and kami shrines were built within the precincts of Buddhist temples. Sino-Korean influences continued in the Taika (645–710) and reached a peak in the Nara period (A.D. 710–794). Nara was the capital and the main Buddhist schools and monasteries were built here.[3]

As early as 624, the Empress Suiko (593–629) regulated the Buddhist priesthood and established supervision of nuns and monks. The latter was also part of the Taiho code of 702. The code included a Shinto bureau and the bureau of onmyo (yin and yang) for Taoism. The latter started as a department of government and only later spread to the people. Partly this was because Japan's seasonal calendar simply followed the agricultural year, but Taoism brought a national calendar that was initially the concern of the central government.

Government control included the rites of enthronement, the worship of national divinities, the upkeep of shrines, etc. Earhart points out it was only natural for the emperor, as the divine ruler, to be concerned with ritual and administrative propriety. If government controlled religion, the religion tended to unify and support the state. Religion received privileges and the state received divine legitimization and service. The relationship continued throughout most of Japanese history.

Shinto is frequently seen as an instrument of Japanese militarism as a matter of government policy, with the emperor as head of both Shinto and the government. The use of religion by government and military is, of course, quite common. The relationship of religion and state is a major feature of many traditions. The Byzantine (Eastern Roman) emperor Constantine incorporated Christianity into the empire, both controlling it and being supported by it. The Hindu emperor Ashoka converted to Buddhism and was supported by his new religion. Later, we will see the opposite view as well in Japan — the military is the instrument of Shinto for spreading the worship of the kami, or the emperor, or the sun goddess. This position is well known in other traditions such as Christianity and Islam.[4]

The Traditions

Shinto, like Hinduism, had no founder. Unlike Hinduism, with its multiple volumes of scripture, Shinto has none. There are, however, some ancient writings which come close to that category of literature. It may be that the ancient writings were composed partly to preserve older traditions, and partly to offset the new. The Kojiki, The Chronicle of Ancient Events, was written circa A.D. 712. Emperor Temmu (673–686) ordered the records preserved in the face of the growing power of Buddhism. In his court was Hieda-no-Are who knew many of the traditions. When Temmu died, his widow, Jito, had Are's words written by O-no-Yasumaro (d. 723). The Nihon Shoki (Nihongi), Chronicles of Japan, was produced in 720 by Futo-no-Yasumaro-no-Ason and Prince Toneri.

The Kogoshui, Gleanings from Ancient Stories, was written by Hironari Imbe, circa A.D. 806, early in the Heian era (794–1193), when Kyoto was the capital. The Gleanings are a defense of ancient priestly practice. One of their additional values is that they record rivalry among priestly families indicating distinct theological and ritual factions this early. The Engishiki, circa 927, is a 50-part collection of Shinto traditions. The first ten are the ritual prayers called norito which served as models of later Shrine rituals. Norito are based on the idea that spoken words have spiritual power.[5]

The origins of Shinto myths would seem to go back at least to the Yamato, but the first literary record is in the Kojiki. The primeval chaos had separated into heaven and ocean. The primal male, Izanagi, and female, Izanami, appeared. They gave birth to 80 lands, 80 islands, and eight million gods. The last god fatally burned his mother. She went to Yomi, the underworld. Izanagi tried to rescue her but succeeded only in getting polluted. He went to the sea to wash and from his left eye produced the sun goddess, Amaterasu, and Susa-no-wo, the storm god from his right eye (or his left nostril and the moon god from his right eye). Noss suggests the Shinto concern with pollution and ablution are foreshadowed here, but the myth may merely legitimate the common practice, even as it incorporates the storm god into the official pantheon, a process well known in Hinduism, Judaism and other traditions.

Later, Amaterasu did not like the way the storm god was ruling the islands so she sent her grandson, Ni-ni-gi, to rule. He married Kono-hana-sakuya-hime, the goddess of Mount Fuji. Their great-great-grandson, Jimmu, was the first Tenno (imperial), the first human emperor, the Son of Heaven. He set out from Kyushu and conquered the Yamato, unified the islands and set up his capital on Honshu in 660 B.C. Along with this divine descent of the emperor, maintained until MacArthur ordered Hirohito to deny his divinity after World War II, the feudal families and the whole people came to understand themselves as descendants of the lesser kami. Thus the islands and the whole people are considered divine.[6]

Shinto was focused in the family or clan for centuries. Some of the public shrines in the open, around a sacred tree or stone, were gradually developed into temples. The famous torii, a gate of two pillars with a horizontal beam across the top, and a crossbar brace, sets off the sacred precincts from the rest of the world. The Engishiki (A.D. 927) records 6,000 shrines receiving state offerings. Hirai suggests the kami of the Imperial Household and the kami of the powerful clans became the kami of the whole nation with offerings made by the state. These practices were systematized by the Taika ("Great Change") Reformation in A.D. 645, and continued until the end of the Kamakura period (1192–1336) when state Shinto was eclipsed and not revived until the Meiji restoration (1867).[7]

Gifts from Abroad

The Meiji restoration in turn eclipsed the Buddhist Shinto that had developed a thousand years earlier. Saicho, or Dengyo Daishi ("The Master Who Brought the Message") helped Emperor Kwammu to break away from the wealthy and powerful Buddhist priests at Nara. The subsequent Heian period takes its name from Mount Hiei where Saicho meditated, overlooking the site of the new capital at Kyoto. In 804, the emperor sent him to China to study Buddhism and he came back an ardent advocate of the Lotus Sutra. He created Tendai Buddhism (Chinese T'ien T'ai, the rationalist school), or Tendai Shinto, by making Buddhism a Japanese religion. All the kami were forms taken by the one Buddha reality. The result was Ichi-jitsu, or One Reality Shinto.

The Chinese Chen Yen (Mystery school) became Japanese Shingon, founded by Kukai or Kobo Daishi ("The Master Teacher of the Dharma") in the ninth century. The cosmic Buddha, Maha-vairocana (Buddha of Celestial Light) is the source of the whole universe. One can identify with the Buddhas and Bodhisattvas through meditation, repeating magic formulas and hand gestures. The Shinto kami are equated with Buddhist savior beings. The sun goddess, Amaterasu, was equated with the Buddha of the Celestial Light. The result was Ryobu, or Two Aspects Shinto. Through Shingon and Tendai, Buddhism and Shinto were practiced as a single faith for a thousand years.[8]

Shoguns

The Kamakura shogunate, dominated by the military rule of the Minamoto and Hojo families, left the emperor in Kyoto while the real power was in Kamakura, near today's Tokyo. Buddhism continued to develop its Zen, Amida, and Nichiren forms. While most Japanese remain both Buddhist and Shinto today, an anti-Buddhist Shinto developed as early as the thirteenth century in the form of Ise Shinto. The Watarai family of hereditary priests who took care of the Ise shrine suggested reversing Ryobu Shinto — the kami were the originals and the Buddhist deities the appearances.

They also emphasized purification and righteousness. Yoshida Shinto, started by Yoshida Kanetomo (1435–1511) in Kyoto, carried on this tradition with some Taoist influence. It is not unusual for devotees of a tradition to see their god(s) as true and others as worshipping the true under different names or the wrong name. Current Christianity includes the claim of the anonymous Christ and the anonymous Christian. Some Hindus have suggested Jesus was another incarnation of Vishnu. This approach contrasts with the simple judgment that other gods are false or fake.[9]

The Kamakura period was followed by the Warring States period (1336–1573) with the Ashikaga shoguns. This military regime failed to prevent the chaos described under Buddhism, in which monasteries had their own armies. Oda Nobunaga (1534–1582) conquered the feudal lords, destroyed the great Buddhist monastery fortresses and their armies, and unified most of the land. Christianity was introduced in 1549 by Jesuit Francis Xavier. Nobunaga supported Christianity, perhaps as part of his anti-Buddhist campaign. Numbers of the feudal lords whom he dispossessed of power turned to Christianity.

Nobunaga's efforts were continued by Toyotomi Hideyoshi (1536–1598), who invaded Korea but was repulsed by an army of Buddhist monks. He started persecuting Christianity, perhaps because of the dissident feudal lords who had become Christian, and perhaps because he suspected political motives in the European backers of the new faith. Pacification was completed with Tokugawa Ieyasu, who began the Tokugawa period (1603–1867), with its capital in Edo (Tokyo). The emperor was in the shadows and Japan was closed to the outside world. Ieyasu was pro-Buddhist and Buddhism regained state support. But neo-Confucianism also became a part of the state cult because it supported the obedience of subordinates to their superiors. In 1614, he deported the Christian missionaries and his successors virtually stamped out the religion. Shinto was revived. Ieyasu himself was deified with the main shrine at Nikko. Bellah suggests that one of the great blessings the Tokugawa regime bestowed on all people was peace, after 150 years of almost constant warfare.[10]

The shoguns are a reminder of the major role of the warrior in Japanese history. Some claim that the Way of the Kami had a close affinity with the Way of the Warrior from the beginning. It is spelled out in the code of the Bushido, "the warrior-knight way," the Japanese equivalent to the code of chivalry of medieval Europe. The Way of the Samurai goes back at least to Minamoto Yoritomo (1148-1199), who started the shogunate at Kamakura though the term "bushido" dates from the Tokugawa period. Yoritomo drew on Zen for self-discipline, stoic resignation to suffering and death, and unquestioning obedience to one's superior, for the Master was the embodiment of Truth whom one follows without thought or reason. Confucianism gave bushido ethical substance, including obedience to superiors. Shinto supplied devotion to country and obedience to superiors.

Within the military, it is known in the West for its suicide cult, but Noss sees this as a distortion. The willingness to die for one's country became an actual seeking to die for one's country. With support from academic nationalists cited later, Japanese military used bushido as part of their war talk. Conquest was the holy mission of Japan to fulfill its manifest destiny: "The expansion of Great Japan throughout the world and the elevation of the entire world into the land of the Gods is the urgent business of the present . . . it is our eternal and unchanging object." Twentieth century military action was "Holy War" and non-Japanese people can only benefit by being brought under Japan's sway. Its influence continued through World War II, which ended the military perspective. Some would say bushido continues today in the corporation (a continuation of the Tokugawa merchants) and patriotism with less emphasis on the military. In any event, Shinto continues to nourish Japanese national identity.[11]

Early in the Tokugawa shogunate, the Christians were finally put down after a desperate uprising in 1637-1638, the Shimabara Revolt in Kyushu. The government then demanded that everyone get a certificate from a Buddhist temple to prove he or she was not a Christian. Some Shinto priests objected, with support from Japanese Confucian scholars. The latter had been studying the neo-Confucianism of the Sung dynasty (960-1279), especially that of Chu Hsi (1130-1200), called Shushi in Japan. In 1647, the emperor ordered hereditary Confucian scholars to use neo-Confucian commentaries rather than earlier ones. The new proposal was for a Confucian Shinto, to be called Suika Shinto. Scholars such as Yoshikawa

Koretaru (1616–1694) and Yamazaki Ansai (1618–1682) emphasized the unity of the two traditions. The Supreme Ultimate (T'ai Chi) of neo–Confucianism was identified with the first kami of the Nihongi. Yoshikawa emphasized imperial virtues of wisdom, benevolence and courage, and a national ethic of loyalty and filial piety as the way to rule the state. Ansai developed this and advocated emperor worship.[12]

Thus encouraged and with continued support from the masses thankful to Amaterasu for good crops, the Ise priests toured the countryside and promoted what Hirai calls Revival Shinto. One who was influenced by their preaching was Ishida Baigan (1685–1744), who began to propagate Shinto at the age of 23. His movement was called Shingaku. He worked for a Kyoto merchant. In his free time, he learned about Taoism, Buddhism and Confucianism, and found enlightenment at the age of 40 and turned to full-time teaching about the true nature of man and knowing the heart. That means behaving prudently, serving one's lord righteously, respecting parents, and loving humanity, especially the poor. He practiced meditation, an austere life and devotion to social obligations. Unite the heart with Amaterasu and act accordingly. He promoted the work ethic — one's occupation is the foundation of the family, service to the nation, the holy calling of heaven. The life of the merchant thus became as holy as that of the samurai warrior. Selling and moneylending are honorable but they must be honest. Baigan taught that Japan is the Land of the Kami, superior to all other nations.[13]

During the following centuries there was also a revival of ancient learning. In 1728, a priest of the Inari (rice goddess) shrine in Kyoto started the National Scholar Movement with a school of national learning (kokugaku). Motoori Norinaga's (1730–1801) commentary on the Kojiki is still authoritative. He considered the Kojiki to be historically accurate. He claimed the early literature represents the true Japanese spirit before it was spoiled by the foreign influences of Buddhism and Confucianism. He denied that Japanese learning was dependent on Chinese sources. Japan is superior and no other nation has equality with her. The Japanese need no ethics from Confucius or anyone else. As divine, they are naturally upright, have no need for a moral code and never had one. He was followed by Hirata Atsutane (1776–1843), whose call to unite all people under the emperor in the name of Shinto was a factor in the Meiji restoration. He justified Hideyoshi's invasion of Korea with the claim that the sovereigns of Japan are the lords of the whole earth. "The Whole World under One Roof" ("hakko ichi-u") became a part of Japanese militarism in the twentieth century.[14]

The Meiji Restoration

The Hermit Kingdom was not entirely closed to the outside world. The Dutch were allowed in Japanese waters. However, American whalers and other national interests wanted in also. An occasional shipwreck tossed sailors onto Japanese shores. These were either killed outright as foreign devils or repatriated with months of delay through the Dutch. The ships also needed ports to get water and provisions. In 1853, President Millard Fillmore sent Commodore Matthew C. Perry to Tokyo with a letter requesting that a few ports be opened. The shogun shared this with the feudal lords who argued pro and con. Emperor Komei was opposed. In 1854, Perry returned with ten ships and 2,000 men. The shogun made a treaty for shipwrecked sailors, food and water and three ports for trade. The emperor kept the internal peace but a struggle for power followed when he died. The shogun resigned and Emperor Meiji was put in control of the country (1868-1911) in what is called the Meiji restoration. Bellah notes the battle cry of the restoration was revere the emperor and expel the barbarians (non-Japanese). Buddhism was disestablished and State Shinto was reestablished.

The Meiji era did not merely disestablish Buddhism. For five years there was active persecution. Many Buddhist temples were destroyed. Shintoists denounced Buddhism as a foreign religion filled with superstition, magic, immorality and more concern for the dead than the living. Buddhists in turn denounced Shinto as being an artificial construction lacking in philosophical merit and built on mythology. Buddhists went on to claim they were loyal to Japan and had made major contributions in education and charitable works. While holding absolutely to the antiwar principle, in practice, Buddhists proclaimed all of Japan's wars holy. Buddhism is all for peace and all of Japan's wars were wars for peace.[15]

Hirai suggests Shinto exists in three forms. Folk Shinto is the unorganized type without doctrines represented in roadside images and agricultural rites. Shrine Shinto referred to above includes State Shinto (Jinga-Shinto). Sect Shinto (Kyoha-Shinto) emerged at the end of the Tokugawa period. Hirai identifies 13 groups divided into at least five categories: Revival Shinto sects, Confucian sects, purification sects, mountain worship sects, and faith healing groups.

Prominent among the faith healing groups is Tenri-kyo, sometimes called the Christian Science of Japan. Tenri means divine reason or wisdom and kyo means religion or religious body. It was founded by Nakayama Miki (1798-1887), a farmer's wife who had been a Pure Land Buddhist. In 1838, her family became ill. She called in an exorcist who used her as a medium to get rid of the evil spirits. Instead, a kami called Tenri O no Mikoto, God the Parent, spoke through her message. The Shinto pantheon are all aspects of this one deity. By 1980, there were 2,573,709 members. International headquarters are in the city of Tenri (the center of the world) near Nara. Social service and education are main activities and include orphanages, Tenri University, libraries, museums.

Konkokyo (the religion of Golden Light) was founded in 1859 by Kawate Bunjiro (1814-1883). After a long illness, he had a revelation of God as Tenchi Kane no Kami, the Parent God (and the only deity) of the universe. He is perfect goodness and calls his followers to universal brotherhood. Human prosperity is the ultimate purpose of the universe. God's work is completed through people. Social concerns include hospitals, libraries, museums, leper missions and prison work. Shinto rituals are used but have been demythologized.

These groups are sometimes called new religions while others reserve the term for post–World War II developments. In the latter period, hundreds of Shinto sects have been formed, some de novo and some growing out of older groups. An interesting footnote here is that a number of these new traditions have been started by women. But Nakamura Kyoko notes this has not changed the status of women in Japan any more than the numerous priestesses and empresses throughout history. In other words, Shinto, like shamanism in general, has accepted the occasional woman in spiritual roles but this has not altered the low social status of women in society at large. The normal life-style, even for the founders of new religions, was to marry, serve their husbands, have children.[16]

Shinto Outside Japan

Shinto has traveled with the Japanese people and the army, which carried the sun goddess' shrine into every conquered territory. Shinto has also been spread by missionaries. Shinto arrived in Latin America and the United States with immigrants. The first to the U.S. were in Hawaii. The first shrine was built in Hilo in 1898 and the first temple in Honolulu in 1906. From Hawaii, Shinto moved to the mainland. In general, Shinto prospered until the 1930s and the gathering of war clouds. After the eclipse of World War II, the tradition has slowly gathered strength, primarily among people of Japanese ancestry but also among some non–Japanese. Honkyoku, Taishakyo, Jinsha, Inari, Jinga, Tensho Kotai Jingu Kyo, Tenrikyo, Konkokyo, Shinreikyo and Third Civilization are among the forms of Shinto in the United States. The last is a messianic group based on the Kototama principle, which is equated to the Tao as the life principle, which is the source of all. Shinreikyo is a postwar healing group concerned with happiness and prosperity. A number of groups have also spread to Canada and Europe.[17]

State Shinto

With the Meiji restoration (1867–1868), State Shinto was restored. While the Tokugawa shogunate required everyone to register in Buddhist temples, the Meiji government required everyone to register in a Shinto shrine. However, that only lasted five years before resurgent Buddhism and foreign demand for freedom of religion changed the Department of Shinto to the Department of Religion. That soon changed too and in 1882, State

Shinto was started. While the constitution of 1889 guaranteed freedom of religion, Shinto had priority. Under the guise of religious freedom, the 1890 Imperial Rescript on Education removed all religious teaching from the schools. State Shinto was taught in public schools and national holidays were related to Shinto festivals. However, the state cult was presented as a national ethic rather than a religion. National shrine priests were not allowed to preside over Shinto funerals. By 1945 there were 218 national and about 110,000 local shrines.

Earhart warns against the common Western view of Shinto as the nationalistic militaristic cause of World War II. One way to deal with this is to distinguish government motivation, the ritual concerns of the priests and the common people's concern for blessings on their homes and welfare. Earhart has some difficulty, given his own quotations of Shinto scholars and leaders, and the postwar attitude of the people themselves who lamented the war's destruction and blamed Shinto as the tradition most closely allied to the war machine, which he himself cites. While the priests disliked government control, they appreciated Shinto's role in welding a national religious force, and they appreciated government financial support. But he also notes that most religious groups—Buddhist, Christian, etc.—supported the war effort. Confucianism was a major rationale supporting militarism in Korea and Manchuria.

Ferguson is one who claims Shinto was a focal point for militant nationalism. Out of it came Japan's benevolent destiny to rule the world as the world's savior. All of Japan's wars were holy wars. The Imperial Army was the religious instrument that would draw "The Whole World Under One Roof"—the imperial policy. At the height of its power, the Japanese Empire stretched across a major portion of the Pacific to New Guinea and the South Sea Islands, to Indonesia, Singapore, Burma, Indo-China, a major portion of China itself. Before World War II, Japan had annexed several nearby islands, Taiwan, and Korea, before invading and conquering Manchuria, or Manchukuo. Shinto was imposed on all areas, not simply as part of the worship of soldiers but as a missionary faith.

Fujisawa says it is conceivable some wartime military and bureaucratic leaders misinterpreted Shinto as a militaristic ideology, but they were trained in Western politics. He sees all-harmonizing, pure Shinto as the most tolerant and peaceful metareligion imaginable, claiming there has been no religious war in Japan, thanks to Shinto. As a neo–Shintoist, however, he does call for sweeping renovation of Shinto. And he does overlook an enormous amount of bloodletting in Japanese history. It is of interest to note in contrast to Fujisawa that in 1937, the military under General Senjuro Hayashi, minister of education, blamed all the evils of the country on Western culture. D.C. Holtom says, "Japan's religion of conquest was brought to an end on December 15, 1945. On this date State Shinto was disestablished...."[18]

The Postwar Period

At the end of World War II, General MacArthur ordered the disestablishment of State Shinto, which cut off all public funds and official affiliation. This order was put into the 1947 constitution. The Association of Shinto Shrines was organized in 1946. Over 86,000 shrines now belong to the group while about 1,000 are independent or belong to small groups. There are approximately 60 million believers.

While some of the 16,251 Sect Shinto shrines were damaged in the war, Sect Shinto itself was not negated by the occupation policies. Internal discouragement and dissension were problems. In part these were overcome from within. Tenrikyo has continued to develop and expand through missionary programs in East Asia, the Americas, etc. In part, postwar difficulties and freedom of religion opened the way to the development of hundreds of new religions, many Shinto or Shinto oriented, or, as in the mid-1800s, a combination of traditions.[19]

Kitamura Sayo (1900–1967), a southern Honshu farmer's wife, had become a shamaness. In 1944, she believed she was possessed by the female-male Shinto deity, Tensho Kotai Jingu, who directed her to establish the Kingdom of God in a world of sin, described in Buddhist terms of desire. Tensho is the one God of the universe, the heavenly father and the eternal Buddha. The tradition is commonly called Odoru Shukyo, the dancing religion, because it uses ecstatic dance in the redemptive process. While using language from other world religions, it remains Shinto. All other religions are false and only Odoru Shukyo can save. It has about 500,000 members. On a trip to Hawaii in 1959, the foundress advised her followers to burn Shinto and Buddhist relics as belonging to the past.[20]

Deguchi Nao (d. 1918), a shamanistic farmer's daughter, started Omotokyo in 1892. Her suffering brought her a messianic vision. In 1980, the movement had about 165,000 members. Since 1945, several new groups have spun off from the original. These groups include pure Shinto, shamanistic healing, a messianic utopia and the Perfect Liberty Kyodan. The last claims the individual is a manifestation of God. People are to live radiantly in self-realization. Their festivals celebrate the joy of life. Kim says the group was started by Tokuchika Miki (b. 1900) in 1946. His father before him founded the Religion of Man, which was suppressed by the government in 1937. Tokuchika revived the group and renamed it. It is Shinto brought up to date without the disadvantages of State, Shrine and Sect Shinto. His father had worshipped a tree, symbol of the High Tree Deity. He added a wheel-shaped gold emblem of 21 rays emanating from the sun as a symbol of Amaterasu. Kim calls the two the most prominent kami of ancient Shinto. PL is interested in everyday life. It has no concern for hermits or monks. Work is an act of God. By working harmoniously with nature, we can create a world of matchless beauty mirroring God's creativity. It has over 600,000 members.[21]

Summary

The old forms of Shinto continue along with the new. As a basic part of the identity of the Japanese people, and with the spread of several forms of Shinto into other parts of the world, Shinto retains its importance among world religions. Indeed, with Japan's ascending star as a social and economic power, not only in Asia but throughout the world, Shinto is more important than ever.

Hirai summarizes its basic position. Shinto doctrine includes the sacredness of everything, as noted earlier. The kami represent mysterious power and truth. They are the source and guide for human existence. Human nature is focused on the true heart and the pure mind as well as the virtues of loyalty, filial piety, love and faithfulness. Hirai claims this suggests that human life is divine and human personality is worthy of respect. All people, regardless of race, nationality or other distinctions, have basic human rights. There is no original sin but people need purification from the impurities that cover the inner mind. There is no end time as in other traditions, for Japan will last forever. The imperial system, supported by Shinto, is an example of unity and harmony. Shinto was used to unify the people during repeated wars.

Hirai claims that since the end of World War II, the age-old desire for peace has been restressed, though he does not cite any earlier desire than the proclamation of 1956 in *The General Principles of Shinto Life* of the Association of Shinto Shrines. "In accordance with the Emperor's will, let us be harmonious and peaceful, and pray for the nation's development as well as the world's co-prosperity." The emphasis on imperial unity for war suggests that if the emperor should will war instead of harmony, Shinto would return to war rather than peace. One can still applaud his concern for all humanity. In 1919, Shinkichi Uesugi claimed "Subjects have no mind apart from the will of the Emperor. Their individual selves are merged with the Emperor. . . . The organizing will resides inherently in the Emperor and apart from the Imperial mind there exists no organizing will." Holtom notes an interpretation of "the whole world under one roof" as meaning the establishment of peace and righteousness in the earth, covering the whole world with charity, love, virtue, truth and justice. Unfortunately, the date of this interpretation was 1940 and it was followed by world war.[22]

Today, Hirai suggests most Shintoists believe cooperation among different religions could contribute to world peace. They do not want syncretism but maintain their own characteristics while working toward the peaceful coexistence of all people.[23]

Peace

Hirai's concern for peace is the focus of this book. One cannot ignore the adulation of the warrior, bushido, the support of the government and the military, in the past. There is no need to pretend these are not there, just as they are present in other traditions. The concern now is peace and Shinto's resources for peace. The harmony with nature that is common throughout the entire tradition, and appears in Shinto agriculture, art, and gardening and flower arrangements, has a special interest today.[24] If the nuclear holocaust does not wipe out the human race, the race may disappear in the foggy mists of environmental pollution. As with Taoism, one is reminded here of T.S. Eliot's view that the world will not end with a bang but a whimper. This harmony with nature could be the salvation of the world.

To this one can add the concern of Shingaku and other sects with humanity and human universalism. Shinto's view of the sacredness of human life goes beyond its island home to the Global Village. With Perfect Liberty, humanity might very well join hands and celebrate life as art, life as a mirror of the divine. The concern is not of course merely a static anthropology that views human nature as divine. That divinity, or kami, is in the heart and Shinto is concerned with the pure heart and the purification of the heart, with honesty and righteous living that reach out in sincerity and humanitarianism to all.[25] That alone could lead to the end of the nuclear standoff. In a day when more and more of life is largely meaningless, even to the Japanese, the work ethic of Shingaku and Perfect Liberty has a saving grace. Work and life seen as a holy calling can provide meaning and purpose that can turn humanity from its destructive course to constructive activity in a world filled with human need.

Fujisawa, who calls himself a neo–Shintoist, sees the West as groping for meaning in the midst of its scientific materiality, bound up in a dualistic view that opposes the spiritual to the material. Shinto can cure that schizophrenia for it has never had the problem. Shinto blends the spiritual cultures of the East as seen in Buddhism, Confucianism and Taoism with the material civilization of the West with its science and technics. Shinto is both national and universal, merging individual destiny with the destiny of the nation. So it can link the national destiny of Japan with the universal destiny of humanity. It is a planetary theory which can also overcome the split between Communist Russia and Capitalist America by creating a congenial atmosphere among them. As a pantheistic monotheism, it combines transcendence and immanence and avoids on the one hand the opposition of the transcendental God to immanent man in the West and the atheistic materialism of the Soviets.[26]

The standoff between the Soviets and the U.S. carries with it the threat of nuclear war. Having experienced nuclear war firsthand, Shinto and other Japanese traditions are in a position to speak out against it so that the world might know and draw back from that holocaust. One can note in this regard that the constitution, which denies Japanese military rearmament, was imposed by victorious enemies. But many Japanese have welcomed that and a strong element of pacifism has developed in the past 30 years. They have opposed the rather considerable military buildup of recent years which has been achieved under the label of defense forces. The pacifism and opposition to the military are also a message Shinto can share with the world. Without further syncretism, Shinto can also point the way to cooperation among the religions of the world. While historic voices have indeed upheld the supremacy of Shinto, by and large the tradition has a major record of tolerance. The "voices" from the past can help Shintoists avoid both smugness and further triumphalism, or jingoism. The record of tolerance is in turn a solid foundation upon which today's leaders and others can build for a cooperative interfaith community of religions, and a cooperative, and yes, peaceful world.

XI. Traditional Faiths

A number of terms have been used for the traditional religions — tribal, primal, primitive, nonliterate. The referent here is the original or native religion or religions of most of the world as contrasted to the so-called historic religions or the major religions or great religions. These include the religion(s) of the American Indians (North and South), Eskimo, South Sea Islands, Australia, Southeast Asia, African tribal religions, the Bon religion of Tibet, the Shaman traditions of Central and Eastern Asia. The paleolithic cave paintings of France (Lascaux) and India from circa 15,000 B.C. reflect shamanistic practices as do present-day religions. Sam D. Gill suggests shamanism is not a religion but a set of techniques and an ideology. Some have suggested these reflect primitive thought in the evolution of religion. However, communication with deity or spirits, as in prayer, and other dimensions of shamanism, can be seen as fundamental to religion in any stage of development.[1]

The word "shaman" originates in Siberia. It means "he who knows" though one should add there are women shamanesses. In American Indian tradition, there are medicine men and women while African tribal religions have witch doctors and women. It should be noted there are differences among these groups, and the grouping here does not mean they are all alike and the various religious leaders can be simply equated. There are, however, some features in common.[2]

The shaman is in communication with the spirit world. He or she may be trained but is "called" to the task, perhaps through possession by a god or spirit. Even though a parent or other shaman may be the teacher or trainer in shamanistic lore, the true teacher is the god or familiar spirit who has chosen the new shaman-to-be. The shaman may be a king, chief, priest or commoner. The diviner, clairvoyant and dream interpretation functions are part of the communication with spirits. The role often includes healing power, especially of demon or spirit possession. Some suggest healing is the primary function of the shaman. The healing or health includes the fertility of the land, flocks and people. The basis of the concept is a cosmos (heaven, earth, underworld) filled with spirits.[3]

Shinto is a form of shamanism. In some ways it is typical in its belief that every rock or tree, mountain or speck of dust, plant or animal or human has its spirit, along with the air, water, fire, and other natural phenomena. Animism is another term for this. The Polynesian concept of mana is a more general form of the transcendental force. Human beings are affected by this spirit world, for good or ill. The role of the shaman is to enhance the good and protect people from the ill, or after it has arrived in the form of infertility, sickness, famine, etc., to cure the problem. Another basic role is that of psychopomp, escort of souls to the afterlife, as in the ancient Greek traditions of Charon and Hermes, and the Roman god Mercury.

The shaman is often identified by abnormal behavior, frequently resembling psychotic or other disturbed actions. A primary difference is that the shaman enters the ecstatic state by an act of will, often through music, dance, meditation, or other action of choice. In the autohypnotic trance, he or she enters the spirit world, perhaps by way of the world mountain or world pillar or world tree connecting heaven and earth. In some cases, the shaman works through a totem animal such as a bear, or flies to heaven as a bird, or is carried there by a bird such as an owl or eagle.[4]

It has been suggested that this shamanistic tradition is a part of all religion. Prayer is common to most traditions and can be seen as continuous with the shamanic communication with the spirit world. Judaism has long had its holy mountain of Mount Zion, a concept borrowed from the earlier ancient Near Eastern traditions, such as the Mesopotamian ziggurat. Early Christian tradition identified Golgotha, the site of Jesus' crucifixion, as the cosmic mountain, the center of the world, the place where Adam, the first man (Genesis 2) was created and buried. The cross of Jesus' crucifixion has been related to the cosmic tree. The tree of knowledge (Genesis 2:17), or life (Genesis 3:22), has also been compared to the world tree of shamanism. An example of clairvoyance is the prophet Samuel who knew the location of the lost asses of Kish, the father of the future king, Saul (I Samuel 9). Interpretation of dreams is also common in the biblical tradition with the stories of Joseph, the son of Jacob, as perhaps the most familiar (Genesis 40–41).[5]

Ramsay MacMullen has suggested that people were not converted to early Christianity by philosophical regard for the teachings and dogmas of the faith. Magic and miracles "proved" the Christian God was more powerful than others and so must be accepted. The attraction of miracles continued throughout Christian history and is still present, as seen in the avid attention people give to faith healers such as Oral Roberts, or to healing shrines such as the Roman Catholic shrine at Lourdes. Some have noted that the Gospels show Jesus of Nazareth as a faith healer as well as or even more than being a teacher or rabbi.[6]

Parallels have also been drawn between what Eliade calls a nostalgia for paradise and other traditions. In the background of Hebrew tradition is the story of the lost garden of Eden. African tradition records a beginning in which people lived in peace with all of nature which included communication with animals, an attribute of the shaman. Harmony with nature is a basic concept among American Indians. Peaceful coexistence is reflected in the biblical book of Isaiah (11:6–9) and in Christian traditions about St.

Francis of Assissi. The shaman continues this power since the original ability for all people to communicate with the spirit and animal worlds has been lost. Some relate all mysticism here as an effort to achieve union or reunion with the divine. The apocalypse — an end time that destroys the present evil world and ushers in a new order — has been interpreted as the achievement of paradise or a return to it. The New Testament of Christianity has several examples, chiefly the book of Revelation (Greek: apocalypse).[7]

A present-day Episcopal priest, Urban T. Holmes, III, has suggested that the origins of priesthood are in shamanism. While he does not recommend that modern clergy should return to shamanism as such, he calls for a shift from the intellectual/active role to more emphasis on the receptive/intuitive mode. The latter is more at home in the world of symbols, metaphors and stories that mediate God's presence in a special way. The clergy should be the illuminator of meaning for people.[8]

Asia. These parallels or mergers suggest both the continuity and differences of shamanism in various cultures. In Japan, the continuation of shamanism in Shinto remains prominent to the present. The ruling power of shamanesses prior to the rise of the Jimmu tradition of emperors was noted in Chinese records about the islands. Archaeological excavations of the Jomon period have produced fertility figurines and clay masks which may have been worn by shamans. The shamanism of the Yayoi period focused on agriculture and oracles in matters of state. Jimmu's mother may have been a shamaness. Later emperors such as Sujin (tenth emperor) and empresses such as Jingo, both practiced shamanistic traditions and had court shamans for healing, for directions from the spirit world, etc. In the Kofun, or Great Tomb period, burials included mirrors, swords, jewels, and paintings of soul boats to ferry spirits to the other world. After the spread of Buddhism, shamans often adopted the language, stories and ritual of Buddhism while continuing shamanistic practices. Similarly, it was the shamanistic form of Taoism that first spread through Japan.[9]

A number of the new religions continue shamanistic traditions today. Tenrikyo, the Religion of Divine Wisdom, was noted in the chapter on Shinto. It, and several others, originated in an experience of spirit possession in which the Parent God spoke through the chosen one. The place of Nakayama Miki's (1798–1887) experience is marked by a wooden column. The present Patriarch of Tenrikyo regularly leads a mystical dance around the column, while other dancers join in, with the music of drums.

Korea's traditional religion is called Sinkyo. Harvie Conn sees it as a religious way of seeing the world rather than a structured set of beliefs. Heaven, man and nature make a harmony of opposites. The tradition has had a variety of religious figures. The largest group were the Mudangs (shamanesses) while the Paksoos (male) were fewer. There were Pansoos (blind diviners), Chikwan (geomancers), Ilkwan (chose favorable times), and Yubok (blind female fortune-tellers). Shamans sometimes dressed like women and vice versa. Their séances (Koots) involved dancing and drums and occasional blood sacrifices. Some used *Chunsoo Kyung*, a book of Buddhist charms, and others used the *Okchu Kyung*, "Nine Heaven Original Controlling, Thunder Shaking Chunchon Book."

As in Japan, shamanism has been seen as the basic faith of the country. Tangun, the traditional founder of Korea, worshipped Hananim, his grandfather and the shamanic Master of the Sky. Behind the official Confucianism of the Yi dynasty, the real religion was shamanism and in Queen Min's rule, it was the official court religion. After her assassination in 1895, shamanism continued among all classes of people. Small and large shrines continue today.[10]

Today, shamanism has also taken on new forms. It appears in numbers of the over 300 new religions. Ch'ondogyo, the Heavenly way, was founded by Ch'oe Che-u (1824–1864). He was educated in Confucianism, Taoism, Buddhism and Roman Catholicism. In 1860, he had a mystical experience described as direct communication with the spirit world. He was given a Sacred Formula through which people can realize God and man are one and union between man and heaven can be realized. He proclaimed heaven on earth and called his teaching Tonghak, or Eastern learning. The movement was in the forefront of the Korean independence movement in 1919. Somewhat in contrast, Chungsan-gyo emphasizes the spiritual aspect of life, trying to unify all religions and to acquire magical powers through religious exercises to establish paradise on earth. The T'ongil-gyo movement of Rev. Sun Myung Moon, known in the West as the Unification Church, includes unification and paradise, identified with the Christian "Kingdom of God." Con suggests that Moon can be seen as the great link-man between the people and the spirit world.[11]

In China, the Emperor Yu, circa 2208 B.C., legendary founder of the traditional Hsia dynasty, reportedly dressed in a bear skin and became the incarnation of the Bear Spirit. From the following and still legendary Shang dynasty, the oracle bones show a belief in the continuing influence of the spirits of the dead.

The term "wu" for shamans may also be among the oracles though others doubt this. In any event, the term is early. These held séances with spirits and were believed to have healing power. Kim notes the "wu" were female while the male shamans were called "hih." They would dance themselves into a frenzied exhaustion, making the body receptive to the shen, or spirit, which then spoke through the medium. Creel notes they were especially numerous in the southern state of Ch'u and also in Ch'i, today's Shantung province. Magicians were also numerous in the latter. These are part of the background for the later development of Taoism. Shamanism relates to the Taoism of the spiritual healer, the fortune-teller or the holy man, to what Creel calls Hsien Taoism with its magical search for immortality, rather than the philosophical tradition.

Ch'u and Winberg Chai note the intimate and mutual relationship between the dead and the living as part of the background of Confucianism. Ancestor worship is recorded for the Shang and later Chou dynasties

(1122–222 B.C.). It was a legal as well as religious obligation not to neglect this worship. The king's ancestral temple and the "she chi," "the altar of land and grain," were twin foci of spiritual forces assuring prosperity in peace and victory in war. In turn, when a state was conquered, these two centers were destroyed. One interpretation of the ancient beliefs is that "Man and the divine were inextricably intertwined and completely involved with each other. They were inseparable, and they must be kept in harmony."[12]

In Tibet and the surrounding areas still influenced by Tibetan Buddhism, one can still find rituals and other vestiges of the ancient shamanistic tradition of the Bon religion. The famous "Om mani padme hum," "Om, the jewel in the lotus," is a magical formula painted on rocks and printed on prayer flags and prayer wheels. This ancient animistic tradition is especially noted for its demons, ghouls and other spirits. "Many Buddhas and bodhisattvas . . . are worshipped along with their ferocious consorts, or Taras."[13]

Africa. E.M. Zuesse and others note that African traditional religions are so diffused with their respective societies that there is hardly any distinction between sacred and profane. This statement could probably hold for most if not all traditional religions. The separation of life and religion is a relatively recent development. While some speak of African religion in the singular, like Hinduism, others note there may have been a thousand or more different religions. Hinduism itself may have originally been several different religions, but this unity was not imposed or achieved in African religions. In contrast to Hinduism and other book religions, there are no ancient scriptures, and no written histories of these traditions. Reliable information depends on relatively recent observations and oral history.[14]

In the midst of considerable variety in African religions, Parrinder suggests that there is belief in a supreme deity, many lesser nature gods, cults of ancestors and magical practices, including witchcraft. Zuesse and Parrinder use the metaphor of a pyramid, with the last as the base. The many gods may be worshipped in their own right or as the way to the high God. Some claim the many are simply different names for the one. Many myths reflect a golden age in which God lived on earth but human sin or thoughtlessness irritated him so he left, a variation from the Hebrew tradition of people being driven out of paradise.[15]

Booth suggests that in the midst of this variety in traditional African religions, there are five unifying concepts: vitality or life force, humanism, wholeness, continuity and healing. The first is the manifestation of spiritual power in human life. It has been called animism and has been compared to Polynesian mana. Wholeness emphasizes the social nature of life. Continuity relates ancestors and the future in the present. Booth adds that while there are practical elements in African religions, they are not exclusively interested in getting something but celebrate in dance, song, etc.[16]

To the characteristics noted earlier for shamanism, one could add here an emphasis on animal spirits such as the royal leopard (Master of

Animals), masked forest spirits, divine kingship, the fertility spirit in the
snake and the rainbow, and the union of male and female in God. There
is a tendency to associate women with witchcraft and men with sorcery,
with the first more concerned with spiritual powers and the latter more with
healing. East, central and southern Africa also have a number of prophets.
They may be priestly rainmakers with shrines or charismatics called by
God in time of crisis. A universal African belief is in multiple souls for each
person. In addition to ancestor worship, these ancestral spirits occupy the
various souls of their descendants. Health and peace come through living
in harmony with these spirits and the environment. "To be in harmony,
each person must honor both parents and all relatives, and fulfill all traditional norms of loyalty and responsibility."[17]

Of the traditional shamanic elements, fertility and success in the hunt
are major concerns as are divination and spirit possession. The latter
especially stresses the healing role. These concerns continue today in
direct form, but they also live on in varying degrees in African Islam and
Christianity. In addition, there are over 6000 new religions which mix
the three — Islam, Christianity and traditional religions — in varying degrees.[18]

The locus of spiritual life continues to be this world rather than an
afterlife. While some African interpreters differ widely on aspects of traditional religions, e.g., monotheism, they generally agree on this focus on
humanity in the present. The enhancement of life's holiness is part of this,
but religion remains very much a social enterprise rather than a quest for
personal salvation. While Western forms of medicine are widely accepted,
traditional healers are also still important with a continued emphasis on
harmony with the ancestors. The ancestral cult is continued even in the
midst of industrialization, and by highly educated Africans who see
Western empiricism missing the spiritual dimension of life. Indeed, the
traditional faith has even more appeal amid all the anxieties of modern
life — fear of evil spirits, concern about fertility and health. Protection from
social marginality or isolation is perhaps the newest dimension in the
disruptions from rural to urban and tribal to national life. This may include
protection from discrimination, injustice, and oppression. Shorter claims
the traditional African hardly exists any more. His place is taken by the
contemporary African. The shrines, diviners and rituals have dwindled.
Urbanization has brought new structures. But traditional religion lives on
in the minds of Africans. Knappert notes that much, perhaps most, of the
old African religions have been lost but original forms can still be traced.
Booth sees the continuity as noted above — Christians and Muslims continue to practice some aspects of traditional religions while the new
religions combine elements of the three.[19]

America. We can note parallels here with Western interpretations of
African traditional religions. One example is that Indians had no religion
according to Columbus, Vespucci and Darwin. Another is the question of
the one or the many. Some speak of Indian or Native American religion in

the singular, while others claim that there were thousands of different religions among over 2000 tribes. Sam D. Gill says each tribe had its own religious institutions, traditions, practices and beliefs, but then goes on to find many similarities. Today's political climate is encouraging the Indians to see themselves as one. Thus we may be seeing, as suggested for Hinduism, the transformation of many traditions into one. Historically, the differences are numerous — there were jaguar gods in the South but not in what is now New York. However, Lévi-Strauss' structuralism, showing the logic of myths, claims the Amerindians participated in a universe of meaning which extended across both North and South America. As in African traditions, so in the Americas, with the exception of the Maya and the Aztecs, there was no written language. Thus the earliest accounts are those of European missionaries, explorers, anthropologists, etc.[20]

In the pan–Indian tradition, we find the familiar relationship between humans and spirits, rituals in which the events of creation are acted out or which keep the world functioning, rituals relating people to the natural world — maple trees, the sun, thunder, seed planting, beans, corn, harvest, the seasons. Among the Hopi, the spirits of the dead returned to this world as "kachinas," all of whom were believed to take on cloud form — to be "cloud people." Rituals included masked impersonators with the kachinas working through them as messengers of the gods. "All native American groups had religious specialists." Sometimes the role was temporary. Sometimes they operated alone and sometimes as part of a group of practitioners, such as the kachina dancers. The societies might stage dramatizations of the rituals or the creation. Some persons or groups functioned in times of crisis such as illness, while others worked with the regular rituals. As in the shaman traditions elsewhere, they might wear some significant attire, use drums, rattles, dance, chants, drugs, self-torture, etc., to attain their altered state of consciousness — a trance, a vision, a dream. Transvestism, nervous dispositions, unusual physical characteristics, being called by spirits and/or trained by older practitioners — men or women — are part of the picture here as in other cultures. Hieb cautions that they were not all alike. The term medicine men has often been used for American Indians rather than shamans. Many did practice healing, but others, such as the Navajo singers, were more specialized.[21]

Spiritual life was not limited to the specialists. Not all tribes had medicine men. In puberty rites, larger numbers, perhaps parents and perhaps all the males of the village might be involved. The famous vision quest of the adolescent or the young man seeking guidance for the future involved the individual, for whom this might be the only such action in a lifetime. The quest often meant spending the night or perhaps the days alone, perhaps in a sacred place or area, meditating, praying, perhaps fasting and going without sleep or even simply sleeping in a holy place in hopes of a dream. Having obtained guidance, perhaps a revelation from a totem animal, the individual resumed normal life or took his place as a man in society. The individualism here is not the modern narcissism without regard for society. Hieb notes that "religion reinforced the solidarity of society by giving expression to its principles and incorporating its units and relationships within the accepted view of the world."[22]

As in African traditions and Confucianism, the next world is largely taken for granted. The focus is this worldly with the deity(ies) immanent rather than transcendent. The "kingdom of God" is here on earth. The spirits of the departed are all around, as in Shinto. Life is a whole, including the dead and the living. An extension and variation of this among the South American Inca Indians was a preoccupation with life after death and a deeply rooted ancestral cult, centered in the present. The good go to heaven and the evil go to the cold underground.[23]

The impact of the Europeans was largely destructive. In the area of the United States and Canada, an estimated Indian population of 20 million was reduced to one million through murder, war, smallpox, venereal disease, and alcohol. Estimates vary today but there are roughly 750,000 in the United States and 250,000 in Canada. The religion suffered accordingly. As in Africa, some responses were through prophets and creative "new religions." Handsome Lake (1735–1815) was a Seneca prophet who founded the Long House Religion of the Iroquois. He is buried on the Onondaga reservation south of Syracuse, New York. His half brother was Chief Cornplanter (c. 1740–1836), a Seneca allied with the British during the American Revolution. He signed the treaty of Fort Stanwix (1784) and lived on his own land grant on the Allegheny River in today's northwestern Pennsylvania. Lake was raised by Quakers. Later in life, he became an alcoholic. In 1798, while living with Cornplanter, he had a vision in which the Great Spirit called him to be a prophet to his people. One of the major features of his Long House Religion is no alcohol. Witchcraft was banned while traditional rituals were reinstated. Hieb suggests Lake helped make farming socially acceptable to the hunter-warrior Senecas, defeated in war and reduced to reservations. Lake also focused on the nuclear family in a context of maternal lineage. The Code of Handsome Lake also forbids theft, quarrelsomeness, gossip, wife-beating, adultery, abortion and jealousy. It says husbands and wives are to love each other, treat children with kindness, and be reverent to the Great Spirit. "Within a few years . . . a group of sober, devout, orderly, and technologically up-to-date farming communities replaced what Wallace vividly describes as 'demoralized slums in the wilderness'."[24]

The Ghost Dance was started by a Paiute named Wovoko (c. 1858–1932), also known as Jack Wilson. His father was a mystic. He worked for a Christian family and was influenced by the Shaker movement of the time. There was an eclipse of the sun in 1870. He had a vision that all whites would disappear, all Indians — dead and alive — would be reunited, the land would be free of death and disease, and the land would be returned to the Indians. Wovoko himself was a pacifist but as the movement spread, it took on warlike overtones. It was a central feature among the Sioux before the Wounded Knee massacre in 1890 in which American soldiers murdered

200 men, women and children. The Sioux were wearing ghost shirts which they thought were bulletproof. The dance itself was a five-day festival with hypnotic trances and shaking.[25]

The Native American Church began in 1890 among the Kiowa and spread. The hallucenogin peyote is part of its ritual. The movement was incorporated in 1918, banned by the Navajo in 1940 but accepted in 1967. Today, estimated membership from this tribe is 33–80 percent. A long period of prohibition by the government was finally followed by toleration. This tradition has also been seen as a new religion that helped people through the crisis of modernity.[26]

There is something of a revival of traditional Indian religion today though it is not clear if it is a fad, the last bit of spark before the fire goes out, a trumped-up movement to help the court battles to regain Indian lands, or a genuine revival of faith. Some festivals may be tourist attractions while others are genuine expressions of Indian tradition. They can, of course, be both. Indians are cooperating across ancient tribal lines more than ever today though old rivalries remain in some instances. Both cooperation and rivalry involve the religious traditions. While speaking of North American Indians, J.W.E. Newberry claims that primal religions are reviving in many parts of the world. The superior attitude of European civilization has been discredited. Disregard for the earth, for community, for spirituality, have brought the whole human enterprise into jeopardy. The renewal is laying a foundation of hope for a new beginning on the earth.[27]

War and Peace

Vine Deloria, Jr., tells how an Indian chief once refused to allow missionaries on his tribal lands. When asked why, he answered that the missionaries teach people to argue about God. His people were at peace with God. Their religion helped them remain at peace rather than at war. Seneca medicine woman Twylah Nitsch claims there were no Indian wars over religion. Ruth Benedict quotes the Indian saying, "In the old days, there were no fights about hunting grounds or fishing territories. There was no law then, so everybody did what was right."[28]

However, there was a great deal of war. The indexes of the *Smithsonian Handbook* have numerous citations for warfare but none for peace. The Indians of the past are best known as warriors on the warpath. One can argue this is filtered through the eyes and minds of bigoted whites who may have thought the best Indian was a dead one. Brandon notes that "in the untouched [by whites] Indian world, even among peoples of dreaded warlike reputation, there was a great deal more peace than war." When the Indians did fight, there were seldom the massive slaughters and conquests of entire areas, as in the European tradition. Still, one cannot deny that at least according to present evidence, the gods were called on for help in war as well as for peace. In the War of 1812 between the United States and England, the U.S. tried to recruit soldiers from among the Indians. Handsome Lake opposed this and earned the title "The Peace Prophet." However, Chief Tecumseh's brother, the Shawnee prophet Tenskwataya, was known as "The War Prophet" and some have argued that Lake's peaceful concerns came from his Quaker background. While Wovoko was himself a pacifist, his movement became militant. Benedict contrasts the Plains Indians where war was a game and a man was not a man unless he was skilled in it, while among the Pueblo, conflict is opposed and peace is prized. She notes that among the Eskimo, the Mission Indians of California and others, war as known in European culture is beyond understanding.[29]

A similar situation can be found in other traditional religions. In Korea, the Ch'ondogyo movement was in the forefront of the fight for Korean independence from Japan, as in 1919, and in more recent years in North Korea from the Communists. In Africa, some of the new religions, such as the prophet Kinjikitile, became foci for rebellions against colonial regimes. Today they would be called terrorists or freedom fighters. Writing on "War and Peace in Africa," Jan Knappert found abundant evidence of the former, but little of the latter. Peace was imposed by the strong through conquest. The weak sued for peace if they had the chance before being destroyed. The shamans of Siberia were not infrequently the leaders of tribes and armed warriors, sometimes against each other. The Tibetans were a conquering force feared by surrounding peoples. While the Dalai Lama is noted for his efforts at peace, it was an armed revolt and the Chinese reprisals that led to his flight from Tibet. Shintoists claim they never fought any holy wars, but observers note that Shinto blessed all of Japan's wars and made them holy.

Where there was war, there was also peace. The American Indians are noted not only for the warpath, but also for the peace pipe. Joseph E. Brown notes there was a threefold peace. The most important was within the souls of people when they realized their relationship, their oneness with the universe and all its powers, and when they realized that Wakan-Tanka dwells at the center of the universe. This center is everywhere and it is within each of us. This is the real peace — the others are but reflections. The others are peace between two individuals and peace between two nations. The concept is reminiscent of Confucianism's peace in the individual, the family, the nation, the world.[30]

When Europeans first arrived, they were received by the Indians in friendship in both North and South America. It was only after the rapes, murders, robberies, enslavement, tortures, and destruction began that the Indians retaliated. A notable exception to Christian debauchery were the French. For economic reasons (maintaining the fur trade), French relationships with Canadian and other Indians remained more peaceful. There were also notable exceptions, such as William Penn, though it is still not clear the Indians understood what he meant by "buying" their land.

While African tradition contains more war than peace, there are exceptions there also. Parrinder notes that while Shaka of the Zulu (born 1787) conquered an area larger than Europe, the neighboring Swazi kings were peaceful. Noss observes that the BaVenda of southern Africa are not inclined to be warlike as are the other Bantu peoples. Ferguson notes that war is part of life and like all of life, is under the gods. Not infrequently, there is a special god or goddess of war in a given society. However, there are also deities of peace. He also notes that among a number of African tribes such as the Embu, Shona and Nyanja, war is a national calamity sent by God in punishment or retribution for some offense. He adds the studies of Margaret Mead in New Guinea where she found the Mundugumor organized for ferocious aggression but the Arapesh disapproving of aggression. The latter group is "a rare example of a tribal society religiously organized for peace. Normally tribal religion embraces peace and war alike as facts of life."[31]

Traditional religion held other elements of peace, however, that are notable in the present age. One dimension is the personal, inner peace sought by the shaman who resisted the call of the spirits. This was also a part of the healing process in time of illness. In interpersonal relationships, the traditional religion served as a kind of social glue which held people together in social solidarity. It also provided, through rituals and beliefs, a social lubricant which helped people get along. In some instances, a mutual faith brought tribes of people together, as among the Iroquois Indians in today's New York and Canada or among the new religions of Handsome Lake, Wovoko and the Native American Church. The new religions of Africa are now serving a similar purpose across the ancient tribal divisions.

The concern for international or global peace probably does not apply to traditional religions in the past. For the most part, they were local in character. Among nonliterate or untraveled peoples, there was probably no knowledge that a globe even existed. The cosmology is frequently a flat earth with the sky above and the underworld beneath, as in pre–Columbian Europe. There was no international view for most human beings prior to the rise of the mass circulation newspaper, radio and television – the formation of the Global Village. Parrinder, speaking of Africa, noted that traditional religion had a vague and general world view but its obligations were largely local and tribal.[32]

Still, there remains a contribution for traditional religion to world peace. Selected groups such as the Pueblo Indians of the American Southwest or the Eskimo might teach the modern world ways of peace. Just as modern Shinto groups have taken world peace as part of their mission, other traditional faiths are developing a larger world view. The primary contribution, however, remains as with Shinto and Taoism, a concern for harmony with nature and between the physical and spiritual worlds, that may be more important than solving the threat of a nuclear holocaust. The natural world must be cared for rather than raped and exploited, if there is to be any world tomorrow. The materialistic West has largely forgotten the spiritual dimension of life but its importance for human wholeness remains. In traditional terms, the will of God remains for people to live in peace with one another.

Gill claims the idea of the Indians living in harmony with nature is a mistaken view which amplifies a highly romantic picture of people living in harmony and peace. Their lives were filled with hardship, disease, death, discomfort and difficulties. Newberry, however, claims that harmony is the overriding virtue for the Indians — we find contentment by coming to terms rather than in conflict. Give and take, unity in diversity, a sense of wholeness with the universe — these are basic to the goal of harmony and balance in life, seen by primal peoples as the foundation of all health, peace and well-being.[33]

Notes

Introduction

1. Quoted by Jan Knappert, personal communication.
2. Chand, "Jainism," pp. 114–123, and Husain, "Preface," pp. vii–x, in *World Religions and World Peace*, ed. Homer A. Jack; Boston: Beacon, 1968.
3. Husain, op. cit., p. viii.
4. Chand, op. cit., p. 115. Husain, op. cit., p. x.
5. Swearer, "Nonviolence in Theravada Buddhism, Past and Present," *Buddhist Peace Fellowship Newsletter*, **8**, no. 3 (Summer 86), 9. Husain, op. cit., pp. viii–ix.

Chapter I

1. This view sees Christianity as another division of the religion. The Pharisees and Christians survived. Other groups such as the Sadducees (the priestly group) and the ascetic Essenes were destroyed by the Roman conquest. Of the 14 million Jews, 5,728,000 are in the United States and 3,374,000 are in Israel according to the 1984 *American Jewish Year Book* as reported in *The Christian Century* **101**, no. 16 (May 9, 1984). The *Century* is cited hereafter as CC. The report claims "zero population growth." David B. Barrett reports 17 million Jews in 1980. He expects 20 million in 2000, with 7,100,000 in the U.S. *The World Christian Encyclopedia;* NY: Oxford, 1982. Richard N. Ostling and Alistair Matheson, "Counting Every Soul on Earth," *Time* (May 3, 1982), 66–67.

Synagogue, Greek for meeting place, is a translation of the Hebrew Bet Kakeneset. Its origins are obscure but are usually assigned to the Exile (587–516 B.C.E.) when the Temple was destroyed, or to the Diaspora (outside of Palestine) when Jews could meet only in homes or houses of prayer. Jacob A. Agus, "Judaism," pp. 139–157, in *Historical Atlas of the Religions of the World*, ed. Isma'il Ragi al Faruqi and David E. Sopher; NY: Macmillan, 1974. R. Pierce Beaver, et al., eds., *Eerdmans' Handbook to the World's Religions;* Grand Rapids, MI: Eerdmans, 1982. Isidore Epstein, *Judaism;* Baltimore: Penguin, 1970. William H. Harris and Judith S. Levey, eds., *The New Columbia Encyclopedia*, NY: Columbia, 1975, pp. 2125, 2673, 1415. Cited hereafter as NCE. Arthur Hertzberg, *Judaism;* NY: Braziller, 1962. Young Oon Kim, *World Religions*, vol. 1: *Living Religions of the Middle East*, 2nd ed.; NY: Golden Gate, 1982. Myrtle Langley, *Religions;* Elgin, IL: Cook, 1981. Max Margolis and Alexander Marx, *History of the Jewish People;* NY: Meridian, 1958 (original, 1927). Herbert G. May and Bruce M. Metzger, eds., *The Oxford Annotated Bible with the Apocrypha;* NY: Oxford, 1965. Benjamin Mazar, et al., eds., *The World History of the Jewish People;* Tel Aviv: Masada, 1963–. David S. Noss and John B. Noss, *Man's Religions*, 7th ed.; NY: Macmillan, 1984, p. 395 [cited hereafter as Noss]. Abram L. Sachar, *A History of the Jews*, 5th ed.; NY: Knopf,

1967. Leo W. Schwarz, ed., *Great Ages and Ideas of the Jewish People*; NY: Modern Library, 1956. Ninian Smart, *The Long Search*; Boston: Little, Brown, 1977. Leo Trepp, *Eternal Faith, Eternal People*; Englewood Cliffs: Prentice-Hall, 1962.

2. Noss, op. cit., p. 379. Sachar, op. cit., pp. 78–90. Trepp, op. cit., pp. 33–37. Michael J. Cook, "Judaism, Early Rabbinic," pp. 499–505, and, "Judaism, Hellenistic," pp. 505–509, in *Interpreter's Dictionary of the Bible, Supplementary Volume*, ed. Keith Crim, et al.; Nashville: Abingdon, 1976. The Dictionary is cited hereafter as IDB, the Supplement as IDBSV. Alfred Haldar, "Hebrew," IDB 2 (1962), 552–553. Yehezkel Kaufmann, "The Biblical Age," pp. 3–92, in Schwartz, op. cit. Niels C. Nielsen, Jr., et al., *Religions of the World*; NY: St. Martin's, 1983, p. 397. J.A. Sanders, "Jew, Jews, Jewess," IDB 2:897–898. Burton H. Throckmorton, Jr., "Judaism," IDB 2:1005. The definition of "Jew" as one living in the land has been debated for a long time. It means that Jews in the Diaspora — the dispersion outside of ancient Eretz (land) Israel — are not Jews, or not real Jews, or not true Jews. The concept has reappeared in modern Israel among leaders who insist that all Jews return to Israel if they intend to be true or real Jews, implying that Diaspora Jews are not real Jews.

3. Dewey M. Beegle, *Moses, The Servant of Yahweh*; Ann Arbor: Pettengill, 1978. John Bright, *A History of Israel*, 3rd ed.; Philadelphia: Westminster, 1981. Roland de Vaux, *Ancient Israel*; NY: McGraw-Hill, 1961. Robert F. Johnson, "Moses," IDB 3:440–450. George E. Mendenhall, *Law and Covenant in the Ancient Near East*; Pittsburgh: Biblical Colloquium, 1955. Jacob M. Myers, "David," IDB 1:771–782, and, "Saul Son of Kish," IDB 4:228–233. Murray L. Newman, "Moses," IDBSV-604–605. Henry O. Thompson, "The Cosmic Covenant," pp. 320–365, in *The Global Congress of the World's Religions*, ed. Thompson; NY: GCWR, 1982. Gerhard von Rad, *Moses*; London: Lutterworth, 1960.

There is considerable debate over the dates of Moses, the Exodus, the later Conquest, and the earlier Patriarchs. Some deny any history and hence date, to any of this while those who agree there was a Moses and an exodus, put the Exodus as early as 1450 B.C.E., and as late as 1150 B.C.E. If the pharaoh of the Exodus was Ramses II, one can date the Exodus c. 1300 and the Conquest c. 1250. The Patriarchs, if they existed, are dated in the Middle Bronze Age between 2000–1500 B.C. R. Lansing Hicks, "Patriarchs," IDB 3:677–678. John Van Seters, "Patriarchs," IDBSV-645–648.

4. Bernhard W. Anderson, "God, Names of," IDB 2:407–417. Trepp, op. cit., pp. 8–10.

5. From time to time, someone suggests that man creates his God(s) in man's own image. Without debating here the accuracy of either statement, it should be noted that the biblical text is clearly the opposite — women and men were created in God's image.

6. Modern scholarship sometimes sees the two stories as part of two documents — the first story is the Priestly one from about 550 B.C.E., while the second, circa 950 B.C.E., is that of the J writer of Judah or the Yahwist. The theory adds two other documents, circa 850 B.C.E., the E or Elohist writer of Ephraim (an alternate name for the northern kingdom of Israel, 920–721 B.C.E.) and the D writer or Deuteronomist. The first three are interwoven in the tetrateuch, or the first four books of the Bible — Genesis, Exodus, Leviticus and Numbers. The Deuteronomist is largely found in the fifth book of Deuteronomy. Julius Wellhausen, *Prolegomena to the History of Ancient Israel*; Cleveland: World, 1965 (original, 1878). Henry O. Thompson, *Approaches to the Bible*; Syracuse: Center for Instructional Communication, 1967. Bernhard W. Anderson, *Understanding the Old Testament*, 4th

ed.; Englewood Cliffs: Prentice-Hall, 1986. Henk Jagersma, *A History of Israel in the Old Testament Period*; Philadelphia: Fortress, 1983.

7. All of this early tradition is heavily debated in modern scholarship. Opinions range from none of it as historical, to all of it as historical, to parts of it so. Instead of a conquest, one popular view suggests an infiltration of the tribes, especially into the largely unoccupied hill country of eastern Canaan. Roland de Vaux, *The Early History of Israel*; Philadelphia: Westminster, 1978. Norman K. Gottwald, *The Tribes of Yahweh*; Maryknoll, NY: Orbis, 1979. Yehezkel Kaufmann, *The Religion of Israel: From Its Beginnings to the Babylonian Exile*; NY: Schocken, 1972. George E. Mendenhall, *The Tenth Generation: The Origins of the Biblical Tradition*; Baltimore: Johns Hopkins, 1973. J. Maxwell Miller and John H. Hayes, *A History of Ancient Israel and Judah*; Philadelphia: Westminster, 1986. George W. Nickelsburg and Robert Kraft, *Early Judaism and Its Modern Interpreters*; Philadelphia: Fortress, 1985. M. Weippert, "Canaan, Conquest and Settlement," IDBSV-125-130.

8. Margolis & Marx, op. cit., pp. 114-215. Sachar, op. cit., pp. 98-111. Trepp, op. cit., pp. 25-57. Salo W. Baron and Joseph L. Balu, eds., *Judaism: Postbiblical and Talmudic Period*; NY: Liberal Arts, 1954. Henk Jagersma, *A History of Israel from Alexander the Great to Bar Kochba*; Philadelphia: Fortress, 1985. Jacob Neusner, *First Century Judaism in Crisis*; Nashville: Abingdon, 1975. James Parkes, *A History of the Jewish People*; Baltimore: Penguin, 1964. Frederick M. Schweitzer, *A History of the Jews Since the First Century A.D.*; NY: Macmillan, 1971.

9. Gaalyahu Cornfeld, ed., *Adam to Daniel*; NY: Macmillan, 1961, p. 381. Halakah sometimes refers to the unwritten law in contrast to the written Torah. Later the halakah was also written down. Torah as instruction may refer to all Jewish teaching, including the Talmud, or to Judaism itself, or its way of life. Trepp, op. cit., pp. 37-40. J.D. Bleich, *Contemporary Halakhic Problems*; NY: Ktav, 1977.

10. Recently, modern tools such as indexes and concordances have been made for the Talmud, easing the study of it somewhat. Margolis & Marx, op. cit., pp. 216-247, 518-524. NCE-2691, 2687, 93. Trepp, op. cit., pp. 37-40. Gerson D. Cohen, "The Talmudic Age," pp. 143-212, in Schwartz, op. cit. Baron & Blau, op. cit., pp. 101-208. Jacob Neusner, ed., *The Talmud of the Land of Israel*; Chicago: University of Chicago, 1985. Isadore Epstein, ed., *The Babylonian Talmud*, vols. 1-18; London: Soncino, 1935-1948. Adin Steinsaltz, *The Essential Talmud*; NY: Basic, 1976. Sachar, op. cit., pp. 143-154. He calls the Shulhan Arukh part of the degeneration of Judaism because it stifled religious thought and put Judaism in a straightjacket (pp. 232-233, 236-238). Trepp, op. cit., pp. 93-108.

11. Kim, op. cit., pp. 54-79. Margolis & Marx, op. cit., pp. 558-577. NCE-2388, 999. Sachar, op. cit., pp. 238-245. Gershom G. Scholem, *The Messianic Idea in Judaism and Other Essays on Jewish Spirituality*; NY: Schocken, 1971, and, *Sabbatai Sevi*; Princeton: Princeton University, 1975. Trepp, op. cit., pp. 246-247.

12. Antisemitism is pre-Christian in origins but Christianity has promoted it on a vast scale. Henry O. Thompson, "A Study in Antisemitism," pp. 73-133, in *Unity in Diversity*, ed. Thompson; NY: Rose of Sharon, 1984, with bibliography. Carl D. Evans, "The Church's False Witness Against Jews," CC 99, no. 16 (May 5, 1982), 530-533. Charlotte Klein, *Anti-Judaism in Christian Theology*; Philadelphia: Fortress, 1978. Leo Kuper, *Genocide: Its Political Use in the Twentieth Century*; New Haven: Yale, 1981. Samuel Sandmel, "Jews, NT Attitudes Toward," IDBSV-477-479.

13. Eerdmans', op. cit., pp. 272–274. Kim, op. cit., pp. 23–24. Margolis & Marx, op. cit., pp. 285–476. NCE-1664. Nielsen, op. cit., pp. 453–454. Noss, op. cit., pp. 402–404. Sachar, op. cit., pp. 168–231. Trepp, op. cit., pp. 272–280. Jacob R. Marcus, ed., *The Jew and the Medieval World: A Source Book*; NY: Atheneum, 1977. Robert M. Seltzer, *Jewish People, Jewish Thought*; NY: Macmillan, 1980. Isadore Twersky, *Introduction to the Code of Maimonides (Mishneh Torah)*; New Haven: Yale, 1980. Judaism is not usually thought of as a creedal religion but the Shema of Deuteronomy 6:4–9 comes close. "Hear, O Israel: The Lord our God, the Lord is one. Love the Lord your God with all your heart and with all your soul and with all your strength. . . ."

14. Gerald Krefetz, *Jews and Money: The Myths and the Reality*; New Haven: Ticknor and Fields, 1982.

15. Jakob J. Petuchowski, "Judaism Today," pp. 3–58, in *Religion in the Middle East*, ed. A.J. Arberry; Cambridge: University Press, 1969. Baron & Blau, op. cit., pp. 67–97. Noss, op. cit., pp. 389–394. Trepp, op. cit., pp. 57–61. Otto Betz, "Dead Sea Scrolls," IDB 1:790–802. John Bowman, *Samaritan Documents*; Pittsburgh: Pickwick, 1977, and, *The Samaritan Problem: Studies in the Relationships of Samaritans, Judaism and Early Christianity*; Pittsburgh: Pickwick, 1975. R.J. Coggins, *Samaritans and Jews*; Atlanta: Knox, 1975. Frank M. Cross, Jr., *The Ancient Library of Qumran*; Garden City: Doubleday, 1958. Louis Finkelstein, *Pharisaism in the Making*; NY: Ktav, 1972. Allen H. Jones, *Essenes: The Elect of Israel and the Priests of Artemis*; Washington: University Press of America, 1985. James D. Purvis, *The Samaritan Pentateuch and the Origin of the Samaritan Sect*; Cambridge: Harvard, 1968. Ellis Rifkin, *A Hidden Revolution: The Pharisees' Search for the Kingdom Within*; Nashville: Abingdon, 1978. Morton Smith, *Palestinian Parties and Politics That Shaped the Old Testament*; NY: Columbia, 1971. John F. Thomson, *The Samaritans*; NY: Gordon, 1976.

16. Margolis & Marx, op. cit., pp. 258–272. Noss, op. cit., p. 401. Nielsen, op. cit., pp. 449–451. Sachar, op. cit., pp. 155–167. Trepp, op. cit., pp. 106, 265–268. Abraham S. Halkin, "The Judeo-Islamic Age," pp. 215–263, in Schwartz, op. cit. Leon Nemoy, *Karaite Anthology*; New Haven: Yale, 1969 (original 1952).

17. Margolis & Marx, op. cit., pp. 430–439, 578–588. NCE-412. Petuchowski, op. cit., p. 3. Sachar, op. cit., pp. 233–236, calls the Cabala the degeneration of Judaism. He gives Baal Shem Tob high marks but despises the Hasidic movement (pp. 263–266) even though it helped destroy the tyranny of the Talmud. Trepp, op. cit., pp. 250–259. Louis Jacobs, *Hasidic Thought*; NY: Behrman, 1976. G.S. Scholem, *Kabbalah*; NY: Quadrangle, 1974, and, *Major Trends in Jewish Mysticism*; NY: Schocken, 1973 (original 1941), and, *Zohar*; NY: Schocken, 1974 (original 1949). Elie Wiesel, *Souls on Fire: Portraits and Legends of Hasidic Masters*: NY: Random House, 1972. Eerdmans', op. cit., p. 300.

18. Margolis & Marx, op. cit., pp. 659–664, 675–682. Nielsen, op. cit., pp. 462–467. Petuchowski, op. cit., pp. 10–22, 42–46. Sachar, op. cit., 267–308, 323–337. Trepp, op. cit., pp. 302–315. Salo W. Baron, "The Modern Age," pp. 315–484, in Schwartz, op. cit. Nathan Glazer, *American Judaism*; Chicago: University of Chicago, 1972. Will Herberg, *Protestant, Catholic, Jew*; Garden City: Doubleday, 1955, pp. 186–226. Gunther W. Plaut, *The Growth of Reform Judaism*; NY: World Union for Progressive Judaism, 1965.

19. Margolis & Marx, op. cit., pp. 719–724. Nielsen, op. cit., pp. 463–468. Petuchowski, op. cit., pp. 22–28, 49–51. Trepp, op. cit., pp. 387–413. Moshe Davis, *The Emergence of Conservative Judaism*; Philadelphia: Jewish Publication Society, 1963. Agus, op. cit., pp. 150–156.

20. Baron, pp. 378–379, op. cit. Petuchowski, op. cit., pp. 51–52. Trepp, op.

cit., pp. 397–398, 413–414. Mordecai M. Kaplan, *Judaism as a Civilization: Toward a Reconstruction of American-Jewish Life;* NY: Reconstructionist Press, 1957, and, *Questions Jews Ask;* ibid., 1972. Brad Rosenstein, "Radical Rabbis," *City Paper* 121 (December 5–12, 1986), 1, 6–7, 12–13.

21. Baron, op. cit., pp. 420–454. Kim, op. cit., p. 88. Margolis & Marx, op. cit., pp. 702–711. NCE-1237, 3046. Petuchowski, op. cit., pp. 28–31. Sachar, op. cit., pp. 338–371, 405–435. Trepp, op. cit., pp. 321–334. Alex Bein, *Theodore Herzl;* NY: Atheneum, 1970 (original 1940). Norman Bentwich, "Judaism in Israel," pp. 59–112, in Arberry, op. cit. Andrew Handler, *Dori: The Life and Times of Theodor Herzl in Budapest (1860–1878);* University, AL: University of Alabama, 1983. Reconstruction Rabbinical College Catalogue, 1983–1985; Philadelphia: RRC, 1983. Desmond Stewart, *Theodor Herzl;* Garden City, NY: Doubleday, 1974.

22. Sachar, op. cit., pp. 444–470. NCE-1375-1377. Larry Collins and Dominique Lapierre, *O Jerusalem;* NY: Pocket Books, 1973. Conor C. O'Brien, *The Siege: The Saga of Israel and Zionism;* NY: S & S, 1985.

23. Nielsen, op. cit., pp. 464–471. Bentwich, op. cit., pp. 72–3, 92, 98, reports the marranos and some Jews from India have seen Israel and gone back home. Within the country, the Naturay Karta claim the nation is illegal idolatry against the laws of God. Historically one can note the 1911 statement by Felix Goldman, "If Zionism frankly admits that in the sense of nationalism one can be a good Jew and at the same time an atheist who is contemptuous of religion, then in the same moment Zionism would be condemned to death in the eyes of all thinking Jews. The spread of Zionism under such conditions would mean death for Judaism." Quoted by Louis Jacobs, *A Jewish Theology;* NY: Behrman House, 1973, p. 277. More recently, Richard L. Rubenstein has said that many Israelis believe as little in the God of the Bible as Greeks today believe in the gods of Homer. Shlomo Deshen claims all Israeli Judaism is nontraditional. It is a recent development out of traditional Judaism. Quantitative measurements are superficial without the meaning and nature of patterns of religiosity. "Israel: Searching for Identity," pp. 85–118, in *Religions and Societies: Asia and the Middle East,* ed. Carlo Caldarola; NY: Mouton, 1982.

S. Zalman Abramov, *Perpetual Dilemma: Jewish Religion in the Jewish State;* NY: Union of American Hebrew Congregations, 1979. Balfour Brickner, "American Jews, Israel and Public Policy," *Worldview* 15, no. 1 (January 1972), 4–8. Kenneth A. Briggs, "American Jews Split Along Orthodox and Reform Lines," *The New York Times* (August 19, 1984), 20E. Kendig B. Cully, "Interview with Eugene B. Borowitz, Theologian of Judaism," *The Review of Books and Religion* 1, no. 8 (May 1983), 6. James S. Diamond, "Making Sense Out of Israel," *CC* XCVII, no. 39 (December 3, 1980), 1205–1206. Irving L. Horowitz, "Israel Developing," *Worldview* 15, no. 9 (September 1972), 28–31, notes that Israel is a nation of Israelis, not Jews. Don Peretz, "Jewish Particularism and Jewish Universalism," *Occasional Papers: Center for Peace and Conflict Studies* II (Fall 81), 19–21, quotes Zionist Ben Gurion on the Jewish state which does not rob the poor or oppress people or lift up swords against others or study war. Peretz also quotes Zionist and Zionist critic Martin Buber (1878–1965) as saying a person has eyes; nationalism is like having diseased eyes. Peter R. Powell, Jr., "Greater Morality," *CC* 101, no. 16 (May 9, 1984), 500. Jeff Salamon, "Zionist Corrections," *Daily Pennsylvanian* (March 27, 1986), 6. Howard Singer, "On Criticizing Israel," *CC* 101, no. 12 (April 11, 1984), 363–365. Margot Slade and Wayne Biddle, "Look Back in Anger," *The New York Times* (January 9, 1983), 8E.

Christian attitudes toward Israel and Zionism are intriguing. Some oppose and are called antisemites. Thompson, *A Study*, op. cit. Some approve and support. Among these are some who see the injustices done to the Jews and think now it is time to go the other way. One could argue this would mean inviting Jews to come to live in the land where the Christians are. Some conservative and fundamentalist Christians see the establishment of the state of Israel as the sign of the end times when Christ will come again. When that happens, all Jews will either convert to Christianity or be murdered, and the Holocaust will be successful. Interestingly, many Jews welcome such Christian support. Some do not see the Holocaust consequences. Some do not care because it means political and financial support for the state now. Caroline T. Marshall, "Some Christian Responses to Jewish and Palestinian Nationalism," *Fides et historia* XVII, no. 2 (Spring-Summer 1985), 53–68. She notes that money for Israel's future comes from the United States. James M. Wall, "Israelis Accept Fundamentalist Allies," CC 103, no. 34 (November 12, 1986), 995–996.

24. Brickner, "Christian Missionaries and a Jewish Response," *Worldview* 21, no. 5 (May 1978), 37–41. Allen S. Maller, "Jews, Cults and Apostates," *Judaism* 30, no. 3 (Summer 1981), 306–311. David Beard, "Argentina's Jewish population dwindling but thriving," *The Philadelphia Inquirer* (December 22, 1985), 8-F. The 1984 *American Jewish Year Book*, op. cit., lists the Argentina Jewish population as 233,000, a decrease of 9000 because of increased emigration. Briggs, op. cit., notes that 50 percent of American Jews marry non-Jews. Some non-Jewish spouses were part of the 10,000–12,000 converts to Judaism in 1983.

25. Bentwich, op. cit., pp. 88–89. Briggs, op. cit., quotes Orthodox rabbi Irving Greenberg as saying "Jews will be engaged in a religious civil war within a generation" unless action for unity is started soon. Eerdmans', op. cit., p. 292. Horowitz, op. cit., p. 29, notes that Jews may outlast the political state. Kim, op. cit., p. 93. Nielsen, op. cit., p. 462. Mark A. Bernheim, "Jewish Identity," *Judaism* 30, no. 3 (Summer 1981), 322–334. Wolf Leslau, *Falasha Anthology*; New Haven: Yale, 1951.

26. Briggs, op. cit. Nielsen, op. cit., pp. 471, 474. Bentwich, op. cit., pp. 87, 102. "Jewish Theological Seminary Admits Women in Historical Move," *The Philadelphia Prism* (October-November 1984), 1. Michael D. Schaffer, "Decision to let women become rabbis is wrenching change for Jewish law," *The Philadelphia Inquirer* (November 6, 1983), 34. Daniel Winkel, "Rabbis united in marriage as well as in religious life," *The Philadelphia Inquirer* (January 8, 1984), 1-M, shares the story of Rabbi Janet Marder and her husband with some of the pros and cons of being a woman rabbi. Thomas L. Friedman, "Order ignites Israeli debate on converts," *Detroit Free Press* (June 30, 1986), 4A, describes the attempt by the Interior Ministry to stamp "convert" on passports to make sure Orthodox rabbis could check on them. Friedman makes a distinction between the legal system which recognizes all Jews and the rabbinical system which does not recognize Reform and Conservative Judaism or "doubtful" converts—those converted by Reform or Conservative.

27. Note that during the period of the judges and the monarchies, much of the fighting was internecine. Hebrews ferociously butchered other Hebrews as well as non-Hebrews, in conquering Canaan and territory specifically forbidden to them by God—wars of greed and imperialistic expansion. James A. Aho, *Religious Mythology and the Art of War*; Westport, CT: Greenwood, 1981, pp. 165–181. Rudolf Smend, *Yahweh War and Tribal Confederation*; Nashville: Abingdon, 1970, pp. 36–42. For a general discussion of war and the military, see Roland de Vaux, *Ancient Israel*, op. cit., pp. 213–267. George L. Carey, "Biblical-Theological Perspectives on War and Peace," *The Evangelical Quarterly* LVII, no. 2 (April

1985), 163-178. Peter C. Craigie, *The Problem of War in the Old Testament;* Grand Rapids, MI: Eerdmans, 1978. Paul Hanson, "War and Peace in the Hebrew Bible," *Interpretation* 38 (1984), 341-362. Vernard Eller, *War and Peace from Genesis to Revelation;* Scottsdale, PA: Herald, 1981. F. Derek Kidner, "Old Testament Perspectives on War," *The Evangelical Quarterly* LVII, no 2 (April 1985), 99-113. Marvin E. Tate, "War and Peacemaking in the Old Testament," *Review and Expositor* LXXIX, no. 4 (Fall 1982), 587-596. G. Ernest Wright, "The Conquest Theme in the Bible," pp. 509-518, in *A Light Unto My Path,* ed. Howard Bream, et al.; Philadelphia: Temple University, 1974.

28. Aho, op. cit., pp. 169-170. Carey, op. cit., pp. 164-165. Hanson, op. cit., 349-362, notes the continuation of the bloody slaughter of humanity in the apocalyptic tradition, e.g., Isaiah 24-27. Kidner, op. cit., pp. 102-104 notes that "Holy War" is not a biblical phrase. So too, Tate, op. cit., p. 596, who adds that "Yahweh war" or "war of Yahweh" is more accurate (Numbers 21:14; I Samuel 18:17, 25:28). Thompson, op. cit., pp. 95-96. de Vaux, *Ancient Israel,* op. cit., pp. 258-267. Frank M. Cross, *Canaanite Myth and Hebrew Epic;* Cambridge: Harvard, 1973, pp. 91-111. "Editorial," *Interpretation* XXXVIII, no. 4 (October 1984), 339-340. Norman K. Gottwald, "War, Holy," IDBSV-942-944. Marvin H. Pope, "Devoted," IDB 1:838-839. Millard C. Lind, *Yahweh Is a Warrior: The Theology of Warfare in Ancient Israel;* Scottsdale, PA: Herald, 1980. Patrick D. Miller, Jr., *The Divine Warrior in Early Israel;* Cambridge: Harvard, 1973. Lawrence E. Toombs, "War, Ideas of," *Interpreter's Dictionary of the Bible* 4 (1962), 796-801. Gerhard von Rad, *Der Heilige Krieg im alten Israel;* Zurich: Zwingli, 1951. In the Middle Ages, the ban was interpreted as excommunication. Jews excommunicated each other so often, the process lost its effectiveness. Joseph Hausner, "Ban and Excommunication: The Meaning, Usage and Purpose of Herem," unpublished manuscript.

29. Asher Bloc, "The Jewish Tradition of Peace," *Fellowship* (February 1953), reprint. Abraham Cronbach, "Peace," *The Universal Jewish Encyclopedia;* NY: Ktav, 1969, 8:418-421. Bloch and Cronbach cite dozens of examples of the call for peace in the Bible, Talmud and modern times. John Ferguson, *War and Peace in the World's Religions;* NY: Oxford, 1978, pp. 81-83. D.M. Dakin, *Peace and Brotherhood in the Old Testament;* NY: Bannisdale, 1956. Adolf Guttmacher, "Peace," *The Jewish Encyclopedia;* NY: Ktav, n.d., 9:565-566. Louis Jacobs, "Peace," *Encyclopedia Judaica;* Jerusalem: Kater, 1971, 13:columns 194-200. Steven S. Schwarzschild, "Shalom," *Occasional Papers: Center for Peace and Conflict Studies* II (Fall 1981), 23-34, has an extensive bibliography on Judaism and peace, and specifically on pacifism. Marc H. Tannenbaum, *Religious Values in an Age of Violence;* Milwaukee: Marquette University, 1976.

30. Schwarzschild, op. cit., p. 30. Maurice N. Eisendrath, "Judaism," pp. 61-75, in *World Religions and World Peace,* ed. Homer A. Jack; Boston: Beacon, 1968. For a modern example of this spiritualization, see Bruce Birch, "Old Testament Foundations for Peacemaking in the Nuclear Era," CC 102, no. 38 (December 4, 1985), 1115-1119. Reuven Kimelman, "Non-Violence in the Talmud," pp. 441-463, in *The Religious Situation: 1969;* Boston: Beacon, 1969.

31. Birch, op. cit., pp. 1115-1116. Eisendrath, op. cit., p. 74. Hanson, op. cit., pp. 345-362, notes that through his suffering servant, Israel, God extends his shalom to the whole world. Herman N. Cohen, *Religion of Reason out of the Sources of Judaism;* NY: Ungar, 1972, p. 459, notes that "If one were to describe in one word the essence of the Jewish mentality, then the word would have to be 'peace'." Quoted by Schwarzschild, op. cit., who notes the gap between preaching and practice, a gap that exudes the odor of hypocrisy. He also quotes Nietzsche's

doctrine that people seek peace when they are weak and justify aggression when they are strong. Schwarzschild, a Jewish pacifist, prefers to avoid the greeting "Shalom." R.G. Hirsch, *Thy Most Precious Gift: Peace in Jewish Tradition;* NY: Union of American Hebrew Congregations, 1974. W. Sibley Towner, "Tribulation and Peace: The Fate of Shalom in Jewish Apocalyptic," *Horizons in Biblical Theology* 67 (1984), 18.

32. George W. Buchanan, *Revelation and Redemption: Jewish Documents of Deliverance from the Fall of Jerusalem to the Death of Nahmanides;* Dillsboro, NC: Western North Carolina Press, 1978. Moses Nahmanides (1135–1270) was born in Cordova and died in Jerusalem.

33. Kimelman, op. cit., shows how the Palestinian Talmudists promoted Gandhian-style nonviolence. It was better to suffer than to be violent, even for self-defense. Neilsen, op. cit., p. 445. Heszel Klepfisz, "Judaism," pp. 235–236, in *Religion in the Struggle for World Community,* ed. Homer A. Jack; NY: World Conference on Religion and Peace, 1980. Balfour Brickner and W. Gunther W. Plaut, "Jewish Prayers," pp. 217–221, in *Religion for Peace,* ed. Homer A. Jack; New Delhi: Gandhi Peace Foundation, 1973. Hirsch, op. cit.

34. Eisendrath, op. cit., pp. 63, 68. Ferguson, op. cit., pp. 90–91. Schwarzschild, op. cit., pp. 27–30. One is reminded of the claim that Shinto never fought a holy war — it just declared all of Japan's wars as holy. Any war could be designated as one to save Israel or as against an oppressor.

35. Kahane, *The Story of the Jewish Defense League;* Radnor, PA: Chilton, 1975. Steve Marshall and Ken Myers, "Threat to citizenship fails to cool Kahane," *USA Today* (January 10, 1986), 2A. Cronbach, op. cit., pp. 420–421, as noted earlier, cites dozens of examples of Jewish support for peace. Peretz, op. cit., p. 21. The Jewish Peace Fellowship, Box 271, Nyack, NY 10960. Brochure, "Jewish Peace Fellowship." Denise S. Akey, et al., eds., *Encyclopedia of Associations,* 19th ed.; Detroit: Gale, 1985. "The Shalom Network Newsletter" (1980–), P.O. Box 3256, Berkeley, CA 94703. "Peace Now: Peace Is Greater Than Greater Israel" (October 1979) describes activities of the Peace Now Movement, P.O.B. 20422, Jerusalem, Israel. Brochure, Os veShalom, P.O. Box 4433, Jerusalem 91043, Israel [New Israel Fund, 111 W. 40th St., Suite 2600, NY, NY 10018]. Larry Cohler, "Israeli religious peace group: Sanctity of life more important than territories," *Long Island Jewish World* (February 8–14, 1985), reprint. Larry Yudelson, "Raising a religious voice for compromise on West Bank," *Jewish World* May 2–8, 1986), 12. Scharzschild, op. cit., pp. 25–26. Practically speaking, war has had more support than peace. See Steven S. Schwarzschild, "The Religious Demand for Peace," *Judaism* 15, no. 4 (Fall 1966), 412–418.

36. Bentwich, op. cit., pp. 98, 103. Horowtiz, op. cit., p. 28, Rabin as quoted by Eisendrath, op. cit., p. 72. Marshall, op. cit.

37. The Editors, "Jerusalem, City of Universal Peace," *Sidic* IV, no. 2 (1971), 2–3 [reprint]. F. Delpech, "Towards a Better Approach to the Problem of the Holy Places," ibid., pp. 3–22. Abdulaziz Y. Saqqaf, ed., *The Middle East City;* NY: Paragon, 1986.

Chapter II

1. The Christian Gospels of Matthew and Luke record that Jesus' mother, Mary, was a virgin and became pregnant by the Holy Spirit (Matthew 2:18; Luke 1:35). In Roman Catholic Christianity, official doctrine is that Mary remained a virgin for life. The four brothers — James, Joses, Judas, Simon — and the sisters of

Mark 6:3 are assigned to Joseph. Some Christians understand them to be Mary's children. Biblical literalists and conservative Christians insist on the virgin birth of Jesus as an article of faith while others see it as less important or a pious fiction. Some modern interpreters note that on occasion, a virgin birth was ascribed to important persons, such as emperors, in the Roman Empire at the time. [Thomas Boslooper notes this is a mistaken interpretation — important persons were seen as a child of a god or goddess (person communication).] Others suggest this virgin birth is a symbolic way of claiming the fulfillment of the prediction in Isaiah 7:14, "a virgin shall conceive and bear a son, and his name shall be called Emmanuel." "Virgin" is translated "young woman" in other contexts of the Hebrew Bible, and some modern versions of the Bible translate "young woman" in Isaiah 7:14. Matthew traces the geneology of Jesus through Joseph.

Instead of Emmanuel, Joseph was told in a dream to call the baby Joshua (Yahweh is salvation), for he (God or Joshua) shall save his people from their sins (Matthew 2:21). The name was very common at the time. Herbert G. May and Bruce M. Metzger, eds., *The Oxford Annotated Bible with Apocrypha*; NY: Oxford, 1965. This is the Revised Standard Version (RSV) of the Bible. George A. Buttrick, et al., eds., *Interpreter's Dictionary of the Bible*; Nashville: Abingdon, 1962 (cited hereafter as IDB) and Keith Crim, et al., eds., *Supplementary Volume*, 1976 (cited as IDBSV). R. Pierce Beaver, et al., eds., *Eerdmans' Handbook to the World's Religions*; Grand Rapids, MI: Eerdmans', 1982, pp. 335–388. Raymond E. Brown, "Virgin Birth," IDBSV-940–941. Frederick C. Grant, "Jesus Christ," IDB 2:869–896. William H. Harris and Judith S. Levey, eds., *The New Columbia Encyclopedia*; NY: Columbia, 1975, pp. 1412–1413. Cited hereafter as NCE. Van A. Harvey, *A Handbook of Theological Terms*; NY: Macmillan, 1964. Myrtle Langley, *Religions*; Elgin, IL: Cook, pp. 46–51. Kenneth Scott Latourette, *A History of Christianity*; NY: Harper & Row, 1953, pp. 33–62. Cited hereafter as LHC. Arthur C. McGiffert, *A History of Christian Thought*, vols. I–II; NY: Scribner's, 1947 (original 1932). D. Moody, "Virgin Birth," IDB 4:789–791. Niels C. Nielsen, Jr., et al., eds., *Religions of the World*; NY: St. Martin's, 1983. John B. Noss and David S. Noss, *Man's Religions*, 7th ed.; NY: Macmillan, 1984, pp. 412–431.

2. The birth took place in Bethlehem according to Luke 2, because of a census in which people were supposed to enroll in their own city. Joseph went to Bethlehem, since he was a descendant of David (king, c. 1000–960 B.C.), and Bethlehem was the "city of David." This too has been called by some a tradition developed to fulfill a prophecy, Micah 5:2, that a ruler from Israel would come from Bethlehem. Gus W. Van Beek, "Bethlehem," IDB 1:394–395.

3. The mixed population is one reason Judean Jews despised the Galileans. Cf. Henry O. Thompson, "A Study in Antisemitism," pp. 73–133, in *Unity in Diversity*, ed. Thompson; NY: Rose of Sharon, 1984. Herod Antipas was the son of Herod the Great and his fourth wife, Malthace. Herod died in 4 B.C. His will, which was accepted by the Roman emperor Augustus, divided his kingdom among his three remaining sons. Antipas was made tetrarch of Galilee (in the north by the Sea of Galilee) and Perea (west of the Jordan River).

While B.C. is translated "Before Christ," and Jesus' birth would thus be "0," a miscalculation in the sixth century A.D. established "0" some six or more years too late. The actual date of Jesus' birth is unknown but estimates range from 4–12 B.C. LHC-3–30. NCE-1233–1234. K.W. Clark, "Galilee," IDB 2:344–347. "Scholar: Jesus may have been born in summer, 12 B.C.," *The Philadelphia Inquirer* (December 22, 1985), 7-A. Samuel Sandmel, "Herod," IDB 2:585–594.

4. The four Gospels (Anglo-Saxon, "god-spell," a story from or about a god) — Matthew, Mark, Luke and John — are the primary sources for the life of the

historical Jesus. There are minor references in the rest of the Christian scripture, the Greek New Testament, and in early writings, including noncanonical scripture-like materials such as the gnostic Gospel of Thomas.

Over the centuries, there have been numerous biographies of Jesus as well as commentaries and interpretations of the Gospels. The following is only a sample. William Barclay, *Jesus of Nazareth*; Nashville: Nelson, 1985. C.K. Barrett, *Jesus and the Gospel Tradition*; London: SPCK, 1967. Gunther Bornkamm, *Jesus of Nazareth*; NY: Harper & Row, 1960. Rudolph Bultmann, *Jesus Christ and Mythology*; NY: Scribner's, 1968, and, *Jesus and the Word*; NY: Scribner's, 1958. Gaalyahu Cornfeld, *The Historical Jesus*; NY: Macmillan, 1983. R.H. Fuller, *The Mission and Achievement of Jesus*; London: SCM, 1954. Lucas Grollenberg, *Jesus*; Philadelphia: Westminster, 1979. J. Jeremias, *The Parables of Jesus*; NY: Scribner's 1955. Warren S. Kissinger, *The Lives of Jesus: A History and Bibliography*; NY: Garland, 1986 (the author estimates 60,000 "lives" of Jesus). Jaroslav Jan Pelikan, *Jesus Through the Centuries*; New Haven: Yale, 1985. James M. Robinson, *A New Quest of the Historical Jesus*; London: SCM, 1959. Edward Schillebeeckx, *Christ: The Experience of Jesus as Lord*; NY: Crossroads, 1983, and, *Jesus: An Experiment in Christology*; NY: Crossroads, 1979. Albert Schweitzer, *The Quest for the Historical Jesus*; NY: Macmillan, 1968 (original 1910). Fulton J. Sheen, *The Life of Christ*; Garden City, NY: Doubleday, 1977. Gerard S. Sloyan, *Jesus in Focus: A Life in Its Setting*; Mystic, CT: Twenty-Third, 1983. Morton Smith, *Jesus the Magician*; NY: Harper & Row, 1982. David F. Strauss, *The Life of Jesus*; Philadelphia: Fortress, 1972 (original 1835—one of the earliest of the "modern" works of this genre). Geza Vermes, *Jesus the Jew*; Philadelphia: Fortress, 1981.

William F. Albright and David Noel Freedman, eds., *The Anchor Bible*; Garden City, NY: Doubleday, 1964ff. This work of multiple volumes has commentaries on biblical books and parts of books by different scholars—Jewish and Christian (Roman Catholic and Protestant). There are many fine one-volume commentaries also. Raymond E. Brown, et al., eds., *The Jerome Biblical Commentary*; Englewood Cliffs, NJ: Prentice-Hall, 1968. Frederick F. Bruce, ed., *The International Bible Commentary*; Grand Rapids, MI: Zondervan, 1986. Francis Davidson, *The New Bible Commentary*, 2nd ed.; Grand Rapids, MI: Eerdmans, 1954. Reginald C. Fuller, et al., eds., *A New Catholic Commentary on Holy Scripture*; NY: Nelson, 1964. Henry S. Gehman, *The New Westminster Dictionary of the Bible*; Philadelphia: Westminster, 1970. James Hastings, et al., eds., *Dictionary of the Bible*, rev.; NY: Scribner's, 1963. Charles L. Laymon, *The Interpreter's One-Volume Commentary on the Bible*; Nashville: Abingdon, 1971. Charles F. Pfeiffer and Everett F. Harrison, *The Wycliffe Bible Commentary*; Chicago: Moody, 1962.

Introductions to the New Testament are frequently helpful as well. Howard Kee, *Understanding the New Testament*, 4th ed.; Englewood Cliffs, NJ: Prentice-Hall, 1983. W.G. Kummel, *Introduction to the New Testament*, rev.; Nashville: Abingdon, 1975 (based on the work of Paul Feine and Johannes Behm). Charles F.D. Moule, *The Birth of the New Testament*; NY: Harper & Row, 1962. Alan Richardson, *An Introduction to the Theology of the New Testament*; NY: Harper & Row, 1958. Ethelbert Stauffer, *New Testament Theology*; London: SCM, 1955. Joseph B. Tyson, *The New Testament and Early Christianity*; NY: Macmillan, 1984.

The relationship of Jesus to other Jewish groups is heavily debated, especially his identity as a Zealot. Paul Badham, "The Just-War Tradition and Nuclear Deterrence," *International Journal on World Peace* II, no. 2 (April–June 1985), 62–71. Ernest Bammel and C.F.D. Moule, eds., *Jesus and the Politics of His Day*; Cambridge: University Press, 1986, contains 26 essays by 16 authors refuting S.G.F.

Brandon. S.G.F. Brandon, *Jesus and the Zealots:* Manchester: Manchester University, 1967. Oscar Cullmann, *Jesus and the Revolutionaries;* NY: Harper & Row, 1970. John Ferguson, *War and Peace in the World's Religions;* NY: Oxford, 1978, pp. 100–101, notes among Jesus' followers Simon the Zealot, Judas Iscariot ("sicarius," "dagger-man") and Simon Peter Bar-Jona (a revolutionary nickname). He insists, however, that no Zealot would have accepted tax collectors as followers and no Zealot would have healed a Roman soldier or commended a Roman's faith. Victor P. Furnish, "War and Peace in the New Testament," *Interpretation* **XXXVIII,** no. 4 (October 1984), 363–379. Martin Hengel, *Was Jesus a Revolutionist?;* Philadelphia: Fortress, 1971.

    5. The Gospel of John can be interpreted so that Jesus' ministry was only one year instead of three. Dwight M. Beck, "Temptation of Jesus," IDB 4:568–569. Owen E. Evans, "Kingdom of God, of Heaven," IDB 3:17–26. "William F. Flemington, "Baptism," IDB 1:348–353. Richard H. Hiers, "Kingdom of God," IDBSV-516. Ernst Jenni, "Messiah, Jewish," IDB 3:360–365. Ellis Rivkin, "Messiah, Jewish," IDBSV-588–591.

    6. Noss, op cit., pp. 422–427. John H. Burt, "Christianity," pp. 100–108, in *World Religions and World Peace,* ed. Homer A. Jack; Boston: Beacon, 1968. Kenneth Grayston, "Sermon on the Mount," IDB 4:279–289. R.G. Hamerton-Kelly, "Sermon on the Mount," IDBSV-815–817. James E. Wood, Jr., "World Religions and World Community," *Journal of Church and State,* 27, no. 2 (Spring 1985), pp. 217–222.

    7. Johannes Hempel, "Hosanna," IDB 2:648. The money changers helped the pilgrims coming to the temple. The official offering was in shekels so pilgrims would change the money of their homeland for Jewish coins (Exodus 30:13; Leviticus 1:14). The pigeons could be purchased for sacrifice. The accusation of robbery suggests the pilgrims were being overcharged or shortchanged. Money changers normally make a profit on the exchange. Perhaps Jesus considered it excessive or that it should have been a free service for the temple.

    8. Noss, op. cit., pp. 432–433. A later addition to the Gospel of Mark has him appearing to the disciples at mealtime, apparently in Jerusalem, after which he ascended into heaven. John 20–21 describes several meetings in Jerusalem followed by a breakfast meeting in Galilee. Matthew 28 has him meeting his disciples in Galilee. Luke closes with Jesus and his disciples at Bethany on the Mount of Olives from where "he parted from them" in some editions while others add, "and was carried up into heaven" (Luke 24:51). The Book of Acts, presumably written by Luke, opens with Jesus' resurrection appearances over 40 days. They gathered on the Mount of Olives where Jesus ascended into heaven (1:1–11). Theodore H. Gaster, "Resurrection," IDB 4:39–43. James M. Robinson, "Ascension," IDB 1:245–247. John A.T. Robinson, "Resurrection in the NT," IDB 4:43–53.

    9. LHC-65-11. NCE-551, 2083. Noss, op. cit., pp. 434–438. Isma'il R. al Faruqi and David E. Sopher, eds., *Historical Atlas of the Religions of the World;* NY: Macmillan, 1974. Rudolph Bultmann, *Primitive Christianity in Its Contemporary Setting;* NY: Meridian, 1956. Tim Dowley, et al., eds., *Eerdmans' Handbook to the History of Christianity;* Grand Rapids, MI: Eerdmans, 1977. Cited hereafter as EHHC. Martin Dibelius, *Studies in the Acts of the Apostles;* NY: Scribner's, 1956. Dibelius and W.G. Kummel, *Paul;* Philadelphia: Westminster, 1953. Martin Hengel, *Acts and the History of Earliest Christianity;* Philadelphia: Fortress, 1979. John C. Hurd, "Paul the Apostle," IDBSV-648–651. Michael Grant, *Saint Paul;* London: Weidenfeld and Nicolson, 1976. Hubert R. Johnson, *Who Then Is Paul?;* Lanham, MD: University Press of America, 1986. John Knox, *Chapters in a Life of Paul;* NY: Abingdon, 1950. Hyman Macoby, *The Mythmaker: Paul and the*

Invention of Christianity; San Francisco: Harper & Row, 1986. Johannes Munck, *Paul and the Salvation of Mankind;* Atlanta, GA: Knox, 1959. Alexander C. Purdy, "Paul the Apostle," IDB 3:681–704. Herman Ridderbos, *Paul: An Outline of His Theology;* Grand Rapids, MI: Eerdmans, 1975. Williston Walker, *A History of the Christian Church,* rev.; NY: Scribner's, 1959, pp. 24–102.

10. LHC-120–128. NCE-775, 825. We note in passing that in moving into the Greco-Roman world, the Judaism of Jesus was amalgamated to various degrees with the mystery religions on the one hand and with European philosophy on the other. In the latter regard, Plato's philosophy eventually became the philosophical basis of the faith. In the Middle Ages, Thomas Aquinas (1225–1274) replaced Plato with Aristotle. In 1879, the pope declared Thomism eternally valid. Beaver, op. cit., pp. 379–381. EHHC-288. Harvey, op. cit., pp. 48–51, 71–72, 74, 189. Henry Bettenson, ed., *Documents of the Christian Church,* 2nd ed.; NY: Oxford University, 1967, pp. 35–37. Jacques Ellul, *La Subversion du Christianisme;* Paris: Seuil, 1984, sees the syncretism as the betrayal of biblical Christianity. Pagan philosophical ideas subverted the Gospel. Power and greed replaced the service of God. Quoted by David W. Gill, "Why Isn't Christendom More Christian?" *Fides et Historia* XVII, no. 2 (Spring–Summer 1985), 70–77. Justo L. Gonzalez, *A History of Christian Thought;* NY: Abingdon, 1975. Reinhold Seeberg, *Textbook of the History of Doctrines,* vols. I–II; Grand Rapids, MI: Baker, 1954, I:87–91.

At times, syncretism in religion has been criticized and condemned (cf. Ellul). Christianity, however, has always been syncretistic and remains so to this day. In addition to the profundities of philosophy, one can note the Christmas tree (German Druids), Christmas Day (the Roman Saturnalia) and large numbers of pagan deities incorporated as angels, demons, saints, forms of the Virgin Mary, etc. The Egyptian/Semitic god Mekal became the archangel Michael. So too the Teutonic war god, "Wodan, was assimilated in the Christian pantheon as "Michael the Archangel." "One dimension" of the archangel might be another way to phrase it. Wodan's ancient sanctuary at Monte Gargano became a favorite shrine of Norman soldiers. James A. Aho, *Religious Mythology and the Art of War;* Westport, CT: Greenwood, 1981, p. 81. Henry O. Thompson, *Mekal: The God of Beth-shan;* Leiden: Brill, 1970. Some of these syncretistic additions are far more important to many Christians than Jesus or the New Testament. A Protestant pastor was nearly dismissed when he tried to keep Santa Claus out of his church.

Some very interesting combinations are appearing in Latin America and Africa where Christianity is mixed with Indian, African and Muslim traditions. David B. Barrett, *Schism and Renewal in Africa: An Analysis of Six Thousand Contemporary Religious Movements;* Nairobi: Oxford, 1968. John Deedy, "Catholicism and Cultural Shock," *The New York Times* (January 19, 1975), E 11, notes Brazilian Catholics worshipping Iemanja, goddess of an Afro-Brazilian cult who is simultaneously an African saint, a native Indian spirit and the Virgin Mary. Mircea Eliade, *Symbolism, the Sacred, & the Arts;* NY: Crossroads, 1985, discusses the phenomena in southeastern Europe. Bernadino Verastique, "Pilgrimage at Chalma: Indigenous Piety in Mexico," *Harvard Divinity Bulletin* XV, no. 4 (April–June 1985), 7–9, notes that under the altar of the Christo de Chalma, one can still enter the ancient cave that served as a shrine of the pre–Hispanic Oztocteotl (Divinity of the Cave).

11. Fred D. Gealy, "Stephen," IDB 4:441–442. George E. Mendenhall, "Covenant," IDB 1:714–723. Constantine's family, sun worshippers, had been tolerant of Christianity. On his way to claim the throne of the Roman Empire, "he saw a cross in the sky superimposed on the sun, a rare but attested version of the halophenomenon. . . ." He heard the words, "in this sign, conquer." He put chi-rho – the cross and the circle – on his soldiers' shields for the first two letters of "Christ" in

Greek. A fourth-century mosaic shows Christ as the sun god in his chariot, perhaps a reflection of Constantine's syncretism. While he was emperor, pagan gods were honored and there were pagan symbols on his coins. He was baptized on his death bed. Bettenson, op. cit., pp. 1–23. EHHC-130–137. Ferguson, op. cit., p. 105. Harvey, op. cit., pp. 60–61. LHC-112–192. NCE-634. Nielsen, op. cit., pp. 498–501. Noss, op. cit., pp. 438–444. Timothy Barnes, *Constantine and Eusebius;* Cambridge: Harvard University, 1981.

12. Arius (250–336), a priest of Alexandria, taught that Jesus the Son is the first creation of God. Bettenson, op. cit., pp. 24–26, 39–44. EHHC-156–165. Harvey, op. cit., pp. 27–28. NCE-145, 147. Nielsen, op. cit., pp. 502–506. Noss, op. cit., pp. 445–447. Seeberg, op. cit., I:201–243. Walker, op. cit., pp. 105–123. Robert C. Gregg and Dennis E. Groh, *Early Arianism;* Philadelphia: Fortress, 1981. Colm Luibheid, *Eusebius of Caesarea and the Arian Crisis;* Dublin: Irish Academic Press, 1981. The conflict led to the first ecumenical council at Nicea in 325 and the formulation of the Nicene Creed. The battle continued for decades with Arius and his chief opponent Athanasius (295–375) alternately forced into exile and then reinstated. The Council of Constantinople in 381 reaffirmed the Nicene Creed.

The monophysites continue today in the Coptic churches of Egypt and Ethiopia, the Armenian Orthodox Church and the Jacobites (founded by Jacob Baradaeus in the sixth century) of Syria and Iraq. Bettenson, op. cit., pp. 46–52, 89, 91–93, 96–97. EHHC-171–178. Harvey, op. cit., pp. 154, 164–165. NCE-1815, 1912. Noss, op. cit., pp. 447–448. Seeberg, op. cit., I:243–288. Walker, op. cit., pp. 131–150. Roberta C. Chestnut, *Three Monophysite Christologies;* London: Oxford, 1975. W.H.C. Frend, *The Rise of the Monophysite Movement;* Cambridge, England: University Press, 1972. Nestorius, d. 451, Bishop of Constantinople in 428, refused to call the Virgin Mary the "Mother of God." While Jesus was conceived by the Holy Spirit, Mary gave birth to a man. Cyril of Alexandria, a political enemy of Nestorius, raised a protest. Nestorius was condemned by the Council of Ephesus in 431. The Creed of Chalcedon in 451 specified two complete natures in one person. Monophysitism was finally condemned by the Sixth Ecumenical Council (680–681) in Constantinople. A.J. Arberry, ed., *Religion in the Middle East, vol I: Christianity and Judaism;* Cambridge: University Press, 1969. William C. Emhardt and George M. Lamsa, *The Oldest Christian People;* NY: AMS, 1970 (original 1926). Friedrich Loofs, *Nestorius and His Place in the History of Christian Doctrine;* NY: Burt Franklin, 1975 (original 1914).

Bettenson, op. cit., pp. 182–226. EHHC-179–425. LHC-269–922. NCE-2023–2024, 2290, 2346–2347. Nielsen, op. cit., pp. 518–36. Noss, op. cit., pp. 450–483. Seeberg, op. cit., vol. II:221–426. Walker, op. cit., pp. 150–419. William P. Armstrong, ed., *Calvin and the Reformation;* Grand Rapids, MI: Baker, 1980. Archibald G. Baker, ed., *A Short History of Christianity;* Chicago: University of Chicago, 1962 (original 1940). Marshall W. Baldwin, *The Medieval Church;* Ithaca, NY: Cornell University, 1953. Ernst Benz, *The Eastern Orthodox Church;* Garden City, NY: Doubleday, 1963. George Brantl, *Catholicism;* NY: Braziller, 1962. S. Bulgakov, *The Eastern Orthodox Church;* London: Centenary, 1935. G.K. Chesterton, *Orthodoxy;* Garden City, NY: Doubleday, 1973. Demetrios J. Constantelos, *Understanding the Greek Orthodox Church: Its Faith, History and Practice;* Minneapolis: Winston, 1982. F.L. Cross, *Dictionary of the Christian Church;* Oxford: Clarendon, 1957. John Dillenberger, *Martin Luther;* Garden City, NY: Doubleday, 1961. Dillenberger and Claude Welch, *Protestant Christianity;* NY: Scribner's, 1954. J. Leslie Dunstan, *Protestantism;* NY: Braziller, 1962. E. Harris Harbison, *The Age of Reformation;* Ithaca, NY: Cornell University, 1955. M.R.P. McGuire, et al., eds., *New Catholic Encyclopedia,* 15 vols.; NY: McGraw-Hill,

166   Chapter II

1967. John T. McNeill, *The History and Character of Calvinism;* NY: Oxford, 1967. T.H. Parker, *John Calvin;* Philadelphia: Westminster, 1983. Alexander Schmemann, *The Historical Road of Eastern Orthodoxy;* NY: Holt, Rinehart and Winston, 1963. Ninian Smart, *The Long Search;* Boston: Little, Brown, 1977, pp. 105–158. Lee Smith and Wes Bodin, eds., *The Christian Tradition;* Allen, TX: Argus, 1978. Timothy Ware, *The Orthodox Church,* rev.; Baltimore: Penguin, 1969. Nicholas Zernov, *The Church of Eastern Christians;* NY: Macmillan, 1946.

13. One could see this development of efficient killing as climaxing in the Nazis. Aho, op. cit., p. 210. Bettenson, op. cit., pp. 116–132. EHHC-204–216, 300–309, 417–420. LHC-221–235. NCE-1809–1810, 1870. Nielsen, op. cit., pp. 509–510, 515. Noss, op. cit., pp. 448–450. Walker, op. cit., pp. 125–128, 198–201. Otto J. Baab, "Woman," IDB 4:864–867. Derek Baker, *A Short History of Monasticism;* NY: Columbia University, 1982. Anne Bancroft, *The Luminous Vision;* London: Allen & Unwin, 1982. Thomas Boslooper, *The Image of Woman;* NY: Rose of Sharon, 1980. Walter Capps, *The Monastic Impulse;* NY: Crossroads, 1982. Sharon N. Emswiler, *The Ongoing Journey: Women and the Bible;* NY: United Methodist Church, 1977. Ursula King, *Towards a New Mysticism;* NY: Seabury, 1980. David Knowles, *Christian Monasticism;* NY: McGraw-Hill, 1969. Victoria Lincoln, *Teresa: A Woman;* Albany, NY: SUNY, 1984. Martin E. Marty, "Mysticism and the Religious Quest for Freedom," *The Christian Century* 100, no. 8 (March 16, 1983), 242–246. The *Century* is cited hereafter as CC. Thomas Merton, *The Monastic Journey;* Kansas City: Sheed Andrews and McNeel, 1977. Rosemary Radford Ruether, *Religion and Sexism;* NY: Simon and Schuster, 1974. Robin Scroggs, "Woman in the NT," IDBSV-966–968. Henry O. Thompson, "Cooperative Contributions Community," pp. 156–186, in Sexual Stereotypes, *East and West,* ed. Bina Gupta; NY: Paragon House, 1987. Evelyn Underhill wrote a great classic, *Mysticism;* NY: Dutton, 1961 (original 1910). Rachel Conrad Wahlberg, *Jesus According to a Woman;* NY: Paulist, 1975.

14. Christian slavery was an extension of the Roman world. It included slaves of various races. It included other Christians though it was an act of piety to set one's Christian slaves free. The Third Lateran Council in 1179 outlawed the slavery of Christians. Since most of the European world was at least nominally Christian, that left Jews, Muslims and the various peoples of Africa and Asia as potential slaves. With the opening of the New World, the slave trade became profitable. African tribal chiefs sold their enemies to Europeans for transport to the Americas. The Muslim slave trade also was very active. While numbers of these slaves became Christians, in the face of profits, the ban on enslaving Christians was largely ignored. Aho, op. cit., p. 93. EHHC-276, 455, 466, 519–520. LHC-245–246, 558. NCE-2534–2535. Marc Bloch, *Feudal Society,* 2 vols.; Chicago: University of Chicago, 1970, vol. 1:132–133. Isaac Mendelsohn, "Slavery in the OT," IDB 4:383–391. Wayne G. Rollins, "Slavery in the NT," IDBSV-830–832. Walther T. Zimmerli, "Slavery in the OT," ibid., pp. 829–830.

David B. Barrett, ed., *World Christian Encyclopedia;* Nairobi: Oxford, 1982. In 1980, there were 1,433,000,000 Christians in the world, 32.8 percent of the population. There were 809 million Roman Catholics, 345 million Protestants, 124 million Eastern Orthodox and 155 million others. Barrett expects 2,020,000,000 Christians by the year 2000, some 32.3 percent of world population. The United States has 161 million Christians split into 2,050 denominations. Overall there are 20,000 subgroups of Christians in the world. Christianity has touched to some extent some 6,850 of the 8,990 ethnic or linguistic groups on earth. Edwin S. Gaustad, *A Religious History of America;* NY: Harper & Row, 1974. Winthrop Hudson, *The Great Tradition of the American Churches;* NY: Harper & Row, 1963.

15. War is prominent in the Hebrew Scriptures, the Christian Old Testament, and appears in the New Testament as well (Matthew 26:52–54; Revelation 9:15). Many Christians glory in it as we will see in a moment. Pacifists have either repudiated the passages in which God blesses war, or they have claimed that Jesus' teachings superseded the old revelation. Some have spiritualized the verses, as some Jewish rabbis did, e.g., holy war describes the power of those fully committed to God. The book of Joshua is "a sustained meditation on what it means to interpret the word of God. . . ." Robert Pilzin, *Moses and the Deuteronomist*; NY: Seabury, 1980, p. 144. Furnish, op. cit., pp. 367–371. Bruce Birch, "Old Testament Foundations for Peacemaking in the Nuclear Era," CC **102**, no. 38 (December 4, 1985), 1115–1119. George L. Carey, "Biblical-Theological Perspectives on War and Peace," pp. 163–178, and, F. Derek Kidner, "Old Testament Perspectives on War," pp. 99–113, and, I. Howard Marshall, "New Testament Perspectives on War," pp. 115–132, and, David F. Wright, "War in a Church-Historical Perspective," pp. 133–161, *The Evangelical Quarterly* LVII, no. 2 (April 1985). Norman Gottwald, "War, Holy," IDB Supplementary Vol., pp. 942–944. Herbert B. Huffmon, "Exodus 23:4–5: A Comparative Study," pp. 271–278, in *A Light Unto My Path*, ed. Howard N. Bream, et al.; Philadelphia: Temple, 1974. William Klassen, *Love of Enemies: The Way to Peace*; Philadelphia: Fortress, 1984. Paul D. Simmons, "The New Testament Basis of Peacemaking," *Review and Expositor* LXXIX, no. 4 (Fall 1982), 597–605, and, Marvin E. Tate, "War and Peacemaking in the Old Testament," ibid., pp. 587–596. Lawrence E. Toombs, "Wars, Ideas of," IDB 4:796–801. G. Ernest Wright, "The Conquest Theme in the Bible," pp. 509–518, in Bream, op. cit. The peaceful dimensions of the Old Testament are also recognized and utilized in Christianity. E.M. Good, "Peace in the OT," IDB 3:705–706. See the chapter on Judaism, this volume, notes 27–28 and references there. One should add also that the *peaceful* elements of the New Testament are spiritualized or set aside to justify war. David Wright, op. cit., p. 144.

16. Simmons, op. cit., p. 599. Ferguson, op. cit., pp. 100–101. Cf. Ferguson's comment cited earlier that Jesus was not a Zealot. He also notes that Jesus did not pick up the violent messiah concepts. Psalm 2:9 says the messiah will break the nations with a rod of iron. Isaiah 9:4–5 says he will shatter the yoke which fetters Israel. II Esdras 12:31–33 saw the messiah as a lion who would destroy the Roman Empire. In Ezra 4, the messiah is the merciless conqueror of the Gentiles. Acts 5:35–37 refers to Theudas and Judas the Galilean as leaders of revolts. Simon bar Koseba, the leader of the Second Jewish Revolt in A.D. 132–135, was declared messiah by Rabbi Akiba.

Pacifism comes from pax and facere and means to make peace. Some have suggested it is *the* presupposition of Christianity. Others deny this. Badham, op. cit., p. 62. NCE-2042. Hans-Werner Bartsch, "The Foundation and Meaning of Christian Pacifism," pp. 185–198, in *New Theology No. 6*, ed. Martin E. Marty and Dean G. Perrman; NY: Macmillan, 1969. John Helgeland, Robert J. Daly and J. Patout Burns, *Christians and the Military: The Early Experience*; Philadelphia: Fortress, 1985. C. Leslie Mitton, "Peace in the NT," IDB 3:706.

17. Aho, op. cit., p. 83. Bettenson, op. cit., p. 107 notes that Ambrose excommunicated the emperor Theodosius the Great for a savage massacre in Thessalonica in 390 as a reprisal for a riot. EHHC-139–140, 198–200. Ferguson, op. cit., pp. 103–104. Furnish, op. cit., pp. 371–375. Marshall, op. cit., p. 118, claims there is no explicit indication in the New Testament that it is wrong to be a soldier. He sees (pp. 123–128) the problem as a confusion between force and violence. Violence is forbidden. Force is permissible and at times necessary. He notes Jesus came not to bring peace but a sword (Matthew 10:34), though Luke 12:51 says "division" rather

than "sword." He adds (p. 132) that God's people are commanded to live in peace with one another and with all people (Romans 12:18, 14:19; II Corinthians 13:11; Ephesians 4:3; etc.). "If Christ died potentially for all people, then we cannot willingly go to war with the people of any nation." NCE-80, 185, 558–559, 2019, 2719. David Wright, op. cit., pp. 135–148, claims the problem was not war or fighting but idolatry — the soldier had to swear by the emperor. Civil office was forbidden for the same reason (p. 144). The ease with which Christians supported Constantine and his "holy" wars shows the objections to military service in the first three centuries was not ethical but religious (p. 145). Rome's wars for the next several centuries were designated holy wars against pagans and heretics (p. 147). Helgeland, op. cit., documents this view from the writings of Tertullian, Origen, etc. Stephen C. Mott, *Biblical Ethics and Social Change*; NY: Oxford, 1982, chapter 9, argues that the teachings of Jesus do not demand a political doctrine of nonviolence. Quoted by Lisa Sowle Cahill, "Nonresistance, Defense, Violence, and the Kingdom in Christian Tradition," *Interpretation* XXXVIII, no. 4 (October 1984), 380–397.

18. Ferguson, op. cit., pp. 105–106. NCE-904. David Wright, op. cit., pp. 149–154, notes that Augustine was the fountainhead for all discussion of war for medieval Christianity in the West — there were refinements of his theory but nothing new.

19. Ferguson, op. cit., pp. 106–107. Aho, op. cit., pp. 81–5. NCE-2792.

20. Romans 13 has been interpreted as make peace, not war, with the government. Paul is writing to a specific situation and in no way saying people must submit to unjust governments everywhere as Acts 4 and 5, and Revelation 13 make clear. There had been a revolt against the Roman government and another was brewing. Paul called upon the Christians in Rome to make peace with each other, and with the government. Cf. Stassen, op. cit., pp. 633–634, and literature cited in n. 18. Bettenson, op. cit., pp. 132–135. Ferguson, op. cit., pp. 103–104. NCE-1342–1343. Albert C. Shannon, *The Medieval Inquisition*; Washington, D.C.: Augustinian College, 1983.

21. Aho, op. cit., pp. 85–93. Ferguson, op. cit., p. 110. NCE-544, 2059–2061. The Second Lateran Council in 1139 anathematized crossbows, bows and arrows and siege machines as hated by God. Ferguson notes they were manned by commoners and might kill the nobility. Aho says chivalry was equated with knights on horseback. There was no glory in the weapons of commoners. One can note on the positive side that these weapons were not only indiscriminate but efficient in their killing. By banning them, the number of casualties was lowered. Other voices, however, then as now, claim all is fair in war. Richard Barber, *The Knight and Chivalry*; NY: Harper & Row, 1982. Maurice Keen, *Chivalry*; New Haven: Yale, 1984.

In addition to the parallel with Confucian gentlemen, Aho (p. 96) claims the principles were similar in classical Hinduism and in Aztec (Nahuatl) Mexico. One could add Islam at several points. Chivalry demanded giving the party to be attacked an advance notice of three days, allowing surrender rather than death, allowing safe passage and truces under certain circumstances. If the surrender offer was refused and the city captured, the men and children were killed and the women raped by these Christians (Aho, p. 99, n. 32). Islam allowed the enemy to convert or to surrender and pay the poll tax, though when these were refused, the slaughter was carried out. Since adultery was a sin, the women were taken in "battlefield marriage," married at night, divorced in the morning. As noted earlier, in 1179, the Third Lateran Council outlawed the enslavement of Christians which encouraged ransom for the well-to-do, though it may have encouraged death for commoners. When captured, the commoners would have been killed rather than held for ransom. Islam also outlawed the enslavement of brothers in the faith. Both allowed the enslavement of others.

22. There are parallels here with Islam. Muhammad's successor, Abu Bakr, united the warring tribes of Arabia and directed their energy against others. Muslim warriors who died in battle went straight to paradise. The Crusades were holy wars, known in Islam as jihad. Cf. above on Teutonic war also, Aho, op. cit., pp. 83, 220 (quote from Raymond). EHHC-269-275. NCE-690-691. Walker, op. cit., pp. 219-224. Carl Erdmann, *The Origin of the Idea of Crusade*; Princeton: Princeton University, 1977. Ronald C. Finucane, *Soldiers of the Faith: Crusaders and Moslems at War*; NY: St. Martin's, 1984. Tate, op. cit., p. 589. Henry Daniel-Rops, *Bernard of Clairvaux*; NY: Hawthorn, 1964. *Thomas Merton on St. Bernard*; London: Mobray, 1980. Marvin H. Pope, *Song of Songs*; Garden City: Doubleday, 1977, p. 119.

In contrast with the call to war, Pope John Paul II has deplored violence and called for peace, an end to discrimination, respect for human dignity and the fundamental rights of man (not women). Samuel Koo, "Pope Decries Violence," *Detroit Free Press* 155, no. 100 (August 12, 1985), 1A. On the papal states see Thomas F.X. Noble, *The Republic of St. Peter: The Birth of the Papal State, 680-825*; Philadelphia: University of Pennsylvania, 1984.

23. The second century of the Crusades was the time of Thomas Aquinas (1225-1274) noted earlier. Using the techniques of Aristotle, transmitted to Europe through Muslim Spain, Aquinas harmonized reason and revelation. A group of Franciscans led by Roger Bacon (1214-1292) resisted Thomas' methods and laid the groundwork for modern science with empirical studies. Bacon recognized the practical side of his studies and dreamed of a world in which the pope would have an army equipped with new types of weapons. With one blow, the pope could then destroy the Islamic armies and bring peace to the world. EHHC-287, 289. NCE-205, 2726.

24. Aho, op. cit., p. 94. Ferguson, op. cit., pp. 107-108. LHC-474-475, 555, 976, 1474. NCE-2792. Walker, op. cit., p. 199. David Wright, op. cit., p. 156. Carl J. Hemmer, "Truce of God," *Encyclopaedia Britannica* 22 (1968), 272, claims the "Truce of God" is the collective name for both the Peace of God and the "Truce of God."

25. Aho, op. cit., p. 84. Ferguson, op. cit., p. 108. LHC-413, 427-428. NCE-1489-1490, 2720-2721. Walker, op. cit., pp. 221-222, 262. The Hospitalers (Order of the Hospital of St. John of Jerusalem) were originally the Friars of the Hospital organized by Gerard de Martignes, head of the hospital of the Latin rite church in Jerusalem. Initially they cared for sick pilgrims but then began military operations to care for them. They are sometimes called the Knights of St. John, or, the Knights of Jerusalem. Later they were the Knights of Rhodes from their headquarters on that island and still later, Knights of Malta, after Rhodes was captured by the Muslims. Malta was lost to Napoleon and in time the fighting warriors were reconstituted as a charitable organization.

The Templars (Knights of the Temple of Solomon) were organized in 1118 to protect pilgrims on the route to the Holy Land. Bernard wrote rules for them similar to his own Cistercian order, which included chastity. Soldier monks were known earlier in Islam, and even earlier in the Old Testament where the vow of chastity was part of the holy war. In his "De Laude Novae Militae," Bernard declared the Templars ministers of God for the killing of evil. After its publication, the Templars were besieged with recruits from all over Europe. After the Crusades, the Templars retreated to Cyprus. Later they became great bankers and moneylenders and were finally destroyed, officially as heretics, perhaps for their property, in 1314.

The Teutonic Knights or Order (Hospital of St. Mary of the Teutons in Jerusalem) were organized in 1190 during the Third Crusade (1189–1192). They had a continuing history in eastern Europe in the conquest of Prussia, which ended in 1525 through the group lingered in Catholic Europe until 1809. Stephen Howart, *The Knights Templar*; NY: Atheneum, 1982. Desmond Seward, *The Monks of War: The Military Religious Orders*; Hamden, CT: Archon, 1972.

26. Bettenson, op. cit., pp. 182–244. EHHC-379. NCE-3051. Jacques Courvoisier, *Zwingli: A Reformed Theologian*; Richmond, VA: Knox, 1963. George R. Potter, *Zwingli*; NY: Cambridge University, 1976. Robert C. Walton, *Zwingli's Theocracy*; Toronto: University of Toronto, 1967.

27. Cahill, op. cit., pp. 387–394. EHHC-363, 398–402. LHC-778–796. NCE-95–96, 1859, 2090. David Wright, op. cit., pp. 157–161. Martin Brecht, *Martin Luther*; Philadelphia: Fortress, 1985, Robert N. Crossley, *Luther and the Peasants' War*; NY: Exposition 1974. Herbert Kirchner, *Luther and the Peasants' War*; Philadelphia: Fortress, 1972. Kyle C. Sessions, ed., *Reformation and Authority: The Meaning of the Peasants' Revolt*; Lexington, MA: Heath, 1968. James M. Stayer, *The Anabaptists and Thomas Muntzer*; Dubuque, IA: Kendall/Hunt, 1980.

28. Note here as throughout the text, that which group of Christians was right or wrong (both?) is not the issue here. The concern is the attitude toward war. Aho, op. cit., p. 206. Ferguson, op. cit., pp. 115–116. EHHC-24–25. LHC-797–835. NCE-687. Antonio Fraser, *Cromwell, The Lord Protector*; NY: Knopf, 1973. Ivan A. Roots, ed., *Cromwell, A Profile*: NY: Hill & Wang, 1973.

Cromwell's efforts to break the Roman Catholic opposition in Ireland may be part of the historic struggle there between Catholics and Protestants, very much in the news today. For more recent background, see Desmond Bowen, *The Protestant Crusade in Ireland, 1800–70*; Montreal: Gill and Macmillan, 1978. J.L.M. Haire, ed., *Challenge and Conflict*; Antrim, Northern Ireland: W & G Baird, 1981. Eric Gallagher and Stanley Worrall, *Christians in Ulster, 1968–1981*; NY: Oxford, 1982. Robert D. Linder, "'The Integrity of Their Quarrel': Or, Why Irish Christians Kill Each Other," *Fides et Historia* XVII, no. 2 (Spring–Summer 1985), 78–89. Padraig O'Malley, *The Uncivil Wars: Ireland Today*; Boston: Houghton Mifflin, 1983.

29. Aho, op. cit., pp. 194–220. Ferguson, op. cit., p. 117. Albert Ple claims that Christian ethics is fundamentally pathological in his *Christian Morality: Duty or Pleasure?*; NY: Paragon, 1986.

Aho goes on to suggest that reformers recognize themselves as evil and part of the problem. Then in humility, all can work together for the common good. Another approach is the assurance of salvation taught by such groups as Moravians and Methodists. Assured of one's security in God, there is no need to destroy others. Eric Fromm said, "The compulsive quest for certainty is not the expression of genuine faith but is rooted in the need to conquer the unbearable doubt." Quoted by Robert Kaufman, *Inside Scientology*; NY: Olympia, 1972, p. xvii.

30. The tax cuts are reminiscent of Islamic policy in reverse. Non-Muslims paid a poll to Islam. Converts were freed of this economic burden. So here with Russian Orthodoxy for converts to Christianity. EHHC-478. NCE-185, 1285, 2733–2734. Janet G. Gray, *The French Huguenots*; Grand Rapids, MI: Baker, 1981. George E. Reaman, *The Trail of the Huguenots in Europe, the United States, South Africa and Canada*; London: Muller, 1964.

31. Ferguson, op. cit., pp. 119, 120, 157. NCE-1239–1240. Reinhold Niebuhr, *Christianity and Power Politics*; NY: Scribner's, 1940. Paul Ramsey, *The Just War*; NY: Scribner's, 1968. F.H. Russell, *The Just War in the Middle Ages*; Cambridge, England: University Press, 1975. On the relationship of politics and religion, see the modern example of Ireland noted earlier, where the two are tightly interwoven.

Linder, op. cit. Christian groups in the holy land have fought each other for centuries. A Muslim family holds the key to the door of the Holy Sepulchre but that has not stopped the fighting. Derk Kinnane Roelofsma, "In the Holy Land, Christians Feud," *Insight* 2, no. 38 (September 22, 1986), 60–61. Robert L. Wilken, "From Time Immemorial? Dwellers in the Holy Land," *CC* 103, no. 23 (July 30–August 6, 1986), 678–680.

32. Badham, op. cit. Cahill, op. cit., pp. 394–397. Carey, op. cit., pp. 172–177, notes the ubiquity of war in history while peace is unusual. Ferguson, op. cit., pp. 111, 119–120. David Wright, op. cit., p. 147. Thomas P. Murphy, ed., *The Holy War;* Columbus: Ohio State, 1976. Glen Stassen, "A Theological Rationale for Peacemaking," *Review and Expositor* LXXIX, no. 4 (Fall 1982), 623–637.

33. Bettenson, op. cit., pp. 173–182. Ferguson, op. cit., pp. 112–113. NCE-885, 996, 1295–1296, 1604, 2919. Roland Bainton, *Erasmus of Christendom;* NY: Crossroads, 1982 (original 1969). John Bartlett, *Bartlett's Familiar Quotations,* 14th ed.; Boston: Little, Brown, 1968. Leonaro Boff, *Saint Francis;* NY: Crossroads, 1982. J.C. Carrick, *Wycliffe and the Lollards;* NY: Gordon, 1977. Julien Green, *God's Fool: The Life of Francis of Assisi;* San Francisco: Harper & Row, 1985. Johan Huizinga, *Erasmus and the Age of Reformation;* Princeton: Princeton University, 1984.

34. Cahill, op. cit., pp. 389–390. NCE-1748. J.C. Wenger, ed., *The Complete Writings of Menno Simons;* Scottsdale, PA: Herald, 1956. Cornelius J. Dyck, ed., *Mennonite History;* Scottsdale: Herald, 1967. Richard C. Detweiler, *Mennonite Statements on Peace 1915–1966;* Scottsdale: Herald, 1968. J. Howard Kauffman and Leland Harder, *Anabaptists Four Centuries Later;* Scottsdale: Herald, 1975. *The Mennonite Encyclopedia,* 4 vols.; Scottsdale: Mennonite Publishing House, 1957.

35. EHHC-402–403. Ferguson, op. cit., p. 114. LHC-788–790. NCE-364, 1296, 2330. One prominent group today are the Amish, Mennonites stemming from the work of the Swiss, Jacob Amman, who founded the group in 1693. They are noted for their refusal to use electricity, telephones, automobiles, tractors and other modern conveniences. There are over 50,000 Amish in the U.S. Many are in Pennsylvania, especially Lancaster County west of Philadelphia. Richard Gehman, "Plainest of Pennsylvania's Plain People: Amish Folk," *National Geographic* 128, no. 2 (August 1965), 227–253. Among the many splinters of Plain people, one group of Brethren is called Dunkers or Dunkards because their baptism is by immersion. A group along the Susquehanna River is called River Brethren. They are known today, in part, because former President Eisenhower's grandfather was one, though his parents converted to Jehovah's Witnesses, another pacifist group. Jerry Bergman, *Jehovah's Witnesses and Kindred Groups;* NY: Garland, 1984, p. 213. David Flint, *The Hutterites;* Toronto: Oxford, 1975. In contrast to the Amish, the Hutterites use labor-saving machinery but maintain clothing styles and live in communal groups.

The splinters are reminders that even "peace" churches fight among themselves. Other groups do, too, of course. There are over 30 Wesleyan or Methodist groups in the United States alone. Claude Howe notes that Baptists are "better known for fighting than for peacemaking." "Baptists and Peacemaking," *Review and Expositor* LXXIX, no. 4 (Fall 1982), 607–622. Perhaps these groups are less associated with military conflict than others because they have not had the military power of others to extend their fighting to the battlefield.

36. Cahill, op. cit., pp. 390–391. EHHC-480–483. NCE-1017–1018. Margaret H. Bacon, *The Quiet Rebels: The Story of the Quakers in America;* NY: Basic, 1969. Peter Brock, *Pioneers of the Peaceable Kingdom;* Princeton: Princeton University, 1970. Richard S. Dunn and Mary Maples Dunn, eds., *The World of William Penn;* Philadelphia: University of Pennsylvania, 1986. Melvin B. Endy, *William Penn and*

Early Quakerism; Princeton: Princeton University, 1973. Jean Soderlund, ed., *William Penn and the Founding of Pennsylvania*; Philadelphia: University of Pennsylvania, 1983. Henry O. Thompson, "William Penn — The Founder of Philadelphia," pp. 485–489, in *Global Outreach*, ed. Thompson; NY: Rose of Sharon, 1987.

37. "FOR Statement of Purpose," FOR, Box 271, Nyack, NY 10960. The FOR has 86 local groups and 32,000 members. Denise S. Akey, et al., eds., *Encyclopedia of Associations*, 19th ed.; Detroit: Gale, 1985.

38. Steven S. Schwarzschild suggests that in the vague complex called the Peace Movement, the overwhelmingly larger portions have no relationship whatsoever to "organized religion." "The Religious Demand for Peace," *Judaism* 15, no. 4 (Fall 1966), 412–418.

A current list, religious and secular, of organizations (including international groups) in the U.S. appears in Akey, op. cit. A sample of publications includes the following: LHC-977, 1019, 1063, 1270. Lalit K. Aggarwal, *Peace Science: A Bibliography*; Philadelphia: University of Pennsylvania, 1974. Robert McAfee Brown, *Making Peace in the Global Village*; Philadelphia: Westminster, 1981. Berenice A. Carroll, et al., *Peace and War: A Guide to Bibliographies*; Santa Barbara, CA: ABC-Olia, 1983. Charles Chatfield, ed., *Peace Movements in America*; NY: Schocken, 1973. Gordon Cosby and Bill Price, *Handbook for World Peacemaker Groups*; Washington: World Peacemakers, 1982. Karl W. Deutsch, *Peace Research*; Middlebury, VT: Middlebury College, 1972. James E. Dougherty, *The Bishops and Nuclear Weapons: The Catholic Pastoral Letter on War and Peace*; Hamden, CT: Archon, 1984. Judith A. Dwyer, ed., *The Catholic Bishops and Nuclear War: A Critique and Analysis of the Pastoral, The Challenge of Peace*; Washington: Georgetown University, 1984. Christopher Grannis, et al., *The Risk of the Cross: Christian Discipleship in the Nuclear Age*; NY: Seabury, 1982. Mahendra Kumar, *Current Peace Research and India*; Varanasi: Gandhian Institute of Studies, 1968. John Macquarrie, *The Concept of Peace*; NY: Harper & Row, 1973. Ganshyam Pardesi, ed., *Contemporary Peace Research*; Atlantic Highlands, NJ: Humanities, 1982. *Peace on Earth*; NY: UNESCO, 1980. *Peace Studies*; Seoul: Kyung Hee University, 1982. Thomas A. Shannon, *War or Peace?*; Maryknoll: Orbis, 1980. John Somerville, *The Peace Revolution*; Westport, CT: Greenwood, 1975. Joan M. Steffy, *The San Francisco Peace Movement: A Survey*; NY: Professors World Peace Academy, 1985. Jack L. Stotts, *Shalom: The Search for a Peaceable City*; NY: Abingdon, 1973. The United Methodist Council of Bishops, *In Defense of Creation: The Nuclear Crisis and a Just Peace*; Nasvhille: Graded Press, 1986. Lawrence S. Wittner, *Rebels Against War: The American Peace Movement, 1941-1960*; NY: Columbia, 1969. David S. Young, ed., *Study War No More*; Elgin, IL: Brethren Press, 1982.

39. Stassen, op. cit., pp. 626–628. Gleason L. Archer, Jr., et al., *The Rapture*; Grand Rapids, MI: Zondervan, 1984. Hal Lindsey, *The 1980's: Countdown to Armageddon*; NY: Bantam, 1980. Roger Fisher, *International Conflict for Beginners*; NY: Harper & Row, 1969.

40. Stassen, op. cit., pp. 629–632.

Chapter III

1. A modern Muslim scholar, Isma'il R. al Faruqi (1921–1986), claimed Judaism, Christianity and Islam are one. Islam did not appear ex nihilo, out of nothing. It is a reaffirmation of the truth of the earlier religions. He also postulated an unrelated native Arabic tradition called hanifiism, which was ethical mono-

theism going back to Abraham. Al Faruqi, "The Role of Islam in Global Inter-religious Dependence," pp. 19–53, in *Towards a Global Congress of the World's Religions*, ed. Warren Lewis; NY: Rose of Sharon, 1980, and, "Islam," pp. 237–283, in *Historical Atlas of the Religions of the World*, ed. al Faruqi and David E. Sopher; NY: Macmillan, 1974. The latter work is cited hereafter as HARW.

James A. Aho treats ancient Hebraism and ancient Islam as similar if not identical religious traditions—both have one true god, an uncreated creator (Quran Sura [chapter] 2:27–28, 2:256, 3:1, 16:3–77) who is absolutely omniscient and omnipotent (2:100–101, 3:25–27, 6:59062, 13:9–17) and whose love is overshadowed by his might (59:23–24). Moral standards are also included. He suggests that the Day of Judgment and the concepts of Hell and Heaven (Sura 15:35–36, 17:13, 22:5, 30:56, 82:17–18) come from Christianity. *Religious Mythology and the Art of War;* Westport, CT: Greenwood, 1981, pp. 182–183. Kenneth Cragg, *Islam and the Muslim;* Milton Keynes: Open University, 1978, pp. 7–12. H.A.R. Gibb and J.H. Kramers, eds., *Shorter Encyclopedia of Islam;* Ithaca: Cornell, 1953. P.M. Holt, et al., eds., *The Cambridge History of Islam;* Cambridge: University Press, 1970. Young Oon Kim, *World Religions*, vol. 1; NY: Golden Gate, 1982, pp. 175–176, notes that the once popular view that Islam borrowed its beliefs from Judaism has been largely abandoned. Niels C. Nielson, Jr., *Religions of the World;* NY: St. Martin's, 1983, pp. 588–590. Cited hereafter as NRW. John B. Noss and David S. Noss, *Man's Religions*, 7th ed.; NY: Macmillan, 1984, pp. 496–500. Ibrahim M. Shalaby, "Islam and Peace," *Journal of Religious Thought* 34, no. 2 (Fall–Winter 1977), 42–49. Ninian Smart, *The Long Search;* Boston: Little, Brown, 1977, pp. 187, 190–191. Cited hereafter as SLS. Gaston Wiet, et al., eds., *History of Mankind, vol. III: The Great Medieval Civilizations;* NY: Harper & Row, 1975. J. Christy Wilson, *Introducing Islam;* NY: Friendship, 1965, p. 11, notes Sura 10:94 of the Quran, "If thou art in doubt about what we have revealed, ask them who read the Scripture before thee." This presumably refers to the Bible since the earthly Quran did not exist before Muhammad. He adds, pp. 23–24, the widespread idea that Muhammad did not inaugurate a new religion but revived the true religion.

Transliterations from the Arabic vary. Muslim is preferred to Moslem, Mussulman or Muhammedan. Mecca is common though Makkah is also used. Quraysh is also spelled Quaraysh, Qoraysh and Kuraish. Quran is commonly spelled Koran. 'Allah is often simplified to Allah.

2. HARW-240. NRW-591, 612. SLS-187. William H. Harris and Judith S. Levey, eds., *The New Columbia Encyclopedia;* NY: Columbia, 1975, pp. 1443. Cited hereafter as NCE. Richard C. Martin, *Islam;* Englewood Cliffs, NJ: Prentice-Hall, 1982, p. 30. Geoffrey Parrinder, *A Dictionary of Non-Christian Religions;* Philadelphia: Westminster, 1971, pp. 16, 126, 147. Cited hereafter as PDNR. The Ka'ba is about 12 m by 11 m and 15 m high, with a flat roof. It is only open a few times a year. Lamps hang inside. The walls are covered with inscriptions.

3. HARW-238-240. NCE-1733-1734. NRW-591-592. PDNR-181. Wiet, op. cit., pp. 141-145. Philip K. Hitti, *History of the Arabs*, 10th ed; NY: St. Martin's, 1975. Fazlur Rahman, *Islam*, 2nd ed; Chicago: University of Chicago, 1979.

4. Aho, op. cit., p. 182, notes the tradition that the Quraysh were one of the North Arabic tribes descended from Ishmael. NRW-588, 612. PDNR-47, says the Black Stone (al-Hajaru 'l-Aswad) is about 28 cm in diameter and mounted in a circular silver band. It is interesting that for all its sacredness throughout the history of Islam, the city, the Kaaba, and the Black Stone were not safe from attack. The city has been conquered and reconquered several times, most recently by the Saudis. The Black Stone was stolen by the Qarmatians and held for 20 years before being returned at the request of the Fatimids (see later). The sacred Mosque of

Mecca was captured by 350 Muslim fundamentalists on November 20, 1979, and held for two weeks in protest against the Saudi government which captured them and executed 65. Ayman S. Al-Yassini, "Saudi Arabia: The Kingdom of Islam," pp. 59–84, in *Religions and Societies: Asia and the Middle East*, ed. Carlo Caldarola; NY: Mouton, 1982.

5. Cragg, *Islam*, op. cit., pp. 12–22. HARW-240–247. Kim, op. cit., pp. 162–175. Martin, op. cit., pp. 30–38. NCE-1854. Noss, op. cit., pp. 500–505. NRW-593–604. PDNR-192. SLS-187–189. Wiet, op. cit., pp. 145–146. Wilson, op. cit., pp. 6–12. 'Abd-al-Rahman 'Azzam, *The Eternal Message of Muhammad*; NY: Mentor, 1965. John Ferguson, *War and Peace in the World's Religions*; NY: Oxford, 1978, pp. 124–125. Godfrey H. Jansen, *Militant Islam*; London: Pan Books, 1971. Myrtle Langley, *Religions*; Elgin, IL: Cook, 1981. Bernard Lewis, *Islam, From the Prophet Muhammad to the Capture of Constantinople*; NY: Harper & Row, 1974. Sayyid Fayyaz Mahmud, "The Prophet Muhammad," pp. 23–30, in *The Islamic Tradition*, ed. Lee Smith and Wes Bodin; Allen, TX: Argus, 1978. Seyyed Hossein Nasr, *Ideals and Realities of Islam*; Boston: Beacon, 1972, pp. 67–92. Lothar Schmalfus, "Muhammad," p. 310, in *Eerdmans' Handbook to the World's Religions*, ed. R. Pierce Beaver, et al.; Grand Rapids, MI: Eerdmans, 1982. R.B. Sergeant, "Historical Review," pp. 3–30, in A.J. Arberry, ed., *Religion in the Middle East*, vol. 2; Cambridge: University Press, 1969. Arberry is cited hereafter as ARME. Montgomery Watt, "The Way of the Prophet," pp. 307–314, in Eerdmans, op. cit., and, *Muhammad: Prophet and Statesman*; Oxford: Clarendon, 1961. John Alden Williams, *Islam*; NY: Braziller, 1961, pp. 57–80.

6. Noss, op. cit., p. 502, says the other three married associates of Muhammad. Zainab married Aub-al-'As; Ruqayya married Uthman (later the third Caliph), Umm Qulthum married Utayba. After Ruqayya's death, Umm Qulthum married Uthman, giving him a double claim to the succession. PDNR-16, 96, 294–295, 312. Zaid became Zaid ibn Muhammad at adoption. He died in 630 fighting for the Islamic cause.

7. Noss, op. cit., notes the debate over Muhammad's knowledge of the Judeo-Christian tradition and hence the source of his "revelations." Some Muslims believe the revelations are from Allah while recognizing that Muhammad understood the revelations because of his knowledge of history. Rahman, op. cit., p. 7.

8. PDNR-122. The Muslim calendar is a lunar calendar. The Western solar year of 1980 was 1400 A.H. in Islam.

9. Muezzin is from the Arabic, mu'addhim, the caller of adhan (call to prayer). The first muezzin was a Mecca-born Ethiopian named Bilal ibn Rabah. "The white, highborn aristocratic members of the tribe of Quraish . . . were displeased and complained. . . . [Muhammad] replied that a righteous, God-fearing Negro was, in his view, superior to the highest born member of the tribe of Quraish." K.G. Saiyadain, "Islam," pp. 49–57, in *World Religions and World Peace*, ed. Homer A. Jack; Boston: Beacon, 1968. It would appear that the brotherhood of Islam was not part of their conversion. Bernard Lewis, *Race and Color in Islam*; NY: Harper & Row, 1971. Barry Hoberman, "The First Muezzin," *Aramco World Magazine* 34, no. 4 (July–August 1984), 2–3.

Al Faruqi, op. cit., 31–37, noted that each religion is an umma alongside the umma of Islam. Ferguson, op. cit., pp. 124, 129. NCE-1866. PDNR-181, 192, 292. Kenneth Cragg notes the problem of deciding who is a Muslim in *Counsels in Contemporary Islam*; Edinburgh: University Press, 1965. He cites (pp. 163–164) the judges in Pakistan, "if we adopt the definition given by one of the ulema [learned ones], we remain Muslims according to the view of that 'alim but kafirs [infidels] according to the definition of every one else." John A. Williams, *Themes of Islamic*

Civilization; Berkeley: University of California, 1971, pp. 7–55, "The Community."

Muhammad Abdul Rauf, "Wahy (Revelation)," pp. 17–18, in Smith and Bodin, op. cit Yaqub Zaki, "The Concept of Revelation in Islam," pp. 59–71, in *Unity and Diversity,* ed. Henry O. Thompson; NY: Rose of Sharon, 1984.

10. NCE-43. PDNR-37, 112, 153. Shalaby, op. cit., p. 42. Wilson, op. cit., p. 9, notes one wife was Jewish and another was a Coptic Christian. Nabia Abbott, *Aisha, the Beloved of Mohammad;* NY: Arno, 1973 (original 1942). Aisha was the source of 2210 traditions.

11. Aho, op. cit., p. 182, notes Abraham's near sacrifice of Isaac as the paradigm of submission. HARW-247–248. NCE-9. NRW-615–616. PDNR-8, defines Islam as "submission, surrender." The word is variously derived, e.g., from the root "silm" which means peace. Saiyadain, op. cit., p. 51. A.K. Brohi, "Contribution of Islam (Considered as Religio Perennis) to the Problems of World Peace," pp. 1–19, in *Religion in the Struggle for World Community,* ed. Homer A Jack; NY: World Conference on Religion and Peace, 1980. Zafrulla Khan, "The Fundamental Peace," pp. 54–71, in *Religion for Peace,* ed. Homer A. Jack; New Delhi: Gandhi Peace Foundation, 1973. Wilson, op. cit., pp. 22–26, notes however, that commonly across the Islamic world, Muhammad is known as the sinless one who existed before the creation of the world, a worker of miracles, one whose body did not cast a shadow. One follower said, "As regards salvation from sin and punishment, the Prophet will save all believers of all time." Salvation by faith became a part of the tradition at an early date though the Quran consistently combines faith and morality, e.g., 2:62; 5:69. Fazlur Rahman, "The Law of Rebellion in Islam," pp. 1–10, in *Islam in the Modern World,* ed. Jill Riatt; Columbia, MO: University of Missouri, 1983. Rahman is really talking about the laws which prohibit rebellion. "Islam itself, of course, was rebellion against the 'status quo' in 7th-century Arabia.... But after the Islamic movement gained power and generated governments, the lawyers of Islam . . . prohibited all uprisings against an established rule. Nevertheless, throughout Islamic history there have been rebellions...." The first of these were the tribes after Muhammad's death. Abu Bakr forced them to acknowledge the political authority of Medina. He used the law on apostasy (ridda) though the tribes were not apostate, says Rahman. They continued as Muslims but rejected the political authority of Medina. Abu Bakr thus set the tone for Islamic history. Rahman notes that Islamic law prohibits war for political conquest but any war can be justified by declaring it a jihad, a struggle for the Cause of Allah.

12. HARW-248–249. NCE-2820, 2852. NRW-616–617. PDNR-292, 294–295. Parrinder notes that Umar had the site of the Jerusalem Temple (Solomon's, Herod's) cleared. The Dome of the Rock was built by Abd al-Malik in 691 but the earlier work explains why the shrine is often called the mosque of Omar. While the faithful credit Allah, Noss, op. cit., p. 515, notes several other explanations for the rapidity of the conquests by poorly equipped (bows and arrows, bamboo spears) bedouin — the vicious rule of the Byzantine Christians and the magnanimous terms offered by the Muslims made the inhabitants — Christians, Jews and everyone else — welcome Islam. All they had to do was submit and pay the tax (poll tax, jizya, and land tax, kharaj) of non-Muslims. The people of the Book (Ahl el-Kitab) — Jews, Christians and Sabaeans — were normally respected. The mobility of the Arab horse and camel, the skill of Muslim generals, and the devotion to Allah's cause must also be noted. In addition, soldiers kept four-fifths of the spoil and were promised paradise if they were killed in battle. The last later cost the United States a lot of second lieutenants in the Philippines when Moro warriors — Mindanao Muslims — waded through gunfire to machete U.S. officers. No one seems to know why

second lieutenants were a special target — perhaps because they were officers and there were more of them. Patrick L. Townsend, "Requiem for the Colt .45," *Newsweek* (March 18, 1985), 14.

On treatment of people of the Book, see Aho, op. cit., pp. 183–186, Brohi, op. cit., p. 9, and Ferguson, op. cit., p. 127, who notes tolerant treatment of Spanish Christians as facilitating the rapidity of the Muslim conquest there. He notes, p. 125, that acceptance of Allah as the one and only God brought forgiveness of all sins, no matter how bad (compare acceptance of Jesus as Savior) as an attraction of the new faith. He also suggests, p. 126, that over-population from the end of internecine warfare and the end of infanticide was a factor. He credits the jihad with maintaining and encouraging the traditional belligerence of the Arabs while directing that courage against others. In later times, internecine warfare returned and became almost endemic. The jihad against Israel has united some but not all Muslims today. The same can be said for the pan–Arab and pan–Islamic movements of the last 100 years. See later on Islam today.

13. Note that rifts were there from the beginning — among the pre–Islamic tribes, among the clans of Quraysh, among the successors and among individuals, i.e., Aisha's opposition to Uthman and Ali. Noss, op. cit., pp. 514–516, notes three divergent views of the succession. The Companions thought the Caliph should be elected from among them. The Legitimists thought succession should be hereditary, i.e., through Ali. The later Ummayads thought they, as leaders of Muhammad's tribe, should determine the succession. They themselves, however, established an hereditary dynasty. NCE-67, 2502. NRW-617–618, 647, notes that the later jurists (ulama) insisted that election was correct but then accepted the hereditary dynasties already installed. PDNR-16, 97, 254. SLS-205. Rahman, op. cit., pp. 7–8, notes the Quran in 42:38 establishes shura, mutual consultation and discussion, as the proper way of rule. Even the Prophet was instructed to consult the community (3:159). Later rulers distorted this to mean a ruler's consultation with whomever he chose to consult. Rahman claims current dictatorships are in violation of the Quran which teaches democracy. The Quran does not even call the caliphate an institution for rule. Rather, all of humanity are viceregents (khalifas) of God (6:165; 10:14, 73; 35:39).

14. Cragg, *Islam*, op. cit., pp. 24–35. Ferguson, op. cit., p. 125. Kim, op. cit., pp. 171–173. Nasr, op. cit., pp. 41–66. NCE-1496. Noss, op. cit., pp. 506–514. NRW-605–608. PDNR-228, 268–269. SLS-191–192. Wiet, op. cit., pp. 540–573. Williams, Islam, op. cit., pp. 15–56. Wilson, op. cit., pp. 26–29. N.J. Dawood, ed., *The Koran*, rev.; Baltimore: Penguin, 1979. Helmut Gatje, *The Qur'an and Its Exegesis*; Berkeley: University of California, 1976. Muhammad Marmaduke Pickthall, ed., *The Meaning of the Glorious Qur'an: Text and Explanatory Translation*; NY: Muslim World League, 1977. Fazlur Rahman, *Major Themes of the Qur'an*; Chicago: Biblioteca Islamica, 1980. Labib as–Said, *The Recited Koran*; Princeton: Darwin, 1975. W. Montgomery Watt, *Bell's Introduction to the Qur'an*, rev.; Edinburgh: University Press, 1970.

15. Noss, op. cit., pp. 518–519. NRW-624–625. PDNR-112. Williams, Islam, op. cit., pp. 80–91. Wilson, op. cit., p. 30. The Shiites have five additional books of hadith which include words of the Prophet and also the imams. Muhammad Ali, *A Manual of Hadith*; Lahore: Ahmadiyya Anjuman, 1951. A. Suhrawardy, *The Sayings of Muhammad*; London: Murray, 1941. One of the most well-known hadith is on equality. "All people are equal, as equal as the teeth of a comb. There is no claim of merit of an Arab over a non–Arab, or of a white over a black person, or of a male over a female. Only God-fearing people merit a preference with God."

16. Aho, op. cit., pp. 183–185. Ferguson, op. cit., p. 131. Khan, op. cit., pp.

64–65. Kim, op. cit., pp. 169–170, quotes al–Ghazzali as saying every man in paradise will have the companionship of 4000 young girls and 8000 attractive divorcees, though a hadith of Muhammad promises the martyr in paradise marriage to only 72 "huris" according to Williams, *Themes*, p. 259. NCE-2655. PDNR-268. Nasir Ahmed Faruqui, "Islamic Prayers," pp. 213–216, in Jack, *Religion for Peace*, op. cit. Viqar A. Hamdan, "Islam," pp. 230–232, and, "The Muslim Service," pp. 155–157, in Jack, *Religion in the Struggle for World Community*, op. cit. The World Conference on Religion and Peace met in 1979. Most of the 31 Muslim participants signed a statement appealing to governments of Muslim countries to continue to grant freedom to non–Muslim minorities. They appealed to governments of non–Muslim countries to grant freedom of religion to Muslims living there. "In the Name of Allah, the Beneficent, the Merciful," pp. 296–297, in Jack, *Religion in the Struggle for World Community*, op. cit. They specifically called for the right of self-determination for Palestinians and noted difficulties faced by Muslims in India, Eritrea, Ethiopia, Philippines, Thailand, and Uganda. They did not mention Communist Russia or China, nor did they suggest that the government of Iran should stop murdering Baha'is, nor did they call for the observance of self-determination by Jews and others in Muslim countries.

17. There are 99 names known to man. The Muslim rosary consists of 33 beads, each representing three names. Devout Muslims can often be seen moving two beads at a time down to the 33rd and then starting over. Cragg, *Islam*, op. cit., pp. 45–47. PDNR-16. Wilson, op. cit., p. 21.

18. Aho, op. cit., pp. 190–191. Cragg, *Islam*, op. cit., pp. 36–63. Ferguson, op. cit., p. 131. Hamdani, op. cit., p. 231. HARW-265–266. Khan, op. cit., p. 67. Martin, op. cit., p. 12. Noss, op. cit., p. 520, notes the distinction between conservative and liberal interpreters. The latter are more willing to use reason or common sense. NRW-608–614. PDNR-96, 143, 155, 219, 227. SLS-192–193. Smith and Bodin, op. cit., pp. 39–98. Wilson, op. cit., pp. 24, 30–41, 54. Williams, *Themes*, op. cit., pp. 133–187. Mohamed al–Nowaihi, "Religion and Modernization: The General Problem and Islamic Responses," pp. 309–340, in *Modernization*, ed. Richard L. Rubenstein; Washington: Paragon, 1982. Saiyed Abdul Hai, "Free Will and Predestination in Islam," pp. 115–120, in *Thoughts on Islam*, ed. Sharif Abdullah Haroon; Dacca: Islamic Academy, 1970. David Kerr, "The Worship of Islam," pp. 317–321, in *Eerdmans'*, op. cit. Raphael Patai, *The Arab Mind*; NY: Scribner's, 1973, pp. 150–155. Erwin I.J. Rosenthal, *Islam in the Modern National State*; Cambridge: University Press, 1965. W. Montgomery Watt, *Free Will and Predestination in Early Islam*; London: Luzac, 1948.

Women have had greater acceptance in Sufism and among groups like the Druze and Ibadis. For these and the modern situation, see ARME. Lamia L. al Faruqi, "Women's Rights and the Muslim Women," *Islam and the Modern Age 3*, no. 2 (May 1972), 76–99. Denise Carmody, *Women in World Religions*; Nashville: Abingdon, 1979. Assia Djebar, *Women of Islam*; London: Deutsch, 1961. John L. Esposito, "The Changing Role of Muslim Women," *Islam and the Modern Age 7*, no. 1 (February 1976), 29–56. Carolyn Fleuhr-Lobban, "Challenging Some Myths: Women in Shari'a (Islamic) Law in the Sudan," *Expedition 25*, no. 3 (Spring 1983), 32–39. Y. Haddad, "Islam, Women and Revolution in Twentieth-Century Arab Thought," *Muslim World 74*, nos. 2–3 (July–October 1984), 137–160. Haddad and Ellison B. Findly, eds., *Women, Religion and Social Change*; Albany: State University of New York, 1985. Shafiqua Haq, "Problems of Women in the Modern World and How Islam Proposes to Solve Them," pp. 121–130, in Haroon, op. cit. Patricia J. Higgins, "Women in the Islamic Republic of Iran: Legal, Social, and Ideological Changes," *Signs 10*, no. 3 (Spring 1985), 477–494. Orayb Najjar, "Arab Women:

Fact and Fiction," *The Christian Century* 101, no. 8 (March 7, 1984), 247–249. Muhammad Abdul Rauf, *The Islamic View of Women and the Family;* NY: Speller, 1977. Nawal el Saadawi, *The Hidden Face of Eve: Women in the Arab World;* Boston: Beacon, 1982. Jane I. Smith, "Women in Islam: Equity, Equality, and the Search for the Natural Order," *Journal of the American Academy of Religion* XLVII, no. 4 (December 1979), 517–537. Charis Waddy, *The Muslim Mind;* NY: Longman, 1976, pp. 54–74. Walther Wiebke, *Woman in Islam;* Montclair, NJ: Abner Schram, 1981.

In addition to the equality of women and men in the hadith quoted in n. 15 earlier, one can add others. "To seek knowledge is obligatory on every Muslim, male and female." "Whoever has a daughter and educates her and trains her in the best manner, he is regarded as the best one of you."

19. HARW-249–252. NCE-2820. Noss, op. cit., pp. 516–518. NRW-618–619. PDNR-81, 191, says Mu'awiya and Ali divided the empire between them and that Hasan was persuaded to give up his claims at Ali's death. Wiet, op. cit., pp. 146–152. Clifford E. Bosworth, *The Islamic Dynasties;* Edinburgh: University Press, 1967. W. Montgomery Watt, *A History of Islamic Spain;* Edinburgh: University Press, 1965.

20. Aho, p. 186. HARW-266–267, 273, 275. Jansen, op. cit. pp. 16 et passim. NCE-2, 1372–1373, 1802, 2917. NRW-585, 619–622, 658–670. The last three sources note that Islam is winning in Africa by a wide margin through an aggressive missionary campaign. Islam will exceed Christianity in numbers in the world by the year 2000. David B. Barrett, *World Christian Encyclopaedia;* Nairobi: Oxford, 1982, claims 723 million Muslims in 1980 (809 million Christians) and projects 1,201 million Muslims (2,020 million Christians) in the year 2000. PDNR-7, 37, 96–97, 116, 173, 192, 288. SLS-208–210. Wiet, op. cit., pp. 152–163, 240–255.

Anson P. Atterbury, *Islam in Africa;* Westport, CT: Greenwood, 1969. C. George Fry, "Christianity's Greatest Challenge," *Christianity Today* (November 7, 1969), 9–12. Bernard Lewis, *The Origins of Isma'ilism: A Study of the Historical Background of the Fatimid Caliphate;* NY: AMS, 1975 (original 1940). Noel Q. King, *Christian and Muslim in Africa;* NY: Harper & Row, 1971. James Kritzeck and William H. Lewis, eds., *Islam in Africa;* NY: Van Nostrand-Reinhold, 1969. Bruce B. Lawrence, "The Fundamentalist Response to Islam's Decline: A View from the Asian Periphery," pp. 11–40, in *Islam in the Modern World,* op. cit., David W. Littlefield, *The Islamic Northeast and North Africa: An Annotated Guide to Books in English;* Littleton, CO: Libraries Unlimited, 1977. Maurice Lombard, *The Golden Age of Islam;* NY: American Elsevier, 1975, has an extensive discussion of slavery which included Slavs, Turks and others as well as Black Africans. Ali A. Mazrui, "Cultural Synthesis in Africa," *The World & I* 1, no. 2 (February 1986), 171–185. Arye Oded, *Islam in Uganda;* NY: Wiley, 1974. Patrick E. Ofori, *Islam in Africa South of the Sahara: A Select Bibliographic Guide;* Neldeln, Liechtenstein: Kto Press, 1977. John S. Trimingham, *The Influence of Islam Upon Africa,* 2nd ed.; NY: Longman, 1980, and, *A History of Islam in West Africa;* Oxford: Clarendon, 1972. Samir M. Zoghby, *Islam in Sub-Saharan Africa: A Partially Annotated Guide;* Washington: Library of Congress, 1978.

Al-Yassini, "Saudi Arabia: The Kingdom of Islam," op. cit. Aziz Ahmad, *An Intellectual History of Islam in India;* Edinburgh; Edinburgh University, 1969. William Theodore de Bary, et al., eds., *Sources of Indian Tradition;* NY: Columbia, 1966, pp. 367–528. Julia D. Howell, "Indonesia: Searching for Consensus," pp. 497–548, in Caldarola, op. cit. Homer Jack, ed. *World Religion/World Peace;* NY: World Conference on Religion and Peace, 1979, p. 96. Gordon P. Means, "Malaysia: Islam in a Pluralistic Society," pp. 445–496, in Caldarola, op. cit. George

Rentz, "The Wahhabis," ARME-270–284. Wayne S. Vucinich, "Islam in the Balkans," ARME-236–252. Earle H. Waugh, et al., eds., *The Muslim Community in North America;* Alberta: University of Alberta, 1983. Richard V. Weeks, ed., *Muslim Peoples;* Westport, CT: Greenwood, 1978.

21. Ferguson, op. cit., p. 131. HARW-265. Jack, *World Religion/World Peace,* op. cit., p. 96. Noss, op. cit., 519–536. PDNR-153, 194. Williams, *Islam,* op. cit., pp. 213–219. Roberto Rubinacci, "The Ibadis," ARME-302–317.

22. Mahdi, the divinely guided one, is a like Jewish messiah who will come some day, perhaps Jesus, perhaps an imam back from the dead, or spiritual hidden-ness. He will gather his followers to victory for a time of justice and peace before the last judgment. There are similarities here to the Christian concept of the second coming of Christ. A hadith of Muhammad says the Mahdi will be of Muhammad's family. Shiites interpret this to mean the Mahdi will be one of their imams. However, another hadith says "There is no Mahdi but Jesus the Son of Mary!" Noss, op. cit., p. 532. NCE-1663. NRW-650. Out of the several mahdi, the most well-known is Muhammad ibn Abdullah (1844–1885) of the Sudan who set up a kingdom in Khartoum after the death of the British General "Chinese" Gordon. PDNR-172. As recently as November 20, 1979, a mahdi was proclaimed by fundamentalists who took over the sacred Mosque of Mecca. The Saudis recaptured it in two weeks and killed him. Al-Yassini, op. cit., p. 80. Williams, *Islam,* op. cit., p. 225, and, *Themes,* op. cit., pp. 191–251. Abdulaziz A. Sachedina, *Islamic Messianism: The Idea of the Mahdi in Twelver Shi'ism;* Albany: State University of New York, 1981.

23. Some say he died but left a son, Muhammad, who disappeared in India, and will return as Mahdi. Cragg, *Islam,* op. cit., pp. 64–69. Nasr, op. cit., pp. 147–178. Noss, op. cit., p. 532. NRW-647–657. PDNR-254, 312. SLS-211–212. Williams, *Islam,* op. cit., pp. 219–239. Asaf A.A. Fyzee, "The Isma'ilis," ARME-318–329. Kerr, "The Unity and Variety of Islam," pp. 330–332 in *Eerdmans',* op. cit. R.B. Sergeant, "The Zaydis," ARME-285–301.

24. Ferguson, op. cit., p. 131. HARW-260–265. Nasr, op. cit., pp. 94–120. NCE-168, 799–800. Noss, op. cit., p. 521. NRW-623–629, 657. PDNR-12, 31–32, 83, 114, 173, 195, 250. SLS-212–215. Williams, *Islam,* op. cit., pp. 92–172. Norman Anderson, "The Law of Islam," pp. 322–324. N.J. Coulson, *A History of Islamic Law;* Edinburgh: University Press, 1964. Asaf A.A. Fyzee, *Outlines of Muham-madan Law;* London: Oxford, 1955. Ignace Goldziher, *Introduction to Islamic Theology and Law;* Princeton: Princeton University, 1981. H.Z. Hirschberg, "The Druzes," ARME-330–348. Majid Khadduri, *The Islamic Conception of Justice;* Baltimore: Johns Hopkins, 1984. Khadduri and Herbert J. Liebesny, eds., *Law in the Middle East: Origin and Development of Islamic Law;* NY: AMS, 1984 (original 1955). Bernard Lewis, *The Assassins;* NY: Octogon, 1980 (original 1968). Aga Khan, *The Christian Century* 103, no. 14 (April 23, 1986), 409. Kevin Reinhart, "Islamic Law as Islamic Ethics," *Journal of Religious Ethics* 11, no. 2 (Fall 1983), 186–203.

25. Cragg, *Islam,* op. cit., pp. 71–77. HARW-266–269. NCE-1099, 2646. Noss, op. cit., pp. 522–528, NRW-629–646. PDNR-30, 106, 195, 268. SLS-186, 206–208. Williams, *Themes,* op. cit., pp. 307–370. Wilson, op. cit., p. 54, also notes the great unity. Islam "may well be described as one of the most cohesive systems known to man." A.J. Arberry, *Sufism;* NY: Harper & Row, 1970 (original 1950). Peter Awn, "The Ethical Concerns of Classical Sufism," *Journal of Religious Ethics* 11, no. 2 (Fall 1983), 240–263. George F. Hourani, *Islamic Rationalism: The Ethics of 'Abd al-Jabbar;* Oxford: Clarendon, 1971. R. Keddie, *Scholars, Saints, and Sufis;* Berkeley: University of California, 1972. Martin Lings, "Sufism," ARME-253–269. Reynold A. Nicholson, *Studies in Islamic Mysticism;* Cambridge: Cambridge

University, 1978 (original 1921). Ahmad H. Sakr and Karm B. Akhtar, *Islamic Fundamentalism*; Ann Arbor, MI: Crescent, 1984. M. Sa'id Shaykh, *Studies in Muslim Philosophy*; Lahore: Ashraf, n.d. Mohamed Ahmed Sherif, *Ghazali's Theory of Virtue*; Albany: State University of NY, 1975. Margaret Smith, *The Way of the Mystics*; NY: Oxford, 1978 (original 1931). J. Spencer Trimingham, *The Sufi Orders in Islam*; Oxford: Clarendon, 1971. James M. Wall, "Shi'ite Fundamentalism Leads '85 Newsmakers," *The Christian Century* 103, no. 1 (January 1–8, 1986), 3–4. W. Montgomery Watt, *The Faith and Practice of al-Ghazali*; London: Allen & Unwin, 1953, and, *Muslim Intellectual: A Study of al-Ghazzali*; Edinburgh: University Press, 1963.

26. Brohi, op. cit., p. 16. Martin, op. cit., pp. 70–85. NCE-1372, 2684. Noss, op. cit., pp. 536–540. PDNR-272. Wiet, op. cit., pp. 311 et passim. James S. Ackerman, et al., eds., *Islamic Art and Architecture*; NY: Garland, 1976. Ernst Grube, *The World of Islam*; NY: McGraw-Hill, 1966 (Landmarks of the World's Art). Bernard Lewis, ed., *Islam and the Arab World*; NY: Knopf, 1976. Lombard, *Golden Age of Islam*, op. cit. Muhammad Marmaduke Pickthall, *The Cultural Side of Islam*; Madras: Universal, 1959. Abdur Rauf, *Islamic Culture and Civilization in Pakistan*; Lahore: Ferozsons, 1975. Francis Robinson, *Atlas of the Islamic World Since 1500*; NY: Facts on File, 1982. Lothar Schmalfuss, "Science, Art and Culture in Islam," pp. 327–329, in *Eerdmans'*, op. cit. A.M.A. Shushtery, *Outlines of Islamic Culture*; Bangalore: Bangalore Press, 1938. K.A. Waheed, *Islamic Background of Modern Science and Culture*; Karachi: National Book Foundation, 1977. Anthony Welch and Stuart C. Welch, *Arts of the Islamic Book*; Ithaca: Cornell, 1982.

27. Al-Yassini, op. cit. HARW-275. NCE-2431–2432, 2804–2805. Jansen, op. cit., for Turkey and all of Islam today. Noss, op. cit., pp. 540–556. Tom Breen, "The Rich Get Richer—and Lazier," *Insight* 2, no. 37 (September 15, 1986), 38–39. Bernard Lewis, *The Emergence of Modern Turkey*, 2nd ed.; London: Oxford, 1968, p. 350, Turk=Muslim. Serif Mardin, "Turkey: Islam and Westernization," pp. 171–198, in Caldarola, op. cit. Henrik Bering-Jensen, "After Years of Martial Law, Democracy Is Marching Back," *Insight* 2, no. 38 (September 22, 1986), 32–34.

28. Cragg, *Islam*, op. cit., pp. 70, 78–87. For the Muslim Brotherhood and parallel movements, and for the Ahmadiyya, see Cragg, *Counsels*, op. cit., pp. 110–124, 155–166. Lawrence, op. cit. NCE-209, 307, 2045–2047. Noss, op. cit., pp. 554–556, says the name Black Muslims comes from a book by C. Eric Lincoln, *The Black Muslims in America*; Boston: Beacon, 1963. NRW-671–688. PDNR-13, 38–39, 46. Rahman, *The Law*, op. cit., pp. 9–10, suggests neo-fundamentalism is trying to submerge the Quran's democracy and retrogress to medievalism. Wilson, op. cit., p. 54. Munir D. Ahmed, "Pakistan: The Dream of an Islamic State," pp. 261–288, in Caldarola, op. cit. Norman Anderson, "The Future of Islam," pp. 333–334, in *Eerdmans'*, op. cit. Edward Atiyah, *The Arabs*; Baltimore: Penguin, 1958. Harold B. Barclay, "Egypt: Struggling with Secularization," pp. 119–145, in Caldarola, op. cit. Morroe Berger, *The Arab World Today*; Garden City, NY: Doubleday, 1964. Joel Bjorling, *The Baha'i Faith: A Historical Bibliography*; NY: Garland, 1985, presents (p. 11) the Baha'i faith as an independent world religion rather than a sect of Islam, though he quotes (p. 3) others who describe Baha'i as religion renewed rather than a new religion. John E. Esslemont, *Baha'u'llah and the New Era*, 3rd ed.; Wilamette, IL: Baha'i, 1970 (original 1928). Yvonne Haddad, *Contemporary Islam and the Challenge of History*; Albany: SUNY, 1982. Nikki R. Keddie, "Iran: Religious Orthodoxy and Heresy in Political Culture," pp. 199–229, in Caldarola, op. cit. Gilles Kepel, *Muslim Extremism in Egypt*; Berkeley: University of California, 1986 (an analysis of contemporary fundamentalist movements).

John J. Metzler, "U.N. Seeks End to Persecution of Baha'is in Iran," *Religious Freedom Alert* **II**, no. 1 (February 1986), 19. "Ferocity of Iran's Baha'i Persecution Unabated," *Religious Freedom Alert* **III**, no. 1 (January/February 1987), 18. Moojan Momen, ed., *The Babi and Baha'i Religions, 1844–1944;* Oxford: Ronald, 1981. James Robson, "The Ahmadis," ARME-349–362. Derk Kinnane Roelofsma, "Seeking Brotherhood, Finding Hate," *Insight* 3, no. 4 (January 26, 1987), 60–61. Wilfred Cantwell Smith, *Islam in Modern History;* NY: New American Library, 1963. Rahman, *The Law,* op. cit., p. 2.

The journal, *Islam and the Modern Age* (New Delhi) 1, no. 1 (May 1970), is an important source of current thinking about Islam.

29. Al Faruqi, op. cit., p. 45. Aho, op. cit., p. 187, compares the razzia (caravan and oasis raids) of pre–Islamic bedouin as a source of the jihad concept. "Ghazi" originally meant "he who participates in the ghazw (razzia)." Brohi, op. cit., p. 12. Ferguson, op. cit., pp. 125, 130–137, suggests an analogy between striving and holy war, with the English terms striving and strife. HARW-256–257. Noss, op. cit., p. 554. Parrinder, op. cit., p. 143. Saiyadain, op. cit., p. 56. SLS-194–195. Williams, *Themes,* op. cit., pp. 255–303.

Hasan Askari, "Muslim Approaches to Religious Sources for Peace," *World Faiths Insight* 8 (January 1984), 42–46. Joseph D. Ben-Dak, pp. 7–9, in *The Global Congress of the World's Religions,* ed. Henry O. Thompson; NY: Rose of Sharon, 1982. Rahman, *The Law,* op. cit., p. 1, notes that Islamic law forbids war for conquest so every war is declared a jihad, whether it is against other Muslims or against non–Muslims. Ibn Khaldun in his *Muqaddima* describes the Arabs as wild, refractory, tough, proud, of lofty ambition with rivalry for supremacy. This is set aside when they are united under religious law (din). Quoted by Sergeant, "Historical Review," op. cit., p. 3.

Majid Khadduri, *War and Peace in the Law of Islam,* 2nd ed.; Baltimore: Johns Hopkins, 1955. In addition to the Law of War (jihad), pp. 51–137, Khadduri discusses the Law of Peace (pp. 141–296). The latter is a temporary device to regulate international relations until all the world becomes dar al–Islam. Dar al-sulh (world of peace) or dar al-'ahd (world of covenant) were non–Muslims who submitted to Islamic authority. Others were dar al-harb, the world or house of war. Elsewhere, Khadduri and Liebesny, op. cit., p. 350, he notes that Islamic law, like medieval Christianity, "recognizes no other nation than its own since the aim of Islam was the subordination of the whole world to one system of law and religion, to be enforced by the supreme authority of the caliph." Thomas P. Murphy, ed., *The Holy War;* Columbus: Ohio State, 1976.

30. Aho, op. cit., p. 188. Askari, op. cit., p. 43. Ferguson, op. cit., pp. 130–137. Khadduri, op. cit., p. 100. Shalaby, op. cit., p. 48, does not deny Muslim leaders have used force to spread Islam but their unjustified fervor was not grounded in Islamic law. Waddy, op. cit., pp. 91–103. Williams, *Themes,* op. cit., p. 278, claims "it is the Sufi mystics who have most emphasized interior struggle: to conquer one's Self is better than the taking of a city." Shaykh Abu Zahra, *The Concept of War in Islam;* Cairo: Ministry of Waqfs, n.d., pp. 12–13. S.A. Haque, *Islam's Contribution to the Peace of the World;* Lahore: Ahmadiya, n.d., pp. 37–48. Pyarelal Nair, *Thrown to the Wolves: Abdul Ghaffar;* Calcutta: Eastlight, 1966. D.G. Tendulkar, *Abdul Ghaffar Khan: Faith Is a Battle;* Bombay: Popular Prakasham, 1967.

31. Al Faruqi, op. cit., p. 45. Aho, op. cit., pp. 185, 189–190. Askari, op. cit., p. 45. Khadduri, *War and Peace,* op. cit., pp. 76–77, 92, 102, 105–106. Khan, op. cit., p. 69. Saiyadain, op. cit., p. 51.

32. Aho, 185–186. Khadduri, *War and Peace,* op. cit., pp. 91, 126–131. Noss,

op. cit., p. 500. Khan, op. cit., pp. 55, 57, 68, 70. Saiyadain, op. cit., pp. 51–53.

33. Al Faruqi, op. cit., p. 19. Brohi, op. cit., p. 3. Ferguson, op. cit., pp. 134–135. Parrinder, op. cit., p. 241. Saiyadain, op. cit., pp. 51–52. Shalaby, op. cit., p. 43. Ala' Eddin Kharofa, "Muslim Prayers," pp. 148–149, in Jack, *Religion in the Struggle for World Community*, op. cit.

34. Saiyadain, op. cit., pp. 53–54. Brohi, op. cit., pp. 12–15. Hamdani, op. cit., p. 231, notes that injustice should not be done even to those who have animosity toward you. The statement cited earlier includes the words, "We are convinced that Islam stands for Peace, Justice, Mercy, Forgiveness, and the creation of a just and compassionate society based on Divine Law." "In the Name of Allah...," op. cit., p. 296. Riffat Hassan, "Peace and the Islamic World-view," *Occasional Papers: Center for Peace and Conflict Studies* II (Fall 1981), 11–14.

35. Al Faruqi, op. cit., pp. 26–37. Brohi, op. cit., p. 18, Hamdani, op. cit., p. 230, Khan, op. cit., pp. 59–60, and Saiyadain, op. cit., pp. 50–52, Waheed, op. cit., 76–91. Mohammed Rafi-ud-Din, *The Potential Contribution of Islam to World Peace*; Karachi: Hamdard Dawakhana Trust, 1957.

36. Aho, op. cit., pp. 184, 192. Obedience to all rulers, including tyrants, is noted by Ferguson, op. cit., p. 130. Christianity has also exhibited both attitudes. The divine right of kings in western Europe and Russian Orthodox submission to Ivan the Terrible are but two of many examples. Saiyadain, op. cit., pp. 53–54. For details on mass liquidations by the Turks, Aho cites George Horton, *The Blight of Asia*; Indianapolis: Bobbs-Merrill, 1926, "a well-documented, if admittedly clearly biased description...." Shalaby, op. cit., p. 43, says Islam=peace, independent of the behavior of individuals. Their actions do not define Islam. Their actions should be judged by Islam.

37. Zakir Husain, "Preface," *World Religions and World Peace*, op. cit., pp. vii–x. Saiyadain, op. cit., pp. 49–50.

38. Brohi, op. cit., p. 19. Saiyadain, op. cit., p. 50. Wilson, op. cit., pp. 40–41, notes "In Islam, we have the strange paradox of a religion, spread by military conquest and with injunctions to holy war in its basic scripture, becoming the advocate of peace in a world decimated by wars begun in nations that are nominally followers of the Prince of Peace."

Chapter IV

1. There are a number of good general introductions to Hinduism. Philip H. Ashby, *Modern Trends in Hinduism*; NY: Columbia, 1974. Nirad C. Chaudhuri, *Hinduism: A Religion to Live By*; NY: Oxford, 1979. Cromwell Crawford, ed., *In Search of Hinduism*; Barrytown, NY: Unification Theological Seminary, 1986. Wm. Theodore de Bary, et al., compilers, *Sources of Indian Tradition*; NY: Columbia University, 1958. Allie M. Frazier, *Hinduism*; Philadelphia: Westminster, 1969. Hal W. French and Arvind Sharma, *Religious Ferment in Modern India*; NY: St. Martin's, 1981. David R. Kinsley, *Hinduism*; Englewood Cliffs, NJ: Prentice-Hall, 1982. Louis Renou, *Hinduism*; NY: Braziller, 1962. K.M. Sen, *Hinduism*; Baltimore, MD: Penguin, 1970. There is also a variety of volumes on world religions which include Hinduism. R. Pierce Beaver, et al., eds., *Eerdmans' Handbook to the World's Religions*; Grand Rapids, MI: Eerdmans, 1982. Keith Crim, et al., eds., *Abingdon Dictionary of Living Religions*; Nashville, TN: Abingdon, 1981. Young Oon Kim, *World Religions*, 2nd ed.; NY: Golden Gate, 1982. Niels C. Nielsen, Jr., et al., *Religions of the World*; NY: St. Martin's, 1983. David S. Noss

and John B. Noss, *Man's Religions*, 7th ed.; NY: Macmillan, 1984. Venkatarama
Raghavan, "Hinduism," pp. 69–96, *Historical Atlas of the Religions of the World*,
ed. Isma'il R. al Faruqi and David E. Sopher; NY: Macmillan, 1974. Ninian Smart,
The Long Search; Boston: Little, Brown, 1977. Huston Smith, *The Religions of
Man*; NY: Harper & Row, 1965. Lin Yutang, *The Wisdom of China and India*; NY:
Modern Library, 1955 (original 1942). Robert C. Zaener, ed., *The Concise En-
cyclopedia of Living Faiths*; NY: Hawthorn, 1964. Cf. also Raymond B. Williams,
"Hinduism in America," *The Christian Century* **104**, no. 8 (March 11, 1987),
267–269.

    2. Sen, op. cit., p. 17. Arthur L. Basham describes Hinduism as monotheistic
but at the beginning of time, God created innumerable supernatural beings, some
in tune with God and some against (demons). "Hinduism," pp. 661–667, in *Encyclopedia of Bioethics*, ed. Warren Reich; NY: Free Press, 1978. John Ferguson,
War and Peace in the World's Religions; NY: Oxford, 1978, p. 29. In the epic poem
the Mahabharata, the King of Dharma is told to worship the brahmins. William H.
Harris and Judith S. Levey, eds., *The New Columbia Encyclopedia*; NY: Columbia,
1975, pp. 756, 1245. Cited hereafter as NEC. George Kotturan, *Ahimsa: Gautama
to Gandhi*; New Delhi: Sterling, 1973, pp. 64–65. Geoffrey Parrinder suggests
dharma is the form of things and the power that maintains them. The word is variously translated duty, right, right conduct, teaching, virtue, truth, obedience to
caste, inner guidance, intuition, and sometimes, religion. It has been interpreted as
doing that which is appropriate to the circumstances. Parrinder, *A Dictionary of
Non-Christian Religions*; Philadelphia: Westminster, 1974. K.L. Seshagiri Rao,
Mahatma Gandhi and Comparative Religion; New Delhi: Motilal Binarsidass,
1978, p. 13. Dharma is derived from "dhri" meaning to have or maintain. Indira
Rothermund, "Mahatma Gandhi and Hindu Tradition," *Gandhi Marg* **3**, no. 12
(March 1982), 722–733.

    3. Frazier, op. cit., pp. 56–57. Sen, op. cit., p. 47. The Asvins ("horsemen")
are the twin sons of the sun, who rescue people in trouble. James A. Aho, *Religious
Mythology and the Art of War: Comparative Religious Symbolisms of Military
Violence*; Westport, CT: Greenwood, 1981, pp. 60–79. Stuart Piggott, *Prehistoric
India*; Baltimore, MD: Penguin, 1950, p. 250. James B. Pritchard, ed., *Ancient Near
Eastern Texts Relating to the Old Testament*, 3rd ed.; Princeton: Princeton, 1969,
p. 206. Wendy O'Flaherty, *The Rig Veda: An Anthology*; NY: Penguin, 1983, pp.
335, 326.

    4. Bridget and Raymond Allchin, *The Rise of Civilization in India and
Pakistan*; NY: Cambridge, 1982. George F. Dales, "Civilization and Floods in the
Indus Valley," *Expedition* **7**, no. 4 (Summer 1965), 10–19. Sir John Marshall, *A
Guide to Taxila*; NY: Cambridge, 1960, and, *Mohenjo Daro and the Indus Civiliza-
tion*; London: Prosbsthain, 1931. Robert L. Raikes, "The End of the Ancient Cities
of the Indus," *American Anthropologist* **66**, no. 2 (April 1964), 284–299. Sir Mor-
timer Wheeler, *Early India and Pakistan*; NY: Praeger, 1959. Ruth Whitehouse, *The
First Cities*; NY: Dutton, 1977.

    5. Some say there are millions of gods but see again Basham, op. cit., p. 661,
with the idea of one God who created innumerable divine beings at the beginning
of time. Diana L. Eck, *Banaras: City of Light*; NY: Knopf, 1982, pp. 51–54, 146.
Steven J. Gelberg, *Hare Krishna, Hare Krishna*; NY: Grove, 1983. Milton Singer,
ed., *Krishna: Myths, Rites, and Attitudes*; Chicago: University of Chicago, 1968.

    6. Kotturan, op. cit., pp. 66–67. O'Flaherty, op. cit. Sen, op. cit., pp. 115,
122, suggests the dates of circa 1200 B.C. for the Rig Veda and circa 1000 for the
Atharva. Yutang, op. cit., pp. 11–30. Franklin Edgerton, ed., *The Beginning of Indian Philosophy: Selections from the Rig Veda, Atharva Veda, Upanishads and*

Mahabharata; Cambridge: Harvard, 1965. Walter A. Fairservis, Jr., "The Script of the Indus Valley Civilization," *Scientific American* **248**, no. 3 (March 1983), 58–66. James A. Santucci, *An Outline of Vedic Literature;* Missoula: Scholars, 1983. Robert C. Zaener, *Hindu Scriptures;* NY: Dutton, 1966.

7. Sen, op. cit., pp. 53–56, 127–145. Yutang, op. cit., pp. 31–53. Paul J. Deussen, *The Philosophy of the Upanishads;* NY: Dover, 1966. Swami Nikhilanandam, *The Upanishads;* NY: Harper & Row, 1963. Koshelya Walli, *The Conception of Ahimsa in Indian Thought (According to Sanskrit Sources);* Varanasi: Bharata Manisha, 1974, p. viii.

8. Yutang, op. cit., pp. 54–114. James L. Fitzgerald, "The Great Epic of India as Religious Rhetoric: A Fresh Look at the 'Mahabharata'," *Journal of the American Academy of Religion* LI, no. 4 (December 1983), 611–630. Ann Stamford, *The Bhagavad Gita;* NY: Continuum, 1977. J.A.B. Van Buitenen, *The Mahabharata;* Chicago: University of Chicago, 1973–1978, and, *The Bhagavad Gita in the Mahabharata;* Chicago: University of Chicago, 1981.

9. Kim, op. cit., pp. 3–7. Sen, op. cit., pp. 72–85. Yutang, op. cit., pp. 135–269.

10. Basham, op. cit., p. 662, calls the four major groups classes (varna) and the subgroups castes (jati). Rao, op. cit., p. 20. Sen, op. cit., pp. 27–31.

11. She isolated some 8000 verses in the Mahabharata that show the same structure as the Seventh Mandala of the Rig Veda. Here the priests are called "vipra," and are more shamans than keepers of the cows and dharma. Their chief function is composing poems or power songs that make the warriors victorious in getting loot. See her "Warriors: The Originators of the Moral Code of Ancient India," pp. 57–61, in *Asian Religions — History of Religion: 1974*, compiled by Harry Partin; Tallahassee, Florida: American Academy of Religion, 1974.

12. Mary Carroll Smith, op. cit., p. 60, suggests that Yudhisthira is a creation of the brahmins who wanted a generous, stupid king. Kotturan, op. cit., p. 67. John D. Smith, "Old Indian: The Two Sanskrit Epics," pp. 48–78, in *Traditions of Heroic and Epic Poetry*, ed. Arthur T. Hatto; London: Modern Humanities Research Association, 1980, p. 61, suggests that Yudisthira represents the righteous king fatefully acting out his dharma. R.N. Dandekar suggests the Mahabharata represents the end of dharma and the beginning of the Artha Shastra ideal. The old rules of chivalrous warfare were overthrown as Arjuna the hero, under the direction of Krishna, destroys his enemies in violation of the rules of righteous war (dharma-yuddha). The Artha ideal was that the end justifies the means while dharma insisted on the righteousness of both. "Artha, the Second End of Man," pp. 236–257, in de Bary, op. cit.

13. Kinsley, op. cit., pp. 56–60. Gandhi thought the origin of caste was only a division of labor. The social groups were flexible in nature. But the system fell into abuse and was divided into rigid compartments which often led to cruel injustice and discrimination. Rao, op. cit., p. 20. Shri Jagadguru Gahgadhar Rajayogeendra Mahaswamiji of Moorusavirmath has noted that Virashaivism has not only objected to untouchability and caste, it has even said that spiritually women and men are equal. "Dharma or Religion," pp. 145–147, in *Religion for Peace*, ed. Homer A. Jack; New Delhi: Gandhi Peace Foundation, 1974. Wendy D. O'Flaherty, ed., *Karma and Rebirth in Classical Indian Traditions;* Berkeley: University of California, 1980.

14. See Walli, op. cit., p. viii, on Upanishadic replacement of sacrifice with meditation. Joan V. Bondurant, *Conquest of Violence: The Gandhian Philosophy of Conflict;* Princeton: Princeton, 1958, pp. 116–121. Mohandas K. Gandhi, *An Autobiography: The Story of My Experiments with Truth;* Boston: Beacon, 1957

Chapter IV 185

(original 1927-1929), pp. 40-41, 90-91. The Gita interpretation is from *The Gospel of Selfless Action: The Gita According to Gandhi*, tr. Mahadev Desai; Ahmedabad: Navajivan, 1946, p. 130. The inspiration comment is from *Young India* (September 29, 1920).

15. Gandhi, *Young India* (October 6, 1921). Shri Jagadguru sees the Vedagamas and Upanishads as the foundations of Indian culture. He goes on to say that "Hindus derive their faith from the infallible scripture of the Vedas." Op. cit., p. 146. Parrinder, op. cit., p. 103. Rao, op. cit., p. 15.

16. On "vipra" see FN 11, supra. Dandekar, op. cit., pp. 237-246, also suggests that in the works of Kautilya, from 300 b.c., about the same time as the Mahabharata, we have a return to materialism. Kautilya was the minister of Chandragupta Maurya, founder of the Maurya empire. Jan Gonda, "The Vedic Gods and the Sacrifice," *Numen* **XXX**, Fsc. 1 (July 1983), 1-34. The change from dharma warfare to artha warfare was noted earlier.

17. Basham, op. cit., p. 661, suggests three forms of moksha. The once influential Sankhya school and the Jains interpret moksha as complete separation of the soul from matter. The Advaita Vendanta see it as realization of the one impersonal world spirit of Brahman as opposed to the illusory character of all else. The Vishtistadvaita school sees it as union with the personal God, whether Vishnu or Shiva. Sen, op. cit., pp. 51, 61. Krishna Sivaraman, "The Meaning of 'moksha' in Contemporary Hindu Thought and Life," pp. 2-11, in *Living Faiths and Ultimate Goals*, ed. Stanley J. Samartha; Maryknoll: Orbis, 1974.

18. Gandhi said that everything he did was for the purpose of attaining moksha. The way to moksha is through service to all humanity. Detleff Kantowsky, "Sarvodaya: An Indigenous Form of 'innerworldly asceticism' in South Asia," *Gandhi Marg 3*, no. 7 (October 1981), 381-393. Cf. also Rao, op. cit., pp. vii-xii (Diwakar). V. Lakshmi Menon, *Ruskin and Gandhi*; Varanasi: Sarva Seva Sangh Prakashan, 1965, p. 35, notes that in the worship of Vishnu, love more than intelligence is the road to moksha. Gandhi's family was Vaishnavite so he imbibed this at his mother's knee. In *Young India* (July 9, 1925) he said, "Love never claims but gives." Thus one might relate Gandhi to bhakti yoga as well as karma yoga. He responded to a Christian's claim about surrender to Jesus as the only way of deliverance, by citing the path of devotion, "Bhakti-marga," of the Gita. *An Autobiography*, op. cit., p. 234. He also referred to anasakti yoga, the way of selflessness.

19. Aho, op. cit., pp. 60-79, titles his section on Hinduism, "The Dharma of the Kshatriya: The Celebration of Military Violence in Hinduism." Sen, op. cit., pp. 86-90. K.M. de Silva, *A History of Sri Lanka*; Delhi: Oxford, 1981, pp. 3-6. P.A. Saram, "Sri Lanka: The Evolutionary Dialectics of a Buddhist State," pp. 333-370, in *Religions and Societies: Asia and the Middle East*, ed. Carolo Caldarola; NY: Mouton, 1982.

20. Renou, op. cit., pp. 220-222. Gandhi, letter to C.F. Andrews, *Collected Works of Mahatma Gandhi* XIV; Ahmedabad: Ministry of Information and Broadcasting, Government of India, 1958, p. 475. Quoted by Amrut W. Nakhre, *Social Psychology of Nonviolent Action*; Delhi: Chanakya, 1982. For Tulsi Das, see F.R. Allchin, "The Place of Tulsi Das in North Indian Devotional Tradition," *Journal of the Royal Asiatic Society of Great Britain and Ireland* Parts 3 & 4 (October 1966), 123-140. Satya P. Bahadur, *The Ramayana of Goswami Tusidas*; Bombay: Jaico, 1972.

21. Ferguson, op. cit., pp. 34-36. Kim, op. cit., pp. 8-13. In contrast to Nakhre, Kotturan, op. cit., pp. 2-4 suggests that ahimsa, nonviolence, is the essence of Indian spirituality. The recent violence (and presumably the historic violence as well) is foreign to the spirit of Indian humanism. He is presumably talk-

ing about Hinduism though this is not clear. The violence recorded in history has been committed by all Indian religious groups. NEC-1324–1325. Arthur L. Basham, *The Wonder That Was India*, 3rd ed.; NY: Taplinger, 1967. Paul G. Hiebert, "India: The Politicization of a Sacred Society," pp. 289–331, in Caldarola, op. cit. T. Walter Wallbank, *A Short History of India and Pakistan from Ancient Times to the Present*; NY: Mentor, 1958.

22. Parrinder, op. cit., p. 51. Renou, op. cit., pp. 86–105. Sen, op. cit., pp. 108–111.

23. Frazier, op. cit., pp. 166–218. Kinsley, op. cit., pp. 82–104. Kotturan, op. cit., pp. 8, 70. Sen, op. cit., p. 51. Walli, op. cit., pp. vii, 1, 15, 39. Nathaniel Altman, *Ahimsa (Dynamic Compassion)*; Wheaton, IL: Theosophical Publishing House, 1980. R. R. Diwakar, "Ahimsa Culture for Human Survival," *Gandhi Marg* 2, no. 10 (January 1981), 579–587. Schweitzer, *Reverence for Life*; NY: Harper & Row, 1969.

Ahimsa is a compound of the negative prefix, "a" and "himsa." The latter is from "hims," to injure, kill or destroy but it is the desiderative of the root, "han," to slay, kill or damage. In other words, in practicing "no harm," one does not merely mechanically refrain from harm. One does not even *want* to harm. Bondurant, op. cit., pp. 23–24, 111, with bibliography. On the inner sense of not wanting to harm, one might compare the Bible's idea that as a man thinks in his heart, so is he (Proverbs 23:7, KJV), or Jesus' claim that it is not enough to refrain from murder. If you are angry with someone, you have already sinned (Matthew 5:21–22). One notes here too the extensive biblical record of war and destruction, and animal sacrifice.

24. Altman, op. cit., p. 6, notes the caricature of the locusts and goes on, p. 26, to quote Gandhi as saying the use of disinfectants is "himsa," "harm," and yet we cannot do without this. He then goes on, p. 80, to quote Gandhi as saying nonviolence "embraces even sub-human life, not excluding noxious insects and beasts. They have not been created to feed our destructive propensities. If we only knew the mind of the Creator, we should find their proper place." Gandhi, *Autobiography*, pp. 34, 325. Albert Schweitzer used disinfectant in surgical operations, but before applying the disinfectant, he apologized to the bacteria saying it was necessary to kill them to save the sick human. The killing of humans and nonviolence to insects is not entirely caricature according to some. Walli, op. cit., p. 121. She quotes (pp. 56–57) the Brahmana Purana as saying that people should not injure harmful creatures who are devoid of discrimination, such as bugs, lice, flies, mosquitos, etc. To cause pain to such as these sends one to hell. Rao, op. cit., pp. 3, 18. O.P. Jaggai notes that one can see women feeding birds and insects while their own children may not have enough to eat. He also notes that cows are worshiped and yet these animals are comparatively the most malnourished. "The History of Medical Ethics in South and East Asia: India," pp. 906–911, in *Encyclopedia of Bioethics*, op. cit. This is not unique. Americans spend $503 million a year on wild bird seed. "Prime-Time Birds," *USAIR* VII, no. VII (August 1985), 18. Meanwhile, the U.S. president, a self-proclaimed Christian, cut federal monies for school lunches for poor children, claiming this was necessary to balance the budget, while hundreds of billions were spent on armaments. Basham, "Hinduism," op. cit., p. 661, suggests a dual ethic. Ahimsa is required of the ascetic or the priest. Nonviolence is considerably modified for the layman, to permit self-defense, the punishment of criminals and righteous warfare. The just war has been quite popular in Christianity. It has been observed that any war can be justified and called righteous.

25. Walli, op. cit, pp. xii–xxiii, xlii. Peter Brock, "Gandhi's Nonviolence and His War Service," *Gandhi Marg* 2, no. 11 (February 1981), 601–616. Gandhi, *Hindu Dharma*; Ahmedabad: Navajivan, 1958.

26. The hunter as evil contrasts strongly with the glorification of the hunt,

e.g., by the maharajas, but no more so than the glorification of war throughout history.

27. Ferguson, op. cit., pp. 29–30. Walli, op. cit., p. 50.

28. Ferguson, op. cit., pp. 30–32. Kotturan, op. cit., pp. 2–6. Parrinder, op. cit., pp. 13, 216. Walli, op. cit., p. 39, 101–102.

29. Margaret Chatterjee, *Gandhi's Religious Thought;* Notre Dame, IN: University of Notre Dame Press, 1983. S.C. Gangal, "Gandhi and World Order," pp. 160–173, in K.P. Misra and Gangal, eds., *Gandhi and the Contemporary World: Studies in Peace and War;* Delhi: Chanakya, 1981. Gandhi, *Non-Violence in Peace & War,* 2 vols.; Ahmedabad: Navajivan, 1942–1949, 2:5–9, and, *An Auto-biography,* op. cit. Amrut W. Nakhre, *Social Psychology of Nonviolent Action: A Study of Three Satyagrahas;* Delhi: Chanakya, 1982, p. 166. K.J. Shah, "Gandhi's Nonviolence: Its Bases," pp. 51–61, in Misra and Gangal, op. cit.
The remark to the Pathans, traditionally fierce Muslim warriors with a long tradition of violence, came in touring the northern Frontier. The son of a clan chieftain, Kahn Abdul Ghaffar Khan, had organized the Servants of God, the Khudai Khidmatgar, for nonviolent resistance. Khan followed the Quran's concern for peace as well as ahimsa. Bondurant, op. cit., pp. 131–144. Peter Brock has reexamined these perspectives, op. cit. Pyarelal Nair, *Thrown to the Wolves: Abdul Ghaffar;* Calcutta: Eastlight, 1966. There is confusion on Gandhi's expectations of the masses for elsewhere he claims his approach is practical idealism. It is for everyone and not just saints. Gandhi, *Pathway to God;* Ahmedabad: Navajivan, 1971, p. 26. Every individual can develop ahimsa. Thomas Merton, ed., *Gandhi on Non-Violence;* NY: New Directions, 1965, p. 26. Altman, op. cit., pp. 24, 62. Henry O. Thompson, "Mohandas Karmachand Gandhi," *World Problems and Human Responsibilities: Gandhian Perspectives,* ed. K.L. Seshagir Rao and H.O. Thompson, forthcoming.

30. Gandhi, *Autobiography,* op. cit., pp. 204–208, 297–301. Kantowsky, op. cit., p. 381. Menon, op. cit. Rao, op. cit., pp. 4–7. James D. Hunt, "Thoreau and Gandhi: A Re-evaluation of the Legacy," *Gandhi Marg* 14, no. 4 (October 1970), 325–332. Kalidas Nag, *Tolstoy and Gandhi;* Patna: Pustak Bhander, 1950.

31. A modern interpreter notes that any coercion or ego gratification destroys the essence of ahimsa. Altman, op. cit., p. x. Bondurant, op. cit. Gandhi, *Non-Violence in Peace & War,* op. cit. *Satyagraha (Nonviolent Resistance);* Ahmedabad: Navajivan, 1951; *Satyagraha in South Africa;* Ahmedabad: Navajivan, 1950. Nakhre, op. cit., p. 19. Rao, op. cit., pp. 1, 61–67. Ranganath R. Diwakar, *Saga of Satyagraha,* rev.; New Delhi: Gandhi Peace Foundation, 1969.

32. Bondurant, op. cit., pp. 11–12, 18. She notes "satya" comes from "sat," "being" plus a suffix, "-ya" and "agraha," "firm grasping." The latter is from "grah," "seize, grasp," with the prefix, "a," meaning "to, towards." Parrinder, op. cit., pp. 245–246. Menon, op. cit., p. 39. Rothermund, op. cit., pp. 722–725. R.R. Diwakar, "Gandhi: From 'God Is Truth' to 'Truth Is God'," *Gandhi Marg* 2, no. 11 (February 1981), 617–626, and, "Satyagraha: Its Origin and Bases," pp. 30–40, in Misra and Gangal, op. cit.
Gandhi was fond of saying that Jesus was the prince of satyagrahis. Ultimate reality ("sat") was the love incarnated in Jesus. One interpreter claims that Gandhi, like Roy and Vivekananda, rejected Christianity but accepted Christ. L.S.S. O'Malley, ed., *Modern India and the West;* London: Oxford, 1941, pp. 334–336, quoted by Sharma, in French and Sharma, op. cit., p. 155. William R. Miller, "Gandhi and King: Pioneers of Modern Nonviolence," *Gandhi Marg* 13, no. 1 (January 1969), 21–28. The idea of God or the gods fighting on behalf of one's cause is at least as old as recorded history. It appears in the inscriptions of ancient Mesopotamia

as well as the Vedas. It is a standard concept in the Bible. Cf. Judges 4–5 and Revelation.

33. Ferguson, op. cit. 36–40. Diwakar, in Misra & Gangal, op. cit., pp. 169–170. Shah, op. cit., p. 51, quotes Gandhi as saying, "My aim is not to be consistent with my previous statements on a given question, but to be consistent with truth as it may present itself to me at a given moment." The concept of peace and truthfulness is from *Young India* (May 20, 1926), quoted by D.N. Pathak, "Gandhi's World View: Intimations of a Peaceful World Society," *Gandhi Marg* 4, no. 11 (February 1983), 918–926. As noted earlier, modern India has not been nonviolent. Force was used to incorporate the royal state of Hyderabad into India, to occupy Kashmir, disputed with Pakistan, and Goa, simply taken from Portugal. Indian armies resisted Chinese troops in border skirmishes and military force was used against Pakistan in the civil war that made Bangladesh an independent nation and at Amritsar in the dispute with Sikh nationalists. The issue here is violence per se. The justification of each of these actions has been argued pro and con. Miller, op. cit., pp. 22–26. Martin Luther King, Jr., *Stride Toward Freedom;* NY: Harper, 1958, pp. 96–97.

34. French and Sharma, op. cit., p. 156. Gandhi, op. cit., pp. 1–35, 69. Rao, op. cit., pp. 1–3, 17–18, 100.

35. Diwakar, op. cit. The Nehru statement on Gandhi is quoted by Gangal, op. cit., p. 173, n. 31, from Lester Pearson, *Memoirs,* vol. 2; London: 1974, p. 119. Kim, op. cit., p. 60. Hunt, op. cit., pp. 325–326, notes that Gandhi began "civil disobedience" before he read Thoreau. In this case, as in other Western influences, Gandhi found confirmation, or a reawakening of what he had already learned in Hinduism. In any case, Gandhi represents a creative synthesis of East and West. Menon, op. cit., p. 37, claims Gandhi saw an underlying unity in the Bible, the Gita, the Quran, etc. The unity was anasaktiyoga, the way of selflessness. Rao, op. cit., pp. 2, 15. Rothermund, op. cit. Shan, op. cit. Devdutt, "On Studying and Teaching of Gandhi," pp. 208–215 in Misra and Gangal, op. cit.

36. Jones is quoted by Pathak, op. cit., p. 918. Kantlowsky, op. cit., p. 386. Rao, op. cit., p. 141.

37. French and Sharma, op. cit., pp. 128–146. Shri Jagadguru, op. cit., pp. 146–147.

Chapter V

1. Gandhi claimed that three persons influenced him deeply — Tolstoy, Ruskin and the Jaina layman Raychandbhai Mehta. The first two influenced through their books, the last through personal contact. Quoted by Padmanabh S. Jaini, *The Jaina Path of Purification;* Berkeley: University of California Press, 1979, p. 315.

2. Jaini, op. cit., pp. 1–2. Asim Kumar Chatterjee, *A Comprehensive History of Jainism [Up to 1000 A.D.];* Calcutta: Firma KLM, 1978. S.C. Diwaker, *Religion & Peace,* rev.; Mathura, Uttar Pradesh: All India Digamber Jain Sangh, 1962. Champat R. Jain cites the evidence of the Indus Valley Culture for the antiquity of Jainism. He also interprets the Hindu Vedas as reflecting the existence of Jainism. He also claims that modern science says human beings have been around for hundreds of millions of years. *Fundamentals of Jainism;* Meerut, Uttar Pradesh: Veer Nirvan Bharti, 1974, pp. 107–113. Modern anthropology suggests the appearance of humans less than two million years ago. Jyotiprasad Jain, *Religion and Culture of the Jains;* New Delhi: Bharatiya Jnanpith, 1975, p. 5 cites as Indus Valley evidence the nude yogin in Jaina posture on seals along with the bull emblem, and the nude male Harappan torsos seen as the worship of Rishabha. Lal M. Joshi, *Facets of*

Jaina Religiousness in Comparative Light; Ahmedabad: L.D. Institute of Indology, 1981. Balwant Nevaskar, *Capitalists Without Capitalism;* Westport, CT: Greenwood, 1971, pp. 144–145, 152. The Kalpa Sutra describes the lives of the first, twenty-second, twenty-third and twenty-fourth tirthankaras in detail and the rest in outline. This section, Jinacarita, "Lives of Jinas," may have been added in the fourth century A.D. Umakant P. Shah, *Encyclopaedia Britannica* 10 (1978), 8–14. Manu M. Shroff, *Jainism and Modern Thought Which Constitutes Terapanth, Youth, the Riddle of World Peace and Its Solution;* Bombay: Shroff, 1956, pp. 1–3.

There are a number of general sources that include Jainism. Isma'il R. al Faruqi and David E. Sopher, eds., *Historical Atlas of the Religions of the World;* NY: Macmillan, 1974. R. Pierce Beaver, et al., eds., *Eerdmans' Handbook to the World's Religions;* Grand Rapids, MI: Eerdmans, 1982. William Theodore de Bary, *Sources of Indian Tradition;* NY: Columbia University, 1958. William H. Harris and Judith S. Levey, eds., *The New Columbia Encyclopedia;* NY: Columbia University, 1975, p. 1392. Niels C. Nielsen, Jr., et al., eds., *Religions of the World;* NY: St. Martin's, 1983. John B. and David S. Noss, *Man's Religions,* 7th ed.; NY: Macmillan, 1984. Ninian Smart, *The Long Search;* Boston: Little, Brown, 1977.

3. Geoffrey Parrinder, *A Dictionary of Non-Christian Religions;* Philadelphia: Westminster, 1971, p. 236; Young Oon Kim, *World Religions,* vol. 2; New York: Golden Gate, 1982, p. 74.

4. Kim, op. cit., 2:75–77. Walther Schubring, *The Religion of the Jainas;* Calcutta: Sanskrit College, 1966, pp. 2–3. Muni Uttam Kamal Jain, *Jaina Sects and Schools;* Delhi: Concept, 1975, pp. 9–15 gives the birth date as 850 B.C. Nevakar, op. cit., pp. 143–147. Arthur L. Basham, *The Wonder That Was India,* 3rd ed.; NY: Taplinger, 1968, pp. 289–297.

5. Jaini, op. cit., pp. 1–41. Shroff, op. cit., pp. 3–5. Schubring, op. cit., p. 4, translates the name of Mahavira's daughter as Anavadya. Nevaskar, op. cit., p. 147, calls her Anojja. Stuart C. Hackett, *Oriental Philosophy;* Madison: University of Wisconsin, 1979, p. 185. Noss, op. cit., pp. 95–98. Basham notes that Mahavira appears in Buddhist scriptures as Nigantha Nataputta, the naked ascetic of the clan of the Jnatrikas (p. 45). Cf. "Jainism and Buddhism," pp. 37–202, in de Bary, op. cit.

6. Jaini, op. cit., pp. 291–306. Basham, *Sources,* p. 39, suggests that at the time, the Aryan class system and brahmanic religion were relatively recent arrivals in Bihar and eastern Uttar Pradesh. Shah, op. cit., pp. 12–13.

7. NMR-106–117. Parrinder, op. cit., pp. 214–215, 169, Kim, op. cit., 2: 77–80.

8. Jaini, op. cit., pp. 274–284. James A. Aho, *Religious Mythology and the Art of War;* Westport, CT: Greenwood Press, 1981, p. 69. Jain offers a list of 29 early kings who supported Jainism while a few became Jains. Op. cit., p. 21, quoting the Uttaradhyayana, ch. 18, verses 19–20 and 34–54. Tradition says the southern movement was in response to a famine in the north.

9. Jaini, op. cit., pp. 4–6. Some Digambara believe women can achieve moksha. Nevaskar, op. cit., p. 160. Basham, *Sources,* p. 37.

10. Jaini, op. cit., pp. 309–310. Shroff, op. cit., pp. 37–38, describes the reformation of the Sthanakvasis by Swami Bhikhanji in 1761, forming the Terapanth ("thy [Mahavira's] path") dedicated to the true way. Jaini translates the term, "the path of the thirteen" from the story of a holy man seeing Bhikhanji and 12 disciples. He calls Bhikhanji a renegade monk who taught total nonassistance. If you help a sick dog and the dog later bites someone, you are responsible for that violence, so don't help the sick dog or anything or anyone else. This is in strong contrast to the usual Jain belief in positive works of good. Op. cit., p. 314.

11. Jaini, op. cit., pp. 285–291. He notes, however, that there was an emphasis

upon conduct as the basis for caste, i.e., there are brahmins by behavior, not by birth. Hackett, op. cit., p. 185.

12. Kotturan, *Ahimsa: Gautama to Gandhi;* New Delhi: Sterling, 1973, p. 8. Nevaskar, op. cit., p. 157. V.P. Kothari, *The Law of Non-Violence (Ahimsa) and Its Relevance for All Times;* Sholapur: Lalchand Hirachand, 1975, p. 46. Myrtle Langley, "Respect for All Life: Jainism," pp. 207–216 in *Eerdmans' Handbook to the World's Religions,* ed. R. Pierce Beaver, et al.; Grand Rapids: Eerdmans, 1982. Shree Chand Rampuria, *The Cult of Ahimsa: A Jain Point of View;* Calcutta: Sri Jain Swetamber Terapanthi Mahasabha, 1947. Koshelya Walli, *The Conception of Ahimsa in Indian Thought According to Sanskrit Sources;* Varanasi: Bharata Manisha, 1974.

13. Jaini, op. cit., p. 187. The Sutra is quoted by John Ferguson, *War and Peace in the World's Religions;* New York: Oxford, 1978,

14. Nevaskar, op. cit., pp. 184–189. Shah, op. cit., p. 12.

15. Jyotiprasad Jain, op. cit., pp. 97–99.

16. Nevaskar, op. cit., pp. 185–188.

17. Chand, "Jainism," pp. 114–123 in *World Religions and World Peace,* ed. Homer A. Jack; Boston: Beacon, 1968. Kothari, op. cit., pp. 47, 49. Basham, *Wonder,* op. cit., p. 295. Hopman, "To Reach God Within," *Jain Meditation International Center Newsletter* [NYC] (Fall/Winter 1984), pp. 2–5. Gurudev, "Hindu-Jain Temple in Pittsburgh," ibid., p. 6, and, "A Special Time, A Special Feeling," ibid., pp. 8-9, 13, and, "Paryushana 1984: A Joyful Celebration of Amity," ibid., pp. 10–11, and, "Thoughts for Today's World," ibid., pp. 16–17. The last comment on God as love seems inconsistent with the traditional view of Jainism as atheistic. However, one could presumably think of God, and think of God as love, without necessarily believing in a Creator.

18. Nevaskar, op. cit., pp. 159–161. His volume is subtitled, "The Jains of India and the Quakers of the West." Kim, op. cit., 2:83–90. Noss, op. cit., pp. 98–101. NCE-1392. Shropp. op. cit., p. 105. Jaini, op. cit., p. 287, quotes the Upasakadhya-yana, "All worldly practices are valid for the Jainas, as long as there is neither loss of pure insight nor violation of the vratas." Thus Jaina laity could adopt local styles in clothing, language, etc., with a clear conscience.

19. Jaini, op. cit., pp. 179–280. The quote is from "Ganagarajyamam madida Simhanandiacaryar," from the Epigraphica Carnatica. It is of interest, however, that Aho, op. cit., p. 6, claims Jainism is one of a few religions with no military ethic.

20. Jaini, op. cit., p. 281. Ferguson, op. cit., p. 33.

21. Jaini, op. cit., pp. 281–282.

22. Ferguson, op. cit., pp. 33–34.

23. Jaini, op. cit., pp. 282–284. Nevaskar, op. cit., p. 160. Basham, *Sources,* op. cit., p. 89.

24. Jaini, 313–314. Basham, *Sources,* p. 90. Somadevasuri, Yasastilaka-campu: II, 97. The Jaina version of the Ramayana has the hero Laksmana go to the same hell as the wicked Ravana. Chand, op. cit., pp. 117–123.

25. Sung Bae Park, "The Conception of Protecting the Nation in Korean Bud-dhism," pp. 58–64 in *Whither Korea* ed. Wonmo Dong and Harold Hawon Sunoo; Dallas, TX: Association of Korean Christian Scholars in North America, 1975. Park claims Won-Kuang and Sosan misinterpreted the Sila Ahimsa. Champat Rai Jain, op. cit., pp. 100–106. Kothari, op. cit., p. 69.

26. C.R. Jain, op. cit., p. 106. P. Jain, op. cit., pp. 99–101.

27. Shroff, op. cit., pp. 116, 186. Jain, op. cit., pp. 176, 185–186. Hopman, op. cit., p. 3. "The Ahimsa Corner: Jain Peace Fellowship," *JMIC Newsletter,* op. cit., p. 7.

Chapter VI

1. Wazir Singh, *Philosophy of Sikh Religion;* New Delhi: Ess Ess, 1981. The author would like to take this opportunity to extend his appreciation to Dr. Singh for reviewing this chapter on Sikhism and offering many helpful suggestions. J.B. Harrison, "Sikhism," pp. 529–549 in *Sources of Indian Tradition,* ed. William T. de Bary, et al.; NY: Columbia University, 1958. John B. Noss and David S. Noss, *Man's Religions,* 7th ed.; NY: Macmillan, 1984, p. 222. Islam arrived in the Indus Valley in A.D. 712 in the conquest of Muhammad bin Qasim al Thaqafi. Continuous control began several centuries later with the Ghaznavides (1021–1186) of Lahore, the Ghorids (1186–1211) of Delhi and the Delhi Sultanate (1211–1526). The Sufi orders were active from the thirteenth century on, first the Chishti and Suhrawadi, and then the Qadiri and Naqshbandi. Their teachings and the shrines of Sufi saints were venerated by Muslims and Hindus alike. Dadu (1544–1603) is a Sufi whose teachings and followers, the Dadupanthi, are a part of this larger movement of which Sikhism is the prime example. Majid Ali Khan, "Advent of Sufism in the Punjab," *Journal of Religious Studies* X, nos. 1 & 2 (Spring–Autumn 1982), 63–68, notes that Muhammad bin Qasim conquered Multan in the Punjab and that Muslim control was continuous thereafter. Khushwant Singh, *A History of the Sikhs. Vol. 1:1469–1839. Vol. 2:1839–1964;* Princeton: Princeton University, 1963, 1966, vol. 1:25–28, and, 2:310–311.

Numbers of general works include Sikhism. Isma'il R. al Faruqi and David E. Sopher, *Historical Atlas of the Religions of the World;* NY: Macmillan, 1974. R. Pierce Beaver, et al., eds., *Eerdmans' Handbook to the World's Religions;* Grand Rapids, MI: Eerdmans, 1982. Keith Crim, et al., eds., *Abingdon Dictionary of Living Religions;* Nashville: Abingdon, 1981. Young Oon Kim, *World Religions. Vol. 2. India's Religious Quest,* 2nd ed.; NY: Golden Gate, 1982. Myrtle Langley, *Religions;* Elgin, IL: Cook, 1981. Niels C. Nielsen, Jr., et al., eds., *Religions of the World;* NY: St. Martin's, 1983. Ninian Smart, *The Long Search;* Boston: Little, Brown, 1977.

2. W. Hew McLeod, *The Evolution of the Sikh Community;* Oxford: Clarendon Press, 1976, pp. 5–6, 108, nirguna sampradaya, the tradition that God is without form or incarnation. Harrison, op. cit., pp. 529–532. Mark Juergensmeyer and N. Gerald Barrier, eds., *Sikh Studies;* Berkeley, CA: Graduate Theological Union, 1979, pp. 1–9, 65–94. W. Owen Cole and Piara Singh Sambhi, *The Sikhs: Their Religious Beliefs and Practices;* London: Routledge & Kegan Paul, 1978, pp. 1–6.

3. Kim, op. cit., pp. 96–97. Dr. Jan Knappert (personal communication) sees Kabir's name as an abridgement of the common Abdul-Kabir, just as Rahman is shortened from Abd ur Rahman. Charlotte Vaudeville, *Kabir;* NY: Oxford University, 1974. The Mughal dynasty (1526–1757) was started in Kabir's lifetime by Babur, a Turk who conquered the Muslim Lodis dynasty (1451–1526). Mughal is a derivative of Mongol. Babur claimed to be a descendent of Tamerlane the Mongol. Geoffrey Parrinder, *Dictionary of Non-Christian Religions;* Philadelphia: Westminster, 1971, pp. 148, 197.

4. Cole & Sambhi, pp. 8–18. Kim, p. 98. Khushwant Singh, *Religion of the Sikhs;* Madras: University of Madras, 1968, pp. 8–11. Wazir Singh, "The First Century of Sikhism," *Journal of Religious Studies* VIII, no. 1 (Spring 1980), 105–118. M.A. Macauliffe, *The Sikh Religion,* vols. I–VI; Oxford: Clarendon, 1909. The zamindars were retainers of the Delhi Sultanate, ruled at this time by the Lodis, the fifth and last dynasty. The zamindars were given control of an area from which they were allowed to collect whatever taxes they could get. In return, they provided sup-

port for the court, such as troops for the army. The office was continued under the Mughals and the British Raj.

5. Harrison, p. 532. Kathleen Isham, "Messianism in the Sikh Religion," unpublished paper, March 1985. Kim, pp. 97–100. Parrinder, p. 197. W.H. McLeod, *Textual Sources for the Study of Sikhism;* Totowa, NJ: Barnes & Noble, 1984, pp. 18–25. *Nanksar Gurdwara, [Gursikh Temple] and Sikh Religion;* Vancouver: Nanksar Gurdwara, n.d., p. 2, says he provided rations to the poor free of charge. The khatri claim to be kshatriya, the warrior caste of Hinduism. The words are cognates. However, McLeod, *Evolution,* p. 98, claims the khatris are a mercantile caste, which would make them vaishya. If caste were truly excluded from Sikhism, it would of course make no difference, but remnants of caste remain.

6. Pritam Singh, "Religion for Peace and Integration," offprint. Noss, pp. 222–225. Kim, p. 102.

7. As with ancient Hebrew tradition, one should note the "name" is not just a label. "Nam" points to and embodies the true nature of God. McLeod, *Textual Sources,* pp. 39–41. Cole & Sambhi, pp. 89–95. John Ferguson, *War and Peace in the World's Religions;* NY: Oxford, 1978, p. 139. Mrs. Manjeet Kaur McCormack, *An Introduction to Sikh Belief,* 8th ed.; London: Sikh Cultural Society of Great Britain, 1982, pp. 4–5. Sidhu, *Introduction to Sikhism;* Burnaby, B.C.: World Sikh Organization, 1984, pp. 2, 7, 21. McLeod, *Evolution,* pp. 32–34, 72–73. Wazir Singh, "The Sikh Response to Social Reality," *Journal of Religious Studies* IX, nos. 1 & 2 (Spring–Autumn 1981), 99–105.

8. Noss, op. cit., p. 224. Sidhu, op. cit., pp. 16–18, 22–23. Gopal Singh, "Sikhism," pp. 76–83 in *World Religions and World Peace: The International Symposium on Peace,* ed. Homer A. Jack; Boston: Beacon, 1968. Harbans Singh, "Sikhism," pp. 239–242 in *Religion in the Struggle for World Community* ed. Homer A. Jack; NY: World Conference on Religion and Peace, 1980.

9. The extent of Nanak's travels is difficult to determine with historical certainty. Some accounts have him traveling to Sri Lanka, to Mecca, and some even to Rome to meet with the Pope, and to Peking. K. Singh, *History* I:33, 302, notes Sikh temple remains in Dacca and tablets commemorating visits of the first and ninth Gurus, and a tablet (discovered in 1916) reflecting Nanak's visit to Baghdad. Cole and Sambhi, op. cit., p. 11. Harrison, op. cit., pp. 532–533. Kim, op. cit., p. 99. McLeod, *Evolution,* op. cit., p. 23.

10. One son, Sri Chand, started a sect of his own, the ascetic Udasis. Harrison, op. cit., p. 539–540. "Panth" is the old Sanskrit word for "path," related to Arabic "tarika" in the sense of path or way to God or a religious community. Dr. Jan Knappert, personal communication.

11. Harrison, op. cit., pp. 539–540. The new script, different from both Hindu and Muslim traditions, helped form a separate identity for the Sikhs. Wazir Singh, *First Century,* op. cit., p. 113, says Angad popularized the script used by Nanak. The alphabet originated much earlier. K. Singh, op. cit., 2:309–310. Dr. Jan Knappert (personal communication) notes that the Gurmukhi script is certainly based on Devanagari, the old Sanskrit alphabet of India, still used for Hindi and Maharati.

It has also been suggested that Amar Das reinstituted pilgrimage, festival days, ritual, and scriptures, to give his people a sense of identity, though all these had been rejected by Nanak. Khushwant Singh, *Religion,* op. cit., p. 28, says Ram Das bought 700 bighas of land from Akbar. He notes the report here in the text in *History* 1:55 and in f.n. 16 says the grant was from Akbar and the payment of Rs. 700/– was to the Zamindars of Tung who owned the land. Noss, op. cit., p. 226, credits Nanak with establishing sangat, gurdwara and langar, and sees them as promoting social service, democracy and harmony. McLeod, *Evolution,* op. cit., pp.

8, 42, 44, also notes that from Ram Das on, the Guruship was hereditary within the Sodhi family. In *Textual Sources*, pp. 25–38, McLeod has extracts of the stories related to each Guru. Isham, op. cit., p. 12. Parrinder, op. cit., pp. 21, 17, 232–233.

12. Gurbachan Singh Talib, "Sikhism — Some of Its Fundamental Doctrines," *Journal of Religious Studies* X, nos. 1 & 2 (Spring–Autumn 1982), 1–6. Wazir Singh, "Japuji," *Journal of Religious Studies* X, nos. 1 & 2 (1982), 7–21. Parkash Singh, *Guru Nanak and his Japji*; Amritsar, 1969. The word "jap" may be a conceptual borrowing from Islam. The Arabic "dhikr"="remembering, mentioning, repeating God's name." While "Nam"="name," the Sanskrit also means essence or spirit as opposed to "rupa," "shape, outer form." Jan Knappert, personal communication.

The Adi Granth contains poetry from 36 authors including Guru Nanak (974 hymns), Guru Angad (62), Guru Amar Das (907), Guru Ram Das (679), Guru Arjan (2218), Guru Tegh Bahadur (116), Kabir (541), Farid (116; some interpreters say 134), Namdev (60), Ravidas (41), Jaidev (2), Ramananda (1 hymn). Cole and Sambhi, pp. 189–195. McLeod, *Textual Sources*, op. cit., pp. 38–55. Part of the difficulty with Farid's authorship is that there were a series of Farids. Farid Shakarganj is the first and may have authored the 116. Another difficulty in counting is that some verses are repeated, as between the introductory section of the Adi Granth and the main body of the text. Cf. also K. Singh, op. cit., 1:319ff, and 2:310.

13. McCormack, op. cit., p. 3. Parrinder, op. cit., pp. 27, 142. Kim, op. cit., pp. 104, 106. McLeod, *Evolution*, op. cit., p. 43, describes a split in the succession between Ram Das' eldest son, Prithi Chand, and Arjan. The followers of the first continued for a time but the followers of the latter won out. For the later Khalsa, the followers of Chand are Minas, scoundrels to be avoided. The Minas' own literature suggests they were trying to be true to Nanak's religious teachings without the later social concerns. McLeod, *Evolution*, op. cit., pp. 60–61, notes that Amar Das had compiled a two-volume work which Arjan used or incorporated into the Adi Granth. Harrison, op. cit., p. 546.

14. Sidhu, op. cit., p. 7. Wazir Singh, "The Sikh Response..." op. cit., p. 103. Gopal Singh, op. cit., p. 76. McLeod, *Evolution*, op. cit., pp. 10–13, notes that the early Gurus lived in the midst of Jat territory and Jats were probably drawn to Sikhism from an early period. They were agriculturalists in contrast to the urban mercantile caste of the Khatri. Today a substantial majority of Sikhs are Jats. They have been noted for their martial traditions, physical strength and energy, straightforward manner, tremendous generosity, their insistence on the right to take vengeance. McLeod goes on to suggest that the growing numbers of Jats in the Panth, increased its militancy as much as any order from Guru Hargobind, who may even have been influenced in his decision by their presence. Harrison, op. cit., p. 541, says Arjan supported Prince Khusrau's unsuccessful rebellion against his father, Jahangir. Jahangir punished Arjan with a fine which he refused to pay, so Jahangir executed him. Once secure on the throne, he was as tolerant as Akbar but the Sikhs henceforth saw Jahangir and the Muslims as their enemies.

15. Parrinder, op. cit., pp. 116–117, 277. Harbans Singh, *Guru Tegh Bahadur*; New Delhi: Sterling, 1982.

16. McLeod, *Textual Sources*, op. cit., pp. 55–63, annotated selections from the Dasam Granth, pp. 71–85 on the rahit, the khalsa code of conduct up to and including the received version of 1950. Nanaksar Gurdwara, p. 2. Sidhu, op. cit., pp. 12–13. Khushwant Singh, *Religion*, op. cit., p. 36, says the short trousers were simply those in use by soldiers of the time.

17. While the office of Guru had become hereditary, Gobind Singh's four sons were killed — two in the fighting and two by execution. He himself eventually took refuge in the Deccan plateau of central India, where a Muslim retainer stabbed him

to death. McLeod, *Evolution*, op. cit., p. 45, suggests that Guru Singh did not pronounce the Granth Sahib to be the Guru but that this doctrine evolved over time. The 1708 date is noted in "Sikh Religion," *Nanaksar Gurdawara*, p. 1. McLeod also notes, *Evolution*, p. 34, that earlier, haircuts and meat were no problem. The objection to halal meat and intercourse with Muslim women may reflect the struggle with the Muslim Mughals and the Muslim Afghans (p. 52). The five K's also evolved, p. 51, and were only finalized well into the 1700s. Harrison, op. cit., p. 548. Isham, op. cit., pp. 14–15. Juergensmeyer and Barrier, op. cit., p. 2. Kim, op. cit., p. 102. Noss, op. cit., p. 228, Parrinder, op. cit., pp. 107–108, 147, 153.

18. Kim, op. cit., p. 111. McLeod, *Evolution*, op. cit., p. 46.

19. Ferguson, op. cit., pp. 141–147. Noss, op. cit., pp. 229, 235. Parrinder, op. cit., p. 111. Gopal Singh, op. cit., p. 80. William H. Harris and Judith S. Levey, eds., *The New Columbia Encyclopedia*; NY: Columbia University Press, 1975, p. 2517.

20. Harrison, op. cit., pp. 548–549. Isham, op. cit., p. 11. Kim, op. cit., pp. 113–116. McLeod, *Evolution*, op. cit., pp. 54–55, and, *Textual Sources*, op. cit., pp. 121–126 (Nirankaris), 126–131 (Namdhari), 133–147 (Singh Sabha). Khushwant Singh sees the Nirankari as a Hindu-Sikh sect. Dyal Das was a part of a larger Hindu community influenced by Sikhism in the western Punjab. When he died, his sandals were placed on the altar beside the Granth in the Nirankari headquarters temple. The 1891 census listed 50,000 members of whom 12,000 were Sikhs and 39,000 were Hindus. The group claims a present membership of 100,000 but K. Singh claims they are losing their identity and being reabsorbed into Sikhism, a judgment with which Cole and Sambhi, op. cit., pp. 155–156, agree. They suggest, pp. 156–158, that the Namdharis number over 700,000. Another group is the Radha (enjoy) Soamis (Master) founded by a Hindu banker, Shiv Dayal (1818–1878). To reach perfection, one needs a living guru. By the 1960s, under Charan Singh, the community had grown to over 100,000. They accept only the Adi Granth but instead of the Granth on an altar, there is a lecture platform for the guru in their temples. They also reject the Khalsa. Part of the background for the Singh Sabha was the conversion of Maharaja Dulip Singh to Christianity in 1853 and the establishment that year of a Christian school in Amritsar itself. The reform Hindu group of Brahmo Samaj established an office in Lahore in 1864 and the Arya Samaj set up its office there in 1877. K. Singh, op. cit., 2:133–147.

21. Ferguson, op. cit., pp. 147–148. Gopal Singh, op. cit., p. 81, quotes C.F. Andrews' comment on the British assaults against the nonviolent, "I see a Christ being crucified in every Sikh before me." K. Singh, op. cit., 2:204. Mohindar Singh, "Sikhs and Non-Violence," *The Sikh Review* XXX, no. 342 (June 1982), 36–41, says the Akalis were arrested after cutting down a dry tree at Guru-ka-Bagh.

22. Cole and Sambhi, op. cit., pp. 158–161. Harrison, op. cit., p. 549. McLeod, *Evolution*, op. cit., pp. 56–58. K. Singh, op. cit., 2:193–216. Mohinder Singh, *The Akali Movement*; New Delhi: Macmillan, 1978.

23. Harry Anderson and Tony Clifton, "Martyrs of the Golden Temple," *Newsweek* (June 25, 1984), 39. Brahma Chellaney, "Sikhs threaten summer unrest unless more concessions granted," *The Philadelphia Inquirer* (April 13, 1985), 10-A. Mark Fineman, "Gandhi has harsh words for FBI: Silence during Sikh investigation criticized," *The Philadelphia Inquirer* (June 5, 1985), 1-A, 14-A.

24. Isham, op. cit., p. 11. Juergensmeyer and Barrier, op. cit., p. 4. McLeod, *Evolution*, op. cit., p. 39. Nananksar Gurdwara—Gursikh Temple, op. cit., pp. 1–2. Wazir Singh, "The Sikh Response . . ." op. cit., p. 104.

25. Bruce LaBrack, "Sikhs Real and Ideal: A Discussion of Text and Context in the Description of Overseas Sikh Communities," pp. 127–142 in Juergensmeyer

and Barrier, op. cit. Douglas Davies, "Religion of the Gurus: The Sikh Faith," pp. 197–206 in Beaver, op. cit. The first gurdwara in the U.S. was in Stockton, CA in 1912, the second in El Centro (1948) and in 1969, the largest Sikh temple in the world was built at Redwood City, CA. The Sikh Foundation publishes a quarterly, *Sikh Sandar*. Another quarterly, *The Sikh World* is published by the International Sikh Federation, Madison Heights, MI. The 3 H O publishes *Beads of Truth*. Its women's auxiliary, GGM, The Grace of God Movement of Women in America, is actively studying the role of women. Isham, p. 11. Cole & Sambhi, pp. 161–162, cite membership figures for 3 H O of 250,000. J. Gordon Melton, *The Encyclopedia of American Religions;* Wilmington, NC: McGrath, 1978, pp. 388–389. *Sikh Religious Studies Information* is a bibliographical journal published by The Institute for Advanced Studies of World Religions; Stony Brook, NY: SUNY, as material becomes available.

26. Ferguson, op. cit., p. 139–141. Isham, op. cit., p. 16. Noss, op. cit., p. 226. Khushwant Singh, op. cit., p. 88.

27. Ferguson, op. cit., p. 138. McCormack, op. cit., p. 9. Gopal Singh, op. cit., pp. 76, 79. The presence of both Muslim and Hindu elements were noted earlier. Sikhism is sometimes seen as a synthesis of these two religions. Kushwant Singh, *Religion*, op. cit., pp. 3, 26. Others deny that, such as Cole and Sambhi, op. cit., pp. 38–42, 145–151, Talib, op. cit., p. 1, Juergensmeyer, "The Forgotten Tradition: Sikhism in the Study of World Religions," pp. 13–23 in Juergensmeyer and Barrier, op. cit., and, Paul B. Courtright, "Syncretism and the Formation of the Sikh Tradition," *Journal of Religious Studies* VI, no. 1 (Spring 1978), 1–15. McLeod, *Evolution*, op. cit., p. 7. says it is the Sant synthesis cited earlier, which Nanak's genius integrated and then expressed with clarity and compelling beauty. Sikhism is also said to transcend rather than synthesize Hinduism and Islam. It is a new revelation as reported earlier in Nanak's experience of God.

28. McCormack, op. cit., pp. 8–11. McLeod, *Textual Sources*, op. cit., pp. 110–114, annotated selections of the Sukhmani.

29. Harbans Singh, op. cit., pp. 239–242. Gopal Singh, op. cit., p. 77.

30. Gopal Singh, op. cit., pp. 75–83. Wazir Singh, "The Sikh Response..." op. cit., p. 104.

31. Wazir Singh, "Religious Pluralism & Co-existence," (March 20, 1985), pp. 1–7. Offprint.

Chapter VII

1. Anne Bancroft, *The Buddhist World;* London: Macdonald, 1984. Francis H. Cook, "Nirvana," pp. 132–136 in *Buddhism: A Modern Perspective*, ed. Charles S. Prebish; University Park: Pennsylvania State University, 1975. There are differences of opinion about the number of Buddhists today. David B. Barrett put the population at 127 million in 1900, 274 million in 1980, and estimates 359 million by the year 2000. *World Christian Encyclopedia;* Nairobi: Oxford, 1982.

There are numerous general studies of Buddhism available. Kenneth K.S. Chen, *Buddhism: The Light of Asia;* Woodbury: Barrons, 1968. Ananda K. Coomaraswamy, *Buddha and the Gospel of Buddhism;* New Hyde Park, NY: University, 1969. Edward Conze, *Buddhism: Its Essence and Development;* NY: Harper, 1959. Heinrich Dumoulin, ed., *Buddhism in the Modern World;* NY: Macmillan, 1976. Allie M. Frazier, *Buddhism;* Philadelphia: Westminster, 1969. Richard Gard, *Buddhism;* NY: Braziller, 1962. Christmas Humphreys, *Buddhism;* Baltimore, MD: Penguin, 1969. David J. and Indrani Kalupahana, *The Way of*

Siddhartha; Boulder, CO: Shambhala, 1982. Frank E. Reynolds, *Guide to the Buddhist Religion;* Boston: Hall, 1981. R.H. Robinson, *The Buddhist Religion: A Historical Introduction;* Belmont, CA: Dickenson, 1970. Nancy W. Ross, *Buddhism;* NY: Knopf, 1980. H. Saddhatissa, *The Buddha's Way;* NY: Braziller, 1972. Helmuth von Glassnapp, *Buddhism: A Non-Theistic Religion;* NY: Braziller, 1970.

General works also include helpful introductions to Buddhism. Isma'il R. al Faruqi and David E. Sopher, *Historical Atlas of the Religions of the World;* NY: Macmillan, 1974. R. Pierce Beaver, ed., *Eerdmans' Handbook to the World's Religions;* Grand Rapids: Eerdmans, 1982. Carlo Caldarola, *Religions and Societies: Asia and the Middle East;* NY: Mouton, 1982. Keith Crim, et al., eds., *Abingdon Dictionary of Living Religions;* Nashville, TN: Abingdon, 1981. William Theodore de Bary, et al., compilers, *Sources of Chinese Traditions;* NY: Columbia, 1960, and, *Sources of Indian Tradition;* NY: Columbia University, 1958. William H. Harris and Judith S. Levey, eds., *The New Columbia Encyclopedia;* NY: Columbia University, 1975. Cited hereafter as NCE. Young Oon Kim, *World Religions,* 2nd ed.; NY: Golden Gate, 1982. Myrtle Langley, *Religions;* Elgin, IL: Cook, 1981. Niels C. Nielsen, Jr., et al., eds., *Religions of the World;* NY: St. Martin's, 1983. John B. and David S. Noss, *Man's Religions,* 7th ed.; NY: Macmillan, 1984. Ninian Smart, *The Long Search;* Boston: Little, Brown, 1977. Lin Yutang, ed., *The Wisdom of China and India;* NY: Modern Library, 1955.

2. Theravada dates Buddha circa 624–544. The Mahayana dates are more commonly used in the West. Beaver, op. cit., pp. 222–236. Kalupahana, op. cit., pp. ix–xiii. NCE-387–388. Nielsen, op. cit., pp. 186–198. Noss, op. cit., pp. 105–124. G.P. Malalasekera, "Theravada Buddhism," pp. 161–183 in al Faruqi and Sopher, op. cit. For conquest and renunciation, see Stanley J. Tambiah, *World Conqueror and World Renouncer;* Cambridge: Cambridge University, 1976.

3. While Gautama said, "All is suffering," Nolan P. Jacobson says, "Almost alone among the philosophies of humanity, Buddhism says that joy is the natural condition of a human's life." *Buddhism & the Contemporary World: Change and Self-Correction;* Carbondale: Southern Illinois University, 1983.

4. J. Stafford Weeks notes the checkered history of tolerance in Buddhism. He describes "Rissho Kosei-kai: A Cooperative Buddhist Sect," pp. 156–168 in *Religious Ferment in Asia,* ed. Robert J. Miller; Lawrence: University Press of Kansas, 1974. He contrasts this with another Japanese group, the Soka Gakkai, with their "break and destroy" (shakubuku) methods. While this has been downplayed in recent years, it has been traced back to early sutras if not to the Buddha himself. Both groups are part of the tradition of Nichiren (1222–1282) Buddhism. Nichiren is noted for his militancy against other Buddhists, other religions, and the government. However, in his later years, he seems to have been more cooperative. Rissho Kosei-kai President Niwano suggests they follow the later Nichiren while Soka Gakkai follows the earlier Nichiren. See further the military conquests described later. Masaharu Anesak, *Nichiren: The Buddhist Prophet;* Gloucester: Smith, 1966. The Venerable Nichidatsu Fujii, whom Gandhi called Guruji, is the leader of the Nichiren group called Nihonzon Myohoji. Fujii claims the basic message of Nichiren was responsibility to pray and work for peace. Presumably this is the later Nichiren. Paul Jaffe, "The Development of the American Buddhist Peace Movement" (available from the Buddhist Peace Fellowship).

5. Jacobson, op. cit., p. 167. NCE-388. De Silva, *Value Orientations and Nation Building;* Columbo, Sri Lanka: Lake House Investments, 1976, pp. 6–7. The reference is to the doctrine of dependent origination, pratitya-samutpada (Sanskrit) or paticca-samuppada (Pali), the interrelatedness of all. Jacobson, op. cit., pp. 7, 34–64.

6. NCE-166–167. Gunapala Dharmsiri, "Buddhism and the Modern World," pp. 89–103, especially pp. 96–97; Richard A. Gard, "A Forward to the Study of Buddhism," pp. 33–48, especially pp. 36–38; David J. Kalupahana, "Empiricism in Early Buddhism and William James," pp. 76–88; in *A Felicitation Volume Presented to the Ven. Narada Mahathera*, ed. Piyadassi Thera; Kandy, Sri Lanka: Buddhist Publication Society, 1979. See also Kalupahana, "Buddhist Tract on Empiricism," *Philosophy East and West* 19 (1969), 65–67, and, "Buddha's Social and Political Philosophy," *The Young Buddhist* (1982), 121–126. Ven. Phra Khantipalo, "An Interpretation of the Kalama Sutta," *The Young Buddhist* (1982), 115–119. Jacobson, op. cit., p. 19, sees empiricism, self-correction, as the key to Buddhist method and Buddhism the only viable alternative to world annihilation. Perhaps no more striking example of empiricism can be found in Buddhism than that of Chinese Ch'an or Japanese Zen with its tradition of, "If you see the Buddha on the road, kill him." It is not a physical death that is called for but the insistence that no idea of the Buddha should come between the seeker and her own direct experience of truth. This is part of Buddhism's attraction to Westerners along with its emphasis on peace and care for all living creatures. Cf. Bancroft, op. cit., pp. 36, 40. See further later.

7. Gard, op. cit., pp. 41–42, claims there were over 33 groups by the first century. He notes Theravada groups in northern areas like Bangladesh, India, Nepal and Pakistan, while Mahayana has been present in the past in the southern areas. Some half million Theravadins in the Chittagon Hill Tracts northeast of the Bay of Bengal in what is now Bangladesh, are currently being exterminated. Nelson Foster, "Tribal Buddhists in Bangladesh: The Suffering Continues," *Buddhist Peace Fellowship [BPF] Newsletter* 8, no. 3 (Summer 1986), 12–13.

It is unfortunate for world peace that Theravadins, according to Kitagawa and Reynolds, have been very reluctant to cooperate with Mahayana or Mantrayana groups. The various national groups do not cooperate with each other either but tend rather to follow the political perspectives of their various governments. Joseph M. Kitagawa and Frank Reynolds, "Theravada Buddhism in the Twentieth Century," pp. 43–64 in Dumoulin, op. cit. Malalasekera, op. cit., pp. 168–183. C. Weihsun Fu, "Mahayana Buddhism (China)," pp. 185–194, and, Joseph M. Kitagawa, "Mahayana Buddhism (Japan)," pp. 195–199, in al Faruqi and Sopher, op. cit.

8. Beaver, op. cit., pp. 237–244. NCE-3043. Nielsen, op. cit., pp. 199–251. Noss, op. cit., pp. 125–176. Jayatilleke, *Aspects of Buddhist Social Philosophy*; Kandy, Sri Lanka: 1969. Quoted by de Silva, op. cit., p. 8. Minoru Kiyota, "The Buddhist Model for Renewal: An Examination of Contemporary Buddhist Sangha in Asia," pp. 122–139 in Miller, op. cit. See especially pp. 125–129 on "Monks and Laity" and his suggestion that the distinction has often been ignored or violated in the Far East. On intolerance, see more later. The issue with women is clear. If we cannot treat women decently, we will not treat males decently either and there is no hope for peace in the world. With the exception of Sikhism, historically, women in all religions have been treated as chattel. Theravada Buddhism has not had religious orders — nuns, convents — for women for centuries — in contradiction to Gautama's permission for them. There are women renunciates, sikamatas, but no official sisterhoods. An alternative interpretation for the idea that women cannot achieve nirvana, is that they can achieve sainthood (arahat) but cannot become a Buddha in this life span. For that they must be reborn as a male. The distinction is not clear.

9. A number of writers have noted social dimensions of Buddhism. See de Silva, op. cit., pp. 44, 10–17, and, "Buddhism and Social Order," *The Young Buddhist* (1981), 155–158. Jacobson, op. cit., pp. 134, 167. A.T. Ariyaratne, "Sarvodaya — Buddhist Inspired Movement for Universal Awakening," *The Young*

Buddhist (1982), 151–153. Joanna Macy, *Dharma and Development: Religion as Resource in the Sarvodaya Self-Help Movement*, 2nd ed.; West Hartford, CT: Kumarian, 1983. Walpola Rahula, *The Heritage of the Bhikkhu*, 2nd ed.; NY: Grove, 1974. John Ferguson, *War and Peace in the World's Religions*; NY: Oxford, 1978. Hajime Nakamura, *The Ideal of World Community*; Madras: Radhakrishnan Institute, 1981. Sulak Sivaraksa, "Buddhism and Development — A Thai Perspective," *Ching Feng 26*, nos. 2–3 (August 1983), 123–133. Henry O. Thompson, "Value Orientation, Self-Deception and Social Commitment," in *Man's Search for Meaning in a Fragmented Universe*, ed. Padmasiri de Silva and Thompson; NY: Rose of Sharon, 1988. De Silva traces part of the nonsocial stereotype to Max Weber's *Religions of India: The Sociology of Hinduism and Buddhism*; Glencoe, IL: Free Press, 1956. Weber saw the search for nirvana as totally self-centered. Weber failed to see that meditation is not escape from the human predicament but an attempt to master it. De Silva, op. cit., pp. 10–14. In other traditions, one could note Gandhi and Jesus as examples of people who went apart in meditation or prayer to find strength and insight for dealing with social problems. However, the stereotype persists that Buddhism is not for ordinary people and has no message for society. It is concerned with the inner man. Very few passages in the vast literature speak of love, or against war and for peace. Arthur L. Basham, "Jainism and Buddhism," pp. 37–202 in de Bary, *Indian Tradition*, op. cit.

10. For the following, see especially Ferguson, op. cit., pp. 52–55, and Kim, op. cit., 2:219–227.

11. Kiyota, op. cit., p. 130. The quotation on oppression is by Joseph M. Kitagawa, "Buddhism and Asian Politics," *Asian Survey 2*, No. 5 (July 1962), 4. Charles S. Prebish, "Buddhist Councils and Divisions in the Order," pp. 21–26 in Prebish, op. cit. The Duttha-Gamani war was not a single event but a 15-year campaign. The Mahavamsa, the "Great Chronicle" (fifth or sixth century A.D.) of Sri Lankan history extolled the confrontation between Sinhalese and Tamils as a holy war fought in the interests of Buddhism. Elara, the Dravidian ruler of northern Sri Lanka, was a good man and a just ruler, but he had false beliefs. K.M. de Silva, *A History of Sri Lanka*; Delhi: Oxford, 1981, p. 15. Walpola Rahula, "Buddhism — Disarmament and Peace," *The Young Buddhist* (1981), 149–150, has forgotten this history (which he himself recorded (Heritage of the Bhikkhu, op. cit.) when he says "it must be stated in unequivocal terms that Buddhism is definitely against any kind of war, violence and armament and is absolutely for peace." He could of course mean that the long, vast record of violence is not Buddhist but merely done by Buddhists in the name of Buddhism. One can agree with him, however, that universal love and nonviolence are part of the teaching of Buddhism. See further later. P.A. Saram, "Sri Lanka: The Evolutionary Dialects of a Buddhist State," pp. 333–370 in *Religions and Societies: Asia and the Middle East*, ed. Carlo Caldarola; NY: Mouton, 1982. Joanna Macy reminds us that the current problems in Sri Lanka between Buddhist Sinhalese and Sri Lankan Tamils is very complicated. Here we can note her observations that some Buddhist monks promote the cause of Sinhalese nationalism and others are working desperately for peace. The same is true for Tamils. Macy, "Dharma and Civil War: The Prospects for Peace in Sri Lanka," *BPF Newsletter 8*, no. 4 (Autumn 1986), 1, 3–5. A similar report comes from S. Mark Heim, "Struggle Toward Peace in Sri Lanka," *The Christian Century 103*, no. 26 (September 10–17, 1986), 766–767. He describes the work of an interfaith Citizen's Committee for National Harmony.

12. Basham, op. cit., p. 129. Kiyota, pp. 131–132. Ling, *Buddhism, Imperialism and War: Burma and Thailand in Modern History*; London: Allen & Unwin, 1979. Cf. also Steven Piker, "Buddhist Ethics," in de Silva and Thompson,

op. cit. More recently, the Buddhist Peace Fellowship has reported active protest against Thai government policies by monks and sikamatas. BPF, "Exemplars of Engaged Buddhism," offprint.

13. David L. Snellgrove, *The Nine Ways of Bon;* Boulder, CO: Prajna, 1980. Arthur F. Wright, *Buddhism in Chinese History;* Stanford, CA: Stanford University, 1959, p. 67.

14. Jacobson, op. cit., p. 135.

15. Chai-sik Chung, "Korea: The Continuing Syncretism," pp. 607–628 in Caldarola, op. cit. Sung Bae Park claims Won-Kuang is to be condemned because Buddha's teaching prohibits killing of any kind. What the sutras teach is not protection of the nation by the sword but by the ruler having right knowledge. "The Conception of Protecting the Nation in Korean Buddhism," pp. 58–64 in *Whither Korea?*, ed. Wonmo Dong and Harold H. Sunoo; Dallas: Association of Korean Christian Scholars in North America, 1975. The Golden Splendor of Light Sutra speaks of the blessings of peace when India's 84,000 kings are content with their territory. People will be prosperous but not greedy. Basham, op. cit., pp. 184–185. James A. Aho, *Religious Mythology and the Art of War: Comparative Religious Symbolisms of Military Violence;* Westport, CT: Greenwood Press, 1981, pp. 127–142. Kim, op. cit., pp. 271–272. Aho traces bushido and its derivatives such as judo, to the kshatriya background of Buddhism. Daizen Victoria traces the close ties of Zen to the military from its first appearance in Japan to the present day. Besides training troops, Zen leaders promoted war and victory. Historically, absolute loyalty was given to the shogun, then to the emperor, and now to the corporation. "Japanese Corporate Zen," *Bulletin of Concerned Asian Scholars* 12, no. 1 (1980), 64–65. Kiyota, op. cit., p. 134. "Picture Essay: The Benevolent Gods of Ancient Japan," *Northwest Orient* 15, no. 11 (November 1984), 33–38, shows two eleventh-century statues of the Buddhist divinity Fudo-Myoo (steadfast king of light) known for his defense of the faith with sword, lasso and flames.

16. Roger J. Corless, "Chinese Buddhism and the Communist Regime," pp. 208–211 in Prebish, op. cit. The exceptions are simply wrong according to Park, op. cit. The concept of ahimsa condemns killing—those who practice, manipulate, or plan the killing, those who remain silent knowing about the killing and mere bystanders, those who are forced to kill such as draftees, executioners and those who kill in self-defense. Park cites Vasubandhu's Abhidharma Kosa IV:144 and 720.

17. Koller, *Oriental Philosophies;* NY: Scribner's, 1970, pp. 192–193. Koller wrote before the events of the 1970s but after all the violence described historically. Technically, one could argue those who used violence were either not Buddhists, or not propagating the faith but only defending it. While recognizing that Buddhist kings fought each other and others, Sulak Sivaraksa also claims that in the whole of Buddhist history, there has never been a holy war. "Buddhism and Nonviolence": *Gandhi Marg* 2, no. 6 (September 1980), 330–340. Presumably he is excluding the Mahavamsa claim in Sri Lankan history that the war between Tamils and Sinhalese was a holy war (see n. 11). Daniel C. Holtom notes that "If . . . Buddhism has never declared a holy war, it has nonetheless proclaimed all Japanese wars holy." *Modern Japan and Shinto Nationalism*, rev.; Chicago: University of Chicago, 1947, p. 148 (quoted by H. Byron Earhart, *Japanese Religion*, 2nd ed.; Encino and Belmont, CA: Dickenson, 1974, p. 99). Ling, *Buddhism, Imperialism and War*, op. cit., pp. 135–139. Ling suggests the idea of Buddhism as a religion of peace comes from its concept of ahimsa, nonviolence. He notes that the wars of Burmese and Thai kings were not wars of religion. They killed each other, Hindus, Muslims, Christians, etc., without partiality. The parallel between Rama IV's king, religion and country and

England's God, king and country is obvious. The 1910 slogan was still heard in 1976 in Thailand, and in commmunist Laos that same year, minus the king. Ling, ibid., pp. 141-151. The slogan, of course, echoes the ancient history of southeast Asian Buddhism. Here and in other areas such as international disarmament, Buddhist leaders tend to support their respective governments. Kitagawa and Reynolds, op. cit., p. 59. The tragedy of nationalism triumphant over religious principle is of course repeated in other religious traditions. However, the triumph is seldom total. In that same year of 1976, monks and sikamatas attended a student rally protesting Thailand's military dictatorship. Some 30 students were killed. The religious placed themselves between the police and the students to stop the killing.

18. Ling, *Buddha, Marx, and God*, 2nd ed.; NY: St. Martin's, 1979. Ling, *Buddhism, Imperialism and War*, op. cit., p. 135-136. For the situation in Thailand in recent times, see Carlo Caldarola, "Thailand: A Sacred Society in Modern Garb," pp. 371-406 in Caldarola, op. cit.

19. So too, the Ven. Thich Thien-Minh, "Non-Violent Action from a Vietnamese Buddhist Viewpoint," pp. 131-134 in *Religion for Peace: Proceedings of the Kyoto Conference on Religion and Peace*, ed. Homer A. Jack; New Delhi: Gandhi Peace Foundation, 1973. Hajime Nakamura, however, notes that while Buddhism does not necessarily prohibit suicide, according to the texts, suicide is meaningless. The Vietnam suicides were not based on any tenet of Buddhist teachings. Such self-immolation has no scriptural approval. "Buddhism," pp. 134-138 in *Encyclopedia of Bioethics*, ed. Warren Reich; NY: Free Press, 1978. De Silva, personal communication, March 6, 1985. A. Terry Rambo, "Vietnam: Searching for Integration," pp. 407-444 in Caldarola, op. cit.

20. In contrast, the WCRP volume includes warm greetings from Patriarch Thich Tinh Khiet of the Unified Buddhist Church of Vietnam, U Thant, the Vietnam United Buddhists Association of Hanoi, the Singapore Buddhist Youth Organizations, and Tae Keo Kim of the Won Buddhists, along with numerous Hindus, Muslims, Christians and others. Jack, op. cit., pp. 289-303. In addition to Thich Nhat Hanh and Thich Thien Minh of Vietnam, other Buddhist participants included Nenkai Inada (Japan Buddhist Federation), Nikkyo Niwano (Rissho Kosei-kai), Lord Abbott Koso Ohtani (Jodo Shin) and at least 34 others. Niwano closed his address with the sincere hope that the children of Buddha would stand hand in hand in bringing harmony into the world to realize world peace (pp. 30-33). Rissho Kosei-kai has explicitly taken a stand for world peace. Heinrich Dumoulin, "Buddhism in Modern Japan," pp. 215-276 in *Buddhism in the Modern World*, op. cit., p. 251. We are, of course, dealing with a basic problem common to many religious traditions. Who speaks for the faith whether it is Buddhism or any other? The Kyoto Conference of the WCRP was in October 1970.

21. Kim, op. cit., pp. 251-252. Shashi Bhushan, ed., *Buddhist Way to Peace*; New Delhi: Progressive Peoples Sector, 1976, pp. 37, 45, 67, 71. Dalai Lama, *My Land and My People*; NY: McGraw-Hill, 1962. Snellgrove, "Tibetan Buddhism Today," pp. 277-293 in *Buddhism in the Modern World*, ed. Dumoulin, op. cit., pp. 286-287. Henry O. Thompson, ed., *The Global Congress of the World's Religions*; NY: Rose of Sharon, 1982, especially pp. 112-137, with bibliography. For China, see Kim, op. cit., pp. 248-249. Ernst Benz, *Buddhism or Communism*; Garden City, NY: Doubleday, 1965. Raymond Pong and Carlo Caldarola, "China: Religion in a Revolutionary Society," pp. 549-577. For Japan, see Victoria, op. cit. Carlo Caldarola, "Japan: Religious Syncretism in a Secular Society," pp. 629-659 in Caldarola, op. cit.

22. Roy H. Beck, "Christians 'ghettoized' in Bangkok: 90,000 survive as hog slaughterers in Buddhist society," *The United Methodist Reporter* 131, No. 20

(October 19, 1984), 3. Minoru Kiyota, "The Buddhist Model for Renewal: An Examination of Contemporary Buddhist Sangha in Asia," pp. 122–139 in Miller, op. cit. Rahula, "Buddhism — Disarmament and Peace," op. cit. In contrast, the Paekche dynasty of Korea ordered the release of all hunting hawks and the abandonment of fishing and hunting equipment in the seventh century. King Pophung in the Silla dynasty of Korea prohibited any kind of killing after Buddhism was legalized in Silla in 527. Park, op. cit., p. 58.

23. Geoffrey Parrinder, *A Dictionary of Non-Christian Religions;* Philadelphia: Westminster, 1971, p. 259. Frederick J. Streng, *Emptiness: A Study in Religious Meaning;* Nashville, TN: Abingdon, 1967.

24. De Silva, *Value Orientations,* pp. 8, 14. Fromm, *The Heart of Man;* London, 1965.

25. Park, op. cit., p. 58. Ferguson, op. cit., pp. 46–47. Dharmasiri, op. cit., p. 90, puts this in terms that would be amusing if it were not so macabre. A Being from Outer Space visits the earth. It is perplexed to find a scientist making high explosive bombs which will be dropped on his own head.

26. Jacobson, op. cit., pp. 35–64, 151–163. David Kalupahana, *Buddhist Philosophy;* Honolulu: University of Hawaii, 1976, p. 29.

27. Ferguson, op. cit., pp. 46–47. Park, op. cit., p. 58, claims it applies even to accidental killing.

28. On not killing mosquitos, see Jacobson, op. cit., p. 141, who admitted on p. 135 the difficulty ignorant Westerners have freeing themselves of the prejudice that Buddhism is not interested in the improvement of life. He apparently did not think to ask what it did to the monks to be responsible for all the suffering and death of human beings from malaria. And he apparently did not think of suggesting that the monks hire Christians to spray the mosquitos, as in Bangkok, Christians kill hogs. Nor did the self-defense motive seem to apply here. What is really difficult for this Westerner is how monks could have such total regard for mosquitos and such a total lack of concern for human beings. On accepting the death of insects, see Macy, op. cit. In contrast to the above, the Sutra Setting Forth the Last Word of the Buddha, warns the sincere ascetic of Buddhism away from all economic activities, including farming. Nakamura goes on, however, to quote other sources such as the Mahaprajnaparamita Sutra and the Vimalakirti-nirdesa Sutra with their positive appreciation of ordinary life, op. cit., pp. 71–75. Dharmasiri, op. cit., pp. 92–93, notes that monks were forbidden to dig the earth lest they harm (Vinaya) but the Buddha did not require this rule for the laity because of practical difficulties — Ahimsa is an ideal one should approximate as far as possible.

29. Wijesekera, *The Concept of Peace as the Central Notion of Buddhist Social Philosophy;* Berlin: 1960, p. 495. Quoted by de Silva, op. cit., p. 49.

30. Nakamura, op. cit.

31. This presumably means that Zen is not Buddhism. See Victoria, op. cit. Ferguson, op. cit., p. 50. Nakamura, op. cit., p. 56.

32. The Mahaparinibanna Sutta of the Digha-nikaya records the saying about the Vajjians. The Digha also includes the story of the first king, who was chosen by the people themselves. The Majjhima-nikaya describes the people's assembly in Kusinara, where Gautama died.

33. Paul D. Clasper, *The Yogi, the Commissar, and the Third World Church;* Valley Forge, PA: Judson Press, 1972, p. 22. This view echoes the comment of Kitagawa, op. cit., and Trevor Ling's observations about the monastic role in social control in Burma and Thailand. Ling, *Buddhism, Imperialism and War,* op. cit., pp. xiii–iv. John S. Strong, *The Legend of King Asoka;* Princeton: Princeton University, 1983, pp. 131, 134. Ferguson, op. cit., pp. 50–51. Nakamura, op. cit., pp.

22, 25. Basham, op. cit., pp. 145–153. Edict 13 describes Ashoka's conversion and his concern with the horrors of war and the victory of Righteousness. See also the Digha Nikaya with its account of the Universal Emperor who rules by the Law of Righteousness, but his thousand sons are crushers of enemy armies! Basham, pp. 136–142.

34. N.A. Nikam and Richard McKeon, eds., The Edicts of Asoka; Chicago; University of Chicago, 1959. The twelfth edict is especially notable for insisting that by honoring other sects, one honors one's own, and vice versa. It is of interest that Ashoka's conquests have continued to serve as an example but this tolerance has not been so prominent. See the record of conquest and destruction cited earlier, and the riots and agitation against other religions in Burma, the intolerance of Nichiren in Japan, etc. Ling, Buddhism, Imperialism, and War, op. cit., pp. 88f, 129. Ling notes, p. 97, a Thai textbook written by Princess Phun, widely used in schools in the 1930s. The book emphasized morality, good works and consideration of others. The reward of a good life is happiness in this world. Nothing was said about nirvana or Buddhist heavens and hells. The concern with traditional Thai morality was echoed by the prime minister in 1937. The concern did not extend to non–Buddhists, however, as seen in the anti–Muslim riots and laws from 1938 to 1941.

35. De Silva, Value Orientations, pp. 8, 14–15. One might note that love is a common theme throughout Buddhism. Harvey B. Aronson, Love and Sympathy in Theravada Buddhism; Delhi: Motilal Banarsidass, 1980. Leslie S. Kawamura, ed. The Bodhisattva Doctrine in Buddhism; Waterloo, Ontario: Wilfrid Laurier University, 1981. Nakamura, op. cit., p. 68 etc. On the other hand, Kim, op. cit., p. 230, also notes the denial of the family in Buddhism. This was one of the drawbacks to the acceptance of the faith in China. The denial of love is also noteworthy in such sources as the Chinese poet, Seng-ts'an, who wrote that the Great Way is not difficult. "When love and hate are both absent everything becomes clear and undisguised." Bancroft, op. cit., p. 32.

36. De Silva, Value Orientations, pp. 15, 82. Kiyota, op. cit., p. 128, "Prince Shotoku: Faith in Action," "Exemplars of Engaged Buddhism," pp. 7–9, offprint.

37. Ferguson, op. cit., pp. 51–52.

38. Weeks, op. cit., pp. 158, 163, 166. Rissho Kosei-kai; Tokyo: Kosei, 1966. Dumoulin, op. cit., pp. 250–251.

39. NCE-2555. Ikeda, A Lasting Peace; NY: Weatherhill, 1981. Dumoulin, op. cit., pp. 268–269.

40. "The Buddhist Peace Fellowship Statement of Purpose," P.O. Box 4650, Berkeley, CA 94704. Among the founders was Robert Aitken, an American Zen Buddhist who consciously blends Buddhism with the Judeo-Christian tradition. Jaffe, op. cit. The BPF is the first non–Judeo-Christian peace fellowship to join the Fellowship of Reconciliation. The Jain Peace Fellowship is the second. Ryo Imamura, "President's Column," Buddhist Peace Fellowship Newsletter 6, no. 4 (October 1984), 2. Imamura is a seventeenth-generation Jodo Shin Shu priest at a Buddhist Churches of America temple in Alameda, CA. Another member of the Board (both their terms ended in 1984) was Joanna Macy, noted earlier for her study of Sarvodaya Shramadana in Sri Lanka. Most of the impetus for the BPF has come from American Zenists. This is surprising given the militarism of Japanese Zen. Jaffer, op. cit., traces the phenomenon to two early Japanese Zen teachers in America who were pacifist, and to the origin of American Zen in the 1960s from the antiwar cohort of the then disaffected American youth. The BPF, however, has expanded beyond this base to an international fellowship. Nakamura, op. cit., pp. 52–53. For a similar view on benevolence, cf. de Silva, Value Orientations, p. 49, as cited earlier. For engaged Buddhism, see Fred Eppsteiner and Dennis Maloney,

eds., *The Path of Compassion: Contemporary Writings on Engaged Buddhism;* Berkeley: BPF, 1985.

41. "The Buddhist Peace Fellowship Statement of Purpose." James Hughes, "Green Buddhist Declaration," *Buddhist Peace Fellowship Newsletter* 6, no. 4 (October 1984), 8.

42. De Silva, *Value Orientations*, pp. 16-17. Bardwell L. Smith, "Sinhalese Buddhism and the Dilemmas of Reinterpretation," pp. 79-104, especially p. 103, in *The Two Wheels of Dhamma: Essays on the Theravada Tradition in India and Ceylon*, ed. Gannath Obeyesekere, Frank Reynolds, and Smith; Chambersburg, PA; American Academy of Religion, 1972.

43. Jacobson, op. cit., pp. 3-6, 14, 93, 131. In an earlier work, Jacobson pointed out that "the Buddha does not offer man the vision of a new society in which he will be free." Freedom comes from creative solitude in which a person tears away illusion and ignorance. Freedom cannot become social until this battle has been won. People botched by inner conflicts resort to destruction in suicidal wars to protect the institutions that hold their society together. They will not be freed by social revolution or religious revival. *Buddhism: The Religion of Analysis;* Carbondale: Southern Illinois University, 1974.

Chapter VIII

1. Creel, *What Is Taoism?;* Chicago: University of Chicago, 1970. General studies include R.B. Blakney, *The Way of Life;* NY: Mentor, 1955. Stuart C. Hackett, *Oriental Philosophy;* Madison: University of Wisconsin, 1979. William H. Harris and Judith S. Levey, eds., *The New Columbia Encyclopedia;* NY: Columbia, 1975, p. 2693. Young Oon Kim, *World Religions*, vol. 2, 2nd ed.; NY: Golden Gate, 1982. M. Levering, "Taoism, Religious," pp. 742-746 in *Abingdon Dictionary of Living Religions*, ed. Keith Crim, et al.; Nashville: Abingdon, 1981. John B. Noss and David S. Noss, *Man's Religions*, 7th ed.; NY: Macmillan, 1975. Geoffrey Parrinder, *A Dictionary of Non-Christian Religions;* Philadelphia: Westminster, 1971. Anna K. Seidel, "Taoism," *Encyclopaedia Britannica*, (1978), 1032-1044. Michael Strickman, "Taoism, History of," ibid., pp. 1044-1050, and "Taoist Literature," pp. 1051-1055. Holmes Welch, *Taoism: The Parting of the Way;* Boston: Beacon, 1957. D.C. Yu, "Taoism, Philosophical," pp. 738-742 in *Abingdon Dictionary of Living Religions* op. cit. Yu notes that in 1973, a group of silk manuscripts was found in a Han dynasty tomb dating from circa 168 B.C. The manuscripts included two versions of the book of Lao Tzu. These are now the oldest known versions. They have no chapter divisions but are in two sections as later versions are, but the sections are reversed. What are now chapters 1-37 (Tao) come second while what are now chapters 38-81 (Te) come first. Lin Yutang, *The Wisdom of China and India;* NY: Modern Library, 1955 (original 1942).

Dr. Hae Soo Pyun kindly read and commented on this chapter. It is a privilege to thank him for several corrections. Any continuing errors are of course the author's.

2. Quotations from the Tao Te Ching are from Blakney. Blakney, pp. 37-38, 77. Parrinder, p. 274. Welch, pp. 50-83. Ch. 39 of the Tao Te Ching includes the order of the universe.

3. Blakney, pp. 24-26. Seidel, p. 1038. Parrinder, pp. 271, 308-309, notes that the Supreme Ultimate produced the Yang through movement. When it reached its limits, it became quiet and produced Yin. Fung Yu-lan, *History of Chinese Philosophy;* Princeton: Princeton University Press, 1952, p. 32 dates the first

reference to Yin and Yang in 780 B.C. when an earthquake was said to be caused by Yin dominating Yang. Quoted by Kim, p. 104.

4. Blakney, pp. 39–40, 79 (ch. 27 — a good work does not have marks of the worker), 80 (ch. 28 — uncarved block). For the last, see Welch, pp. 35–49. There are a number of ideas here reminiscent of Western thought such as John Locke's "tabula rasa" or "blank tablet" as a description of the child's mind. Taoism's return to nature and the noble savage concepts of Rousseau and the European Enlightenment may also be similar in intent. Rousseau thought man was good by nature but had been corrupted by human civilization. Most cultures have a concept of a Golden Age somewhere in the past to which philosophers and religionists call society to return. In the vernacular the good old days were when men were men, and money was worth what it said though few had any. It is the call to the simple life heard once again in the works of E.F. Schumacher in his *Small Is Beautiful;* London: Blond & Briggs, 1973. The tranquility is reminiscent of Gautama the Buddha's Middle Path. Buddhist influence is clear by the fourth century A.D. but probably not present in earlier Taoism. Perhaps both Gautama and Lao-tzu were influenced by ancient traditions. A future paradise or the return of the Golden Age, either by human effort or by divine or messianic intervention is also part of numbers of traditions such as Jainism, Zoroastrianism, Christianity and Buddhism. Similarly, non-attachment is part of the traditions of India and of mysticism in general. Welch, pp. 50–82, discusses parallels between mysticism and Taoism. On pp. 5–7, he lists 15 parallels between the Christian New Testament and the Tao Te Ching.

5. Noss, p. 256. Charles A. Reed offers interesting examples of relaxed humans in proximity and even friendship with wolves, lions, hyena, etc. "Wild Animals Ain't So Wild, Domesticating Them Not So Difficult," *Expedition* 28, no. 2 (1986), 8–15.

6. Blakney, p. 26, says "no true mystic would know himself to be such. . . . Christ, for example, does not mention religion; he *is* religious . . . but not self-consciously so." He quotes ch. 1 of the Tao Te Ching:

> The secret waits for the insight
> Of eyes unclouded by longing;
> Those who are bound by desire
> See only the outward container.

In contrast to the Occidental-Oriental division noted here, Welch, p. 163, says the Chinese themselves divide Taoism into a school (the philosophy of Lao-tzu and Chuang-tzu) and a sect.

7. Welch, pp. 179–183, feels it was written by one person, possibly an ex-official and ex-soldier, circa 325 B.C., but both author and date remain problematic. Strickman, p. 1051. He notes that the present canon of Taoist scripture dates from the fifteenth century and contains nearly 1500 titles, many from esoteric Taoism along with philosophical works. Other speak of a canon of 1120 volumes from the fifteenth century. Cf. Welch, p. 88.

8. Strickman, p. 1047. John Ferguson, *War and Peace in the World's Religions;* NY: Oxford, 1978, p. 73.

9. Parrinder, pp. 140, 160–161. Strickman, p. 1052. Welch, pp. 135–141.

10. Seidel, p. 1043. Strickman, pp. 1046, 1050. Welch, pp. 151–158. Lin Yutang, op. cit., p. 690.

11. Levering, op. cit., p. 745. Welch, pp. 133, 163–178.

12. Strickman, pp. 1045–1046. Welch, pp. 151–158, It is of interest that this same problem appears in the Roman Empire with its religio licita and religio illicita. This was the one point of cooperation between the Roman Catholics and the

Protestants during the Reformation — they were united against the Anabaptists. The early Wesleyans were looked at askance and the so-called Free Churches were not accepted for centuries. Methodism did not become legal in Germany until the 1920s. Today, history repeats itself or continues with organized or mainline religions largely opposed to the so-called New Religions.

13. Ferguson, p. 71. Strickman, p. 1046. Welch, p. 157.
14. Blakney, pp. 82–83, 116. Noss, p. 257. Welch, pp. 20–25.
15. Ferguson, p. 68.
16. Kim, p. 297. Noss, p. 243.
17. Welch, pp. 177–178, suggests that the majority of the survivors of a nuclear war will be peasants and savages — the ones far enough away from nuclear blasts. This could ironically make it possible to live in the small simple communities advocated by the Tao Te Ching in ch. 80. Lin Yutang, op. cit., p. 581 suggested that if the chapters on war and peace in the book of Lao Tze were required reading for the delegates to the peace conference, we would have a totally different world.
18. Kim, p. 300. Tao Te Ching, ch. 57. Welch, p. 26.
19. Welch, pp. 168, 26, quoting Ruth Benedict, *Patterns of Culture*, p. 233. Twylah Nitsch, a Seneca Indian, claims (as other traditions do) that the American Indians never fought a religious war. *Global Outreach*, ed. Henry O Thompson; NY: Rose of Sharon, 1987, p. 112.

Chapter IX

1. There are many sources on Confucious. "Confucianism," *Encyclopaedia Britannica* (1978), 1108–1109. The Encyclopaedia is cited hereafter as EB. Ch'u Chai and Winberg Chai, *Confucianism*; Woodbury, NY: Barron's, 1973. Herrlee G. Creel, *Confucius: The Man and the Myth*; Westport, CT: Greenwood, 1975 (original, 1949). Lawrence Faucett, *The Sayings of Confucius: A New Translation of the Analects*; San Diego, CA: 1978. Betty Kelen, *Confucius in Life and Legend*; NY: Thomas Nelson, 1971, pp. 17–33. Cheng Tien-Hsi, *China Moulded by Confucius: The Chinese Way in Western Light*; Westport, CT: Hyperion, 1973 (original 1946). Confucianism is included in many general works as well. Isma'il Ragi al Faruqi and David E. Sopher, eds., *Historical Atlas of the Religions of the World*; NY: Macmillan, 1974. R. Pierce Beaver, et al., eds., *Eerdmans' Handbook to the World's Religions*; Grand Rapids, MI: Eerdmans, 1982. Keith Crim, et al., eds., *Abingdon Dictionary of Living Religions*; Nashville: Abingdon, 1981. William Theodore de Bary, et al., eds., *Sources of Chinese Tradition*; NY: Columbia, 1960. William H. Harris and Judith S. Levey, *The New Columbia Encyclopedia*; NY: Columbia University, 1975. Young Oon Kim, *World Religions. Vol. 3. Faiths of the Far East*, 2nd ed.; NY: Golden Gate, 1982, pp. 121–160. Myrtle Langley, *Religion*; Elgin, IL: Cook, 1981. Niels C. Nielsen, Jr., et al., *Religions of the World*; NY: St. Martin's, 1983. John B. Noss and David S. Noss, *Man's Religions*, 7th ed.; NY: Macmillan, 1984. Geoffrey Parrinder, *A Dictionary of Non-Christian Religions*; Philadelphia: Westminster, 1971, pp. 65, 265. Ninian Smart, *The Long Search*; Boston: Little, Brown, 1977. Theodore T. Yeh, *Confucianism, Christianity and China*; NY: Philosophical Library, 1969. Lin Yutang, *The Wisdom of China and India*; NY: Modern Library, 1955.

2. The tradition also says she was 16 and had been seduced by a 73-year-old man who had eight daughters by his wives. Father Shu-liang Ho (624–549 B.C.) was the military commander of a district in Lu. The K'ung family were from the neighboring state of Sung and among the traditions is one that says he was a descendant of royalty. Among the K'ungs were generals, philosophers, musicians

and government officials. After a revolution, the K'ungs fled to Lu where in time, Shu-liang Ho was born. He helped the Mengs, a family of the nobility. They gave him a job and in time he became a soldier and won some fame which resulted in the military command with his home in the village of Tsou, near Ch'u-fu. Two years after Ch'iu's birth, his father died. For these traditions, Kelen, op. cit., draws on the first biography of Confucius in the *Records of the Historians* written by Ssu-Ma T'an (d. 110 B.C.) and his son Sse-Ma Ch'ien (d. 85 B.C.), called the Herodotus of China. Each was successively Grand Historian in the Han dynasty court of Emperor Wu. Creel, op. cit., p. 7, quotes Ts'ui Shu (c. 1800) that the biography in *Historical Records* is 80 percent slander. He presents a detailed critique of the biography on pp. 243–248. Noss, op. cit., pp. 265–301, claims the Analects are the best source of information but they are short on biography. Chai, op. cit., p. 28, says Confucius was born in Lu, modern Ch'u Fu in Shantung. The K'ung family was part of the ducal house of Sung, descendants of the Shang dynasty. Creel, op. cit., p. 25, notes this data in the 300 B.C. historical work, Tso Chuan, but claims it is doubtful. EB-1108–1109. Kim, op. cit., pp. 121ff. Parrinder, op. cit., pp. 65, 265.

    3. Kelen, op. cit., pp. 143–148, Chai, op. cit., pp. 29–31, 170. Cheng, op. cit., p. 57, gives the son's name as Lee, meaning carp. Yeh, op. cit., p. 82, calls the son, Li, and says Confucius had a concubine rather than a wife.

    4. Creel, op. cit., pp. 4, 222–253, dates the misuse of Confucianism to justify despotism to the Han dynasty's Emperor Wu. He calls this state Confucianism. Perhaps there is a parallel here with State Shinto in Japan.

    5. Cheng, op. cit., pp. 46–47, 50, 65–66. Creel, op. cit., pp. 113–122. Kim, op. cit., pp. 333–334. Mei, op. cit., p. 1093.

    6. Noss, op. cit., pp. 296–298. Robert N. Bellah, *Tokugawa Religion*; Boston: Beacon, 1970, pp. 55, 87. H. Byron Earhart, *Japanese Religion: Unity and Diversity*, 2nd ed.; Encino and Belmont, CA: Dickenson, 1974. Yi Pao Mei, "Confucianism," EB-1091–1099.

    7. Creel, op. cit., pp. 5, 254–278. Mei, op. cit., p. 1099.

    8. Chai, op. cit., p. 31. Creel, op. cit., pp. 75–99. Confucius' view that being a gentleman was a matter of practicing the standards of conduct appropriate to a gentleman is reminiscent of the Buddha's idea that one is a brahmin by conduct rather than by birth. John Ferguson, *War and Peace in the World's Religions*; NY: Oxford, 1978, pp. 63–64. Yeh, op. cit., pp. 82–83, notes, however, that Confucius did not educate women. The gentleman or superior man (chun tzu or jiun tze) is a central concept in Confucius thought. The Chun-tzu literally means "prince-son" but the concept of superior man is not limited to rulers. "Anyone can be a superior man. It is only necessary to decide to be one."

    9. Dr. Hae Soo Pyun, personal communication. Chai, op. cit., pp. 34–37. Kim, op. cit., p. 335. Yi Pao Mei, op. cit., p. 1092. Noss, op. cit., pp. 272–275. Stuart C. Hackett, *Oriental Philosophy*; Madison: University of Wisconsin, 1979, pp. 31–33. The five relationships appear in the Chung Yang, the Doctrine of the Mean. Their stress on loyalty was the basis for feudalistic ethics in Tokugawa Japan. By that time, they were filtered through neo–Confucianism (see later) and were used to support the status quo. There was no revolution against the Son of Heaven in Japan. This form of Confucianism also contributed to the Samurai Way of the Warrior called Bushido with its emphasis on self-control and loyalty to one's master. Earhart, op. cit., p. 89.

    10. Cheng, op. cit., pp. 30–37. Hackett, op. cit., pp. 36–38. Yi Pao Mei, op. cit., p. 1092. Noss, op. cit., pp. 271–273. James A. Aho, *Religious Mythology and the Art of War: Comparative Religious Symbolisms of Military Violence*; Westport, CT: Greenwood, 1981, p. 103. Chai, op. cit., p. 87.

11. Dr. Hae Soo Pyun, personal communication. Aho, op. cit., pp. 113–114. Yi Pao Mei, op. cit., p. 1092. The moral imperative has Western echoes in the ethics of Immanuel Kant (1726–1804). The concept of virtue has taken on new life in the West with such works as Alasdair MacIntyre, *After Virtue;* Notre Dame: University of Notre Dame, 1981. Creel, op. cit., pp. 129–130.

12. Cheng, op. cit., pp. 37–42, 129–134, 169. Kelen, op. cit., pp. 107–111. Yi Pao Mei, op. cit., p. 1092.

13. Cheng, op. cit., pp. 164, 175–189. For the world equality see his p. 189, f.n. 1. Creel, op. cit., pp. 280–285. Noss, op. cit., pp. 274–278. Yeh, op. cit., pp. 82–83. Mencius Bk. III, Pt. II, Ch. II.

14. Bellah, op. cit., pp. 108–110. Schumacher, *Small Is Beautiful;* London: Blond and Briggs, 1973.

15. Cheng, op. cit., pp. 57–64. Cheng, p. 57, names Tseng Tze as the author of the Great Learning. Creel, op. cit., pp. 100–108. De Bary, op. cit., pp. 4–5, 17, 100–135. The latter notes Ta Hsueh means education for the adult or higher education. Chung yung refers to centrality and normality, harmony with the universe. Its central teaching is ch'eng, sincerity or the truth-fullness of virtue, equivalent to jen. Kim, op. cit., pp. 328–331. Noss, op. cit., pp. 268–270. Yutang, op. cit., pp. 811–864.

16. Chai, op. cit., pp. 48–64. Cheng, op. cit., pp. 136–159. Creel, op. cit., pp. 189–194. De Bary, op. cit., pp. 100–112. Mei, op. cit., p. 1093. Noss, op. cit., pp. 284–287. Yutang, op. cit., pp. 743–784. For Immanuel Kant's rejection of total depravity while recognizing human sinfulness, see the discussion by James C. Livingston, *Modern Christian Thought;* NY: Macmillan, 1971, pp. 71–76. He is working primarily with Kant's *Religion Within the Limits of Reason Alone* (1793), ed. T.M. Green and J. Silber; NY: Harper, 1960. For the comparison with Mencius, see Philip Whang, "The Philosophy of Mencius," forthcoming.

17. Chai, op. cit., pp. 65–82, 112–155. De Bary, op. cit., pp. 112–127, 534–557. Hackett, op. cit., pp. 36–40. Mei, op. cit., pp. 1094–1097. Noss, op. cit., pp. 292–296.

18. Aho, op. cit., p. 101. In Book V, Sec. 5 of the Book of History (Shu Ching), Duke Chou tells how the Shang lost the Mandate, and adds, "I dare not say with certainty that our heritage will forever remain with fortune." Chai, op. cit., p. 24. Creel, op. cit., pp. 113–114. De Bary, op. cit., pp. 7–16, 213–214.

19. Creel, op. cit., pp. 1, 18, 142–172. Ferguson, op. cit., pp. 62–63.

20. Chai, op. cit., pp. 83–85. De Bary, op. cit., pp. 260–264. Mei, op. cit., p. 1094. Noss, op. cit., p. 270.

21. Creel, op. cit., pp. 279–285. De Bary, op. cit., p. 21. Earhart, op. cit., p. 99. Ferguson, op. cit., pp. 72–73. Mei, op. cit., pp. 1094–1099. Noss, op. cit., p. 298. One could note the use of Confucianism for militarism and totalitarianism violates the essence of the tradition. See later on Confucius' attitude toward war.

22. Woodward, "The Soul of Confucius Meets the System of Mao," *Psychology Today* 18, no. 4 (April 1984), 40–45.

23. Chai, op. cit., pp. 168–173. Earhart, op. cit., p. 99. Mei, op. cit., p. 1098. Noss, op. cit., pp. 274–275, 299–300. Woodward, op. cit., p. 42. Raymond Pong and Carlo Caldarola, "China: Religion in a Revolutionary Society," pp. 549–605 in *Religions and Societies: Asia and the Middle East,* ed. Caldarola; NY: Mouton, 1982.

24. Noss, op. cit., p. 275.

25. Kelen, op. cit., p. 26.

26. Aho, op. cit., p. 101.

27. Aho, op. cit., p. 105. Cheng, op. cit., p. 33, citing also Mencius Bk. VII,

Pt. II, Ch. 4, Sec. 1, and, IV, Pt. I, Ch. 14, Sec. 2. Creel, op. cit., p. 171. Ferguson, op. cit., pp. 64, 68. Kelen, op. cit., p. 58. Yeh, op. cit., pp. 145–151.

28. Aho, op. cit., pp. 103–112. While much modern effort has focused on transcending the concept of "us" versus "them" mentality, it has been noted for other traditions. Thus while it appears to be bigotry or jingoism, the belief that non-Chinese were considered barbarians compares with a common human phenomenon. The Greeks considered others to be barbarians. The Jews divided the world between themselves and the goyim. Non-Christians are called heathen by those called to love their neighbors. C.P. Fitzgerald, *The Chinese View of Their Place in the World;* NY: Oxford, 1976, sees this view continuing today. Cheng, op. cit., p. 26, *says* virtually the opposite in one sense, that the Chinese knew/know human nature is more or less the same in all lands and times. All humans have the same feelings – pleasure, anger, grief, fear, love, hate and desire (Book of Li, Bk. XXII). And yet his entire text glorifies his people. Chinese civilization always aims at peace and harmony (p. 20) though elsewhere he cites enormous destruction and persecution by Chinese (e.g., pp. 26–28). He does not claim all Chinese are great, however, and cites at length the Confucian distinction between the superior and inferior man (pp. 37–42).

29. Aho, op. cit., pp. 114–119. He notes that Sun Tzu was introduced into Japan in the eighth century during China's T'ang dynasty. In the Tokugawa period of Japan, bloodless victory, combat without "naked blades" was interpreted as the struggle for enlightenment.

30. Quoted by Kelen, op. cit., pp. 103–104. Cheng, op. cit., p. 8.

31. Chai, op. cit., pp. 95–97, 156–173. S.G.F. Brandon, ed., *A Dictionary of Comparative Religion;* NY: Scribner's, 1970.

32. Cheng, op. cit., pp. 47–48. Mei, op. cit., pp. 1091–1092. "Let There Be Peace on Earth," © 1955. Reprinted as no. 27, *Come Share the Spirit*, compiled by William G. Shorney; Carol Stream, IL: Hope, 1978. The tolerance represented in the above is also reminiscent of the concept cited earlier that all men are brothers.

Chapter X

1. Robert N. Bellah, *Tokugawa Religion;* Boston: Beacon, 1970 (original 1957), p. 104 for "sincere." He quotes (p. 66) Shinto theologian Imbe-no-Masamichi (1367) as saying kami comes from "kagami," "mirror." H. Byron Earhart, *Japanese Religion; Unity and Diversity*, 2nd ed.; Encino and Belmont, CA: Dickenson, 1974, p. 5. John Ferguson, *War and Peace in the World's Religions;* NY: Oxford, 1978. Chikao Fujisawa, *Zen and Shinto;* Westport, CT: Greenwood, 1974 (original 1959), pp. 17, 26–27. D.C. Holtom, *Modern Japan and Shinto Nationalism,* rev.; NY: Paragon, 1963 (original 1943), p. 41. Young Oon Kim, *World Religions. Vol. 3. Faiths of the Far East*, 2nd ed.; NY: Golden Gate, 1982, pp. 191–201. J. Gordon Melton, *Encyclopedia of American Religions*, 2 vols.; Wilmington, NC: McGrath, 1978, 2:438. John B. Noss and David S. Noss, *Man's Religions*, 7th edition; NY: Macmillan, 1984, pp. 302–327. Michale Pye, "A Tapestry of Traditions: Japanese Religions," pp. 255–267 in *Eerdmans' Handbook to the World's Religions*, ed. R. Pierce Beaver, et al.; Grand Rapids: Eerdmans, 1982.

Niels C. Nielsen, Jr., et al., quote Motoori Norinaga (1730–1801) as deriving kami from a word for high, lifted up, unusual, mysterious, divine. *Religions of the World;* NY: St. Martin's, 1983, p. 322. Motoori Norinaga also claimed the kami were human beings in ancient times who were raised to a divine status by later ages. Yoshito Tanaka in 1938 claimed the kami were ancestors now worshipped as gods.

Quoted by Noss, op. cit., p. 313. In 1910, Knitake Kume said the emperor is a living kami. In 1919, Genchi Kato claimed the emperor was the Shinto equivalent to Jehovah among the Jews. Quoted by Holtom, op. cit., pp. 9–10, 12. He notes, p. 41, that if one looks at only the larger shrines, the number of kami falls from the millions to slightly over 200. State Shinto, however, made all the warriors who fell in battle into kami, both as a reward for their sacrifice and to encourage others. It presented some interesting moral problems as when known wrongdoers died on the battlefield and then became kami, a rather dubious example for the moral education of the young. Holtom, pp. 46–54. The problem, of course, appears in other traditions as in Christianity when a pornographer claims to be born again but goes on publishing pornography.

For the Ainu and the physical anthropology of the early inhabitants, cf. J. Edward Kidder, Jr., *Japan Before Buddhism*, rev.; NY: Praeger, 1966, pp. 85–89. Noss suggests the early wars with the aborigines may have set the military tone for subsequent Japanese religion and life, with its respect for great warriors. Op. cit., p. 303. Historically, we can note early tribal wars in Hebrew, Hindu and other traditions, but fighting gods seem to be a part of the tradition from the beginning. Cult and military grew together. Ferguson, op. cit., p. 74. Earhart, op. cit., p. 13 says the Ainu are Caucasian rather than Japanese but he also notes the divine appears in the former as kamui, which is very similar to kami.

The following paragraphs also draw on James A. Aho, *Religious Mythology and the Art of War*; Westport, CT: Greenwood, 1981. Wm. Theodore de Bary, et al., eds., *Sources of Japanese Tradition*; NY: Columbia University, 1958. William H. Harris and Judith S. Levey, eds., *The New Columbia Encyclopedia*; NY: Columbia University, 1975, "Shinto," pp. 2502–2503, "Japan," pp. 1397–1400. Naofusa Hirai, "Shinto," *Encyclopaedia Britannica* (1978), 671–676. Ninian Smart, *The Long Search*; Boston: Little, Brown, 1977.

2. Earhart, op. cit., pp. 11–13. Hirai, op. cit., p. 672. Kidder, op. cit., p. 21, estimates there are 100,000 archaeological sites from pre–Buddhist Japan. He notes, p. 22, that modern archaeology dates from 1877 and Edward S. Morse's excavation of the neolithic shell mounds at Omori between Tokyo and Yokohama. Kidder suggests the Cacausoid Ainu were immigrants and the mongoloid characteristics did not predominate until the Yayoi period. He interprets the mixed physical features in both ancient and modern times to mean there is no distinct race of Japanese. Nielsen, op. cit., pp. 331–332. Noss, op. cit., p. 303. Oka Masao claims there were five major ethnic groups: Austro-Asians from south of the Yangtse (matrilinear, worshipped goddesses such as Amaterasu), absorbed by Melanesians (matriarchal; horizontal cosmology), Micronesians (patrilinear; water field rice cultivation), Tungustic from Siberia (vertical cosmology — gods descended from heaven), and Altaic from northern Asia. Their chief deity was transformed into the sun goddess. Their conquest of the central region called Yamato in the Tomb (Kofun) period (A.D. 250–600) replaced the Yayoi period (250 B.C.–A.D. 250) clans. Quoted by Joseph M. Kitagawa, "Shinto," pp. 127–132 in *Historical Atlas of the Religions of the World*, ed. Isma'il Ragi al Faruqi and David E. Sopher; NY: Macmillan, 1974.

3. The traditional date for the arrival of Buddhism is A.D. 538. Earhart, op. cit., 27–30. Noss, op. cit., pp. 304–305. The interaction of the faiths is in a tradition attributed to Prince Regent Shotoku (573–621). A convert to Buddhism, he did not neglect the kami. He called Shinto the root and stem, Confucianism the leaves and branches, and Buddhism the flowers and fruit. Fujisawa, op. cit., pp. 1–2.

4. Earhart, op. cit., pp. 20, 26–27. Joseph Kitagawa notes the government was not the patron of religion but the religious police. *Religion in Japanese History*; NY: Columbia, 1966, p. 34. Quoted by Aho, op. cit., pp. 129, 139.

5. Earhart, op. cit., pp. 18-20. Hirai, op. cit., p. 674. The Kojiki begins with the Deity Lord of the August Center of Heaven, which later Christian apologists related to God. They compared Paul's statement in Athens about "The Lord of the Universe and the Maker of the World and All Things Therein" (Acts 17:24). They continued with the next two kami, the "High August Producing Deity" and the "Divine Producing Deity" and claim the three are one and equivalent to the Christian Trinity. Before his death in 1843, Hirata Atsutane had also suggested a spiritual monism in the Kojiki. Holtom, op. cit., pp. 111-122. Parrinder, op. cit., pp. 90, 155-156, 202. Donald L. Philippi, tr., Kojiki; Princeton: Princeton University, 1969. Post Wheeler, The Sacred Scriptures of the Japanese; Westport, CT: Greenwood, 1976 (original 1952).

6. This is one of at least four versions of the myth of origins. One might note that while Amaterasu held the chief place, with hers the holiest of shrines at Ise (on the seacoast 200 miles southwest of Tokyo), she was only first among equals. Ferguson, op. cit., p. 74. Hirai, op. cit., pp. 672-673, notes two different world views were present in ancient Shinto. The myth here reflects the heaven, earth, underworld concept of Siberian and Mongolian shamanism. There was also a two dimension view of the present world and Perpetual Country in horizontal order. The latter is known from southeast Asia, Melanesia and Micronesia (see above). Hirata Atsutane in the nineteenth century declared the Japanese islands were produced first by the greatest of the kami. The inferiority of the rest of the world is indicated by their creation out of sea foam and mud. Noss, op. cit., pp. 304-307, 316. Parrinder, op. cit., pp. 17, 101, 143.

An alternate view of Jimmu Tenno's role is that he was the chief and high priest of the Yamato, who conquered the rest of the land. Another is that he led the Mongoloids or Altaic peoples who conquered the islands in the Tomb period. Still others suggest the emperor never conquered anything but was a religious figure. Nielsen, op. cit., pp. 331-332. Kidder, op. cit., p. 209, suggests an historical date of the first century B.C. for Jimmu.

The present Emperor Hirohito marked his 85th birthday in April 1986. He is the longest-lived emperor of 124 successive monarchs. Emperor Gomizunoo (1596-1680), the 108th ruler, lived 84 years and 3 months. Emperor Hirohito ascended the throne on December 25, 1926, at the death of his father, Emperor Taisho. A very human person, he likes to wear a comfortable American shoe called "Hush Puppies." Rick Ratliff, "Hirohito's sole shoemaker sizes him for Hush Puppies," Detroit Free Press (June 30, 1986), 4B

7. Earhart, op. cit., pp. 17, 21-23, 32, 75. He notes, p. 73, the Ryobu, Two Aspect Shinto, has two smaller poles attached to each upright in the torii gate. The two smaller poles refer to the dual character of the world, transcended by the overarching unity. Parrinder suggests the torii represent perches for birds (tori) who helped the gods. There are more than 20 types of torii. Op. cit., p. 285. Hirai, op. cit., p. 675. Noss, op. cit., p. 321.

8. Earhart, op. cit., pp. 49-58. He notes, p. 74, that at first, the Buddha was the original and the kami were representatives of Buddha. The later Shinto perspective reversed this so the kami were the original and the Buddhas and bodhisattvas were representatives of the kami. Hirai, op. cit., p. 672. Noss, op. cit., pp. 160-163, 307-309.

9. "Shogun" has been seen as abbreviated from "Sei-i-tai-shogun," "barbarian subduing generalissimo," the emperor's deputy. William G. Beasley, The Meiji Restoration; Stanford, CA: Stanford University, 1972, p. 43. Nielsen, op. cit., pp. 346, claim this is the title, which means military dictator, given by the imperial court to Tokugawa Ieyasu.

10. Hirai, op. cit., pp. 672–674, notes that children are raised with Shinto rituals and weddings are Shinto but funerals are Buddhist. Traditional Japanese homes have two family altars — one for kami and one for Buddha. Earhart, op. cit., pp. 1–2, 19–25, 79, 89, 104. He adds Taoism and Confucianism in terms of magical beliefs and ethics, respectively, to Hirai's observation. Noss, op. cit., pp. 304–305, 309–311, 324–325.

Earhart adds that there is no single organized religion called "Japanese religion" contrary to the view of some that Shinto is *the* Japanese religion. One explanation for this is that apart from Jodo Shin and Nichiren Buddhism, and the imported Christianity, Japanese religions do not claim absolute truth to the exclusion of other traditions. Some would add here the Nichiren offshoot, Soka Gakkai, but more importantly, at least some Shintoists have made exclusive claims for Shinto and he admits the Japanese person cannot divorce himself from Shinto. One can add the view of some Shintoists that the first kami of the Kojiki is the god of all other religions by different names — Buddha, Jesus, etc. were all Shinto missionaries. He notes (pp. 74–75) Kitabatake Chikafusa (1293–1354) who supported the divine descent of the emperor and claimed the superiority of Shinto over foreign traditions. He quotes (p. 45) Yoshida Kanetomo (1435–1511), "All foreign doctrines are offshoots of Shinto." (Cited by Noss also, op. cit., p. 320.) Earhart also admits that Buddhism was not accepted when it first appeared in 538. Prince Shotoku was an ardent Buddhist but acceptance was a process that took some time. Attempts to purify Shinto often included rejecting other traditions. See further, later, Motoori (d. 1801) and the Meiji era effort to make Shinto the only Japanese religion (his p. 94).

Hirai, op. cit., p. 676, claims that Shintoists today want cooperation but not syncretism. This, of course, is in contrast to the extensive syncretism which began when Buddhism, etc., arrived and continues in sect Shinto and in the new religions which combine Shinto with Christianity, etc. The issue of Japanese religion or religions is complicated by the Japanese language which does not usually distinguish between the singular and the plural. Pye, op. cit., pp. 255–257. On peace, Bellah, op. cit., p. 21.

11. Noss, op. cit., pp. 318–321. The willingness and even eagerness to die for one's faith or one's country may or may not be a distortion but it is quite common in history. The 1000 Jewish murderers and suicides of Masada in A.D. 72 are national heroes for modern Israel. Christians have courted martyrdom, "baptism by blood" from earliest times. Mahatma Gandhi advised his followers "not to fear death, but to face it and welcome it when it comes in the performance of duty." Quoted from *Indian Opinion* (March 18, 1914) by Mark Juergensmeyer, *Fighting with Gandhi*; San Francisco: Harper & Row, 1984, p. 52. Herrlee G. Creel quotes numerous references in the *Chung Tzu* "that for the enlightened Taoist both death and life are matters of indifference, and in some passages death is even called desirable." *What Is Taoism?*; Chicago: University of Chicago, 1970, p. 14.

The "Holy War" comment is from Holtom, op. cit., p. 19. One can compare the Christian crusades, the holy war of Judaism and Islam's "jihad." He notes (p. 20) the bitterly inconsistent severity toward conquered people. The "war stories" of captured Americans after World War II, the revolts of Koreans, and anti–Japanese guerilla activity in occupied territories suggest that others did not see the "benefits" of Japanese rule. Earhart, op. cit., pp. 65, 99, notes that all religious traditions fed into Japanese nationalism and militarism. Among Buddhist groups, he explicitly cites the Nichiren sect. Aho, op. cit., pp. 129–138, notes that in the Tokugawa period, bushido was converted from military discipline to spiritual discipline, from warfare with others to warfare with oneself. Through bushido, one could become a kami. It is of interest that in the 1930s and 1940s, when Christianity was attacked as a "foreign" religion, Christian apologists responded by comparing their faith with bushido — moral obligation, sacrifice, firm conviction, compassion, loyalty to ruler and country, and devoted public service. Holtom, op. cit., pp. 104–111. It is understood, of course, that the obedience as an ideal was often reinforced by financial support. When the money was not forthcoming, loyalty weakened. Bellah, op. cit., pp. 23, 26, suggests the failure to pay the loyal followers led to the downfall of the Tokugawa regime. See pp. 89–98 for his description of bushido and its incorporation by the merchant class as part of their code in the Tokugawa period.

12. Earhart, op. cit., p. 80, claims the Shimabara Revolt was a peasant rebellion rather than a religious uprising. He adds that by 1650, Christianity had become an underground religion and it then took on a Japanese character.

13. Bellah, op. cit., pp. 33, 133–177. The work ethic and service is reminiscent of Ferguson's view of Shinto as activity. Op. cit., p. 74. There is a parallel in Mahatma Gandhi's concept of physical labor as divine service. Gandhi, *Bread Labor*; Ahmedabad: Navijivan, 1960. Joseph W. Elder, "The Gandhian Ethic of Work in India," pp. 51–62 in *Religious Ferment in Asia*, ed. Robert J. Miller; Lawrence: University of Kansas, 1974. Kim, op. cit., pp. 196–197.

14. Bellah, op. cit., pp. 100–101. Earhart, op. cit., p. 91. Hirai, op. cit., pp. 672–673. Noss, op. cit., pp. 310–311. The National Scholars development is described by Nielsen, op. cit., pp. 348–349. Hirata is quoted by Holtom, op. cit., p. 21. Harris and Levy, op. cit., p. 2503, on no need for a moral code. A similar suggestion has been made for the American Indians. Holmes Welch, *Taoism*; Boston: Beacon, 1957, pp. 168, 26. The concept also appears in the Hebrew prophets who prophesied a Day when the Law would be written on the heart so there would be no need for a written Torah. However, cf. the earlier note about wrongdoers becoming kami when they died on the battlefield. Holtom, pp. 44–54. Perhaps "moral" is a matter of definition or perhaps it is only after death that one reaches a pure moral state. H. Neill McFarland, "The Spirit of Japan: A Thematic Review of Japanese History," *The Search for Absolute Values and the Creation of the New World*; NY: ICF, 1982, II:967–979.

15. Noss, op. cit., pp. 305, 311–312. This period was followed by the Taisho (1912–1925) and the Showa (1926 to the present with the Emperor Hirohito). Sometimes the 1868–1945 time is called the modern period and the time since, the postwar period. Earhart, op. cit., p. xi. Holtom, op. cit., pp. 127–151. He notes, p. 209, Shinto apologist Genchi Kato in 1926, saying the Shinto shrine at Ise is a splendid mausoleum and Japan is the classical land of necrolatry — the worship of the dead. On the Meiji Restoration, see Beasley, op. cit. On the battle cry, Bellah, op. cit., p. 184.

16. Earhart, op. cit., pp. 90–91, uses the term "Restoration Shinto." He discusses Tenrikyo on pp. 110–114. He sees it as a return to peasant values — gratitude to the sacredness of the cosmos and the ethics of placing social good before individual profit. Ferguson, op. cit., pp. 75–76. Hirai, op. cit., p. 673. Kim, op. cit., pp. 187–190, 192, lists Tenrikyo as a shamanistic religion as well as an example of sectarian Shinto. Earhart agrees in seeing Miki's revelation as shamanistic possession. Melton, op. cit., 2:440–442. Noss, op. cit., p. 325. Parrinder, op. cit., pp. 156, 247, 278–279.

For extended discussion on the New Religions see H. Neill McFarland, *The Rush Hour of the Gods*; NY: Macmillan, 1967. Harry Thomsen, *The New Religions of Japan*; Westport, CT: Greenwood, 1978 (original 1963). Tenrikyo and Konkoyo are discussed in Robert S. Ellwood, Jr., *The Eagle and the Rising Sun: Americans and the New Religions of Japan*; Philadelphia: Westminster, 1974. On women —

Nakamura Kyoko, "Revelatory Experience in the Female Life Cycle: A Biographical Study of Women Religionists in Modern Japan," *Japanese Journal of Religious Studies* 8, nos. 3–4 (September–December 1981), 187–205. Nielsen, op. cit., pp. 329, 332, 355, suggests the role of women in the new religions does represent an increased role for women in religion and society. Historically, they suggest most "miko" or shamans have been women. They also quote a tradition that the empress was the miko and the emperor her interpreter rather than a political ruler.

17. Ellwood, op. cit. Holtom, op. cit., p. 55. Melton, op. cit., pp. 437–443. In 1985, the Rev. Alfred Tsuyuki of the Konko Church in Los Angeles, traveled to Flat Rock, MI. There he led the Shinto "Sacred Groundbreaking Ceremony with the Principal Parent of the Universe" for a new Mazda auto factory. Martin E. Marty, "Shinto's Turn," *The Christian Century* (October 9, 1985), 903.

18. Earhart, op. cit., pp. 96–99, 105, 120–121. Ferguson, op. cit., p. 75. Holtom, op. cit., pp. iii, 153–172. "All the wars of Japan are holy wars since they are under the supreme command of an emperor who can do nothing wrong" (p. 54). The army is the principal agency for the fulfillment of Japan's destiny (p. 23). He quotes (p. 158) Hideo Hori as saying in 1939 that Shinto and the state are so intimately connected, they cannot be separated. Fujisawa, op. cit., pp. 46, 50. General Hayashi is quoted by Holtom, op. cit., p. 89.

19. Noss, op. cit., pp. 312–315, 321, notes that Japan is becoming steadily more secular. In 1973, only 25 percent of the people preferred some form of religion. The source is not indicated but one might question it. The new religions alone account for more than that. By 1960, one in three Japanese were associated with one of these. Ellwood, op. cit., p. 14. Pye, op. cit., p. 255. But, Noss says, most Japanese do not understand these new religions which take personal involvement in contrast to mere respect. Myrtle Langley reports on a 1970 census in which a population of 100 million had a religious affiliation of 177 million (many listed two traditions such as Shinto and Buddhism). *A Book of Beliefs: Religions;* Elgin, IL: Cook, 1981.

20. Kyoko, op. cit., for 1980 statistics. Melton, op. cit., p. 440. Noss, op. cit., pp. 325–326. Thomsen, op. cit., pp. 199–219 for Odoru Shukyu.

21. Kim, op. cit., pp. 199–201. McFarland, op. cit., pp. 123–144 for PL Kyodan. Noss, op. cit., p. 326. Thomsen, op. cit., pp. 127–198 for the Omoto group, p. 249 for PL membership.

22. Hirai, op. cit., pp. 673–674. Uesugi is quoted by Holtom, op. cit., p. 10. For "under one roof" as meaning peace, Holtom, p. 23.

23. Hirai, op. cit., p. 676. Cf. f.n. 10. Ono Sokyo of Kokugakuin University in Tokyo (the intellectual center of Shinto since its founding in 1890) also claims a universalism for Shinto while acknowledging that nationalism, the imperial institution and Shinto are inextricably bound together. Quoted by Nielsen, op. cit., pp. 357–358.

24. Ono Sokyo, op. cit., Bellah, op. cit., p. 62, says "Nature is both a benevolent and nurturing force toward whom man should express gratitude, and a manifestation of the ground of being. . . . Nature is not alien to the divine or to man but is united with both."

25. Holtom, op. cit., pp. 158–160, quoting Hideo Hori (1939) and Genchi Kato (1938). The latter said Shinto is more than "an ethical spark of universalism." It is part of the human soul and universal human nature. The seventeenth century scholar, Nobuyosh Watarai said, "Perfect sincerity is the supreme principle of Shinto." Earlier, Christianity was condemned for its universalism. Holtom, pp. 80–88. Christians responded with the record of their charitable works and claimed they believed in holy living for Japan rather than merely dying for their country. On universalism, Ono Sokyo, op. cit.

26. Fujisawa, op. cit., pp. 22, 28, 32. One could hear echoes here if one wished of the extreme nationalism and triumphalism cited earlier. But note Fujisawa's own earlier comment on the need for Shinto itself to go through a sweeping renovation to return to its true state. Whether one agrees with his high evaluation of Shinto or not, his point is the contribution Shinto can make to world peace. Nielsen, op. cit., p. 325, notes that while some kami are destructive, Amaterasu and her descendant, the emperor, are concerned with peace and order in the world of nature and humanity.

Chapter XI

1. Gill, "Shamanism," pp. 674–677 in *Abingdon Dictionary of Living Religions*, ed. Keith Crim, et al.; Nashville: Abingdon, 1981 (cited hereafter as ADLR), and, *Beyond "The Primitive"—The Religions of Nonliterate Peoples*; Englewood Cliffs, NJ: Prentice-Hall, 1982, pp. 89–92. Vilmas Dioszegi, "Shamanism," pp. 638–641 in *The New Encyclopaedia Britannica, Macropedia*; London: EB, 1978. The following paragraphs also draw on *Eerdmans' Handbook to the World's Religions*; Grand Rapids: Eerdmans, 1982, pp. 128–168. Mircea Eliade, *Shamanism*, rev.; Princeton: Princeton University, 1964 (original 1951). Robert S. Ellwood, Jr., *Religious and Spiritual Groups in Modern America*; Englewood Cliffs: Prentice-Hall, 1973. John Ferguson, *War and Peace in the World's Religions*; NY: Oxford, 1978. Michael Harner, *The Way of the Shaman: A Guide to Power and Healing*; NY: Bantam, 1982. William H. Harris and Judith S. Levey, eds., *The New Columbia Encyclopedia*; NY: Columbia, 1975, pp. 2491, 107. This volume is cited hereafter as NCE. Young Oon Kim, *World Religions. Vol. 3. Faiths of the Far East*, 2nd ed.; NY: Golden Gate, 1982. Lawrence Krader, "Shamanism," pp. 45–49 in *Historical Atlas of the Religions of the World*, ed. Isma'il R. al Faruqi and David E. Sopher; NY: Macmillan, 1974. Myrtle Langley, *A Book of Beliefs: Religions*; Elgin, IL: Cook, 1981. Stephen Larson, *The Shaman's Doorway*; NY: Harper & Row, 1976. Ioan M. Lewis, *Ecstatic Religion: An Anthropological Study of Spirit Possession and Shamanism*; Baltimore: Penguin, 1971. Bronislaw Malinowski, *Magic, Science and Religion*; Garden City: Doubleday, 1948. Robert C. Mitchell, *African Primal Religions*; Niles, IL: Argus, 1977. John B. Noss and David S. Noss, *Man's Religions*, 7th ed.; NY: Macmillan, 1984, pp. 1–31.

2. ADLR-674, 677, suggests "shaman" comes through Russian from Siberian Tungusic "shaman." There are cognate words in many Siberian and Central Asian languages. The word may also have derived from the Pali "samana" through the Chinese "sha-men." Geoffrey Parrinder, *A Dictionary of Non-Christian Religions*; Philadelphia: Westminster, 1971, p. 251 (cited hereafter as PDNR). Eliade, op. cit., pp. 495–496.

3. While dream interpretation is still held in high regard by some traditions today, it has been largely taken over in the West by psychology. Psychiatrists have been called the high priests of today's society. Perhaps "shamans" would be more correct. Ellwood, op. cit., p. 13, emphasizes the healing dimension and also notes (p. 16) a detailed comparison between the peak experience concept of psychologist Abraham Maslow and the shamanistic experience. The following are examples of the healing tradition. *Border Healing Woman: The Story of Jewel Babb* as told to Pat Ellis Taylor; Austin: University of Texas, 1981. Eduardo Calderon, Richard Cowan, Douglas Sharon, and F. Kaye Sharon, *Eduardo el Curandero: The Words of a Peruvian Healer*; Richmond, CA: North Atlantic Books, 1982. Jerome D. Frank, *Persuasion and Healing: A Comparative Study of Psychotherapy*, rev.; NY:

Schocken, 1974. Ramesh M. Shrestha with Mark Lediard, *Faith Healers: A Force for Change;* NY: UNICEF, 1980 (Nepal). On the spirit world, see Harold Turner, "World of Spirits," pp. 128–132 in *Eerdmans' Handbook,* op. cit.

4. PDNR-60, 121, 151, 182, 224. Ellwood, op. cit., p. 15, suggests that Dante's *Divine Comedy* recapitulated the shaman's journey and made it part of Western tradition. Lewis, op. cit., pp. 178–205, has an extensive discussion on the differences between shamanistic possession and psychiatric problems. See also Frank, op. cit., for a general comparison of shamanism and psychotherapy.

5. Gill, op. cit., p. 675. Kim, op. cit., pp. 366–369.

6. MacMullen, *Christianizing the Roman Empire (A.D. 100–400);* New Haven, CT: Yale University, 1984. G.R.H. Wright, "The Upside Down Tree on the Vatican Hill," in *Put Your Future in Ruins,* ed. Henry O. Thompson; Bristol, IN: Wyndham Hall Press, 1985. Wright notes the apocryphal "Acts of Peter" dated circa A.D. 200 as a striking example of the attraction of the miraculous.

7. Eliade, "Nostalgia for Paradise in the Primitive Traditions," *Myths, Dreams and Mysteries;* NY: Harper, 1960, pp. 59–72. See also Eliade's "Gods, Goddesses and Myths of Creation," chapters 1–2 of *From Primitives to Zen;* NY: Harper & Row, 1974, and, *The Myth of the Eternal Return, or, Cosmos and History;* Princeton: Princeton University, 1971 (original 1949). Kim, op. cit., pp. 370–373. ADLR-675. Some have suggested the concept of communication with nonhuman life continues today in the idea of talking to plants as a way to give them attention and keep them healthy. Peter Tompkins and Christopher Bird, *The Secret Life of Plants;* NY: Harper & Row, 1973. On mysticism, see Huston Smith, *Forgotten Truth;* NY: Harper & Row, 1976, and, Anne Bancroft, *The Luminous Vision;* London: Allen & Unwin, 1982. Ellwood, op. cit., p. 17, suggests that shamanism is antihistorical, trying to escape external time. It does this through two modes: mysticism and apocalypticism.

8. Holmes, *The Priest in Community;* NY: Seabury, 1978. See especially ch. 3, "The Shamanistic Roots of Priesthood." One can note the clergy escort of the dead body to burial or cremation as equivalent to the role of the psychopomp.

9. Robert S. Ellwood and Richard Pilgrim, *Japanese Religion;* Englewood Cliffs, NJ: Prentice-Hall, 1985. Kim, op. cit., pp. 374–376. Eliade, *Shamanism,* op. cit., pp. 461–465.

10. Kim, op. cit., pp. 377–386. Eliade, *Shamanism,* op. cit., pp. 447–461.

11. Conn, "Korea," pp. 138–139 in *Eerdmans' Handbook,* op. cit. Kim, op. cit., pp. 388–391. Gernot Prunner, "The New Religions in Korean Society," *Korea Journal* (February 1980), 4–15. Alan C. Covel, *Ecstasy: Shamanism in Korea;* Elizabeth, NJ: Hollyum International Corporation, 1984.

12. Chai and Chai, *Confucianism;* Woodbury, NY: Barron's, 1969. Eliade, *Shamanism,* op. cit., pp. 458–460. Kim, op. cit., pp. 374–376. Herrlee G. Creel, *What Is Taoism?* Chicago: University of Chicago, 1970. Walter Heissig, *The Religions of Mongolia;* Berkeley: University of California, 1980.

13. NCE-2745. Helmut Hoffman, et al., *Tibet: A Handbook;* Bloomington, IN: Indiana University, 1975, pp. 94–173. The first 27 kings of Tibet were of the Bon religion. Bon continued through several more reigns before Tibet was converted to Buddhism. The latter is known as Lamaism which "has preserved the Bon shamanic tradition almost in its entirety." Eliade, *Shamanism,* op. cit., pp. 430–441. David L. Snellgrove, *The Nine Ways of Bon;* Boulder, CO: Prajna, 1980 (original 1967), p. 1, notes that "bon" means invite, entreat, invoker and seed and chant (the chant invokes the spirits). Bonpos (followers of bon) have suffered serious hostility in the past. Now others take as little account of their existence as possible.

14. Zuesse, "African Traditional Religion," pp. 5–12 in ADLR. PDNR-12, and,

216 Chapter XI

African Traditional Religion; Westport: Greenwood, 1975 (original 1954). Gill, op. cit., p. 8. Booth suggests this diffusion of religion throughout society was the reason the first Portuguese visitors to southern Africa thought the Africans had no religion. The Europeans were used to seeing religion as something separate from life. Newell S. Booth, Jr., ed., *African Religions: A Symposium;* NY: NOK, 1977, p. 1. Ferguson, op. cit., p. 1. Wande Abimbola, "The Notion of Sacrifice in the Yoruba Religion," pp. 175–181 in *Restoring the Kingdom,* ed. Deane William Ferm; NY: Paragon, 1984. Jan Knappert, "The Religions of Africa," pp. 223–233 in *The Global Congress of the World's Religions,* ed. Henry O. Thompson; NY: Rose of Sharon, 1982. E. Bolaji Idowu, *African Traditional Religion: A Definition;* Maryknoll: Orbis, 1973. Myrtle Langley, "There Is No African Religion...?" pp. 239–249 in *Towards a Global Congress of World Religion,* ed. Warren Lewis; NY: Rose of Sharon, 1978. Niels C. Nielsen, Jr., et al., *Religions of the World;* NY: St. Martin's, 1983, pp. 24–32, "Religious Symbolism Among the Dogon and Yoruba." Aylward Shorter, "African Traditional Religion: Its Relevance in the Contemporary World," *Cross Currents* **28**, no. 4 (Winter 1978–1979), 421–431. Fred Wellbourn, "There Is No African Religion," pp. 234–239 in *Towards,* op. cit. Gaston Wiet, et al., *History of Mankind. Vol. III. The Great Medieval Civilizations;* NY: Harper & Row, 1975, pp. 827–868, "The Prehistory of Africa." William C. Willoughby, *The Soul of the Bantu;* Garden City: Doubleday, 1928. Dominique Zahan, *The Religion, Spirituality, and Thought of Traditional Africa;* Chicago: University of Chicago, 1979 (original 1970).

15. Samuel Erivwo, "God and Man in African Belief," pp. 117–127 in *Towards,* op. cit. Kwame Gyekye, "The Unitive Elements in African Philosophies and Theologies," pp. 216–229 in *Towards,* op. cit. John Mbiti, "The Encounter of Christian Faith and African Religion," *The Christian Century* **97**, no. 27 (August 27–September 3, 1980), 817–820. Here, and in his *African Religions and Philosophy;* NY: Praeger, 1969, and, *Concepts of God in Africa;* NY: Praeger, 1970, Mbiti claims African traditional religion is monotheistic. In "Traditional Religions in Africa," pp. 61–68 in *Historical Atlas,* op. cit., Mbiti treats traditional faith as a unity. Okot p'Bitek, *African Religions in Western Scholarship;* Nairobi: East African Literature Bureau, 1971, p. 47, claims the monotheism of Mbiti and others is due to their Western orientation. Geoffrey Parrinder, *Religion in Africa;* NY: Praeger, 1969, p. 31.

16. Booth, op. cit., pp. 6–8. Parrinder, Religion in Africa, op. cit., pp. 26–27, 233. One is reminded here of Hebrew concepts of time — there is no past, present or future. Language expresses completed, present and ongoing action.

17. Zuesse, op. cit., pp. 7–8. Nathaniel I. Ndiokwere, *Prophecy and Revolution: The Role of Prophets in the Independent African Churches and in Biblical Tradition;* London: SPCK, 1981. Knappert, op. cit., p. 227, suggests the concept of soul is too vague to speak clearly of different souls. There may be simply different ways of understanding the phenomenon. For an example of healing, see Jean Buxton, *Religion and Healing in Manderi;* Oxford: Clarendon, 1973.

18. Harold W. Turner, *Religious Innovation in Africa;* Boston: Hall, 1979. Friday M. Mbon, "Africa's New Religious Movements," *ICF Report* **3**, no. 1 (May 1985), 8–9, 12. He cites an estimated 33 million Traditionalists as too conservative. David B. Garrett, *Schism and Renewal in Africa: An Analysis of Six Thousand Contemporary Religious Movements;* Nairobi: Oxford, 1968. Gregory Jaynes describes a Roman Catholic Mass in which people dance with hand clapping and ululation. The priest carries a long knife as a symbol of his authority. Praise of ancestors is mixed with prayers to saints. "Pope Seeks to Feed the Flock Whose Increase Is Most Rapid," *The New York Times* (May 4, 1980) 1, E7. The article notes

over 200 million Christians out of a total population of 450 million. Ali A. Mazrui, "Cultural Synthesis in Africa," *The World & I* 1, no. 2 (February 1986), 171–185.
19. Zuesse, op. cit., p. 12. Shorter, op. cit., pp. 421–422. Knappert, op. cit., p. 223. Booth, op. cit., p. 9. Harold W. Turner, "The Relationship Between Development and New Religious Movements in the Tribal Societies of the Third World," pp. 84–110 in *God & Global Justice;* NY: Paragon, 1985.
20. L.A. Hieb, "Native American Tribal Religion," ADLR-526–533. Robert F. Berkhofer, Jr., *The White Man's Indian: Images of the American Indian from Columbus to the Present;* NY: Knopf, 1978, pp. 6 (Columbus) and 8 (Vespucci). He notes, p. 1, that the "Indian" is a White invention. Native Americans neither called themselves by a single term nor understood themselves as a collectivity — if they knew about each other at all (very doubtful!). But today's Indians are beginning to claim oneness, at least in part for political power (p. 195). Francis Paul Prucha, *The Indians in American Society from the Revolutionary War to the Present;* Berkeley: University of California, 1986. William Brandon, *The American Heritage Book of Indians;* NY: Dell, 1961. Eliade, *Shamanism*, op. cit., pp. 288–336. Sam D. Gill, *Native American Religions;* Belmont, CA: Wadsworth, 1982, and, *Native American Traditions;* Wadsworth, 1983. Religions, p. 15, for differences and the whole text for similarities. Aake Hultkrantz, *The Religions of the American Indians*, rev.; Berkeley: University of California, 1979 (original 1967), p. 3 notes that it is only from a superficial perspective that the Indian religions constitute a unity. Weston La Barre, "Amerindian Religions," pp. 51–57 in *Historical Atlas*, op. cit. William C. Sturtevant, ed., *Handbook of North American Indians*, 20 vols.; Washington: Smithsonian, 1978–. Turner, *Eerdmans' Handbook*, op. cit., p. 129, cites Darwin on the Patagonia Indians. Wiet, op. cit., pp. 869–952, "Prehistoric New World Cultural Development." For some insight on the Indians in the United States today, see Glenn Emery, "On Native Ground: The American Indian Today," *Insight* 2, no. 35 (September 1, 1986), 8–19.
21. Hieb, op. cit., pp. 531–532. Michael J. Harner, *Hallucinogens and Shamanism;* NY: Oxford, 1973. Hultkrantz, op. cit., pp. 84–102. Gill, op. cit., pp. 74–76, 92. James S. Griffith, "Kachinas and Masking," pp. 764–777 in *Handbook*, vol. 10 (1983), op. cit., Ethelou Yazzie, "Navaho Wisdom," *The World & I* 1, no. 1 (January 1986), 282–291.
22. Hieb, op. cit., p. 532. Gill, *Beyond the Primitive*, op. cit., pp. 74–97; *Religions*, op. cit., pp. 97–101; *Traditions*, op. cit., pp. 90–104. John Lame Deer and Richard Erdoes, *Lame Deer: Seeker of Visions;* NY: Simon and Schuster, 1972. Hultkrantz, op. cit., pp. 3–4 et passim.
23. PDNR-135.
24. Hieb, op. cit., p. 533. A.F.C. Wallace, "Origins of the Long House Religion," pp. 442–448 in *Handbook*, op. cit., vol. 15 (1978), and, *Death and Rebirth of the Seneca;* NY: Knopf, 1969. As with the new religions in Africa, Wallace sees the Long House Religion as assisting people to come to grips with the crisis of modernity. NCE-658, 1180. Gill, *Traditions*, op. cit., pp. 145–150. On tradition and change in American Indian religion, see Gill, *Religion*, op. cit., pp. 140ff.
25. NCE-1080, 3010. Gill, op. cit., pp. 104–107. Weston La Barre, *The Ghost Dance;* Garden City: Doubleday, 1970. Gill, *Religion*, op. cit., pp. 164–167, and, *Traditions*, op. cit., pp. 157–162.
26. David F. Aberle, "Peyote Religion Among the Navajo," pp. 558–569 in *Handbook*, op. cit., vol. 10 (1983). Edward F. Anderson, *Peyote: The Divine Cactus;* Tucson, AZ: University of Arizona, 1980. Weston La Barre, *The Peyote Cult*, 4th ed.; Archon Books, 1975. Alice Lee Marriott, *Native American Church of*

North America; NY: Mentor, 1972. James S. Slotkin, *The Peyote Religion;* Glencoe, IL: Free, 1956. Gill, *Religion,* op. cit., pp. 167–171, and, *Traditions,* op. cit., pp. 162–166.

27. Newberry, "North American Indians," pp. 165–166 in *Eerdmans' Handbook,* op. cit.

28. Deloria, *God Is Red;* NY: Delta, 1973. Nitsch, *Global Outreach;* NY: Rose of Sharon, 1987. Benedict, *Patterns of Culture;* Boston: Houghton Mifflin, 1959 (original 1934), pp. 252–253. Benedict explains this phenomenon as suggesting the Indians were so tuned in to the social order, they did not think of it as being imposed from without. In contrast, Gill suggests the motif of the trickster — coyote in the Plains Indian tradition — is a desire to be free of rules, to be unbound by time, space or society. Gill, *Religions,* op. cit., pp. 26–29. That would suggest people were aware. Cf. further, Paul Radin, *The Trickster;* NY: Philosophical Library, 1956.

29. *Handbook,* op. cit. There are three references to peace and many references to war in Julian H. Steward, ed., *Handbook of South American Indians,* 7 vols.; Washington: United States Government Printing Office, 1947–1963. Brandon, op. cit., p. 151. He includes the peaceful Pueblo in his descriptions. He also notes that all was not peace and light — Indians lived in fear of ghosts, goblins, and other supernatural spirits. Wallace, *Handbook,* op. cit., p. 447. Benedict, op. cit., pp. 30–32, 98–99. For a detailed description of the wars and human sacrifices of the Aztecs, see James A. Aho, *Religious Mythology and the Art of War;* Westport, CT: Greenwood, 1981, pp. 41–59.

30. Knappert, "War and Peace in Africa," manuscript. Ake Hultkrantz, "Nomads of the Steppes," pp. 122–126 in *Eerdmans' Handbook,* op. cit. Brown, ed., *The Sacred Pipe: Black Elk's Account of the Seven Rites of the Oglala Sioux;* Norman: University of Oklahoma, 1953, p. 115. The text as a whole describes a variety of purposes for the pipe.

31. Parrinder, *Religion in Africa,* op. cit., p. 91. Noss, op. cit., p. 26. Ferguson, op. cit., p. 16.

32. Parrinder, op. cit., p. 90. The "local" concern comment, could, or course, be made about many of the so-called world religions. The average church congregation in Christianity is primarily concerned with its own affairs and its world view is apt to be rather vague.

33. Gill, *Religions,* op. cit., p. 36. Newberry, op. cit. Cf. also, Leslie Hoggarth, *Eerdmans',* pp. 167–168, speaking about the Indians of the Andes Mountains in South America.

Bibliography

Abbott, Nabia. *Aisha, The Beloved of Mohammad.* NY: Arno, 1973 (original 1942).

Abramov, S. Zalman. *Perpetual Dilemma: Jewish Religion in the Jewish State.* NY: Union of American Hebrew Congregations, 1979.

Ackerman, James S., et al., eds. *Islamic Art and Architecture.* NY: Garland, 1976.

Aggarwal, Lalit K. *Peace Science: A Bibliography.* Philadelphia: University of Pennsylvania, 1974.

Ahmad, Aziz. *An Intellectual History of Islam in India.* Edinburgh: Edinburgh University, 1969.

Aho, James A. *Religious Mythology and the Art of War: Comparative Religious Symbolisms of Military Violence.* Westport, CT: Greenwood, 1981.

Albright, William F. and David Noel Freedman, eds. *The Anchor Bible.* Garden City: Doubleday, 1964ff.

Ali, Muhammad. *A Manual of Hadith.* Lahore: Ahmadiyya Anjuman, 1951.

Allchin, Bridget and Raymond. *The Rise of Civilization in India and Pakistan.* NY: Cambridge, 1982.

Altman, Nathaniel. *Ahimsa: Dynamic Compassion.* Wheaton, IL: Theosophical Publishing House, 1980.

Anderson, Bernhard W. *Understanding the Old Testament.* 4th ed. Englewood Cliffs, NJ: Prentice-Hall, 1986.

Anderson, Edward F. *Peyote: The Divine Cactus.* Tucson: University of Arizona, 1980.

Anesak, Masaharu. *Nichiren: The Buddhist Prophet.* Gloucester: Smith, 1966.

Arberry, A.J., ed. *Religion in the Middle East.* Cambridge, England: University Press, 1969.

Archer, Gleason L., Jr., et al. *The Rapture.* Grand Rapids, MI: Zondervan, 1984.

Armstrong, William P., ed. *Calvin and the Reformation.* Grand Rapids, MI: Baker, 1980.

Aronson, Harvey B. *Love and Sympathy in Theravada Buddhism.* Delhi: Motilal Banarsidass, 1980.

Ashby, Philip H. *Modern Trends in Hinduism.* NY: Columbia, 1974.

Atterbury, Anson P. *Islam in Africa.* Westport, CT: Greenwood, 1969.

'Azzam, 'Abd-al-Rahman. *The Eternal Message of Muhammad.* NY: Mentor, 1965.

Bacon, Margaret H. *The Quiet Rebels: The Story of the Quakers in America.* NY: Basic, 1969.

Bahadur, Satya P. *The Ramayana of Goswami Tulsidas.* Bombay: Jaico, 1972.

Bainton, Roland. *Erasmus of Christendom.* NY: Crossroads, 1982 (original 1969).

Baker, Archibald G., ed. *A Short History of Christianity.* Chicago: University of Chicago, 1962 (original 1940).

Baker, Derek. *A Short History of Monasticism.* NY: Columbia, 1982.

Baldwin, Marshall W. *The Medieval Church.* Ithaca, NY: Cornell, 1953.

Bammel, Ernest, and C.F.D. Moule, eds. *Jesus and the Politics of His Day.* Cambridge, England: University Press, 1986.

Bancroft, Anne. *The Buddhist World.* London: Macdonald, 1984.
_____. *The Luminous Vision.* London: Allen & Unwin, 1982.
Banerjee, Nitya N. "Peace Through Hinduism," pp. 417–429 in *Dr. Satkari Moo-kerji Felicitation Volume,* ed. B.P. Sinha, et al. Varanasi Chowkhamba San-skrit Series, 1969.
Barber, Richard. *The Knight and Chivalry.* NY: Harper & Row, 1982.
Barclay, William. *Jesus of Nazareth.* Nashville, TN: Nelson, 1985.
Barnes, Timothy. *Constantine and Eusebius.* Cambridge: Harvard, 1981.
Baron, Salo W. and Joseph L. Balu, eds. *Judaism: Postbiblical and Talmudic Period.* NY: Liberal Arts, 1954.
Barrett, C.K. *Jesus and the Gospel Tradition.* London: SPCK, 1967.
Barrett, David B. *Schism and Renewal in Africa: An Analysis of Six Thousand Contemporary Religious Movements.* Nairobi: Oxford, 1982.
_____, ed. *The World Christian Encyclopedia.* NY: Oxford, 1982.
Basham, Arthur L. "Hinduism," pp. 661–667 in *Encyclopedia of Bioethics,* ed. War-ren Reich. NY: Free Press, 1978.
_____. *The Wonder That Was India.* 3rd ed. NY: Taplinger, 1967.
Beasley, William G. *The Meiji Restoration.* Stanford, CA: Stanford University, 1972.
Beaver, R. Pierce, et al., eds. *Eerdmans' Handbook to the World's Religions.* Grand Rapids, MI: Eerdmans, 1982.
Beegle, Dewey M. *Moses, the Servant of Yahweh.* Ann Arbor, MI: Pettengill, 1978.
Bein, Alex. *Theodore Herzl.* NY: Atheneum, 1970 (original 1940).
Bellah, Robert N. *Tokugawa Religion.* Boston: Beacon, 1970.
Benedict, Ruth. *Patterns of Culture.* Boston: Houghton Mifflin, 1959 (original 1934).
Benz, Ernst. *Buddhism or Communism.* Garden City, NY: Doubleday, 1965.
_____. *The Eastern Orthodox Church.* Garden City, NY: Doubleday, 1963.
Berger, Morroe. *The Arab World Today.* Garden City, NY: Doubleday, 1964.
Bergman, Jerry. *Jehovah's Witnesses and Kindred Groups.* NY: Garland, 1984.
Berkhofer, Robert F., Jr. *The White Man's Indian: Images of the American Indian from Columbus to the Present.* NY: Knopf, 1978.
Bettenson, Henry, ed. *Documents of the Christian Church.* 2nd ed. NY: Oxford, 1967.
Bhushan, Shashi, ed. *Buddhist Way to Peace.* New Delhi: Progressive Peoples Sec-tor, 1976.
Bjorling, Joel. *The Baha'i Faith: A Historical Bibliography.* NY: Garland, 1985.
Blakney, R.B. *The Way of Life.* NY: Mentor, 1955.
Bleich, J.D. *Contemporary Halakhic Problems.* NY: Ktav, 1977.
Bloch, Marc. *Feudal Society.* Chicago: University of Chicago, 1970.
Boff, Leonard. *Saint Francis.* NY: Crossroads, 1982.
Bondurant, Joan. *Conquest of Violence.* Princeton, Princeton, 1958.
Booth, Newell S., Jr., ed. *African Religions: A Symposium.* NY: NOK, 1977.
Bornkamm, Gunther. *Jesus of Nazareth.* NY: Harper & Row, 1960.
Boslooper, Thomas. *The Image of Woman.* NY: Rose of Sharon, 1980.
Bosworth, Clifford E. *The Islamic Dynasties.* Edinburgh: University Press, 1967.
Bowen, Desmond. *The Protestant Crusade in Ireland, 1800–70.* Montreal: Gill and Macmillan, 1978.
Bowman, John. *Samaritan Documents.* Pittsburgh: Pickwick, 1977.
_____. *The Samaritan Problem: Studies in Relationships of Samaritans, Judaism and Early Christianity.* Pittsburgh: Pickwick, 1975.

Brandon, S.G.F. *A Dictionary of Comparative Religion.* NY: Scribner's, 1970.
_____. *Jesus and the Zealots.* Manchester: Manchester University, 1967.
Brandon, William. *The American Heritage Book of Indians.* NY: Dell, 1961.
Brantl, George. *Catholicism.* NY: Braziller, 1962.
Bream, Howard, et al., eds. *A Light Unto My Path.* Philadelphia: Temple University, 1974.
Brecht, Martin. *Martin Luther.* Philadelphia: Fortress, 1985.
Bright, John. *A History of Israel.* 3rd ed. Philadelphia: Westminster, 1981.
Brock, Peter. "Gandhi's Nonviolence and His War Service," *Gandhi Marg* 2, no. 11 (February 1981), 601–616.
_____. *Pioneers of the Peaceable Kingdom.* Princeton: Princeton University, 1970.
Brown, Joseph E., ed. *The Sacred Pipe: Black Elk's Account of the Seven Rites of the Oglala Sioux.* Norman: University of Oklahoma, 1953.
Brown, Raymond E., et al., eds. *The Jerome Biblical Commentary.* Englewood Cliffs, NJ: Prentice-Hall, 1968.
_____. *Making Peace in the Global Village.* Philadelphia: Westminster, 1981.
Bruce, Frederick F., ed. *The International Bible Commentary.* Grand Rapids, MI: Zondervan, 1986.
Buchanan, George W. *Revelation and Redemption: Jewish Documents of Deliverance from the Fall of Jerusalem to the Death of Nahmanides.* Dillsboro, NC: Western North Carolina, 1978.
Buddhist Peace Fellowship Newsletter. Berkeley, CA: BPF, continuing.
Bulgakov, S. *The Eastern Orthodox Church.* London: Centenary, 1935.
Bultmann, Rudolph. *Jesus and the Word.* NY: Scribner's, 1958.
_____, *Jesus Christ and Mythology.* NY: Scribner's, 1968.
_____. *Primitive Christianity in Its Contemporary Setting.* NY: Meridian, 1956.
Buttrick, George A., et al., eds. *Interpreter's Dictionary of the Bible.* Nashville, TN: Abingdon, 1962ff.
Buxton, Jean. *Religion and Healing in Manderi.* Oxford: Clarendon, 1973.
Caldarola, Carlo, ed. *Religions and Societies: Asia and the Middle East.* NY: Mouton, 1982.
Calderon, Eduardo, et al. *Eduardo el Curandero: The Words of a Peruvian Healer.* Richmond, CA: North Atlantic Books, 1982.
Capps, Walter. *The Monastic Impulse.* NY: Crossroads, 1982.
Carmody, Denise. *Women in World Religions.* Nashville, TN: Abingdon, 1979.
Carrick, J.C. *Wycliffe and the Lollards.* NY: Gordon, 1977.
Carroll, Berenice A., et al. *Peace and War: A Guide to Bibliographies.* Santa Barbara, CA: ABC-Olia, 1983.
Chai, Ch'u and Winberg. *Confucianism.* Woodbury, NY: Barron's, 1973.
Chatfield, Charles, ed. *Peace Movements in America.* NY: Schocken, 1973.
Chatterjee, Asim Kumar. *A Comprehensive History of Jainism (Up to A.D. 1000.)* Calcutta: Firma KLM, 1978.
Chatterjee, Margaret. *Gandhi's Religious Thought.* Notre Dame, IN: Notre Dame University Press, 1983.
Chaudhuri, Nirad C. *Hinduism: A Religion to Live By.* NY: Oxford, 1979.
Chen, Kenneth K.S. *Buddhism: The Light of Asia.* Woodbury, NY: Barrons, 1968.
Chesteron, G.K. *Orthodoxy.* Garden City, NY: Doubleday, 1973.
Chestnut, Roberta C. *Three Monophysite Christologies.* London: Oxford, 1975.
Clasper, Paul D. *The Yogi, the Commissar, and the Third World Church.* Valley Forge, PA: Judson Press, 1972.
Coggins, R.J. *Samaritans and Jews.* Atlanta: Knox, 1975.

Cohen, Herman N. *Religion of Reason Out of the Sources of Judaism*. NY: Ungar, 1972.
Cole, W. Owen and Piara Singh Sambhi. *The Sikhs: Their Religious Beliefs and Practices*. London: Routledge & Kegan Paul, 1978.
Collins, Larry and Dominique Lapierre. *O Jerusalem*. NY: Pocket, 1973.
Constantelos, Demetrios J. *Understanding the Greek Orthodox Church: Its Faith, History and Practice*. Minneapolis: Winston, 1982.
Conze, Edward. *Buddhism: Its Essence and Development*. NY: Harper, 1959.
Coomaraswamy, Ananda K. *Buddha and the Gospel of Buddhism*. New Hyde Park, NY: University, 1969.
Cornfeld, Gaalyahu, ed. *Adam to Daniel*. NY: Macmillan, 1961.
_____. *The Historical Jesus*. NY: Macmillan, 1983.
Cosby, Gordon and Bill Price. *Handbook for World Peacemaker Groups*. Washington: World Peacemakers, 1982.
Coulson, N.J. *A History of Islamic Law*. Edinburgh: University Press, 1964.
Courvoisier, Jacques. *Zwingli: A Reformed Theologian*. Richmond, VA: Knox, 1963.
Covel, Alan C. *Ecstasy: Shamanism in Korea*. Elizabeth, NJ: Hollyum International, 1984.
Cragg, Kenneth. *Counsels in Contemporary Islam*. Edinburgh: University Press, 1965.
_____. *Islam and the Muslim*. Milton Keynes: Open University, 1978.
Crawford, Cromwell, ed. *In Search of Hinduism*. Barytown, NY: Unification Theological Seminary, 1986.
Creel, Herrlee G. *Confucius: The Man and the Myth*. Westport, CT: Greenwood, 1975 (original 1949).
_____. *What Is Taoism?* Chicago: University of Chicago, 1970.
Crim, Keith, et al., eds. *Interpreter's Dictionary of the Bible, Supplementary Volume*. Nashville, TN: Abingdon, 1976.
Cross, F.L. *Dictionary of the Christian Church*. Oxford: Clarendon, 1957.
Cross, Frank M., Jr. *The Ancient Library of Qumran*. Garden City: Doubleday, 1958.
_____. *Canaanite Myth and Hebrew Epic*. Cambridge: Harvard, 1973.
Crossley, Robert N. *Luther and the Peasants' War*. NY: Exposition, 1974.
Cullman, Oscar. *Jesus and the Revolutionaries*. NY: Harper & Row, 1970.
Cully, Kendig B. "Interview with Eugene B. Borowitz, Theologian of Judaism," *The Review of Books and Religion* 1, no. 8 (May 1983), 6.
Dakin, D.M. *Peace and Brotherhood in the Old Testament*. NY: Bannisdale, 1956.
Dales, George F. "Civilization and Floods in the Indus Valley," *Expedition* 7, no. 4 (Summer 1965), 10–19.
Daniel-Rops, Henry. *Bernard of Clairvaux*. NY: Hawthorn, 1964.
Davidson, Francis. *The New Bible Commentary*. 2nd ed. Grand Rapids, MI: Eerdmans, 1954.
Davis, Moshe. *The Emergence of Conservative Judaism*. Philadelphia: Jewish Publication Society, 1963.
de Bary, William Theodore, et al., eds. *Sources of Chinese Tradition*. NY: Columbia, 1960.
_____. *Sources of Indian Tradition*. NY: Columbia, 1966.
Deloria, Vine. *God Is Red*. NY: Delta, 1973.
de Silva, K.M. *A History of Sri Lanka*. Delhi: Oxford, 1981.
de Silva, Padmasiri. *Value Orientations and Nation Building*. Columbo, Sri Lanka: Lake House Investments, 1976.

_____ and Henry O. Thompson, eds. *Man's Search for Meaning in a Fragmented Universe.* NY: Rose of Sharon, 1988.

Detweiler, Richard C. *Mennonite Statements on Peace 1915–1966.* Scottsdale, PA: Herald, 1968.

Deussen, Paul J. *The Philosophy of the Upanishads.* NY: Dover, 1966.

Deutsch, Karl W. *Peace Research.* Middlebury, VT: Middlebury College, 1972.

de Vaux, Roland. *Ancient Israel.* NY: McGraw-Hill, 1961.

_____. *The Early History of Israel.* Philadelphia: Westminster, 1978.

Dibelius, Martin. *Studies in the Acts of the Apostles.* NY: Scribner's, 1956.

_____ and W.G. Kummel. *Paul.* Philadelphia: Westminster, 1953.

Dillenberger, John. *Martin Luther.* Garden City, NY: Doubleday, 1961.

_____ and Claude Welch. *Protestant Christianity.* NY: Scribner's, 1954.

Diwakar, Ranganath R. "Ahimsa Culture for Human Survival," *Gandhi Marg* 2, no. 10 (January 1981), 579–587.

_____. "Gandhi: From 'God Is Truth' to 'Truth Is God'," *Gandhi Marg* 1, no. 11 (February 1981), 617–626.

_____. *Saga of Satyagraha,* rev. New Delhi: Gandhi Peace Foundation, 1969.

Diwaker, S.C. *Religion and Peace,* rev. Mathura, Uttar Pradesh: All India Digamber Jain Sangh, 1962.

Djebar, Assia. *Women of Islam.* London: Deutsch, 1961.

Dong, Wonmo and Harold Hawon Sunoo, ed. *Whither Korea.* Dallas, TX: Association of Korean Christian Scholars in North America, 1975.

Dougherty, James E. *The Bishops and Nuclear Weapons: The Catholic Pastoral Letter on War and Peace.* Hamden, CT: Archon, 1984.

Dowley, Tim, et al., eds. *Eerdmans' Handbook to the History of Christianity.* Grand Rapids, MI: Eerdmans, 1977.

Dumoulin, Heinrich, ed. *Buddhism in the Modern World.* NY: Macmillan, 1976.

Dunn, Richard S. and Mary Maples Dunn, eds. *The World of William Penn.* Philadelphia: University of Pennsylvania, 1986.

Dunstan, J. Leslie. *Protestantism.* NY: Braziller, 1962.

Dwyer, Judith A., ed. *The Catholic Bishops and Nuclear War: A Critique and Analysis of the Pastoral, the Challenge of Peace.* Washington: Georgetown University, 1984.

Dyck, Cornelius J., ed. *Mennonite History.* Scottsdale, PA: Herald, 1967.

Earhart, H. Byron. *Japanese Religion,* 2nd ed. Encino and Belmont, CA: Dickenson, 1974.

Eck, Diana L. *Banaras: City of Light.* NY: Knopf, 1982.

Edgerton, Franklin, ed. *The Beginning of Indian Philosophy: Selections from the Rig Veda, Atharva Veda, Upanishads and Mahabharata.* Cambridge: Harvard, 1965.

Eliade, Mircea. *From Primitives to Zen.* NY: Harper & Row, 1974.

_____. *The Myth of the Eternal Return, or, Cosmos and History.* Princeton: Princeton University, 1971 (original 1949).

_____. *Myths, Dreams and Mysteries.* NY: Harper, 1960.

_____. *Symbolism, the Sacred & the Arts.* NY: Crossroads, 1985.

Eller, Vernard. *War and Peace from Genesis to Revelation.* Scottsdale, PA: Herald, 1981.

Ellul, Jacques. *La Subversion du Christianisme.* Paris: Seuil, 1984.

Ellwood, Robert S., Jr. *The Eagle and the Rising Sun: Americans and the New Religions of Japan.* Philadelphia: Westminster, 1974.

_____. *Religious and Spiritual Groups in Modern America.* Englewood Cliffs, NJ: Prentice-Hall, 1973.

_____ and Richard Pilgrim. *Japanese Religion*. Englewood Cliffs, NJ: Prentice-Hall, 1985.

Emhardt, William C. and George M. Lamsa. *The Oldest Christian People*. NY: AMS, 1970 (original 1926).

Emswiler, Sharon N. *The Ongoing Journey: Women and the Bible*. NY: United Methodist Church, 1977.

Endy, Melvin B. *William Penn and Early Quakerism*. Princeton: Princeton University, 1973.

Eppsteiner, Fred and Dennis Maloney, eds. *The Path of Compassion: Contemporary Writings on Engaged Buddhism*. Berkeley, CA: BPF, 1985.

Epstein, Isidore, ed. *The Babylonian Talmud*, Vols. *1–18*. London: Soncino, 1935–1948.

_____. *Judaism*. Baltimore: Penguin, 1970.

Erdmann, Carl. *The Origin of the Idea of Crusade*. Princeton: Princeton University, 1977.

Esslemont, John E. *Baha'u'llah and the New Era*, 3rd ed. Wilamette, IL: Baha'i, 1970 (original 1928).

Fairservis, Walter A., Jr. "The Script of the Indus Valley Civilization," *Scientific American* **248**, no. 3 (March 1983), 58–66.

Faruqi, Isma'il Ragi al and David E. Sopher, eds. *Historical Atlas of the Religions of the World*. NY: Macmillan, 1974.

Ferguson, John. *War and Peace in the World's Religions*. NY: Oxford, 1978.

Ferm, Deane William, ed. *Restoring the Kingdom*. NY: Paragon House, 1984.

Finkelstein, Louis. *Pharisees in the Making*. NY: Ktav, 1972.

Finucane, Ronald C. *Soldiers of the Faith: Crusaders and Moslems at War*. NY: St. Martin's, 1984.

Fisher, Roger. *International Conflict for Beginners*. NY: Harper & Row, 1969.

Fitzgerald, C.P. *The Chinese View of Their Place in the World*. NY: Oxford, 1976.

Fitzgerald, James L. "The Great Epic of India as Religious Rhetoric: A Fresh Look at the 'Mahabharata'," *Journal of the American Academy of Religion* **LI**, no. 4 (December 1983), 611–630.

Flint, David. *The Hutterites*. Toronto: Oxford, 1975.

Frank, Jerome D. *Persuasion and Healing*, rev. NY: Schocken, 1974.

Fraser, Antonio. *Cromwell, the Lord Protector*. NY: Knopf, 1973.

Frazier, Allie M. *Buddhism*. NY: Braziller, 1962.

_____, ed. *Hinduism*. Philadelphia: Westminster, 1969.

French, Hal W. and Arvind Sharma. *Religious Ferment in Modern India*. NY: St. Martin's, 1981.

Frend, W.H.C. *The Rise of the Monophysite Movement*. Cambridge, England: University Press, 1972.

Fuller, Reginald H. *The Mission and Achievement of Jesus*. London: SCM, 1954.

_____, et al., eds. *A New Catholic Commentary on the Holy Scripture*. NY: Nelson, 1964.

Fyzee, Asaf A.A. *Outlines of Muhammadan Law*. London: Oxford, 1955.

Gallagher, Eric and Stanley Worrall. *Christians in Ulster, 1968–1981*. NY: Oxford, 1982.

Gandhi, Mohandas K. *An Autobiography: The Story of My Experiments with Truth*. Boston: Beacon, 1957.

_____. *Collected Works of Mahatma Gandhi*. Ahmedabad: Ministry of Information and Broadcasting, Government of India, 1958.

_____. *The Gospel of Selfless Action: The Gita According to Gandhi*. Ahmedabad: Navajivan, 1946.

_____. *Hindu Dharma*. Ahmedabad: Navajivan, 1958.

_____. *Non-Violence in Peace & War*. Ahmedabad: Navajivan, 1942–1949.

_____. *Pathway to God*. Ahmedabad: Navajivan, 1971.

_____. *Sarvodaya*. Ahmedabad: Navajivan, 1951.

_____. *Satyagraha in South Africa*. Ahmedabad: Navajivan, 1950.

_____. *Women and Social Injustice*. Ahmedabad: Navajivan, 1954.

_____. *Young India, Vols. I (1919–1922), II (1924–1926), III (1927–1928)*. Madras: 1922, 1927, 1935.

Gard, Richard. *Buddhism*. NY: Braziller, 1962.

Gatje, Helmut. *The Qur'an and Its Exegesis*. Berkeley: Univ. of California, 1976.

Gaustad, Edwin S. *A Religious History of America*. NY: Harper & Row, 1974.

Gehman, Henry S. *The New Westminster Dictionary of the Bible*. Philadelphia: Westminster, 1970.

Gelberg, Steven J., ed. *Hare Krishna, Hare Krishna*. NY: Grove, 1983.

Gibb, H.A.R. and J.H. Kramers, eds. *Shorter Encyclopedia of Islam*. Ithaca, NY: Cornell, 1953.

Gill, Sam D. *Beyond "The Primitive"—The Religions of Nonliterate Peoples*. Englewood Cliffs, NJ: Prentice-Hall, 1982.

_____. *Native American Religions*. Belmont, CA: Wadsworth, 1982.

_____. *Native American Traditions*. Wadsworth, 1983.

Glazer, Nathan. *American Judaism*. Chicago: University of Chicago, 1972.

Goldziher, Ignace. *Introduction to Islamic Theology and Law*. Princeton: Princeton University, 1981.

Gonda, J. "The Vedic Gods and the Sacrifice," *Numen* XXX, Fsc. 1 (July 1983), 1–34.

Gonzalez, Justo L. *A History of Christian Thought*. NY: Abingdon, 1975.

Gottwald, Norman K. *The Tribes of Yahweh*. Maryknoll, NY: Orbis, 1979.

Grannis, Christopher, et al. *The Risk of the Cross: Christian Discipleship in the Nuclear Age*. NY: Seabury, 1982.

Grant, Michael. *Saint Paul*. London: Weidenfeld and Nicolson, 1976.

Gray, Janet G. *The French Huguenots*. Grand Rapids, MI: Baker, 1981.

Green, Julien. *God's Fool: The Life of Francis of Assisi*. San Francisco: Harper & Row, 1985.

Gregg, Robert C. and Dennis E. Groh. *Early Arianism*. Philadelphia: Fortress, 1981.

Grollenberg, Lucas. *Jesus*. Philadelphia: Westminster, 1979.

Grube, Ernst. *The World of Islam*. NY: McGraw-Hill, 1966.

Hackett, Stuart C. *Oriental Philosophy*. Madison: University of Wisconsin, 1979.

Haddad, Yvonne. *Contemporary Islam and the Challenge of History*. Albany: SUNY, 1982.

_____ and Ellison B. Findly, eds. *Women, Religion and Social Change*. Albany: SUNY, 1985.

Haire, J.L.M., ed. *Challenge and Conflict*. Antrim, Northern Ireland: W & G Baird, 1981.

Handler, Andrew. *Dori: The Life and Times of Theoldor Herzl in Budapest (1860–1878)*. University, AL: University of Alabama, 1983.

Haque, S.A. *Islam's Contribution to the Peace of the World*. Lahore: Ahmadiya, n.d.

Harbison, E. Harris. *The Age of Reformation*. Ithaca, NY: Cornell, 1955.

Harner, Michael J. *Hallucinogens and Shamanism*. NY: Oxford: 1973.

_____. *The Way of the Shaman: A Guide to Power and Healing*. NY: Bantam, 1982.

Haroon, Sharif Abdullah, ed. *Thoughts on Islam*. Dacca: Islamic Academy, 1970.

Harris, William H. and Judith S. Levey, eds. *The New Columbia Encyclopedia.* NY: Columbia, 1975.

Harvey, Van A. *A Handbook of Theological Terms.* NY: Macmillan, 1964.

Hastings, James, et al., eds. *Dictionary of the Bible,* rev. NY: Scribner's, 1963.

Hatto, Arthur T., ed. *Traditions of Epic and Heroic Poetry.* London: Modern Humanities Research Association, 1980.

Heissig, Walter. *The Religions of Mongolia.* Berkeley: Univ. of California, 1980.

Helgeland, John, Robert J. Daly and J. Patout Burns. *Christians and the Military: The Early Experience.* Philadelphia: Fortress, 1985.

Hengel, Martin. *Acts and the History of Earliest Christianity.* Philadelphia: Fortress, 1979.

_____. *Was Jesus a Revolutionary?* Philadelphia: Fortress, 1971.

Herberg, Will. *Protestant, Catholic, Jew.* Garden City: Doubleday, 1955.

Hertzberg, Arthur. *Judaism.* NY: Braziller, 1962.

Hirsch, R.G. *Thy Most Precious Gift: Peace in Jewish Tradition.* NY: Union of American Hebrew Congregations, 1974.

Hitti, Philip K. *History of the Arabs,* 10th ed. NY: St. Martin's, 1975.

Hoffman, Helmut, et al. *Tibet: A Handbook.* Bloomington: Indiana Univ., 1975.

Holmes, Urban T. *The Priest in Community.* NY: Seabury, 1978.

Holt, P.M., et al., eds. *The Cambridge History of Islam.* Cambridge, England: University Press, 1970.

Holtom, Daniel C. *Modern Japan and Shinto Nationalism,* rev. Chicago: University of Chicago, 1947.

Horton, George. *The Blight of Asia.* Indianapolis: Bobbs-Merrill, 1926.

Hourani, George F. *Islamic Rationalism.* Oxford: Clarendon, 1971.

Howart, Stephen. *The Knights Templar.* NY: Atheneum, 1982.

Hudson, Winthrop. *The Great Tradition of the American Churches.* NY: Harper & Row, 1963.

Huizinga, Johan. *Erasmus and the Age of Reformation.* Princeton: Princeton University, 1984.

Hultkrantz, Aake. *The Religions of the American Indians,* rev. Berkeley: University of California, 1979.

Humphreys, Christmas. *Buddhism.* Baltimore: Penguin, 1969.

Hunt, James D. "Thoreau and Gandhi: A Re-evaluation of the Legacy," *Gandhi Marg* 14, no. 4 (October 1970), 325–332.

Idowu, E. Bolaji. *African Traditional Religion.* Maryknoll, NY: Orbis, 1973.

Ikeda, Daisaku. *A Lasting Peace.* NY: Weatherhill, 1981.

Jack, Homer A., ed. *Religion for Peace: Proceedings of the Kyoto Conference on Religion and Peace.* New Delhi: Gandhi Peace Foundation, 1974.

_____. *Religion in the Struggle for World Community.* NY: World Conference on Religion and Peace, 1980.

_____. *World Religion/World Peace.* NY: World Conference on Religion and Peace, 1979.

_____. *World Religions and World Peace.* Boston: Beacon, 1968.

Jacobs, Louis. *Hasidic Thought.* NY: Behrman, 1976.

_____. *A Jewish Theology.* NY: Behrman House, 1973.

Jacobson, Nolan P. *Buddhism & the Contemporary World: Change and Self-Correction.* Carbondale: Southern Illinois University, 1983.

_____. *Buddhism: The Religion of Analysis.* Carbondale: Southern Illinois University, 1974.

Jagersma, Henk. *A History of Israel from Alexander the Great to Bar Kochba.* Philadelphia: Fortress, 1985.

_____. *A History of Israel in the Old Testament Period*. Philadelphia: Fortress, 1983.

Jain, Champat R. *Fundamentals of Jainism*. Meerut, Uttar Pradesh: Veer Nirvan Bharti, 1974.

Jain, Jyotiprasad. *Religion and Culture of the Jains*. New Delhi: Bharatiya Jnanpith, 1975.

Jain, Muni Uttam Kamal. *Jaina Sects and Schools*. Delhi: Concept, 1975.

Jaini, Padmanabh S. *The Jaina Path of Purification*. Berkeley: University of California, 1979.

Jansen, Godfrey H. *Militant Islam*. London: Pan Books, 1971.

Jeremias, J. *The Parables of Jesus*. NY: Scribner's, 1955.

Johnson, Hubert R. *Who Then Is Paul?* Lanham, MD: University Press of America, 1986.

Jones, Allen H. *Essenes*. Washington: University Press of America, 1985.

Joshi, Lal M. *Facets of Jaina Religiousness in Comparative Light*. Ahmedabad: L.D. Institute of Indology, 1981.

Journal of Religious Studies. Department of Religious Studies, University of Punjab, Patiala, India.

Juergensmeyer, Mark. *Fighting with Gandhi*. San Francisco: Harper & Row, 1984.

_____ and N. Gerald Barrier, eds. *Sikh Studies*. Berkeley, CA: Graduate Theological Union, 1979.

Kahane, Meir. *The Story of the Jewish Defense League*. Radnor, PA: Chilton, 1975.

Kalupahana, David. *Buddhist Philosophy*. Honolulu: University of Hawaii, 1976.

_____ and Indrani Kalupahana. *The Way of Siddhartha*. Boulder, CO: Shambhala, 1982.

Kantowsky, Detleff. "Sarvodaya: An Indigenous Form of 'innerworldly asceticism' in South Asia," *Gandhi Marg* 3, no. 7 (October 1981), 381–393.

Kaplan, Mardecai M. *Judaism As a Civilization*. NY: Reconstructionist Press, 1957.

_____. *Questions Jews Ask*. ibid., 1972.

Kauffman, J. Howard and Leland Harder. *Anabaptists Four Centuries Later*. Scottsdale, PA: Herald, 1975.

Kaufman, Robert. *Inside Scientology*. NY: Olympia, 1972.

Kaufmann, Yehezkel. *The Religion of Israel: From Its Beginnings to the Babylonian Exile*. NY: Schocken, 1972.

Kawamura, Leslie S., ed. *The Bodhisattva Doctrine in Buddhism*. Waterloo, Ontario: Wilfrid Laurier University, 1981.

Keddie, R. *Scholars, Saints, and Sufis*. Berkeley: University of California, 1972.

Kee, Howard. *Understanding the New Testament*, 4th ed. Englewood Cliffs, NJ: Prentice-Hall, 1983.

Keen, Maurice. *Chivalry*. New Haven: Yale, 1984.

Kelen, Betty. *Confucius in Life and Legend*. NY: Nelson, 1971.

Kepel, Gilles. *Muslim Extremism in Egypt*. Berkeley: University of California, 1986.

Khadduri, Majid. *The Islamic Conception of Justice*. Baltimore: Johns Hopkins, 1984.

_____. *War and Peace in the Law of Islam*, 2nd ed. Baltimore: Johns Hopkins, 1955.

_____ and Herbert J. Liebesny, eds. *Law in the Middle East: Origin and Development of Islamic Law*. NY: AMS, 1984 (original 1955).

Kidder, J. Edward, Jr. *Japan Before Buddhism*, rev. NY: Praeger, 1966.

Kim, Young Oon. *World Religions*, 3 vols., 2nd ed. NY: Golden Gate, 1982.

King, Martin Luther, Jr. *Stride Toward Freedom*. NY: Harper, 1958.

King, Noel Q. *Christian and Muslim in Africa*. NY: Harper & Row, 1971.

King, Ursula. *Towards a New Mysticism*. NY: Seabury, 1980.

Kinsley, David R. *Hinduism*. Englewood Cliffs, NJ: Prentice-Hall, 1982.

Kirchner, Herbert. *Luther and the Peasants' War*. Philadelphia: Fortress, 1972.

Kissinger, Warren S. *The Lives of Jesus: A History and Bibliography*. NY: Garland, 1986.

Kitagawa, Joseph. *Religion in Japanese History*. NY: Columbia, 1966.

Klassen, William. *Love of Enemies: The Way to Peace*. Philadelphia: Fortress, 1984.

Klein, Charlotte. *Anti-Judaism in Christian Theology*. Philadelphia: Fortress, 1978.

Knowles, David. *Christian Monasticism*. NY: McGraw-Hill, 1969.

Knox, John. *Chapters in a Life of Paul*. NY: Abingdon, 1950.

Koller, John M. *Oriental Philosophies*. NY: Scribner's, 1970.

Kothari, V.P. *The Law of Non-Violence (Ahimsa) and Its Relevance for All Times*. Sholapur: Lalchand Hirachand, 1975.

Kotturan, George. *Ahimsa: Gautama to Gandhi*. New Delhi: Sterling, 1973.

Krefetz, Gerald. *Jews and Money: The Myths and the Reality*. New Haven: Ticknor and Fields, 1982.

Kritzeck, James and William H. Lewis, eds. *Islam in Africa*. NY: Van Nostrand-Reinhold, 1969.

Kumar, Mahendra. *Current Peace Research and India*. Varanasi: Gandhian Institute of Studies, 1968.

Kummel, W.G. *Introduction to the New Testament*, rev. Nashville, TN: Abingdon, 1975.

Kuper, Leo. *Genocide: Its Political Use in the Twentieth Century*. New Haven: Yale, 1981.

La Barre, Weston. *The Ghost Dance*. Garden City, NY: Doubleday, 1970.

————. *The Peyote Cult*, 4th ed. NY: Archon, 1975.

Lama, Dalai. *My Land and My People*. NY: McGraw-Hill, 1962.

Lame Deer, John and Richard Erdoes. *Lame Deer: Seeker of Visions*. NY: Simon and Schuster, 1972.

Langley, Myrtle. *Religions*. Elgin, IL: Cook, 1981.

Larson, Stephen. *The Shaman's Doorway*. NY: Harper & Row, 1976.

Latourette, Kenneth Scott. *A History of Christianity*. NY: Harper & Row, 1953.

Laymon, Charles L., ed. *The Interpreter's One-Volume Commentary on the Bible*. Nashville, TN: Abingdon, 1971.

Leslau, Wolf. *Falasha Anthology*. New Haven: Yale, 1951.

Lewis, Bernard. *The Assassins*. NY: Octogon, 1980 (original 1968).

————. *The Emergence of Modern Turkey*, 2nd ed. London: Oxford, 1968.

————, ed. *Islam and the Arab World*. NY: Knopf, 1976.

————. *Islam, From the Prophet Muhammad to the Capture of Constantinople*. NY: Harper & Row, 1974.

————. *The Origins of Isma'ilism: A Study of the Historical Background of the Fatimid Caliphate*. NY: AMS, 1975 (original 1940).

————. *Race and Color in Islam*. NY: Harper & Row, 1971.

Lewis, Ioan M. *Ecstatic Religion: An Anthropological Study of Spirit Possession and Shamanism*. Baltimore: Penguin, 1971.

Lewis, Warren, ed. *Towards a Global Congress of the World's Religions*. NY: Rose of Sharon, 1980.

Lincoln, C. Eric. *The Black Muslims in America*. Boston: Beacon, 1963.

Lincoln, Victoria. *Teresa: A Woman*. Albany, NY: SUNY, 1984.

Lind, Millard C. *Yahweh Is a Warrior: The Theology of Warfare in Ancient Israel*. Scottsdale, PA: Herald, 1980.

Lindsey, Hal. *The 1980s: Countdown to Armageddon.* NY: Bantam, 1980.

Ling, Trevor. *Buddha, Marx, and God,* 2nd ed. NY: St. Martin's, 1979.

_____. *Buddhism, Imperialism and War: Burma and Thailand in Modern History.* London: Allen & Unwin, 1979.

Littlefield, David W. *The Islamic Northeast and North Africa: An Annotated Guide to Books in English.* Littleton, CO: Libraries Unlimited, 1977.

Livingston, James C. *Modern Christian Thought.* NY: Macmillan, 1971.

Lombard, Maurice. *The Golden Age of Islam.* NY: American Elsevier, 1975.

Loofs, Friedrich. *Nestorius and His Place in the History of Christian Doctrine.* NY: Franklin, 1975 (original 1914).

Luibheid, Colm. *Eusebius of Caesarea and the Arian Crisis.* Dublin: Irish Academic Press, 1981.

Macauliffe, M.A. *The Sikh Religion.* Oxford: Clarendon, 1909.

McCormack, Manjeet Kaur. *An Introduction to Sikh Belief,* 8th ed. London: Sikh Cultural Society of Great Britain, 1982.

McFarland, H. Neill. *The Rush Hour of the Gods.* NY: Macmillan, 1967.

McGiffert, Arthur C. *A History of Christian Thought.* NY: Scribner's, 1947 (original 1932).

McGuire, M.R.P., et al., eds. *New Catholic Encyclopedia.* NY: McGraw-Hill, 1967.

MacIntyre, Alasdair. *After Virtue.* Notre Dame: University of Notre Dame, 1981.

McLeod, W. Hew. *The Evolution of the Sikh Community.* Oxford: Clarendon, 1976.

_____. *Textual Sources for the Study of Sikhism.* Totowa, NJ: Barnes & Noble, 1984.

McNeill, John T. *The History and Character of Calvinism.* NY: Oxford, 1967.

Macoby, Hyman. *The Mythmaker: Paul and the Invention of Christianity.* San Francisco: Harper & Row, 1986.

Macquarrie, John. *The Concept of Peace.* NY: Harper & Row, 1973.

Macy, Joanna. *Dharma and Development: Religion as Resource for Sarvodaya Self-Help Movement,* 2nd ed. West Hartford, CT: Kumarian, 1983.

Malinowski, Bronislaw. *Magic, Science and Religion.* Garden City, NY: Doubleday, 1948.

Marcus, Jacob R., ed. *The Jew and the Medieval World.* NY: Atheneum, 1977.

Margolis, Max and Alexander Marx. *History of the Jewish People.* NY: Meridian, 1958 (original 1927).

Marriott, Alice Lee. *Native American Church of North America.* NY: Mentor, 1972.

Marshall, Sir John. *A Guide to Taxila.* NY: Cambridge, 1960.

_____. *Mohenjo Daro and the Indus Civilization.* London: Prosbsthain, 1931.

Martin, Richard C. *Islam.* Englewood Cliffs, NJ: Prentice-Hall, 1982.

Marty, Martin E. and Dean G. Peerman, eds. *New Theology No. 6.* NY: Macmillan, 1969.

May, Herbert G. and Bruce M. Metzger, eds. *The Oxford Annotated Bible with the Apocrypha.* NY: Oxford, 1965.

Mazar, Benjamin, et al., eds. *The World History of the Jewish People.* Tel Aviv: Masada, 1963ff.

Mbiti, John. *African Religions and Philosophy.* NY: Praeger, 1969.

_____. *Concepts of God in Africa.* NY: Praeger, 1970.

Melton, J. Gordon. *The Encyclopedia of American Religions.* Wilmington, NC: McGrath, 1978.

Mendenhall, George E. *Law and Covenant in the Ancient Near East.* Pittsburgh: Biblical Colloquium, 1955.

_____. *The Tenth Generation: The Origins of the Biblical Tradition*. Baltimore: Johns Hopkins, 1973.

The Mennonite Encyclopedia. Scottsdale, PA: Mennonite Publishing House, 1957.

Menon, V. Lakshmi. *Ruskin and Gandhi*. Varanasi: Sarva Seva Sangh Prakashan, 1965.

Merton, Thomas, ed. *Gandhi on Non-Violence*. NY: New Directions, 1965.

_____. *The Monastic Journey*. Kansas City: Sheed, Andrews and McNeel, 1977.

Miller, J. Maxwell and John H. Hayes. *A History of Ancient Israel and Judah*. Philadelphia: Westminster, 1986.

Miller, Patrick D., Jr. *The Divine Warrior in Early Israel*. Cambridge: Harvard, 1973.

Miller, Robert J., ed. *Religious Ferment in Asia*. Lawrence: University Press of Kansas, 1974.

Miller, William R. "Gandhi and King: Pioneers of Modern Nonviolence," *Gandhi Marg* 13, no. 1 (January 1969), 21–28.

Misra, K.P. and S.C. Gangal, eds. *Gandhi and the Contemporary World: Studies in Peace and War*. Delhi: Chanakya, 1981.

Mitchell, Robert C. *African Primal Religions*. Niles, IL: Argus, 1977.

Momen, Moojan, ed. *The Babi and Baha'i Religions, 1844–1944*. Oxford: Ronald, 1981.

Mott, Stephen C. *Biblical Ethics and Social Change*. NY: Oxford, 1982.

Moule, Charles F.D. *The Birth of the New Testament*. NY: Harper & Row, 1962.

Munck, Johannes. *Paul and the Salvation of Mankind*. Atlanta, GA: Knox, 1959.

Murphy, Thomas P., ed. *The Holy War*. Columbus: Ohio State, 1976.

Nag, Kalidas. *Tolstoy and Gandhi*. Patna: Pustak Bhander, 1950.

Nair, Pyarelal. *Thrown to the Wolves: Abdul Ghaffar*. Calcutta: Eastlight, 1966.

Nakamura, Hajime. *The Ideal World Community*. Madras: Radhakrishnan Institute, 1981.

Nakhre, Amrut W. *Social Psychology of Nonviolent Action*. Delhi: Chanakya, 1982.

Narayan, Shriman, ed. *The Selected Works of Mahatma Gandhi*. Ahmedabad: Navajivan, 1968.

Nasr, Seyyed Hossein. *Ideals and Realities of Islam*. Boston: Beacon, 1972.

Ndiokwere, Nathaniel I. *Prophecy and Revolution: The Role of Prophets in the Independent African Churches and in Biblical Tradition*. London: SPCK, 1981.

Nemoy, Leon. *Karaite Anthology*. New Haven: Yale, 1969 (original 1952).

Neusner, Jacob. *First Century Judaism in Crisis*. Nashville, TN: Abingdon, 1975.

_____, ed. *The Talmud of the Land of Israel*. Chicago: University of Chicago, 1985.

Nevaskar, Balwant. *Capitalists Without Capitalism*. Westport, CT: Greenwood, 1971.

Nicholson, Reynold A. *Studies in Islamic Mysticism*. Cambridge: Cambridge University, 1978 (original 1921).

Nickelsburg, George W. and Robert Kraft. *Early Judaism and Its Modern Interpreters*. Philadelphia: Fortress, 1985.

Niebuhr, Reinhold. *Christianity and Power Politics*. NY: Scribner's, 1940.

Nielsen, Niels C., Jr., et al. *Religions of the World*. NY: St. Martin's, 1983.

Nikam, N.A. and Richard McKeon, eds. *The Edicts of Asoka*. Chicago: University of Chicago, 1959.

Nikhilanandam, Swami. *The Upanishads*. NY: Harper & Row, 1963.

Noble, Thomas F.X. *The Republic of St. Peter: The Birth of the Papal State, 680–825*. Philadelphia: University of Pennsylvania, 1984.

Noss, David S. and John B. Noss. *Man's Religions*, 7th ed. NY: Macmillan, 1984.

Obeyesekere, Gannath, et al., eds. *The Two Wheels of Dhamma: Essays on the Theravada Tradition in India and Ceylon.* Chambersburg, PA: American Academy of Religion, 1972.

O'Brien, Conor C. *The Siege: The Saga of Israel and Zionism.* NY: S & S, 1985.

Oded, Arye. *Islam in Uganda.* NY: Wiley, 1974.

O'Flaherty, Wendy D., ed. *Karma and Rebirth in Classical Indian Traditions.* Berkeley: University of California, 1980.

_____, tr. *The Rig Veda: An Anthology.* NY: Penguin, 1983.

Ofori, Patrick E. *Islam in Africa South of the Sahara: A Select Bibliographic Guide.* Neldeln, Liechtenstein: Kto Press, 1977.

O'Malley, L.S.S., ed. *Modern India and the West.* London: Oxford, 1941.

O'Malley, Padraig. *The Uncivil Wars: Ireland Today.* Boston: Houghton Mifflin, 1983.

Pardesi, Ganshyam, ed. *Contemporary Peace Research.* Atlantic Highlands, NJ: Humanities, 1982.

Parker, T.H. *John Calvin.* Philadelphia: Westminster, 1983.

Parkes, James. *A History of the Jewish People.* Baltimore: Penguin, 1964.

Parrinder, Geoffrey. *African Traditional Religion.* Westport, CT: Greenwood, 1975.

_____. *A Dictionary of Non-Christian Religions.* Philadelphia: Westminster, 1974.

_____. *Religion in Africa.* NY: Praeger, 1969.

Partin, Harry, compiler. *Asian Religions—History of Religion: 1974.* Tallahassee, FL: American Academy of Religion, 1974.

Patai, Raphael. *The Arab Mind.* NY: Scribner's, 1973.

Pathak, D.N. "Gandhi's World View: Intimations of a Peaceful World Society," *Gandhi Marg* 4, no. 11 (February 1983), 918–926.

p'Bitek, Okot. *African Religions in Western Scholarship.* Nairobi: East African Literature Bureau, 1971.

Pelikan, Jaroslav J. *Jesus Through the Centuries.* New Haven: Yale, 1985.

Pfeiffer, Charles F. and Everett E. Harrison. *The Wycliffe Bible Commentary.* Chicago: Moody, 1962.

Philippi, Donald L., tr. *Kojiki.* Princeton: Princeton University, 1969.

Pickthall, Muhammad Marmaduke. *The Cultural Side of Islam.* Madras: Universal, 1959.

_____, ed. *The Meaning of the Glorious Qur'an.* NY: Muslim World League, 1977.

Piggott, Stuart. *Prehistoric India.* Baltimore, MD: Penguin, 1950.

Plaut, Gunther W. *The Growth of Reform Judaism.* NY: World Union for Progressive Judaism, 1965.

Ple, Albert. *Christian Morality: Duty or Pleasure?* NY: Paragon, 1986.

Polzin, Robert. *Moses and the Deuteronomist.* NY: Seabury, 1980.

Pope, Marvin H. *Song of Songs.* Garden City, NY: Doubleday, 1977.

Potter, George R. *Zwingli.* NY: Cambridge University, 1976.

Prebish, Charles S., ed. *Buddhism: A Modern Perspective.* University Park: Pennsylvania State University, 1975.

Pritchard, James B., ed. *Ancient Near Eastern Texts Relating to the Old Testament*, 3rd ed. Princeton: Princeton, 1969.

Prucha, Francis Paul. *The Indians in American Society from the Revolutionary War to the Present.* Berkeley: University of California, 1986.

Purvis, James D. *The Samaritan Pentateuch and the Origin of the Samaritan Sect.* Cambridge: Harvard, 1968.

Radin, Paul. *The Trickster.* NY: Philosophical Library, 1956.

Rafi-ud-Din, Mohammed. *The Potential Contributions of Islam to World Peace.* Karachi: Hamdard Dawakhana Trust, 1957.

Rahman, Fazlur. *Islam,* 2nd ed. Chicago: University of Chicago, 1979.

_____. *Major Themes of the Qur'an.* Chicago: Biblioteca Islamica, 1980.

Rahula, Walpola. *The Heritage of the Bhikkhu,* 2nd ed. NY: Grove, 1974.

Raikes, Robert L. "The End of the Ancient Cities of the Indus," *American Anthropologist* 66, no. 2 (April 1964), 284–299.

Rampuria, Shree Chand. *The Cult of Ahimsa: A Jain Point of View.* Calcutta: Sri Jain Swetamber Terapanthi Mahasabha, 1947.

Ramsey, Paul. *The Just War.* NY: Scribner's, 1968.

Rao, K.L. Seshagiri. *Mahatma Gandhi and Comparative Religion.* Delhi: Motilal Banarsidass, 1978.

Rauf, Abdur. *Islamic Culture and Civilization in Pakistan.* Lahore: Ferozsons, 1975.

Rauf, Muhammad Abdul. *The Islamic View of Women and the Family.* NY: Speller, 1977.

Reaman, George E. *The Trail of the Huguenots in Europe, the United States, South Africa and Canada.* London: Muller, 1964.

Reich, Warren, ed. *Encyclopedia of Bioethics.* NY: Free Press, 1978.

Renou, Louis, ed. *Hinduism.* NY: Braziller, 1961.

Reynolds, Frank E. *Guide to the Buddhist Religion.* Boston: Hall, 1981.

Riatt, Jill, ed. *Islam in the Modern World.* Columbia, MO: University of Missouri, 1983.

Richardson, Alan. *An Introduction to the Theology of the New Testament.* NY: Harper & Row, 1958.

Ridderbos, Herman. *Paul: An Outline of His Theology.* Grand Rapids, MI: Eerdmans, 1975.

Rifkin, Ellis. *A Hidden Revolution: The Pharisees' Search for the Kingdom Within.* Nashville, TN: Abingdon, 1978.

Robinson, Francis. *Atlas of the Islamic World Since 1500.* NY: Facts on File, 1982.

Robinson, James M. *A New Quest of the Historical Jesus.* London: SCM, 1959.

Robinson, R.H. *The Buddhist Religion: A Historical Introduction.* Belmont, CA: Dickenson, 1970.

Roots, Ivan A., ed. *Cromwell, A Profile.* NY: Hill & Wang, 1973.

Rosenthal, Erwin I.J. *Islam in the Modern National State.* Cambridge, England: University Press, 1965.

Ross, Nancy W. *Buddhism.* NY: Knopf, 1980.

Rothermund, Indira. "Mahatma Gandhi and Hindu Tradition," *Gandhi Marg* 3, no. 12 (March 1982), 722–733.

Rubenstein, Richard L., ed. *Modernization.* Washington: Paragon, 1982.

Ruether, Rosemary Radford. *Religion and Sexism.* NY: Simon and Schuster, 1974.

Russell, F.H. *The Just War in the Middle Ages.* Cambridge, England: University Press, 1975.

Saadawi, Nawal el. *The Hidden Face of Eve: Women in the Arab World.* Boston: Beacon, 1982.

Sachar, Abram L. *A History of the Jews,* 5th ed. NY: Knopf, 1967.

Sachedina, Abdulaziz A. *Islamic Messianism: The Idea of the Mahdi in Twelver Shi'ism.* Albany: SUNY, 1981.

Saddhatissa, H. *The Buddha's Way.* NY: Braziller, 1972.

as-Said, Labib. *The Recited Koran.* Princeton: Darwin, 1975.

Sakr, Ahmad H. and Karm B. Akhtar. *Islamic Fundamentalism.* Ann Arbor, MI: Crescent, 1984.

Samartha, Stanley J., ed. *Living Faiths and Ultimate Goals.* Maryknoll: Orbis, 1974.

Santucci, James A. *An Outline of Vedic Literature.* Missoula, MT: Scholars, 1983.

Saqqaf, Abdulaziz Y., ed. *The Middle East City.* NY: Paragon, 1986.

Schillebeeckx, Edward. *Christ: The Experience of Jesus as Lord.* NY: Crossroads, 1983.

_____. *Jesus: An Experiment in Christology.* NY: Crossroads, 1979.

Schmemann, Alexander. *The Historical Road of Eastern Orthodoxy.* NY: Holt, Rinehart and Winston, 1963.

Scholem, Gershom S. *Kabbalah.* Quadrangle, 1974.

_____. *Major Trends in Jewish Mysticism.* NY: Schocken, 1973 (original 1941).

_____. *The Messianic Idea in Judaism and Other Essays on Jewish Spirituality.* NY: Schocken, 1971.

_____. *Sabbatai Sevi.* Princeton: Princeton University, 1975.

_____. *Zohar.* NY: Schocken, 1974.

Schubring, Walther. *The Religion of the Jainas.* Calcutta: Sanskrit College, 1966.

Schumacher, E.F. *Small Is Beautiful.* London: Blond & Briggs, 1973.

Schwartz, Leo M., ed. *Great Ages and Ideas of the Jewish People.* NY: Modern Library, 1956.

Schweitzer, Albert. *The Quest for the Historical Jesus.* NY: Macmillan, 1968 (original 1910).

_____. *Reverence for Life.* NY: Harper & Row, 1969.

Schweitzer, Frederick M. *A History of the Jews Since the First Century A.D.* NY: Macmillan, 1971.

Seeberg, Reinhold. *Textbook of the History of Doctrines.* Grand Rapids, MI: Baker, 1954.

Seltzer, Robert M. *Jewish People, Jewish Thought.* NY: Macmillan, 1980.

Sen, K.M. *Hinduism.* NY: Penguin, 1970.

Sessions, Kyle C., ed. *Reformation and Authority: The Meaning of the Peasants' Revolt.* Lexington, MA: Heath, 1968.

Seward, Desmond. *The Monks of War: The Military Religious Orders.* Hamden, CT: Archon, 1972.

Shannon, Albert C. *The Medieval Inquisition.* Washington, D.C.: Augustinian College, 1983.

Shannon, Thomas A. *War or Peace?* Maryknoll, NY: Orbis, 1980.

Shaykh, M. Sa'id. *Studies in Muslim Philosophy.* Lahore: Ashraf, n.d.

Sheen, Fulton J. *The Life of Christ.* Garden City: Doubleday, 1977.

Sherif, Mohamed Ahmed. *Ghazali's Theory of Virtue.* Albany: SUNY, 1975.

Shrestha, Ramesh M. with Mark Lediard. *Faith Healers.* NY: UNICEF, 1980.

Shroff, Manu M. *Jainism and Modern Thought Which Constitutes Terapanth, Youth, the Riddle of World Peace and Its Solution.* Bombay: Shroff, 1956.

Shushtery, A.M.A. *Outlines of Islamic Culture.* Bangalore: Bangalore Press, 1938.

Sidhu, Introduction to Sikhism. Burnaby, B.C.: World Sikh Organization, 1984.

Sikh Religious Studies Information. Stony Brook, NY: SUNY, continuing.

Singer, Milton, ed. *Krishna: Myths, Rites, and Attitudes.* Chicago: University of Chicago, 1968.

Singh, Harbans. *Guru Tegh Bahadur.* New Delhi: Sterling, 1982.

Singh, Khushwant. *A History of the Sikhs.* Princeton: Princeton University, 1963, 1966.

————. *Religion of the Sikhs*. Madras: University of Madras, 1968.
Singh, Mohinder. *The Akali Movement*. New Delhi: Macmillan, 1978.
Singh, Parkash. *Guru Nanak and His Japji*. Amritsar, 1969.
Singh, Wazir. *Philosophy of Sikh Religion*. New Delhi: Ess Ess, 1981.
Slotkin, James S. *The Peyote Religion*. Glencoe, IL: Free Press, 1956.
Sloyan, Gerard S. *Jesus in Focus*. Mystic, CT: Twenty-Third, 1983.
Smart, Ninian. *The Long Search*. Boston: Little, Brown, 1977.
Smend, Rudolf. *Yahweh War and Tribal Confederacy*. Nashville: Abingdon, 1970.
Smith, Huston. *Forgotten Truth*. NY: Harper & Row, 1976.
————. *The Religions of Man*. NY: Harper & Row, 1965.
Smith, Lee and Wes Bodin, eds. *The Christian Tradition*. Allen, TX: Argus, 1978.
————. *The Islamic Tradition*. Allen, TX: Argus, 1978.
Smith, Margaret. *The Way of the Mystics*. NY: Oxford, 1978 (original 1931).
Smith, Morton. *Jesus the Magician*. NY: Harper & Row, 1982.
————. *Palestinian Parties and Politics That Shaped the Old Testament*. NY: Columbia, 1971.
Smith, Wilfred Cantwell. *Islam in Modern History*. NY: New American Library, 1963.
Snellgrove, David L. *The Nine Ways of Bon*. Boulder, CO: Prajna, 1980.
Soderlund, Jean, ed. *William Penn and the Founding of Pennsylvania*. Philadelphia: University of Pennsylvania, 1983.
Somerville, John. *The Peace Revolution*. Westport, CT: Greenwood, 1975.
Stamford, Ann. *The Bhagavad Gita*. NY: Continuum, 1977.
Stauffer, Ethelbert. *New Testament Theology*. London: SCM, 1955.
Stayer, James M. *The Anabaptists and Thomas Muntzer*. Dubuque, IA: Kendal/Hunt, 1980.
Steffy, Joan M. *The San Francisco Peace Movement*. NY: Professors World Peace Academy, 1985.
Steinsaltz, Adin. *The Essential Talmud*. NY: Basic, 1976.
Steward, Julian H., ed. *Handbook of South American Indians*. Washington: U.S. Government Printing Office, 1947–63.
Stewart, Desmond. *Theodor Herzl*. Garden City, NY: Doubleday, 1974.
Stotts, Jack L. *Shalom: The Search for a Peaceable City*. NY: Abingdon, 1973.
Strauss, David F. *The Life of Jesus*. Philadelphia: Fortress, 1972 (original 1835).
Streng, Frederick J. *Emptiness: A Study in Religious Meaning*. Nashville, TN: Abingdon, 1967.
Strong, John S. *The Legend of King Asoka*. Princeton: Princeton University, 1983.
Sturtevant, William C., ed. *Handbook of North American Indians*. Washington: Smithsonian, 1978ff.
Suhrawardy, A. *The Sayings of Muhammad*. London: Murray, 1941.
Tambiah, Stanley J. *World Conqueror and World Renouncer*. Cambridge: Cambridge University, 1976.
Taylor, Pat Ellis. *Border Healing Woman*. Austin: University of Texas, 1981.
Tendulkar, D.G. *Abdul Ghaffar Khan: Faith Is a Battle*. Bombay: Popular Prakasham, 1967.
Thekkinedath, Joseph. *Love of Neighbour in Mahatma Gandhi*. Alwaye, Kerala, India: Pontifical Institute of Theology and Philosophy, 1973.
Thera, Piyadassi, ed. *A Felicitation Volume Presented to the Ven. Narada Mahathera*. Kandy, Sri Lanka: Buddhist Publication Society, 1979.
Thompson, Henry O. *Approaches to the Bible*. Syracuse: Center for Instructional Communication, 1967.

_____. *The Global Congress of the World's Religions*. NY: Rose of Sharon, 1982.

_____. *Global Outreach*. NY: Rose of Sharon, 1987.

_____. *Mekal: The God of Beth-shan*. Leiden: Brill, 1970.

_____, ed. *Put Your Future in Ruins*. Bristol, IN: Wyndam Hall, 1985.

_____, ed. *Unity in Diversity*. NY: Rose of Sharon, 1984.

Thompson, John F. *The Samaritans*. NY: Gordon, 1976.

Thomsen, Harry. *The New Religions of Japan*. Westport, CT: Greenwood, 1978.

Tien-Hsi, Cheng. *China Moulded by Confucius: The Chinese Way in Western Light*. Westport, CT: Hyperion, 1973 (original 1946).

Tompkins, Peter and Christopher Bird. *The Secret Life of Plants*. NY: Harper & Row, 1973.

Trepp, Leo. *Eternal Faith, Eternal People*. Englewood Cliffs, NJ: Prentice-Hall, 1962.

Trimmingham, John S. *A History of Islam in West Africa*. Oxford: Clarendon, 1972.

_____. *The Influence of Islam Upon Africa*, 2nd ed. NY: Longham, 1980.

_____. *The Sufi Orders in Islam*. Oxford: Clarendon, 1971.

Turner, Harold W. *Religious Innovation in Africa*. Boston: Hall, 1979.

Twersky, Isadore. *Introduction to the Code of Maimonides (Mishneh Torah)*. New Haven: Yale, 1980.

Tyson, Joseph B. *The New Testament and Early Christianity*. NY: Macmillan, 1984.

Underhill, Evelyn. *Mysticism*. NY: Dutton, 1961 (original 1910).

Van Buitenen, J.A.B. *The Bhagavad Gita in the Mahabharata*. Chicago: University of Chicago, 1981.

_____. *The Mahabharata*. Chicago: University of Chicago, 1973-1978.

Vaudeville, Charlotte. *Kabir*. NY: Oxford University, 1974.

Vermes, Geza. *Jesus the Jew*. Philadelphia: Fortress, 1981.

von Glassnapp, Helmuth. *Buddhism: A Non-Theistic Religion*. NY: Braziller, 1970.

von Rad, Gerhard. *Der Heilige Krieg im alten Israel*. Zurich: Zwingli, 1951.

Waddy, Charis. *The Muslim Mind*. NY: Longman, 1976.

Waheed, K.A. *Islamic Background of Modern Science and Culture*. Karachi: National Book Foundation, 1977.

Wahlberg, Rachel Conrad. *Jesus According to a Woman*. NY: Paulist, 1975.

Walker, Williston. *A History of the Christian Church*, rev. NY: Scribner's, 1959.

Wallbank, T. Walter. *A Short History of India and Pakistan*. NY: Mentor, 1958.

Walli, Koshelya. *The Conception of Ahimsa in Indian Thought (According to Sanskrit Sources)*. Varanasi: Bharata Manisha, 1974.

Walton, Robert C. *Zwingli's Theocracy*. Toronto: University of Toronto, 1967.

Ware, Timothy. *The Orthodox Church*, rev. Baltimore: Penguin, 1969.

Watt, W. Montgomery. *Bell's Introduction to the Qur'an*, rev. Edinburgh: University Press, 1970.

_____. *The Faith and Practice of al-Ghazzali*. London: Allen & Unwin, 1953.

_____. *Free Will and Predestination in Early Islam*. London: Luzac, 1948.

_____. *A History of Islamic Spain*. Edinburgh: University Press, 1965.

_____. *Muhammad: Prophet and Statesman*. Oxford, Clarendon, 1961.

_____. *Muslim Intellectual: A Study of al-Ghazzali*. Edinburgh: University Press, 1963.

Waugh, Earl H., et al., eds. *The Muslim Community in North America*. Alberta: University of Alberta, 1983.

Weber, Max. *Religions of India: The Sociology of Hinduism and Buddhism*. Glencoe, IL: Free Press, 1956.

Weeks, Richard V., ed. *Muslim Peoples.* Westport, CT: Greenwood, 1978.
Welch, Anthony and Stuart C. Welch. *Arts of the Islamic Book.* Ithaca, NY: Cornell, 1982.
Welch, Holmes. *Taoism: The Parting of the Way.* Boston: Beacon, 1957.
Wellhausen, Julius. *Proglegomena to the History of Ancient Israel.* Cleveland: World, 1965 (original 1878).
Wenger, J.C., ed. *The Complete Writings of Menno Simons.* Scottsdale, PA: Herald, 1956.
Wheeler, Sir Mortimer. *Early India and Pakistan.* NY: Praeger, 1959.
Wheeler, Post. *The Sacred Scripture of the Japanese.* Westport, CT: Greenwood, 1976.
Whitehouse, Ruth. *The First Cities.* NY: Dutton, 1977.
Wiebke, Walther. *Woman in Islam.* Montclair, NJ: Schram, 1981.
Wiesel, Elie. *Souls on Fire: Portraits and Legends of Hasidic Masters.* NY: Random House, 1972.
Wiet, Gaston, et al., eds. *History of Mankind. Vol. III. The Great Medieval Civilization.* NY: Harper & Row, 1975.
Williams, John Alden. *Islam.* NY: Braziller, 1961.
_____. *Themes of Islamic Civilization.* Berkeley: University of California, 1971.
Willoughby, William C. *The Soul of the Bantu.* Garden City, NY: Doubleday, 1928.
Wilson, J. Christy. *Introducing Islam.* NY: Friendship, 1965.
Wittner, Lawrence S. *Rebels Against War: The American Peace Movement, 1941–1960.* NY: Columbia, 1969.
Wright, Arthur F. *Buddhism in Chinese History.* Stanford, CA: Stanford University, 1959.
Yeh, Theodore T. *Confucianism, Christianity and China.* NY: Philosophical Library, 1969.
Young, David S., ed. *Study War No More.* Elgin, IL: Brethren Press, 1982.
Yulan, Fung. *History of Chinese Philosophy.* Princeton: Princeton University, 1952.
Yutang, Lin. *The Wisdom of China and India.* NY: Modern Library, 1955 (original 1942).
Zaener, Robert C., ed. *The Concise Encyclopedia of Living Faiths.* NY: Hawthorn, 1964.
_____. *Hindu Scriptures.* NY: Dutton, 1966.
Zahan, Dominique. *The Religion, Spirituality, and Thought of Traditional Africa.* Chicago: University of Chicago, 1979.
Zahra, Shaykh Abu. *The Concept of War in Islam.* Cairo: Ministry of Waqfs, n.d.
Zernov, Nicholas. *The Church of Eastern Christians.* NY: Macmillan, 1946.
Zoghby, Samir M. *Islam in Sub-Saharan Africa: A Partially Annotated Guide.* Washington: Library of Congress, 1978.

Index